BAMBOO BLADE ⑥

MASAHIRO TOTSUKA
AGURI IGARASHI

Translation: Stephen Paul

Lettering: Terri Delgado

BAMBOO BLADE Vol. 6 © 2007 Masahiro Totsuka, Aguri Igarashi / SQUARE ENIX CO., LTD. All rights reserved. First published in Japan in 2007 by SQUARE ENIX CO., LTD. English translation rights arranged with SQUARE ENIX CO., LTD. and Hachette Book Group through Tuttle-Mori Agency, Inc.

Translation © 2010 by SQUARE ENIX CO., LTD.

Yen Press
Hachette Book Group
237 Park Avenue, New York, NY 10017

www.HachetteBookGroup.com
www.YenPress.com

Yen Press is an imprint of Hachette Book Group, Inc. The Yen Press name and logo are trademarks of Hachette Book Group, Inc.

First Yen Press Edition: September 2010

ISBN: 978-0-316-07299-1

10 9 8 7 6 5 4 3 2 1

BVG

Printed in the United States of America

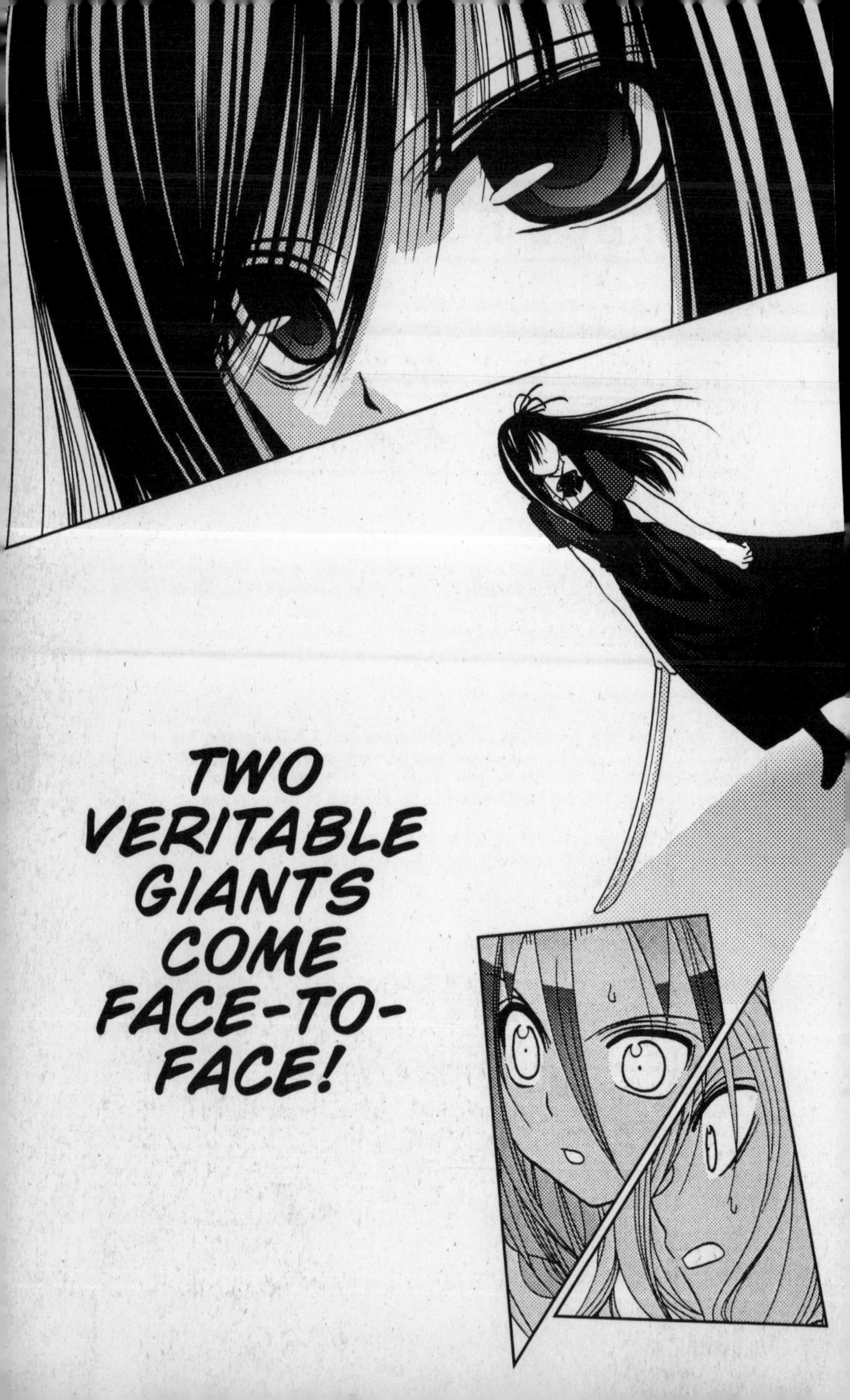
TWO VERITABLE GIANTS COME FACE-TO-FACE!

BAMBOO BLADE 6
CONTENTS

Story: Masahiro Totsuka / Art: Aguri Igarashi

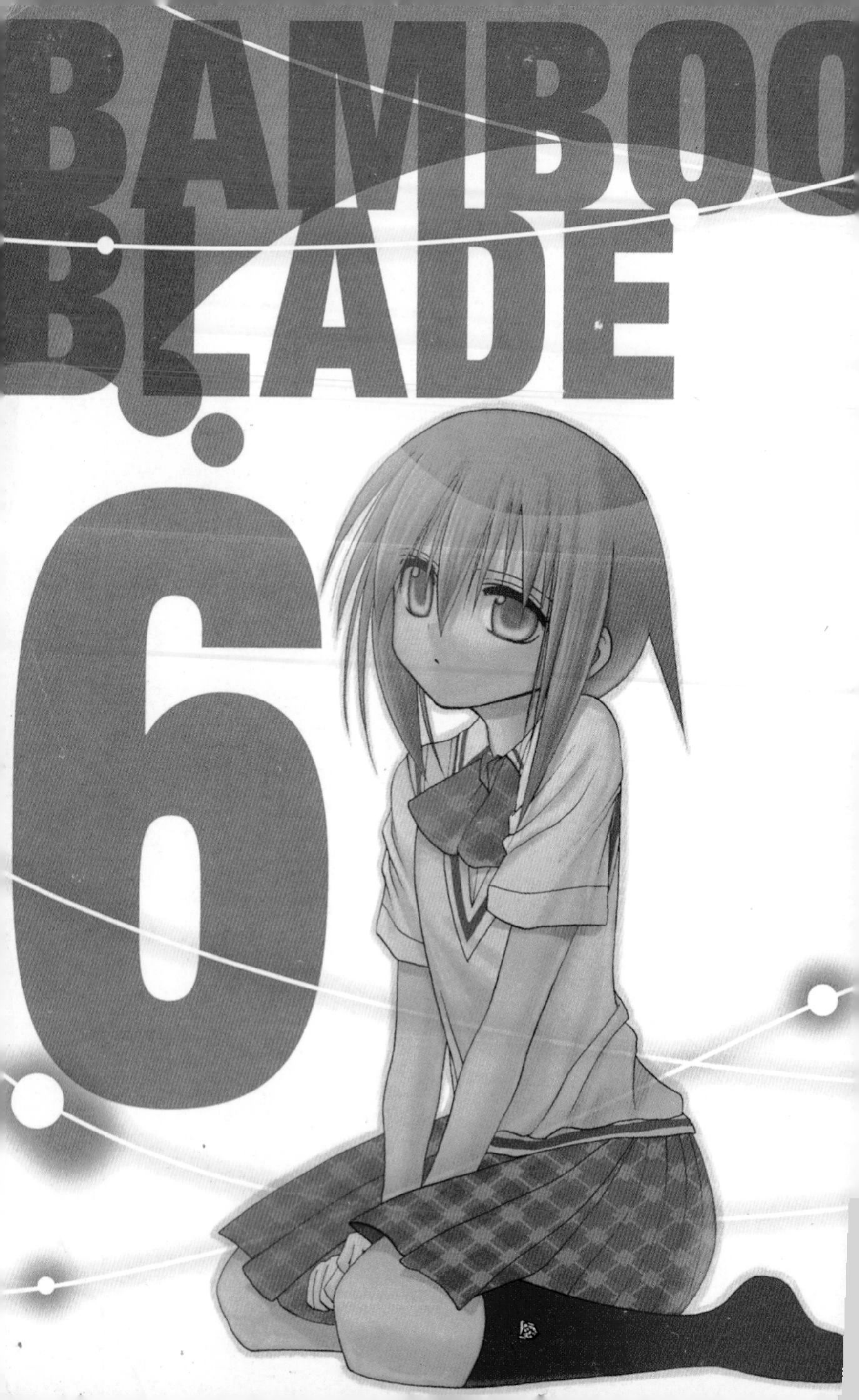
BAMBOO
BLADE
6

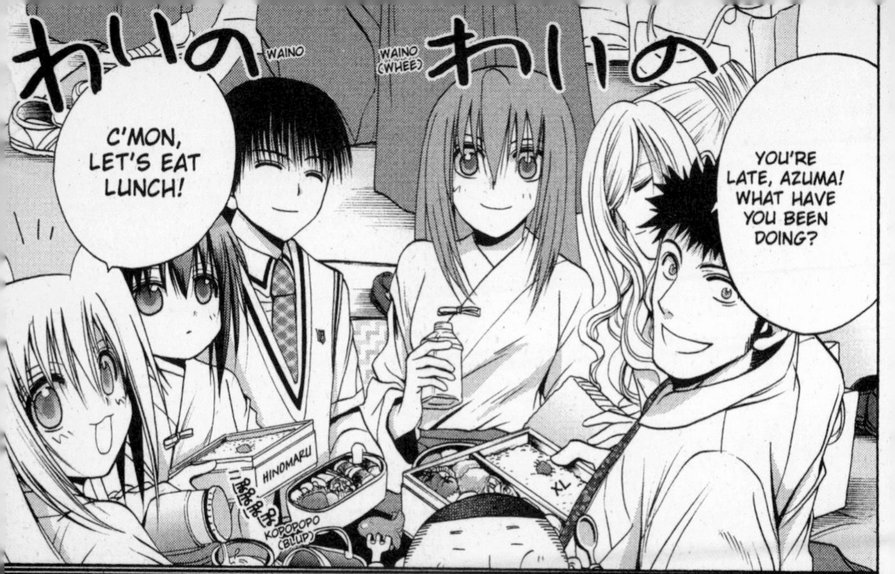
わいの
WAINO (WHEE)
わいの
WAINO
YOU'RE LATE, AZUMA! WHAT HAVE YOU BEEN DOING?
C'MON, LET'S EAT LUNCH!
XL
HINOMARU
KOROPOPO (BLUP)

CHAPTER 49
TAMAKI AND THE PARKING LOT

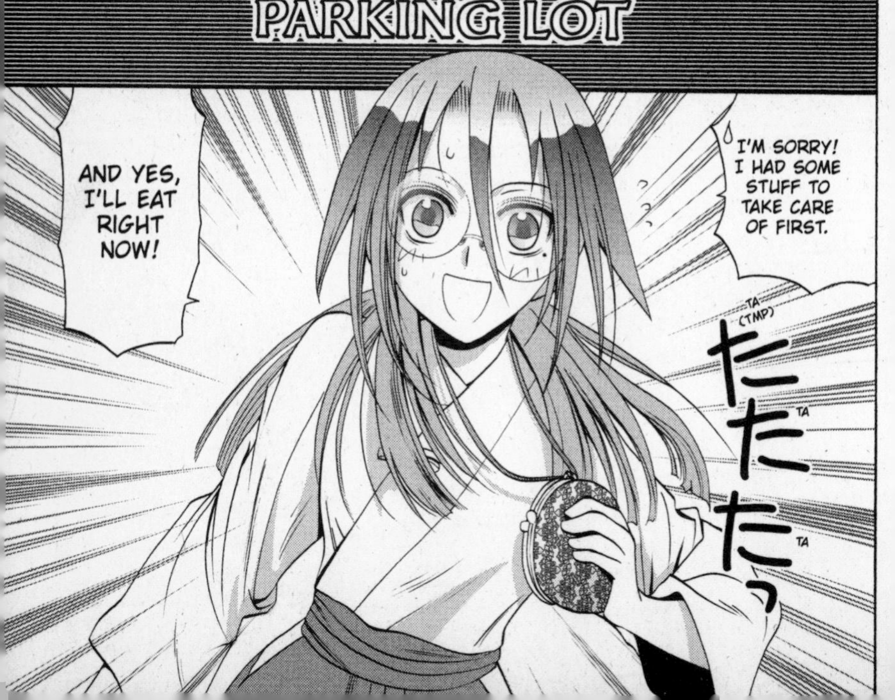
I'M SORRY! I HAD SOME STUFF TO TAKE CARE OF FIRST.
AND YES, I'LL EAT RIGHT NOW!
たたたっ
TA (TMP)
TA
TA

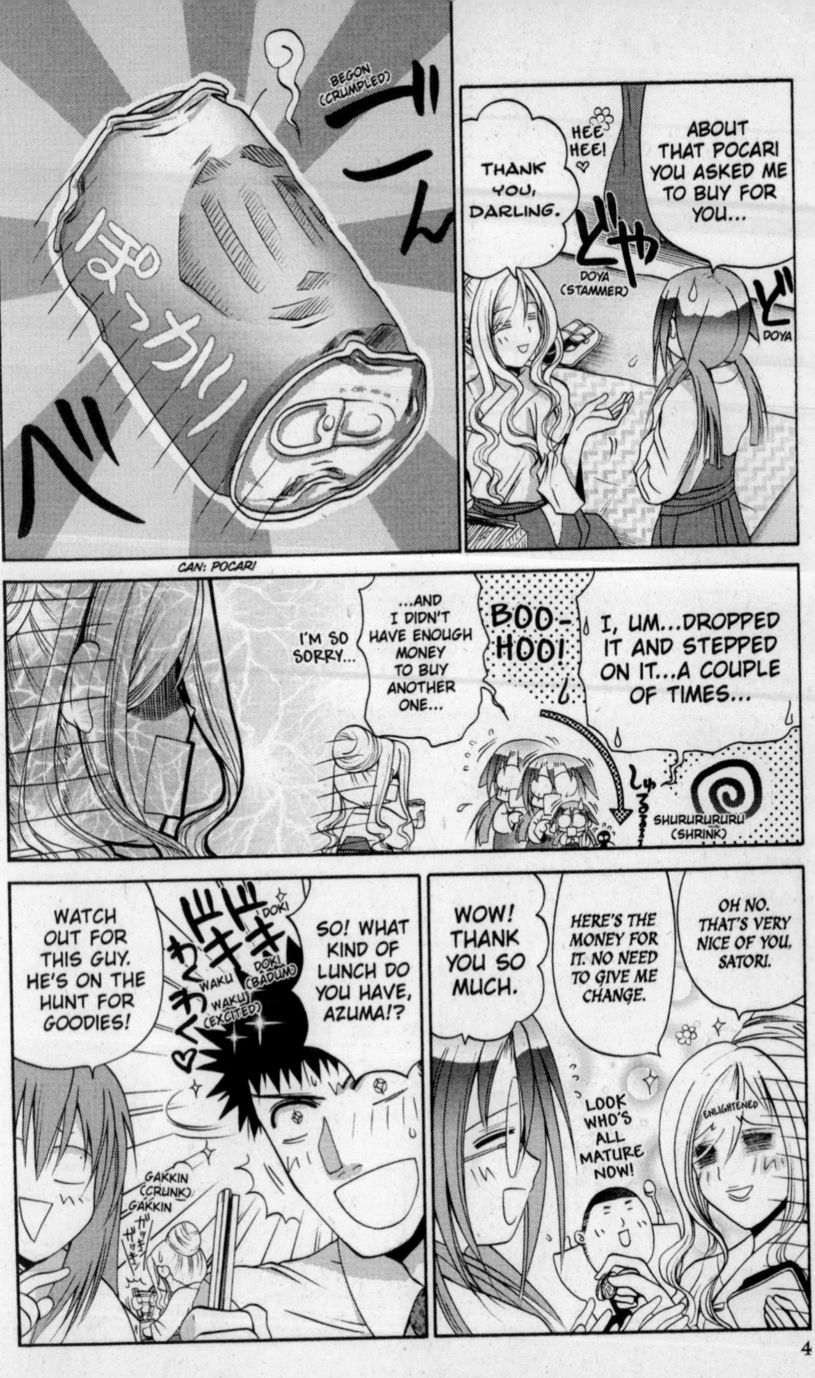
ABOUT THAT POCARI YOU ASKED ME TO BUY FOR YOU...
HEE HEE!
THANK YOU, DARLING.
DOYA (STAMMER)
DOYA
BEGON (CRUMPLED)
CAN: POCARI
I, UM...DROPPED IT AND STEPPED ON IT...A COUPLE OF TIMES...
SHURURURURU (SHRINK)
BOO-HOO!
...AND I DIDN'T HAVE ENOUGH MONEY TO BUY ANOTHER ONE...
I'M SO SORRY...
OH NO. THAT'S VERY NICE OF YOU, SATORI.
HERE'S THE MONEY FOR IT. NO NEED TO GIVE ME CHANGE.
WOW! THANK YOU SO MUCH.
ENLIGHTENED
LOOK WHO'S ALL MATURE NOW!
SO! WHAT KIND OF LUNCH DO YOU HAVE, AZUMA!?
DOKI
DOKI (BADUMP)
WAKU
WAKU (EXCITED)
WATCH OUT FOR THIS GUY. HE'S ON THE HUNT FOR GOODIES!
GAKKIN (CRUNK)
GAKKIN

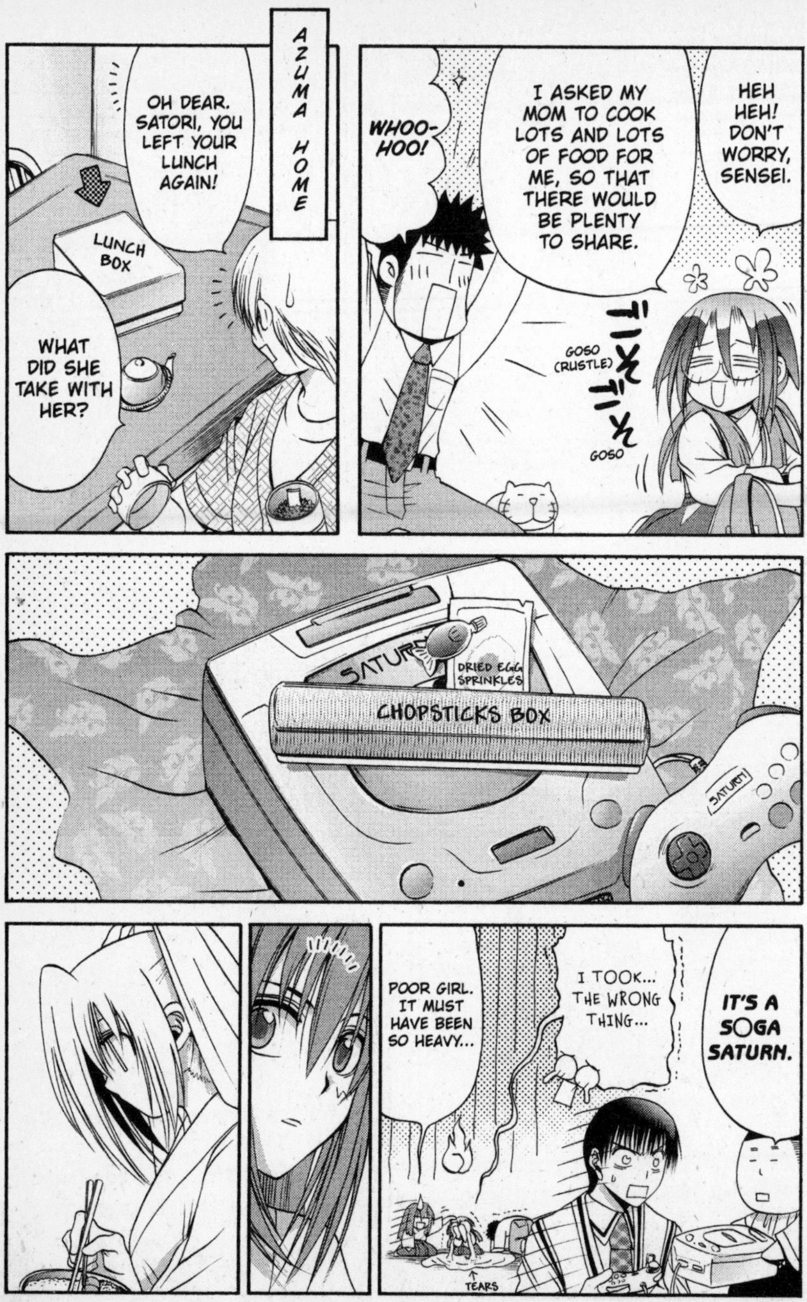
HEH HEH! DON'T WORRY, SENSEI.
I ASKED MY MOM TO COOK LOTS AND LOTS OF FOOD FOR ME, SO THAT THERE WOULD BE PLENTY TO SHARE.
WHOO-HOO!
GOSO (RUSTLE)
GOSO
AZUMA HOME
OH DEAR. SATORI, YOU LEFT YOUR LUNCH AGAIN!
LUNCH BOX
WHAT DID SHE TAKE WITH HER?
DRIED EGG SPRINKLES
CHOPSTICKS BOX
SATURN
IT'S A SOGA SATURN.
I TOOK... THE WRONG THING...
POOR GIRL. IT MUST HAVE BEEN SO HEAVY...
TEARS

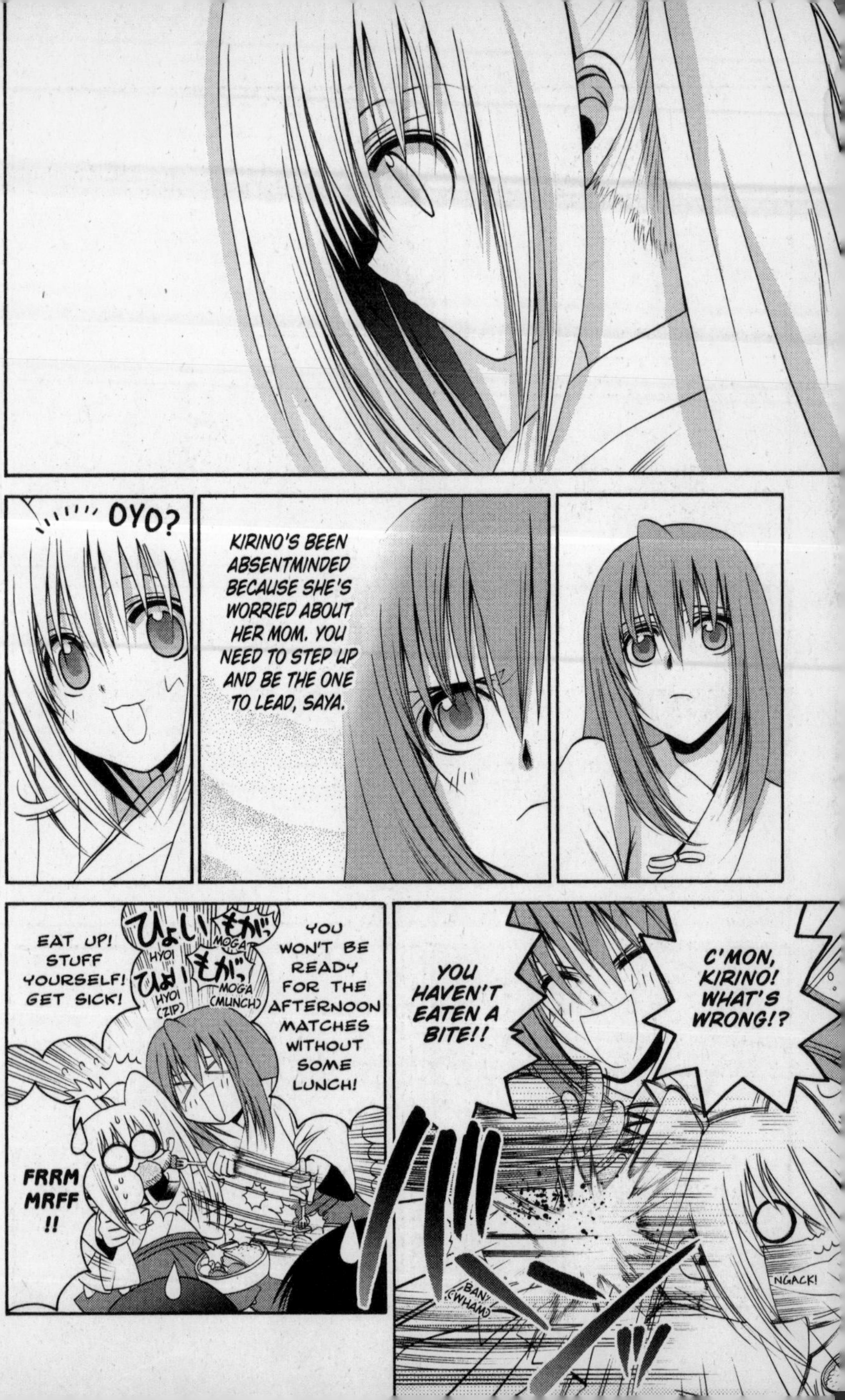
KIRINO'S BEEN ABSENTMINDED BECAUSE SHE'S WORRIED ABOUT HER MOM. YOU NEED TO STEP UP AND BE THE ONE TO LEAD, SAYA.
OYO?
C'MON, KIRINO! WHAT'S WRONG!?
YOU HAVEN'T EATEN A BITE!!
BAN (WHAM)
NGACK!
YOU WON'T BE READY FOR THE AFTERNOON MATCHES WITHOUT SOME LUNCH!
もがっ MOGA
もがっ MOGA (MUNCH)
ひょい HYOI
ひょい HYOI (ZIP)
EAT UP! STUFF YOURSELF! GET SICK!
FRRM MRFF !!

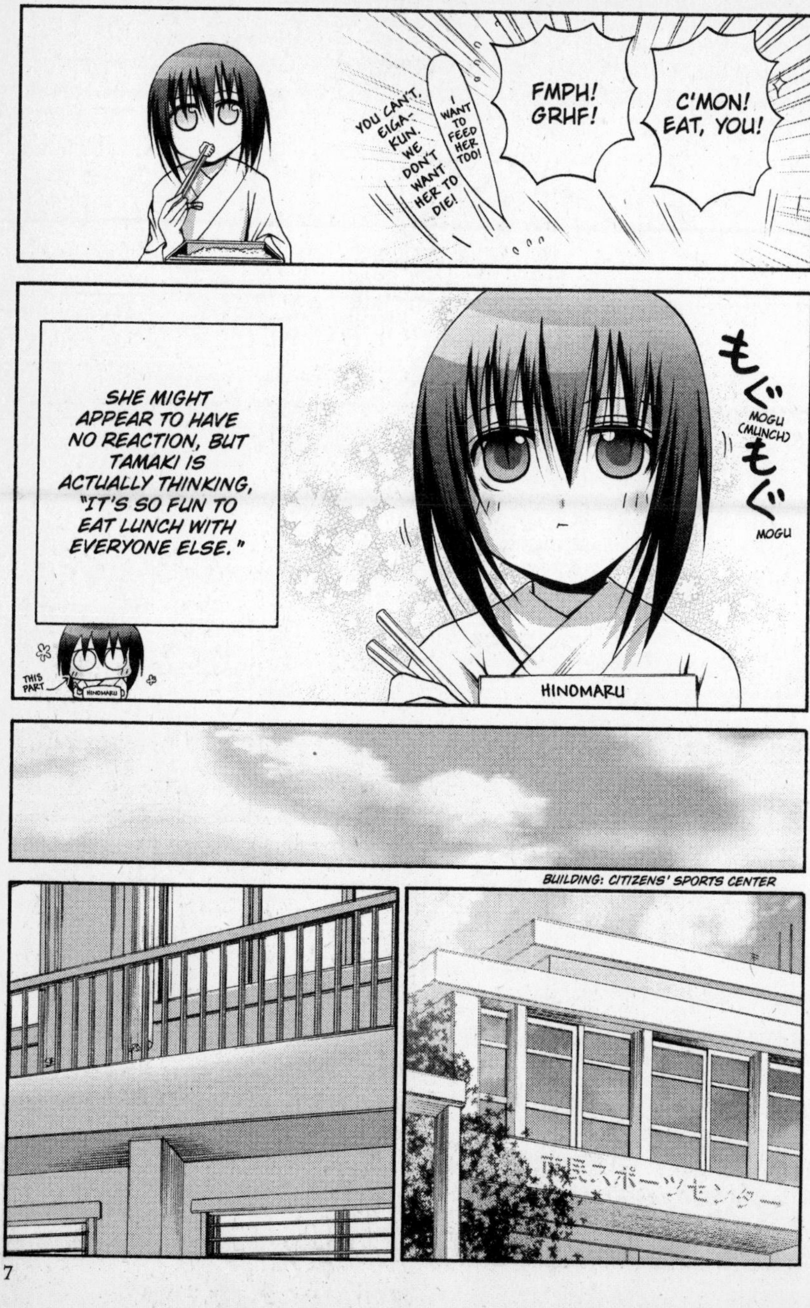
C'MON! EAT, YOU!
FMPH! GRHF!
I WANT TO FEED HER TOO!
YOU CAN'T, EIGA-KUN. WE DON'T WANT HER TO DIE!
もぐもぐ
MOGU (MUNCH) MOGU
HINOMARU
SHE MIGHT APPEAR TO HAVE NO REACTION, BUT TAMAKI IS ACTUALLY THINKING, "IT'S SO FUN TO EAT LUNCH WITH EVERYONE ELSE."
THIS PART
HINOMARU
BUILDING: CITIZENS' SPORTS CENTER
市民スポーツセンター

WOMEN'S
RESTROOM

カリ
KARI

カリ
KARI

カリ
KARI

カリ
KARI

カ
！！
KARI

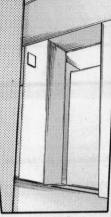

カ
リ
KARI

カ
リ
KARI

KARI
(SCRATCH)

カ
リ
KARI

カ
リ
KARI

カリ
KARI

カリ
KARI

カリ
KARI

カリ
KARI

カリ
KARI

カリ
KARI

カリ
KARI

カリ
KARI

カリ
KARI

カリ
KARI

カリ
KARI

KONISHI-
SENPAAAI?

MAYBE
SHE'S
IN THE
BATH-
ROOM!

わた
わた
WATA

わた
わた
WATA
(FLUSTER)

KONISHI-
SENPAI!
WHERE
COULD
SHE BE?

バタバタ
BATA

BATA
(STOMP)

バタ
BATA

SENPAI!

8

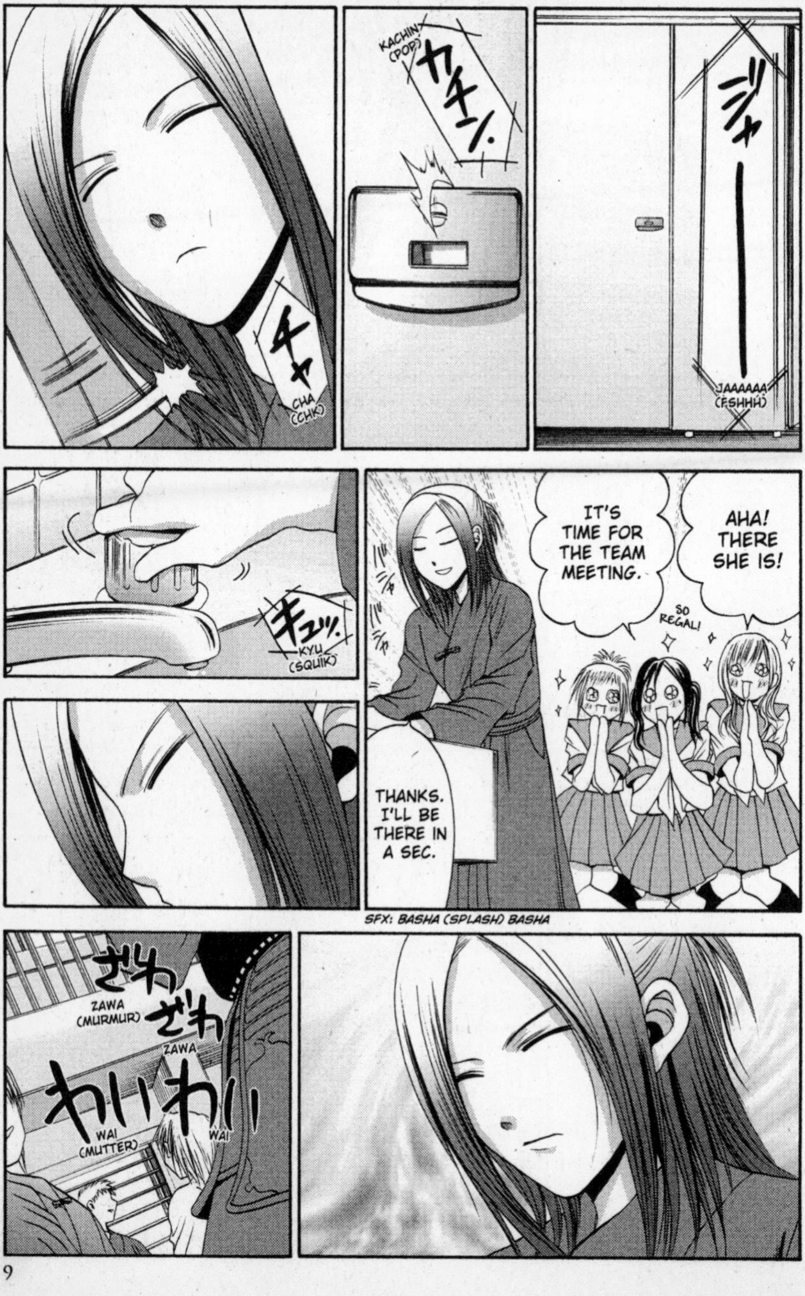
ジャー
JAAAAAA (FSHHH)
カチン
KACHIN (POP)
チャ
CHA (CHK)
AHA! THERE SHE IS!
SO REGAL!
IT'S TIME FOR THE TEAM MEETING.
THANKS. I'LL BE THERE IN A SEC.
SFX: BASHA (SPLASH) BASHA
キュッ
KYU (SQUIK)
ざわ ざわ
ZAWA (MURMUR) ZAWA
わいわい
WAI (MUTTER) WAI

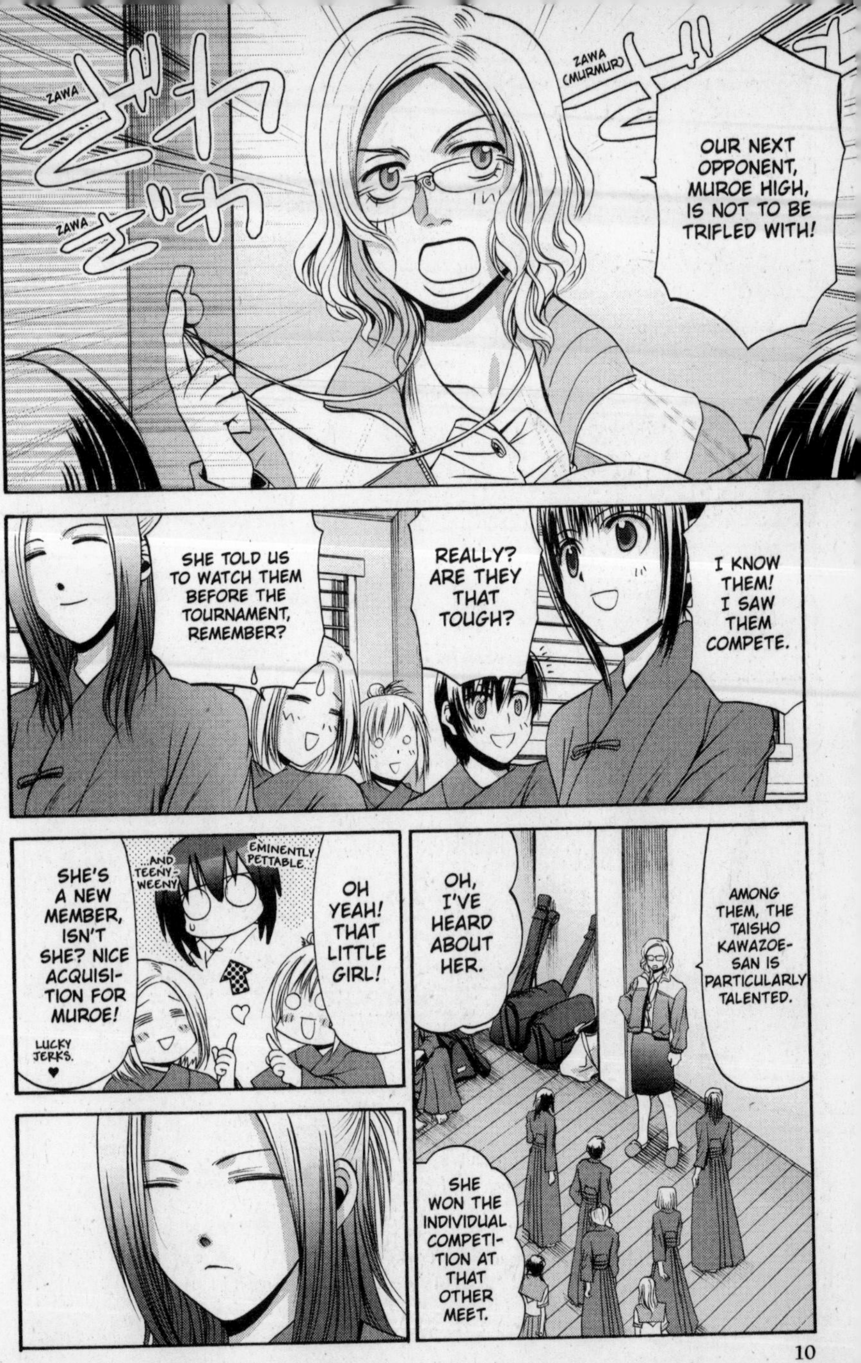
ZAWA (MURMUR)
OUR NEXT OPPONENT, MUROE HIGH, IS NOT TO BE TRIFLED WITH!
ZAWA
ZAWA
I KNOW THEM! I SAW THEM COMPETE.
REALLY? ARE THEY THAT TOUGH?
SHE TOLD US TO WATCH THEM BEFORE THE TOURNAMENT, REMEMBER?
AMONG THEM, THE TAISHO KAWAZOE-SAN IS PARTICULARLY TALENTED.
OH, I'VE HEARD ABOUT HER.
SHE WON THE INDIVIDUAL COMPETITION AT THAT OTHER MEET.
OH YEAH! THAT LITTLE GIRL!
EMINENTLY PETTABLE.
...AND TEENY-WEENY
SHE'S A NEW MEMBER, ISN'T SHE? NICE ACQUISITION FOR MUROE!
LUCKY JERKS. ♥

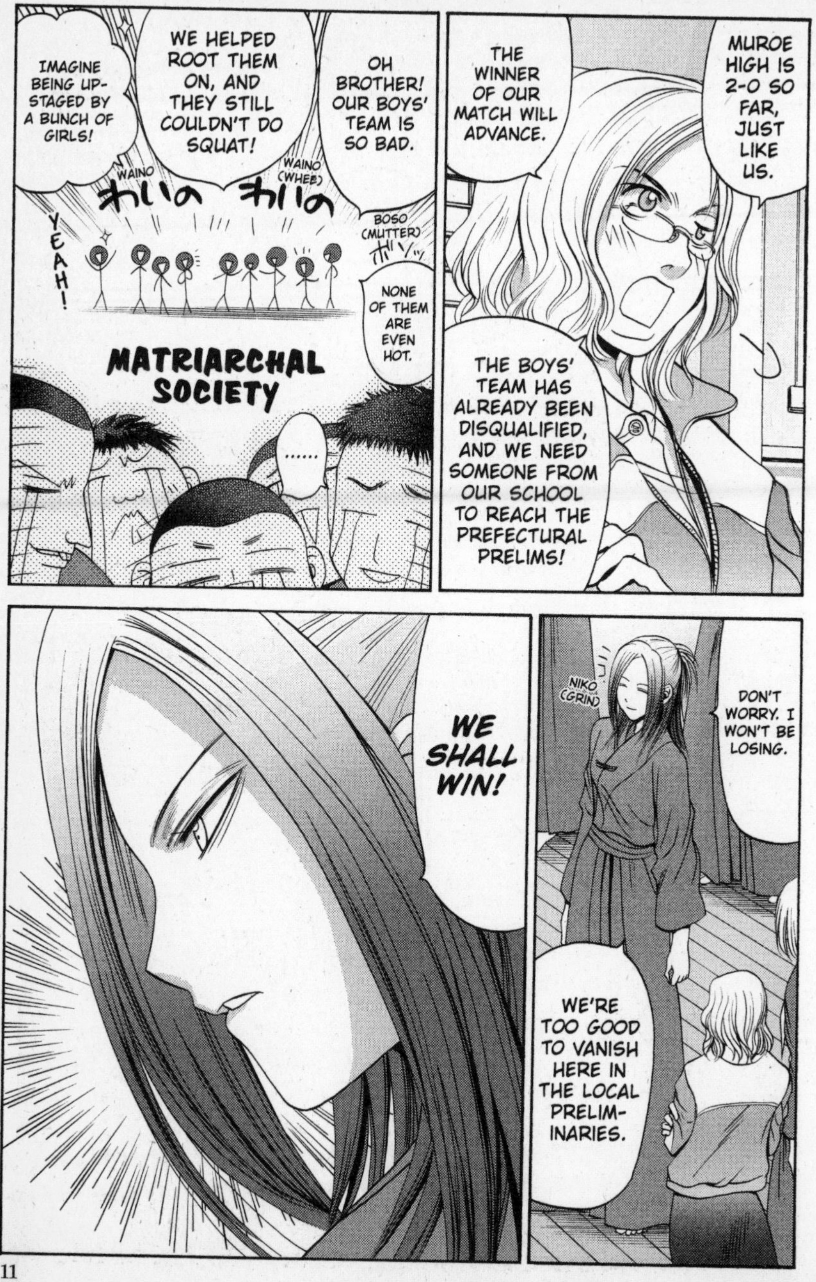
MUROE HIGH IS 2-0 SO FAR, JUST LIKE US.
THE WINNER OF OUR MATCH WILL ADVANCE.
THE BOYS' TEAM HAS ALREADY BEEN DISQUALIFIED, AND WE NEED SOMEONE FROM OUR SCHOOL TO REACH THE PREFECTURAL PRELIMS!
OH BROTHER! OUR BOYS' TEAM IS SO BAD.
WE HELPED ROOT THEM ON, AND THEY STILL COULDN'T DO SQUAT!
IMAGINE BEING UP-STAGED BY A BUNCH OF GIRLS!
WAINO (WHEE)
わいの わいの
WAINO
BOSO (MUTTER)
YEAH!
NONE OF THEM ARE EVEN HOT.
MATRIARCHAL SOCIETY
......
DON'T WORRY. I WON'T BE LOSING.
NIKO (GRIN)
WE'RE TOO GOOD TO VANISH HERE IN THE LOCAL PRELIMINARIES.
WE SHALL WIN!

THANKS, GIRLS.

I'LL DO MY BEST.

KYAAA!!

IF KONISHI-SENPAI HAD COMPETED IN THAT INDIVIDUAL MEET, SHE WOULD HAVE DESTROYED HER!

KYAA KYAA

SHE'S RIGHT! THAT LITTLE SHRIMPER DOESN'T STAND A CHANCE AGAINST KONISHI-SENPAI!

IT'S KONISHI'S SUPPORT TEAM AGAIN.

SO...

OOOH...♡

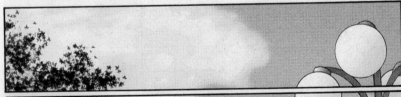

ZZZ.

12

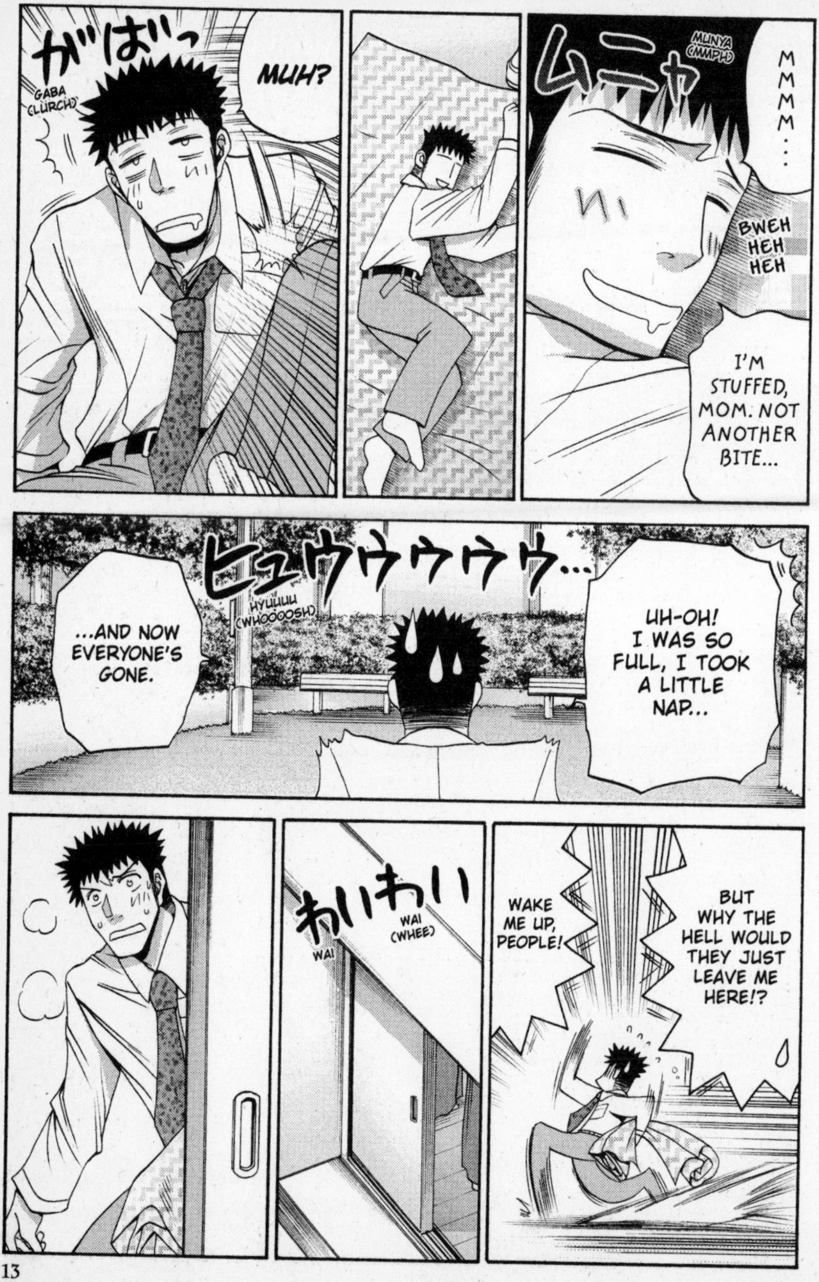
ムニャ
MUNYA (MMPH)
MMMM...
BWEH HEH HEH
I'M STUFFED, MOM. NOT ANOTHER BITE...
MUH?
がばっ
GABA (LURCH)
UH-OH! I WAS SO FULL, I TOOK A LITTLE NAP...
ヒュウウウウウ...
HYUUUU (WHOOOOSH)
...AND NOW EVERYONE'S GONE.
BUT WHY THE HELL WOULD THEY JUST LEAVE ME HERE!?
WAKE ME UP, PEOPLE!
わいわい
WAI (WHEE)
WAI

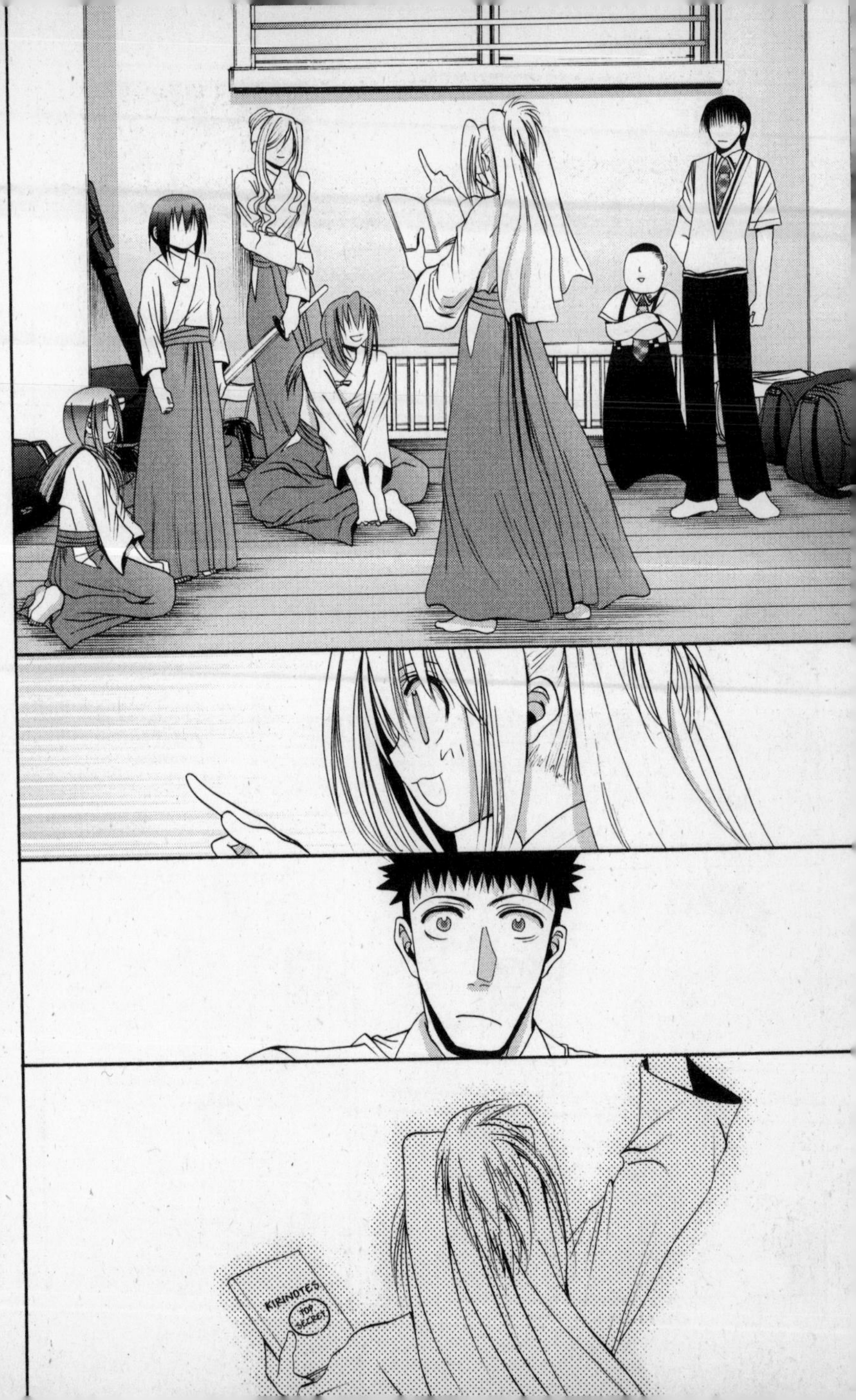
KIRINOTES
TOP SECRET

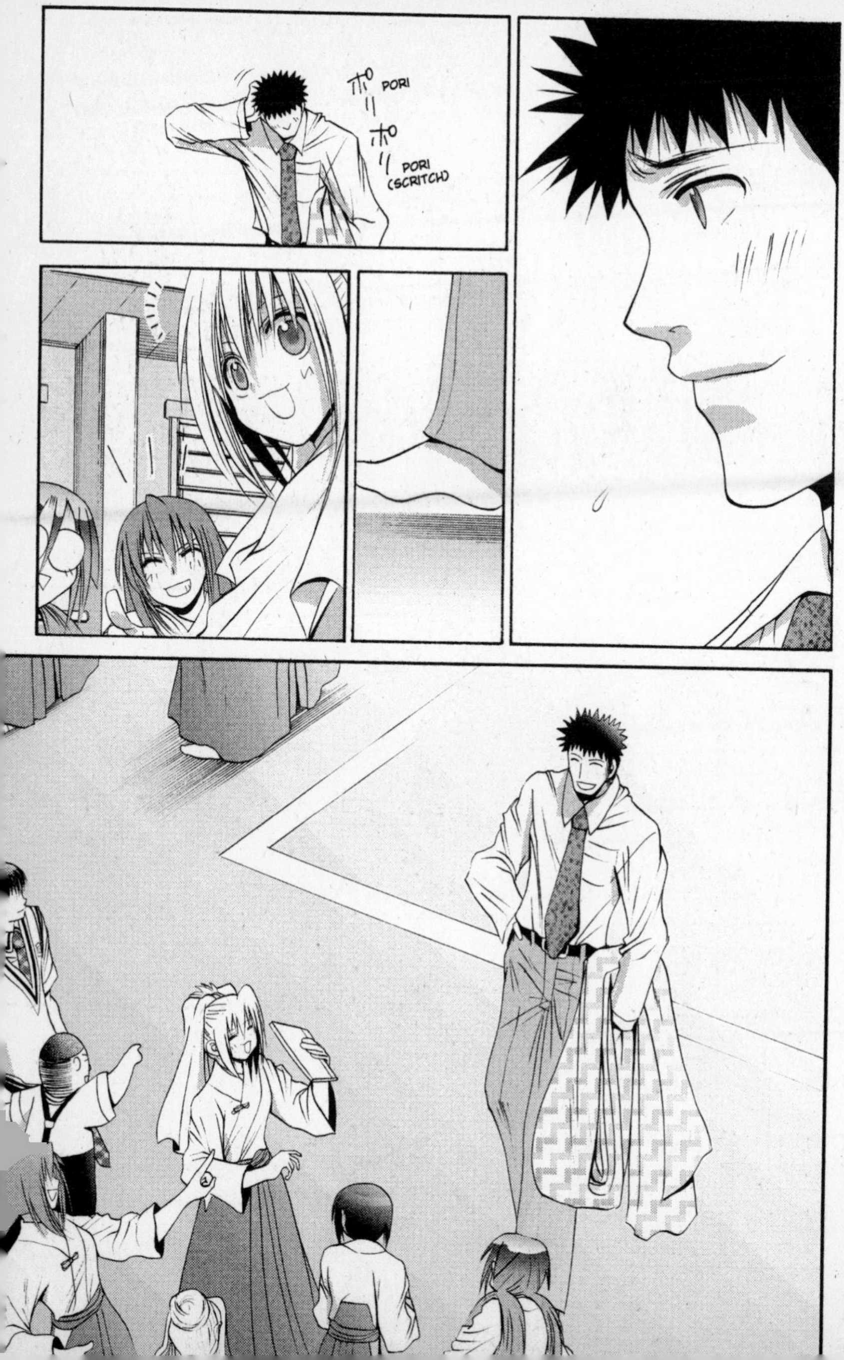
ポリ
PORI
ポリ
PORI (SCRITCH)

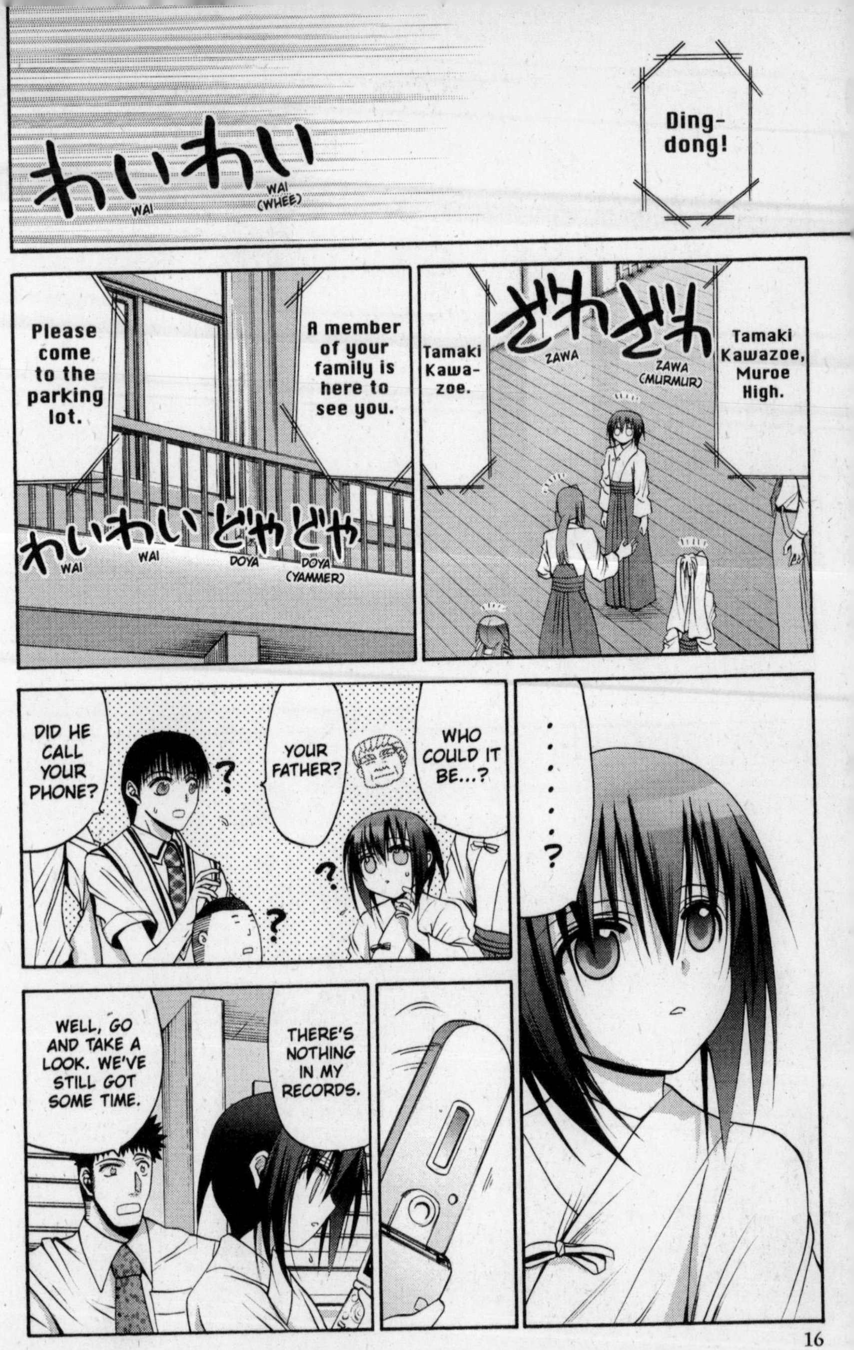
Ding-dong!
わいわい
WAI WAI (WHEE)
Tamaki Kawazoe, Muroe High.
ざわざわ
ZAWA ZAWA (MURMUR)
Tamaki Kawazoe.
A member of your family is here to see you.
Please come to the parking lot.
わいわいどやどや
WAI WAI DOYA DOYA (YAMMER)
. . . . . . ?
WHO COULD IT BE...?
YOUR FATHER?
DID HE CALL YOUR PHONE?
THERE'S NOTHING IN MY RECORDS.
WELL, GO AND TAKE A LOOK. WE'VE STILL GOT SOME TIME.

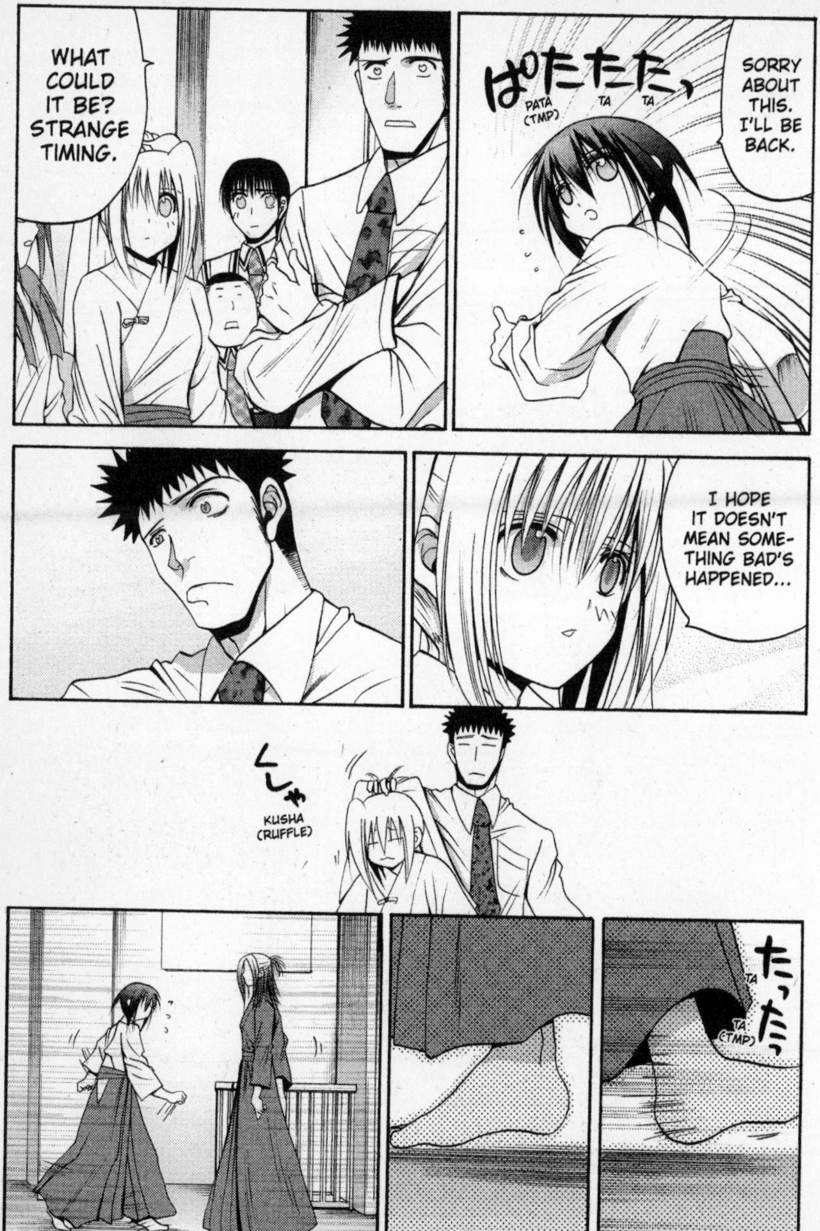
ぱたたた、
PATA (TMP) TA TA
SORRY ABOUT THIS. I'LL BE BACK.
WHAT COULD IT BE? STRANGE TIMING.
I HOPE IT DOESN'T MEAN SOME-THING BAD'S HAPPENED...
くしゃ
KUSHA (RUFFLE)
たったっ
TA TA (TMP)

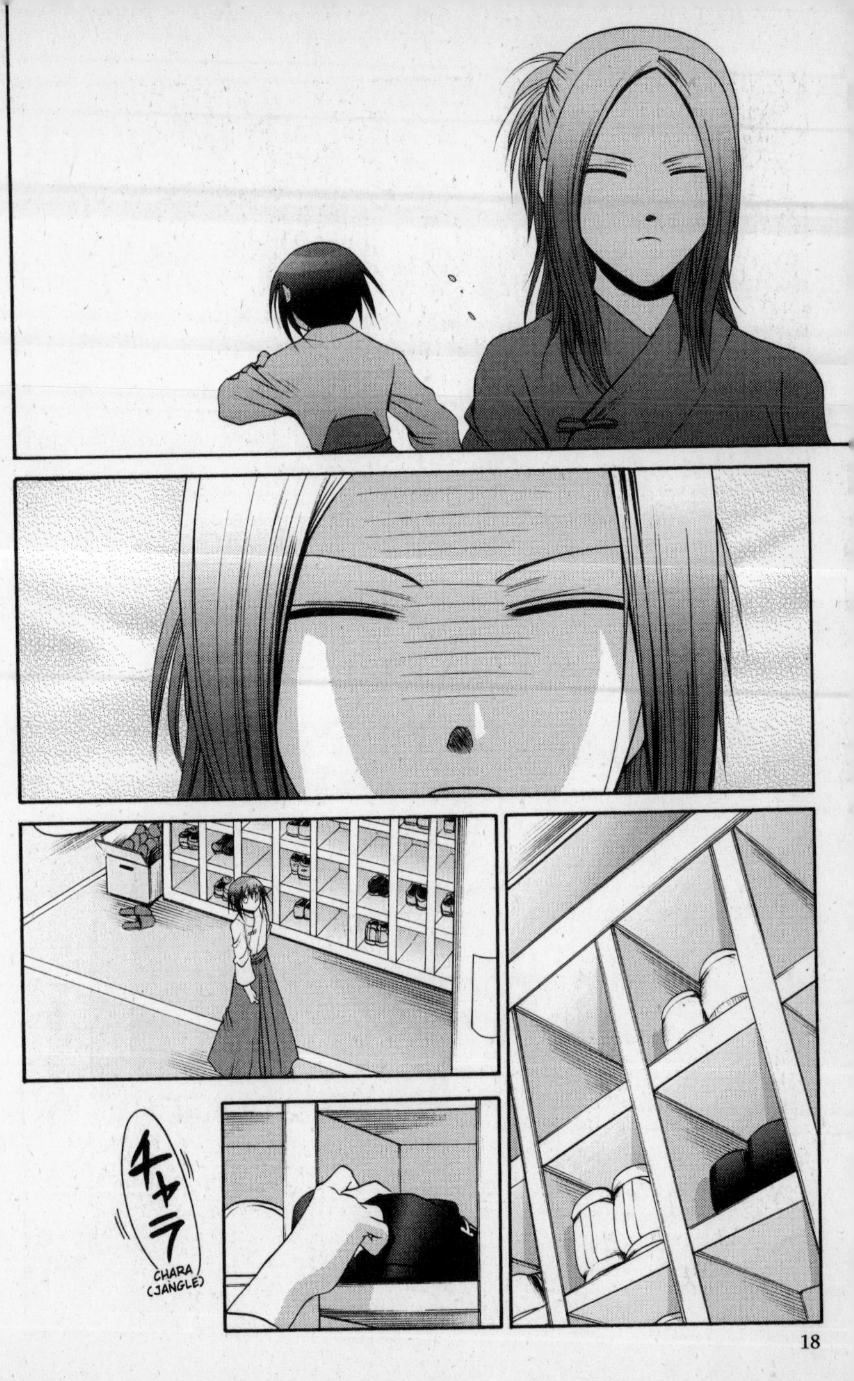
チャラ
CHARA
(JANGLE)

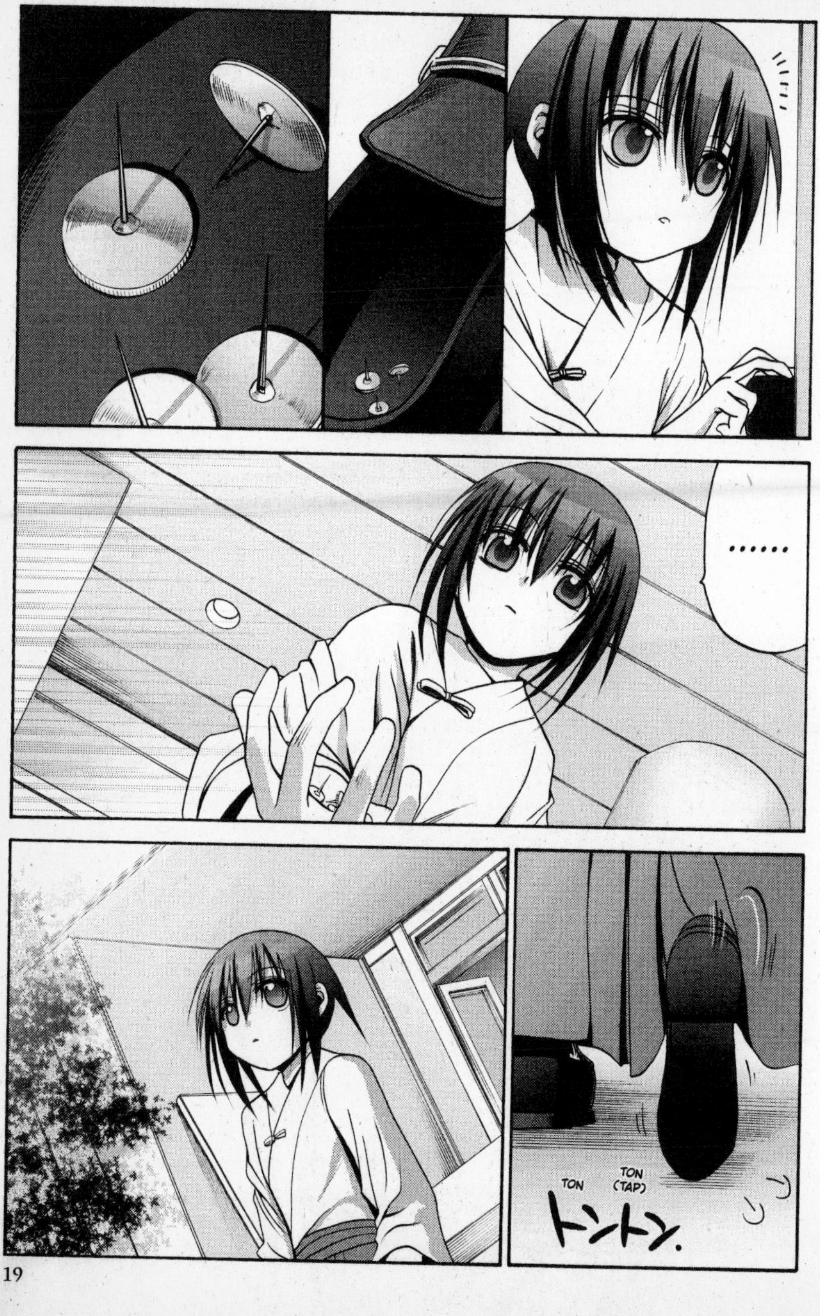

......
TON TON (TAP)
トントン.

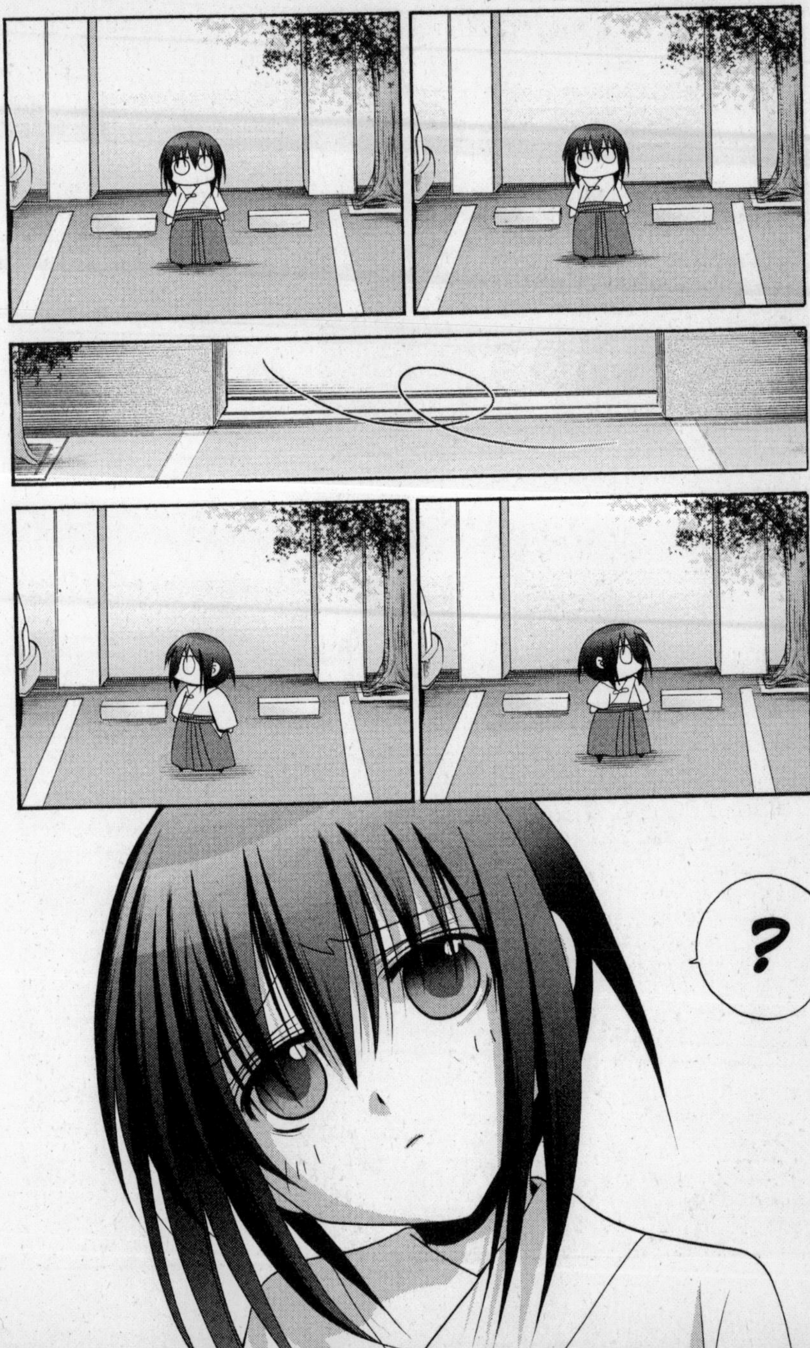
?

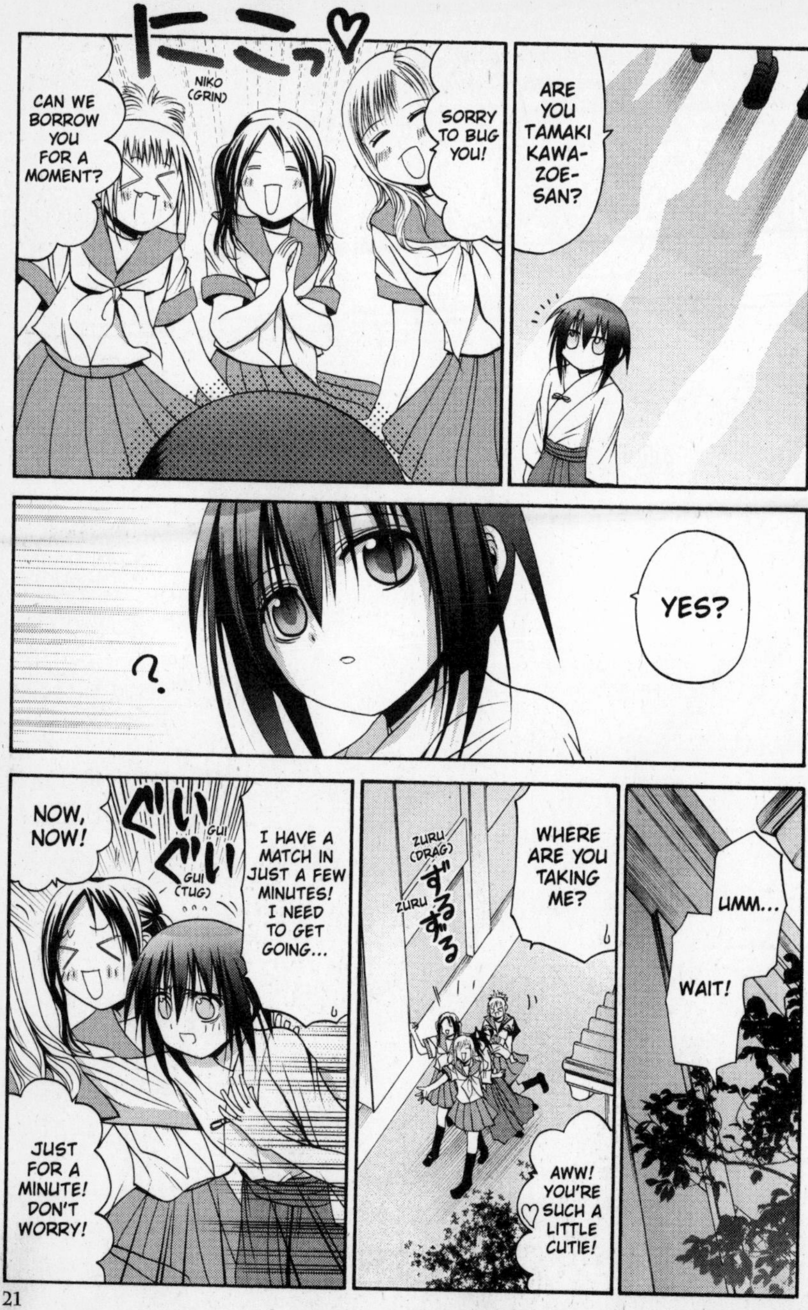
ARE YOU TAMAKI KAWAZOE-SAN?
SORRY TO BUG YOU!
にこっ
NIKO (GRIN)
CAN WE BORROW YOU FOR A MOMENT?
YES?
?
UMM...
WAIT!
WHERE ARE YOU TAKING ME?
ずるずる
ZURU (DRAG) ZURU
AWW! YOU'RE SUCH A LITTLE CUTIE!
I HAVE A MATCH IN JUST A FEW MINUTES! I NEED TO GET GOING...
ぐいぐい
GUI GUI (TUG)
NOW, NOW!
JUST FOR A MINUTE! DON'T WORRY!

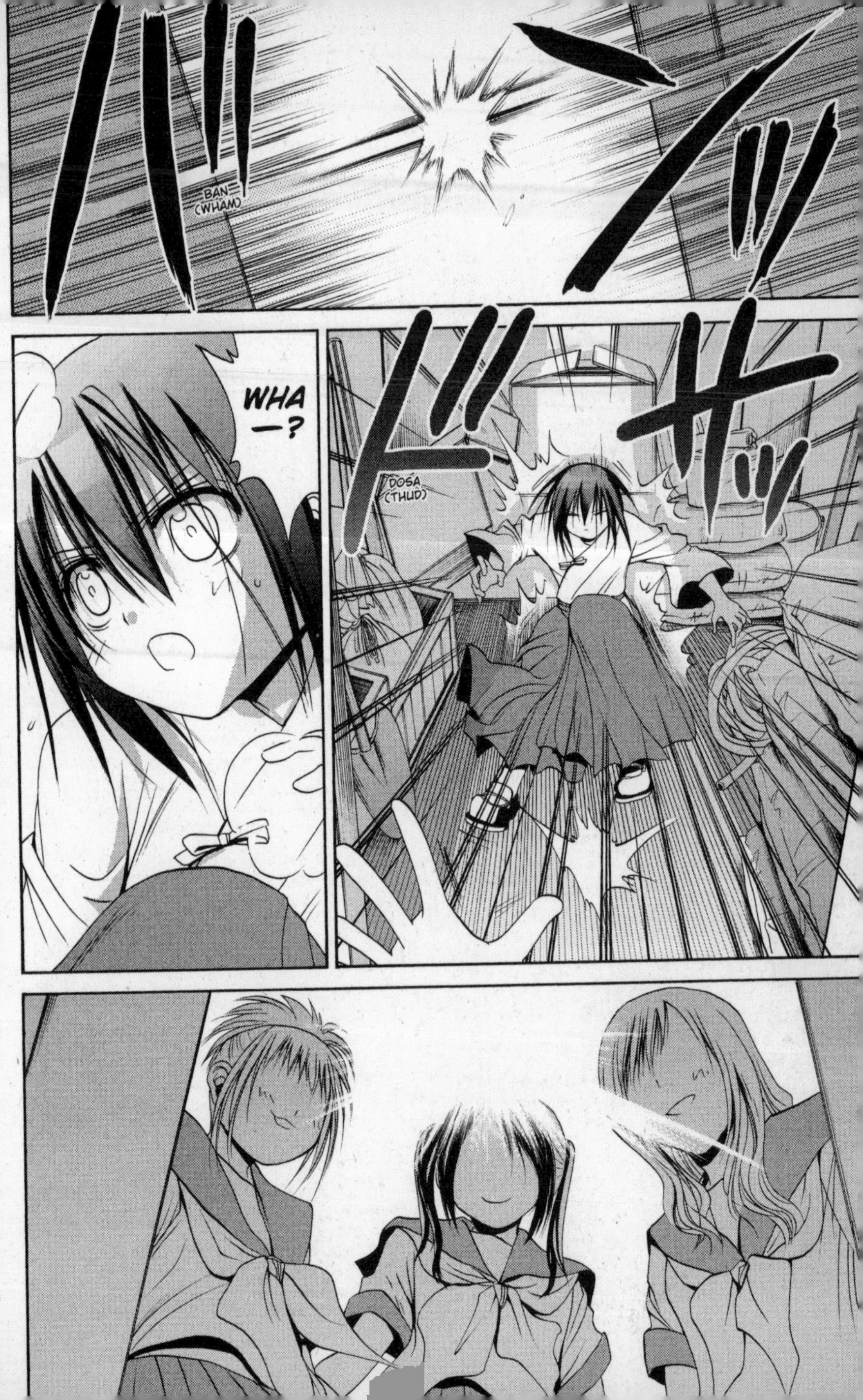
BAN (WHAM)
DOSA (THUD)
WHA—?

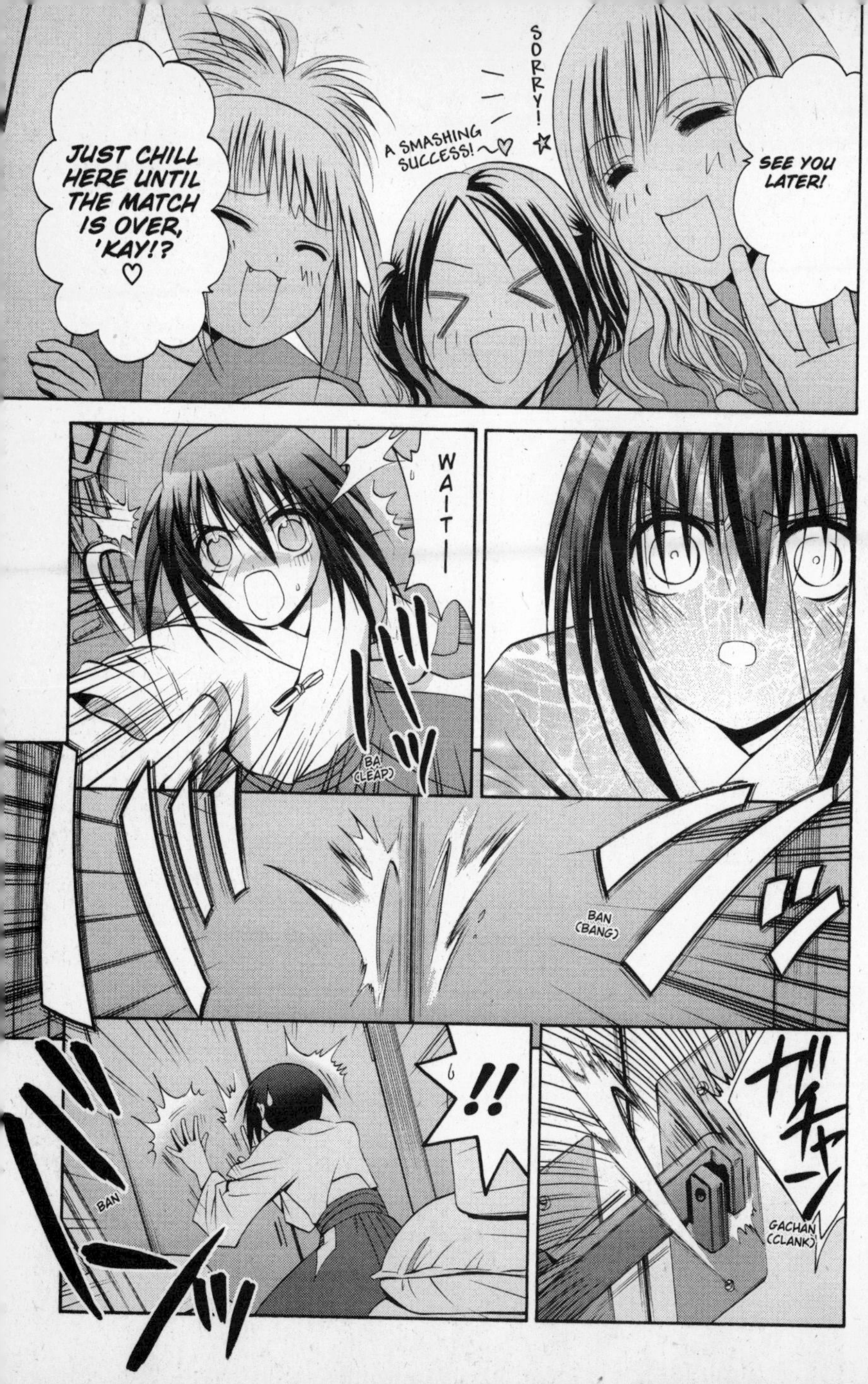
SEE YOU LATER!
SORRY! ☆
A SMASHING SUCCESS! ~♡
JUST CHILL HERE UNTIL THE MATCH IS OVER, 'KAY!? ♡
WAIT!
BA (LEAP)
BAN (BANG)
GACHAN (CLANK)
!!
BAN

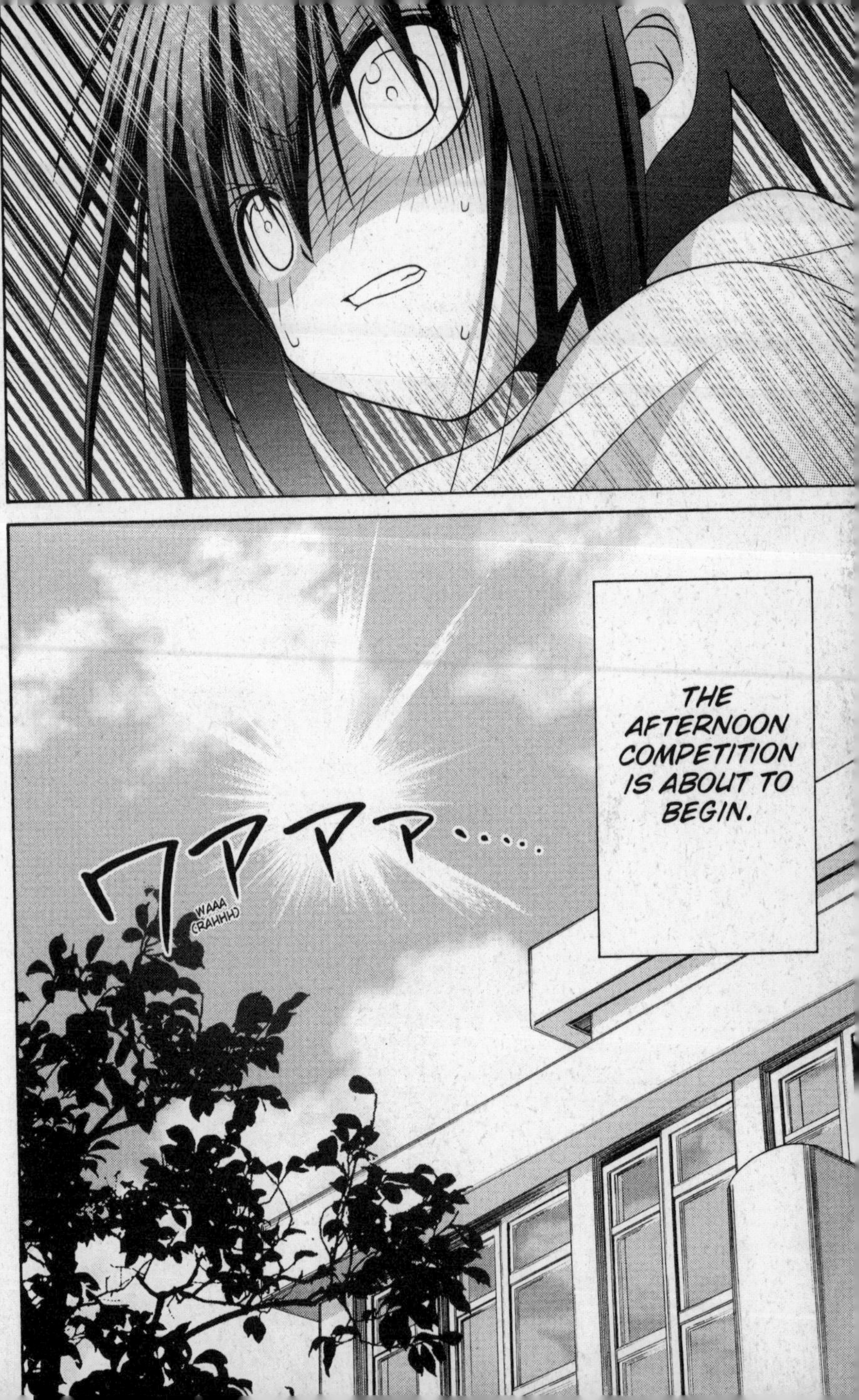
THE AFTERNOON COMPETITION IS ABOUT TO BEGIN.
ワアアア・・・・
WAAA (RAHHH)

BAMBOO BLADE

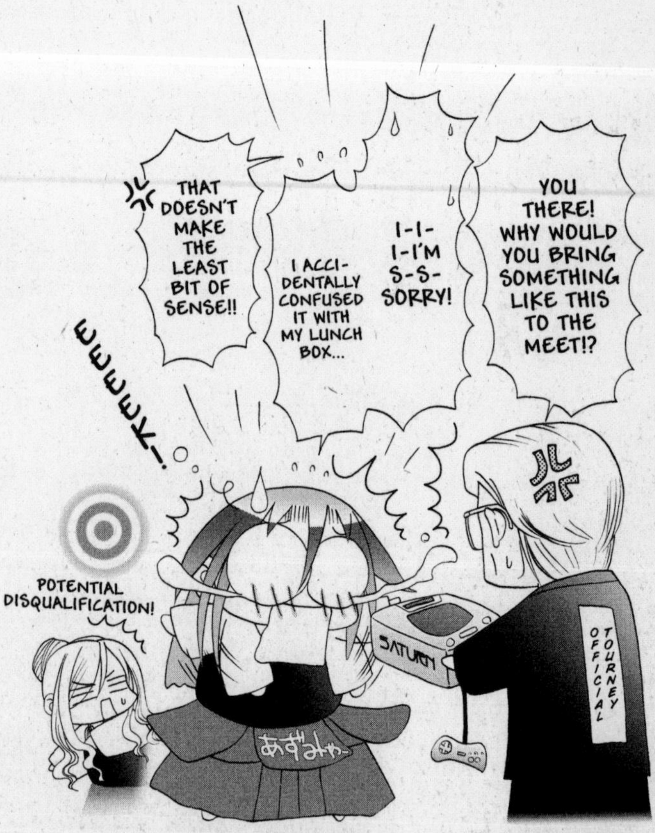
YOU THERE! WHY WOULD YOU BRING SOMETHING LIKE THIS TO THE MEET!?
I-I-I-I'M S-S-SORRY!
I ACCIDENTALLY CONFUSED IT WITH MY LUNCH BOX...
THAT DOESN'T MAKE THE LEAST BIT OF SENSE!!
EEEEK-!
POTENTIAL DISQUALIFICATION!
OFFICIAL TOURNEY
SATURN
あずみや

ARMOR: AZUMIYA

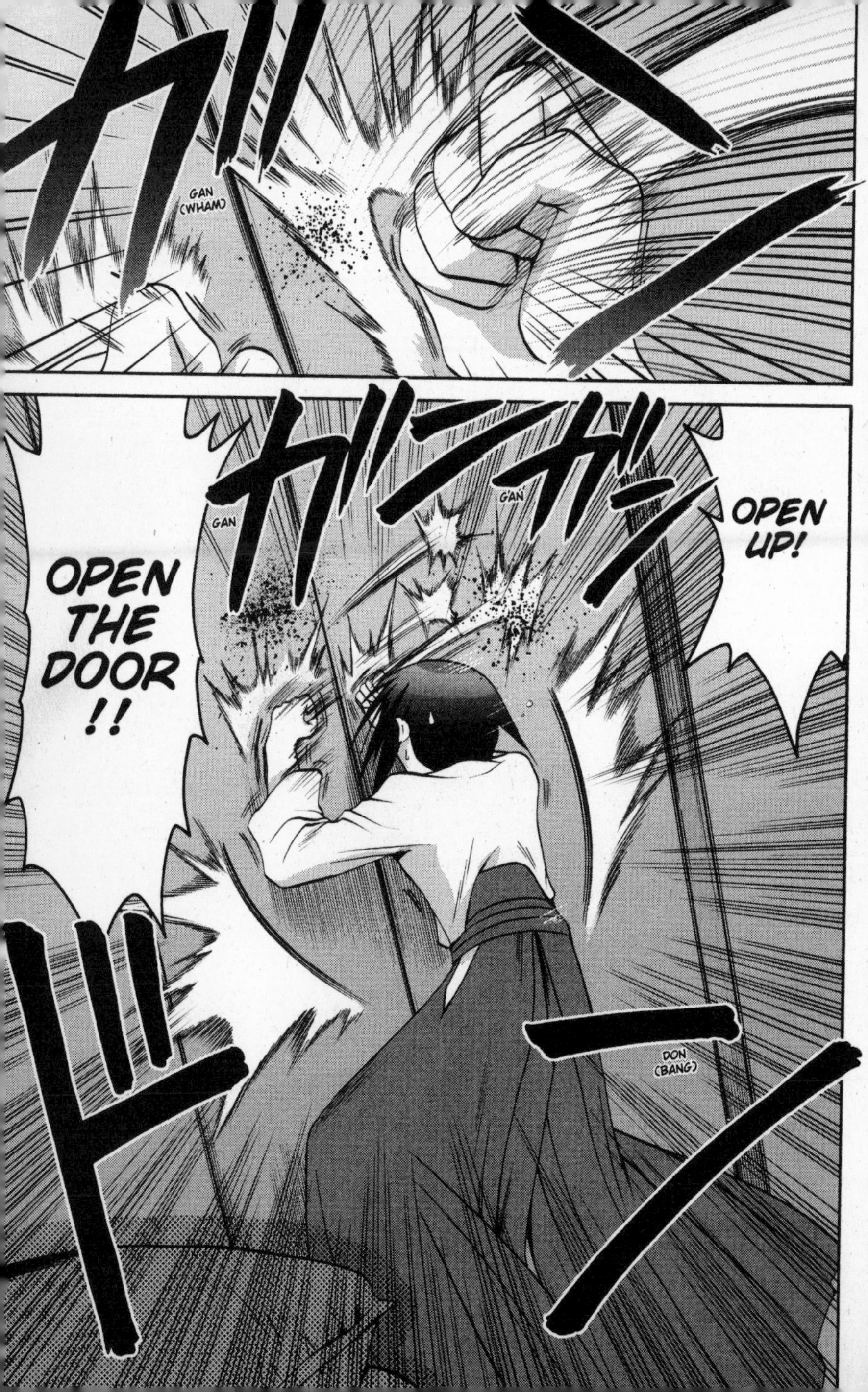
GAN (WHAM)
OPEN UP!
GAN
GAN
OPEN THE DOOR !!
DON (BANG)

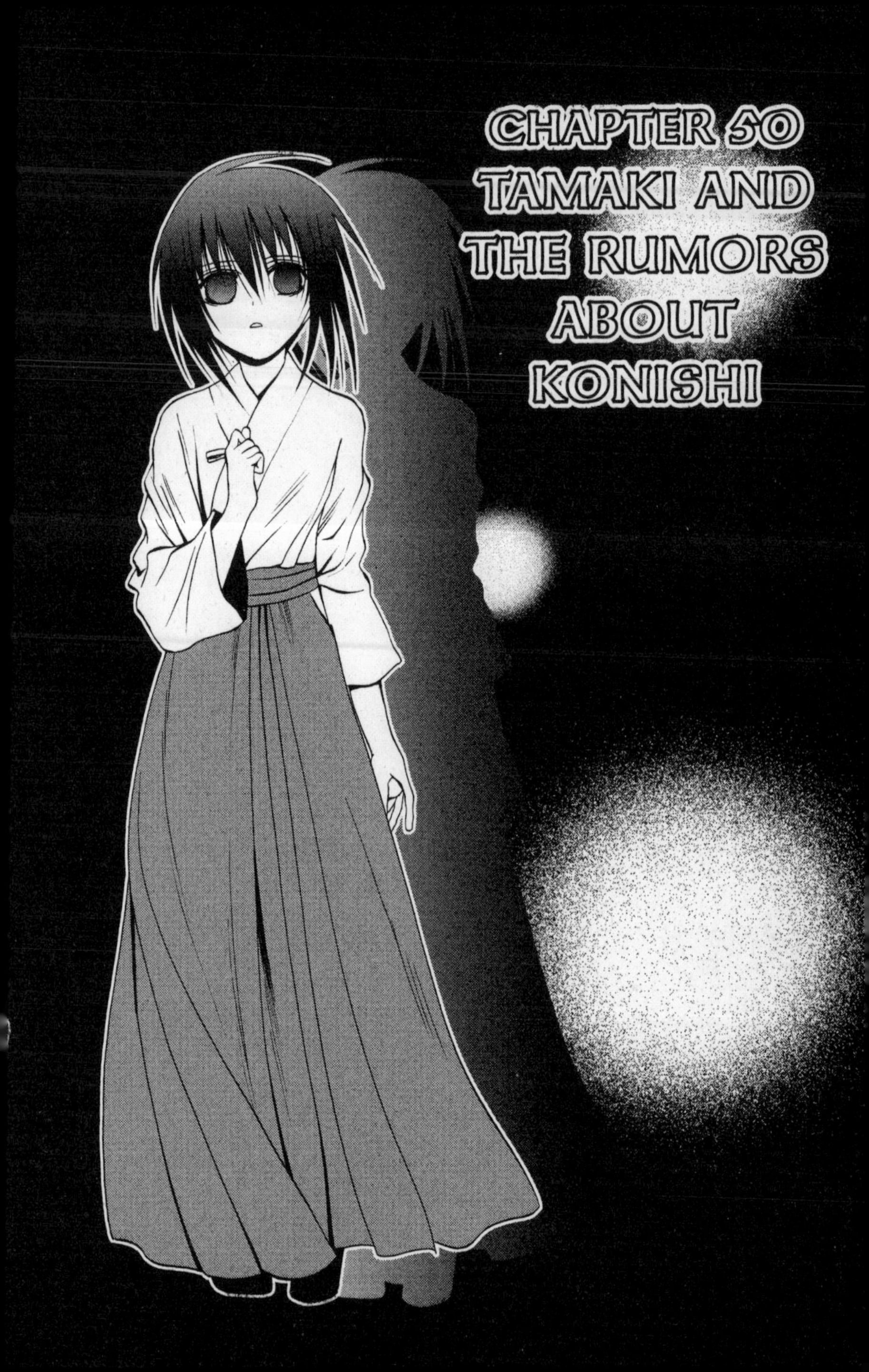
CHAPTER 50
TAMAKI AND THE RUMORS ABOUT KONISHI

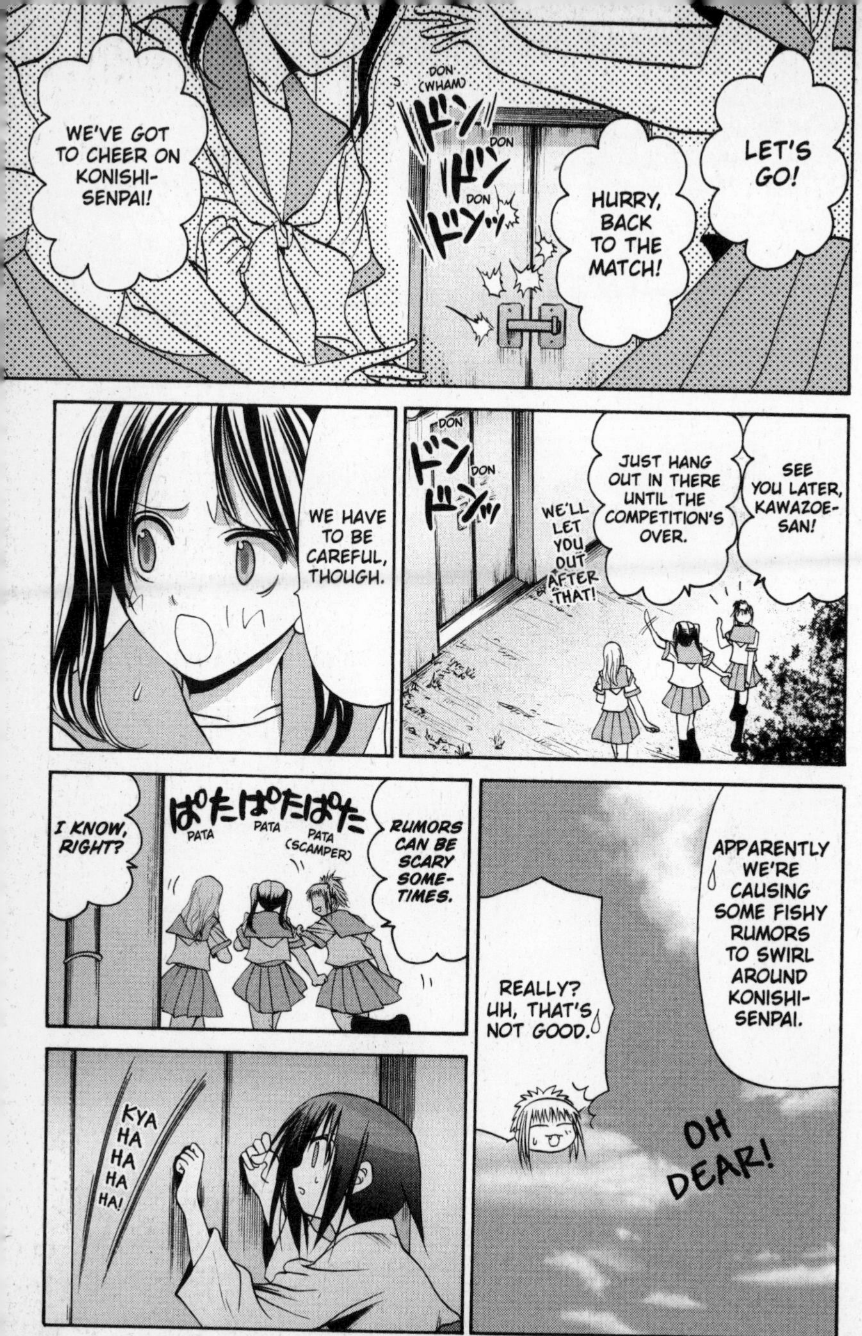
LET'S GO!
HURRY, BACK TO THE MATCH!
DON (WHAM)
ドン
DON
ドン
DON
ドンッ
WE'VE GOT TO CHEER ON KONISHI-SENPAI!
SEE YOU LATER, KAWAZOE-SAN!
JUST HANG OUT IN THERE UNTIL THE COMPETITION'S OVER.
WE'LL LET YOU OUT AFTER THAT!
DON
ドン
DON
ドンッ
WE HAVE TO BE CAREFUL, THOUGH.
APPARENTLY WE'RE CAUSING SOME FISHY RUMORS TO SWIRL AROUND KONISHI-SENPAI.
REALLY? UH, THAT'S NOT GOOD.
OH DEAR!
RUMORS CAN BE SCARY SOMETIMES.
ぱたぱたぱた
PATA PATA PATA (SCAMPER)
I KNOW, RIGHT?
KYA HA HA HA HA HA!

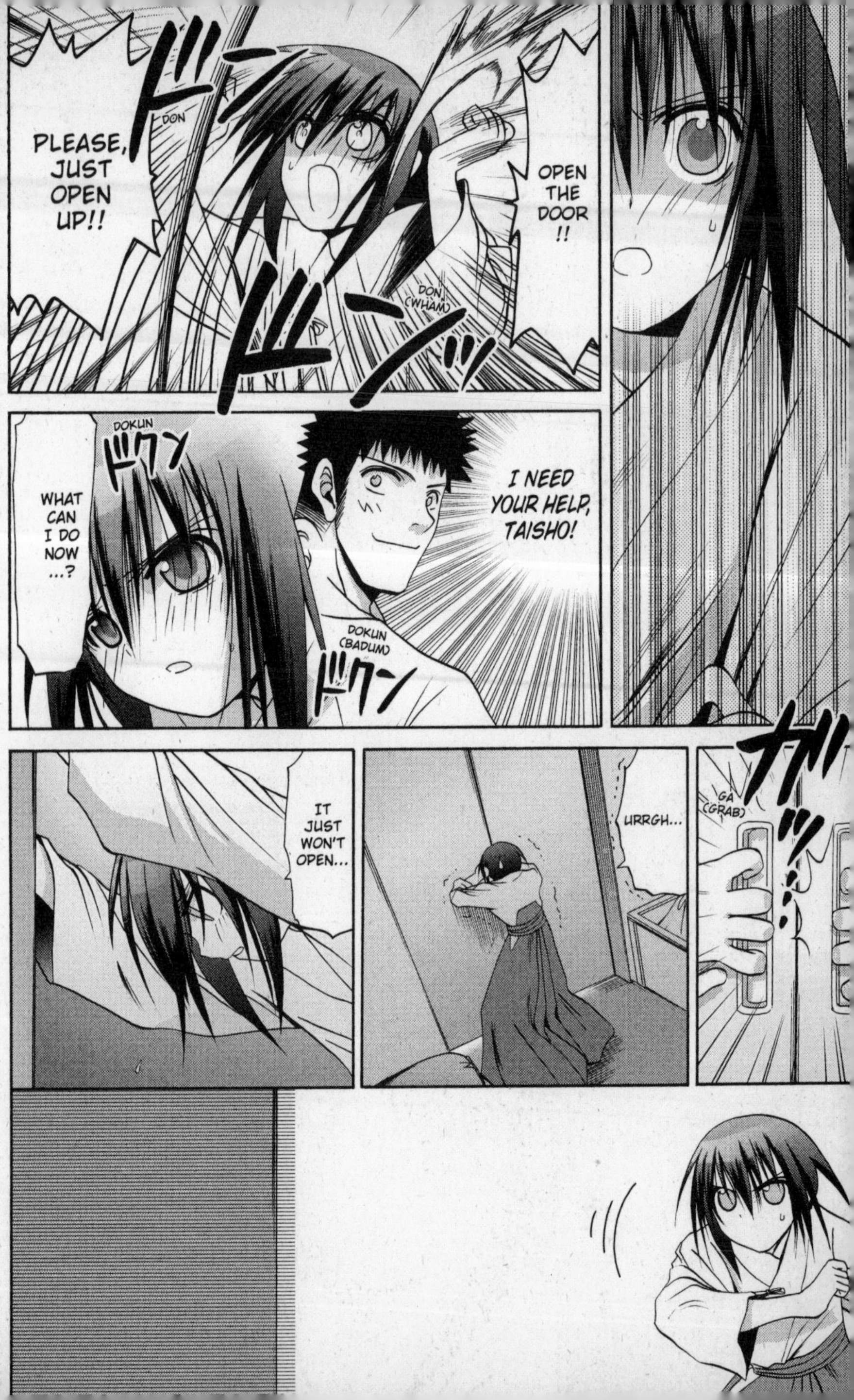
OPEN THE DOOR !!
DON
PLEASE, JUST OPEN UP!!
DON (WHAM)
I NEED YOUR HELP, TAISHO!
DOKUN
WHAT CAN I DO NOW ...?
DOKUN (BADUM)
GA (GRAB)
URRGH...
IT JUST WON'T OPEN...

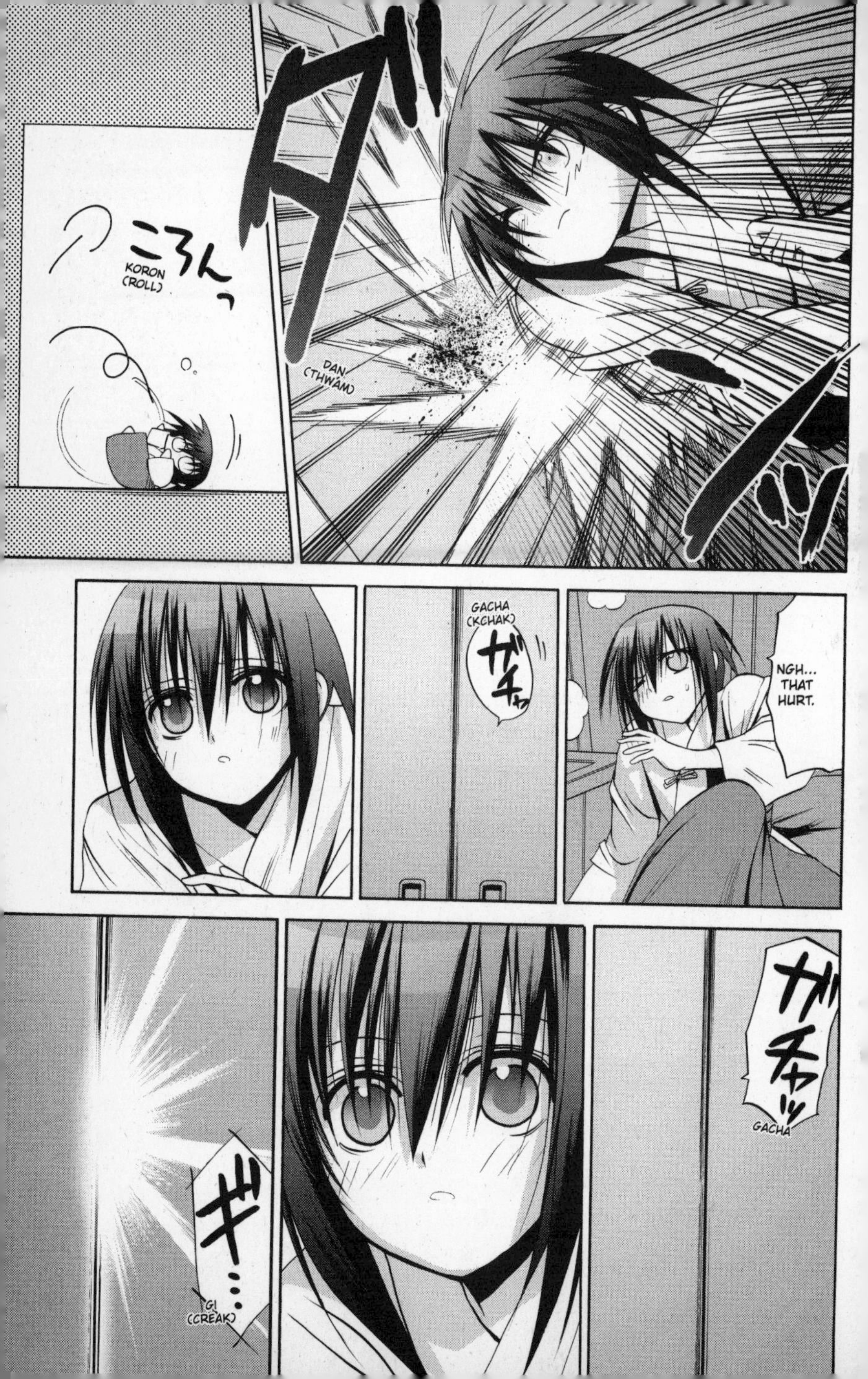
DAN (THWAM)
ころん
KORON (ROLL)
NGH... THAT HURT.
ガチャ
GACHA (KCHAK)
ガチャッ
GACHA
ギ…
GI (CREAK)

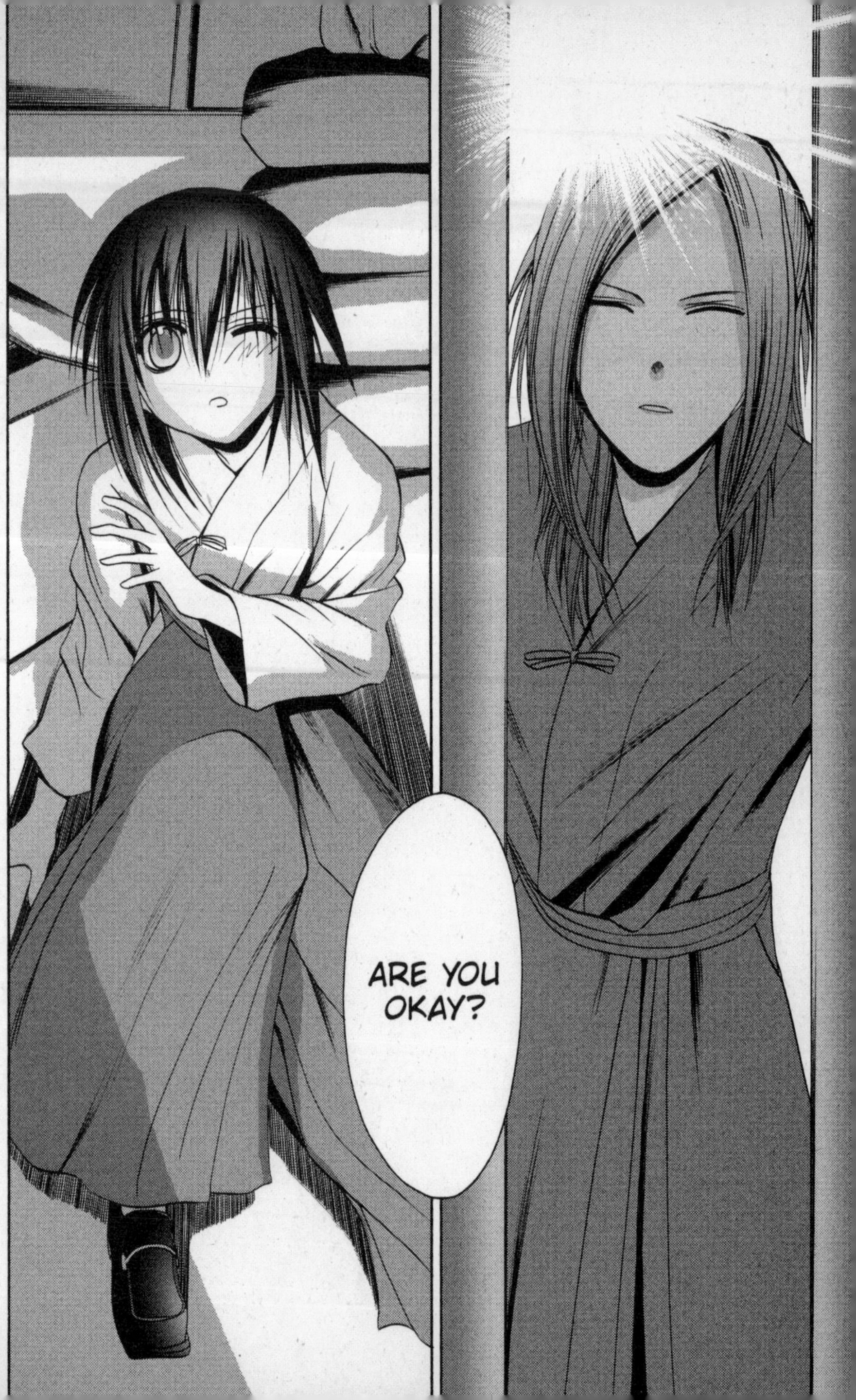
ARE YOU OKAY?

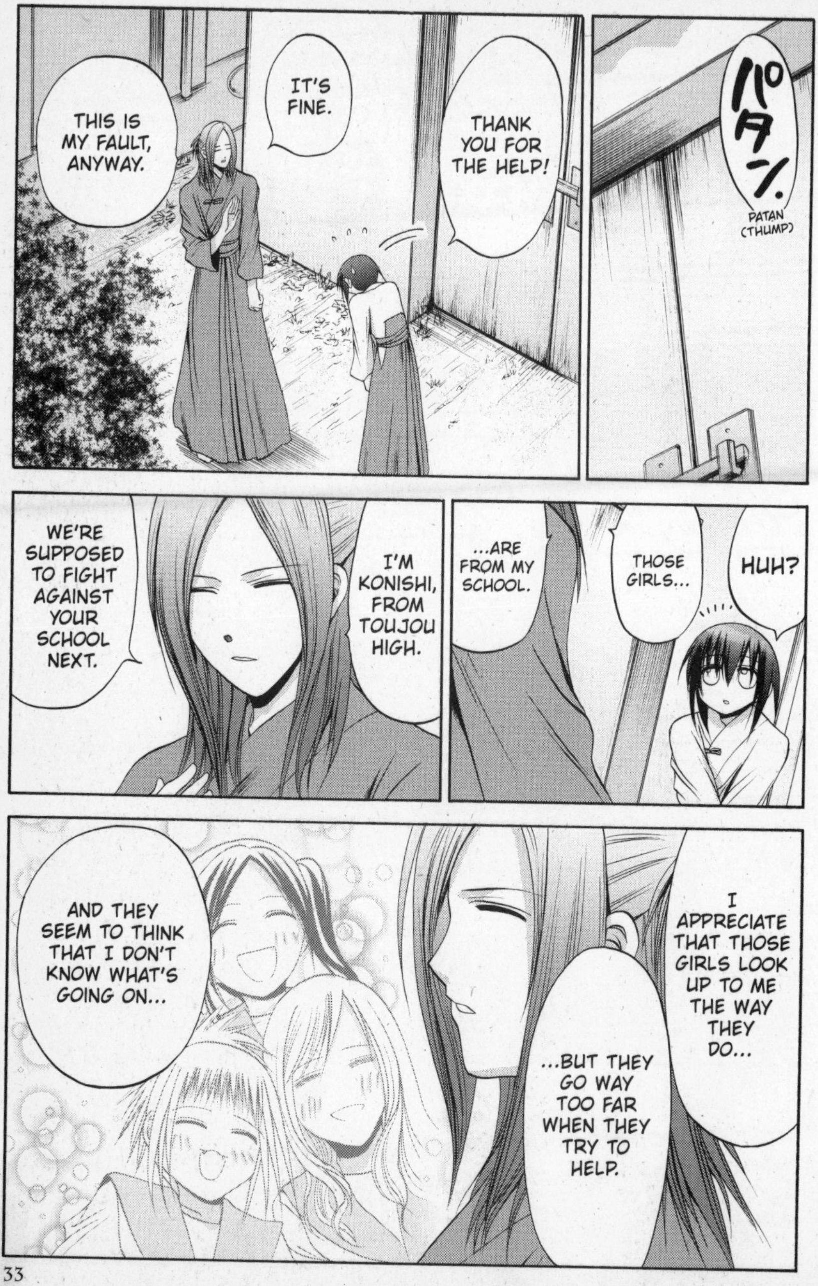
パタン.
PATAN (THUMP)
THANK YOU FOR THE HELP!
IT'S FINE.
THIS IS MY FAULT, ANYWAY.
HUH?
THOSE GIRLS...
...ARE FROM MY SCHOOL.
I'M KONISHI, FROM TOUJOU HIGH.
WE'RE SUPPOSED TO FIGHT AGAINST YOUR SCHOOL NEXT.
I APPRECIATE THAT THOSE GIRLS LOOK UP TO ME THE WAY THEY DO...
...BUT THEY GO WAY TOO FAR WHEN THEY TRY TO HELP.
AND THEY SEEM TO THINK THAT I DON'T KNOW WHAT'S GOING ON...

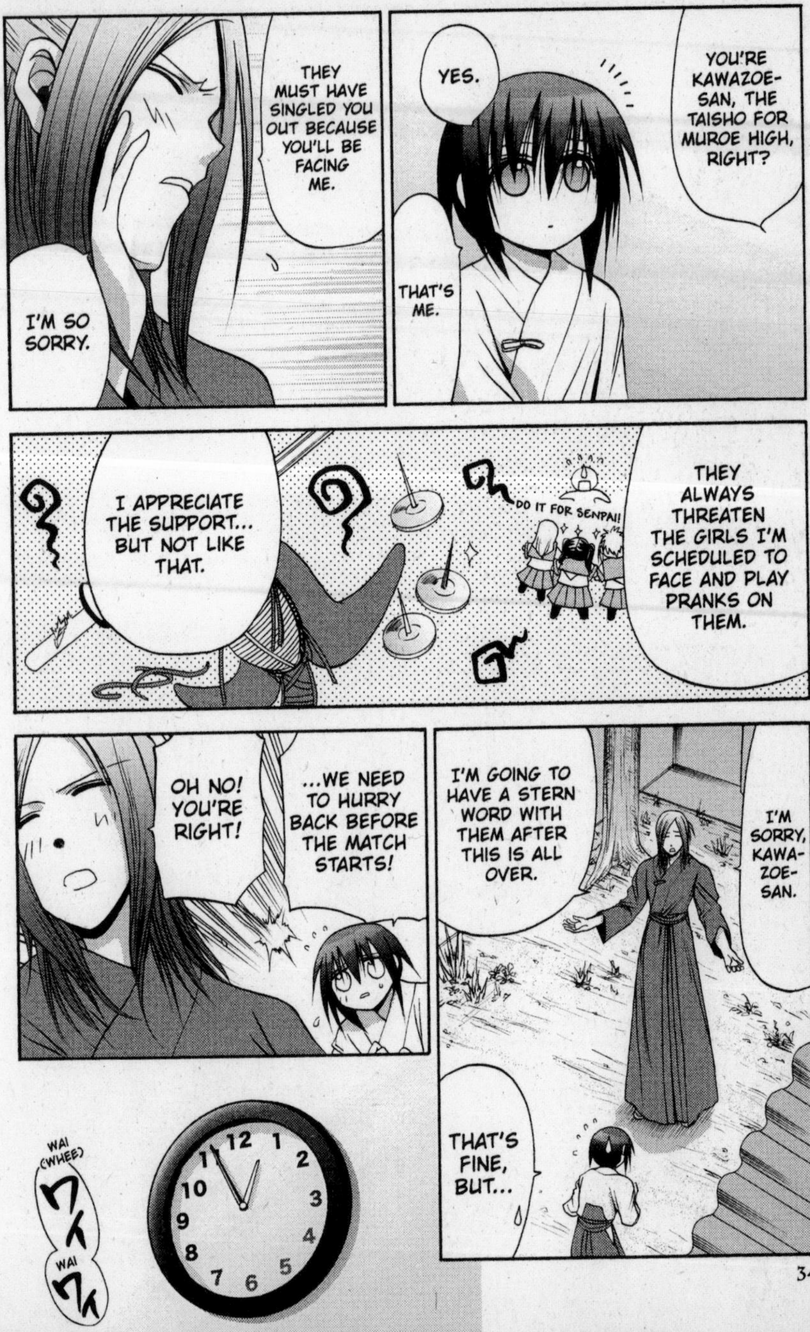
YOU'RE KAWAZOE-SAN, THE TAISHO FOR MUROE HIGH, RIGHT?
YES.
THAT'S ME.
THEY MUST HAVE SINGLED YOU OUT BECAUSE YOU'LL BE FACING ME.
I'M SO SORRY.
THEY ALWAYS THREATEN THE GIRLS I'M SCHEDULED TO FACE AND PLAY PRANKS ON THEM.
DO IT FOR SENPAI!
I APPRECIATE THE SUPPORT... BUT NOT LIKE THAT.
I'M SORRY, KAWAZOE-SAN.
I'M GOING TO HAVE A STERN WORD WITH THEM AFTER THIS IS ALL OVER.
THAT'S FINE, BUT...
...WE NEED TO HURRY BACK BEFORE THE MATCH STARTS!
OH NO! YOU'RE RIGHT!
WAI (WHEE)
ワイ
WAI
ワイ

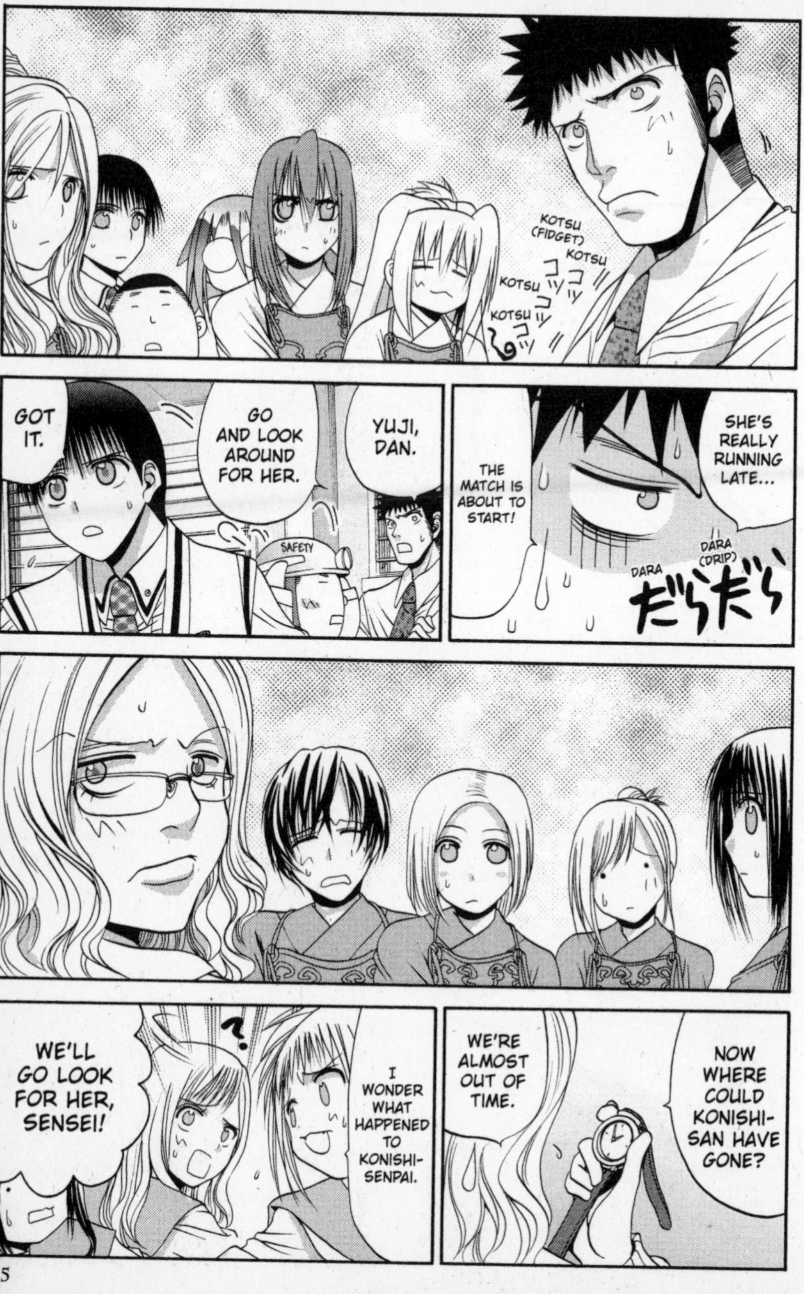
KOTSU (FIDGET)
KOTSU
KOTSU
KOTSU
コツコツコツコツ
SHE'S REALLY RUNNING LATE...
THE MATCH IS ABOUT TO START!
DARA (DRIP)
DARA
だらだら
YUJI, DAN.
GO AND LOOK AROUND FOR HER.
GOT IT.
SAFETY
NOW WHERE COULD KONISHI-SAN HAVE GONE?
WE'RE ALMOST OUT OF TIME.
I WONDER WHAT HAPPENED TO KONISHI-SENPAI.
?
WE'LL GO LOOK FOR HER, SENSEI!

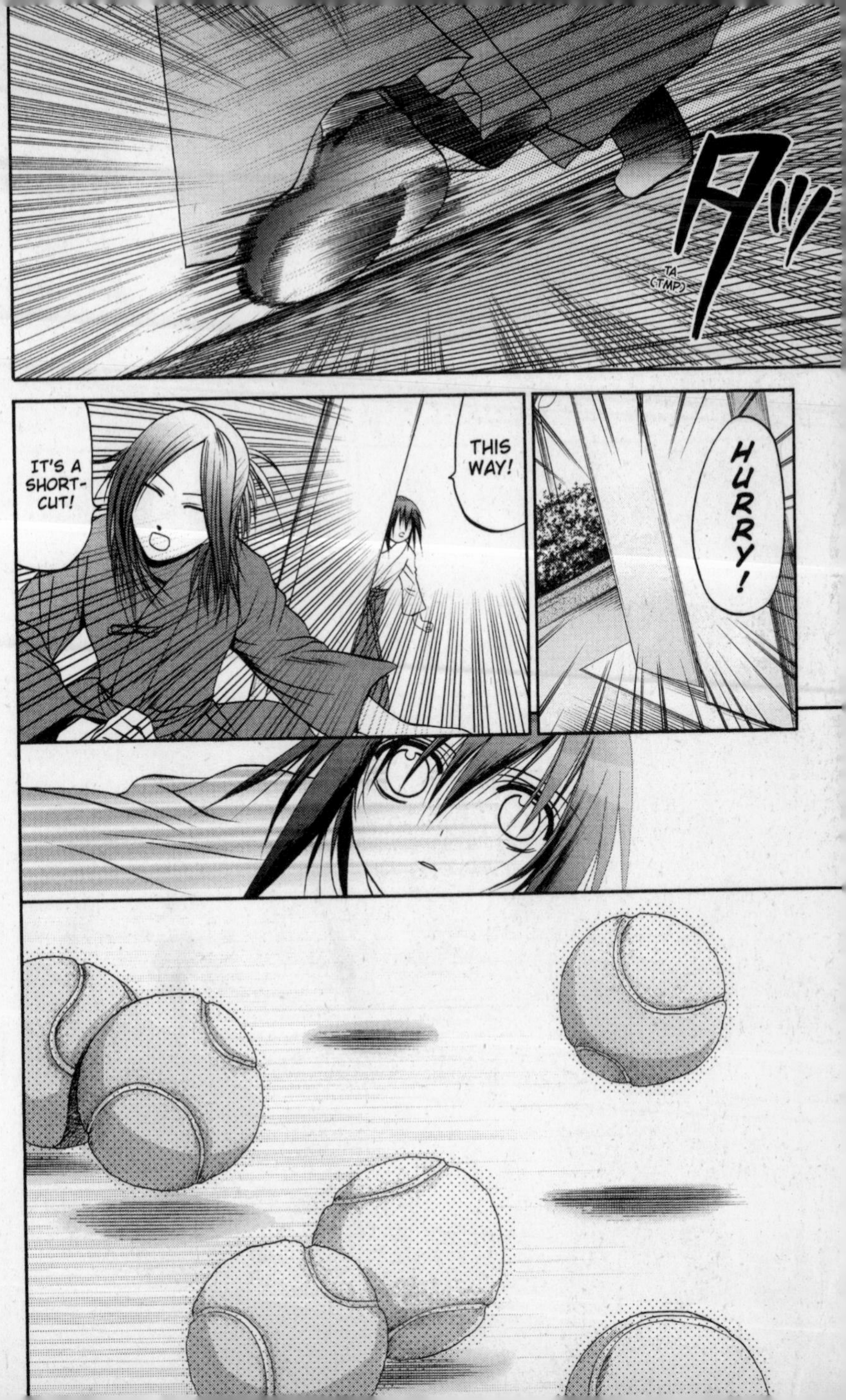
タッ
TA (TMP)
HURRY!
THIS WAY!
IT'S A SHORT-CUT!

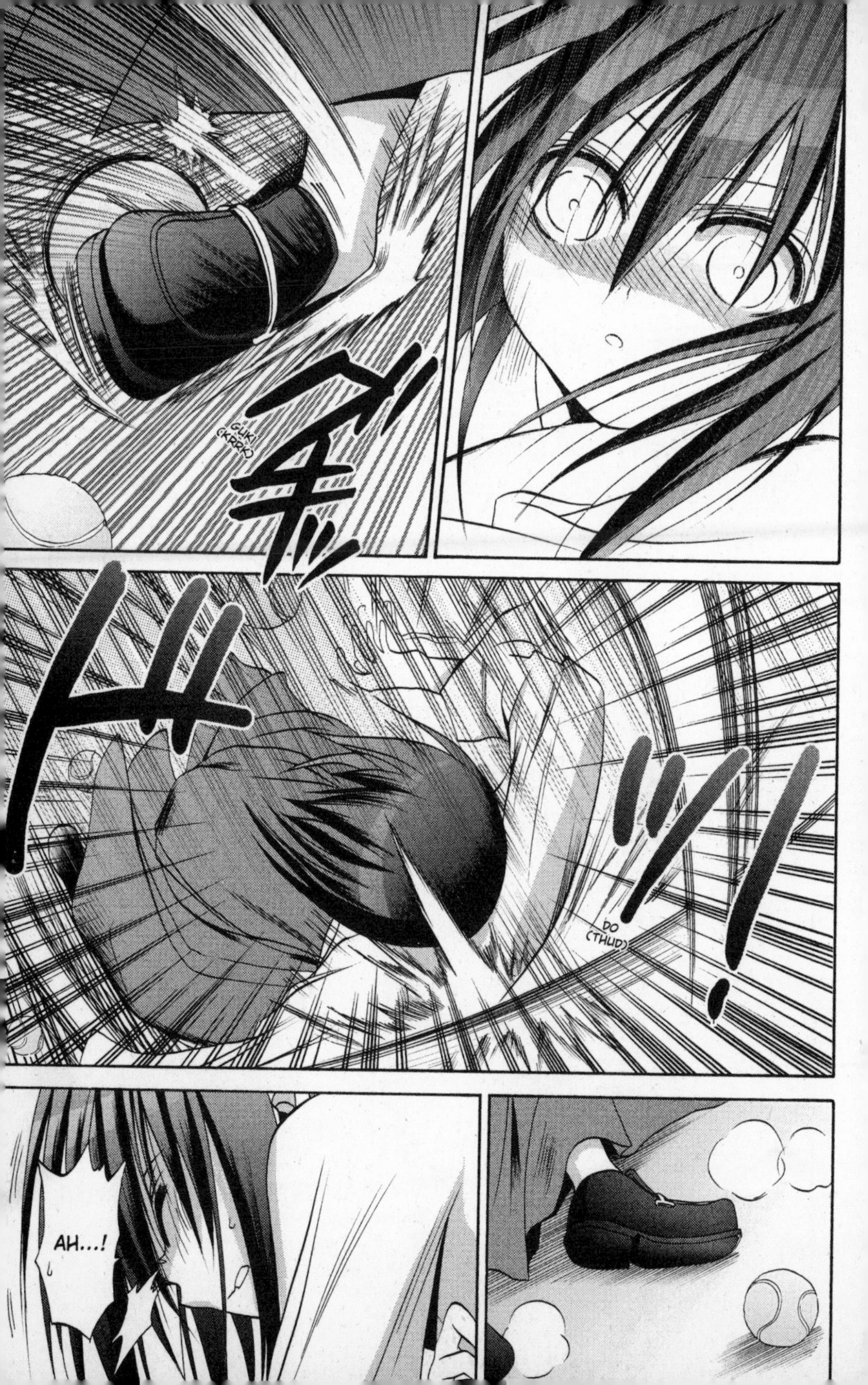
GUKI (KRRK)
DO (THUD)
AH...!

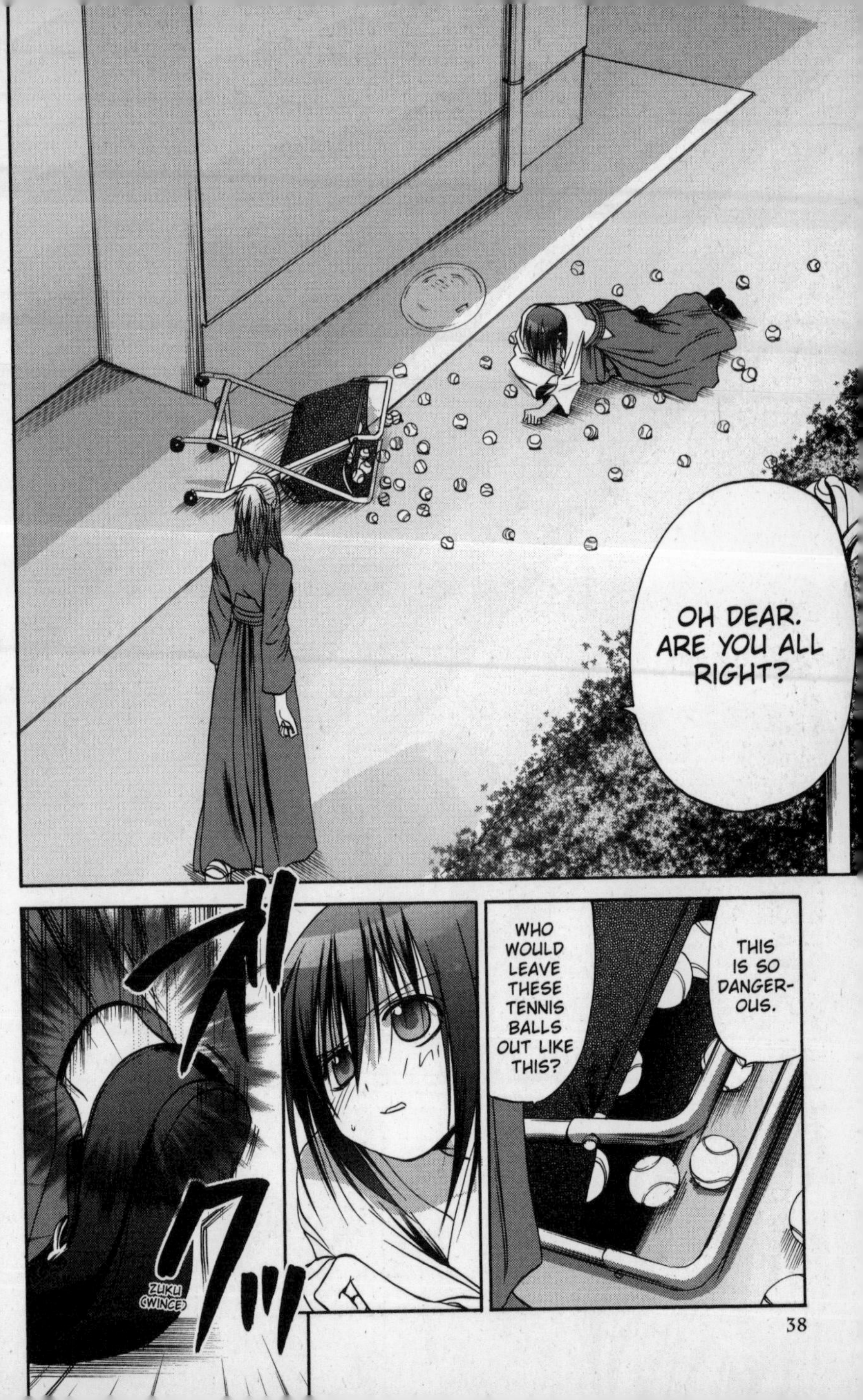
OH DEAR. ARE YOU ALL RIGHT?
THIS IS SO DANGER-OUS.
WHO WOULD LEAVE THESE TENNIS BALLS OUT LIKE THIS?
ZUKU (WINCE)

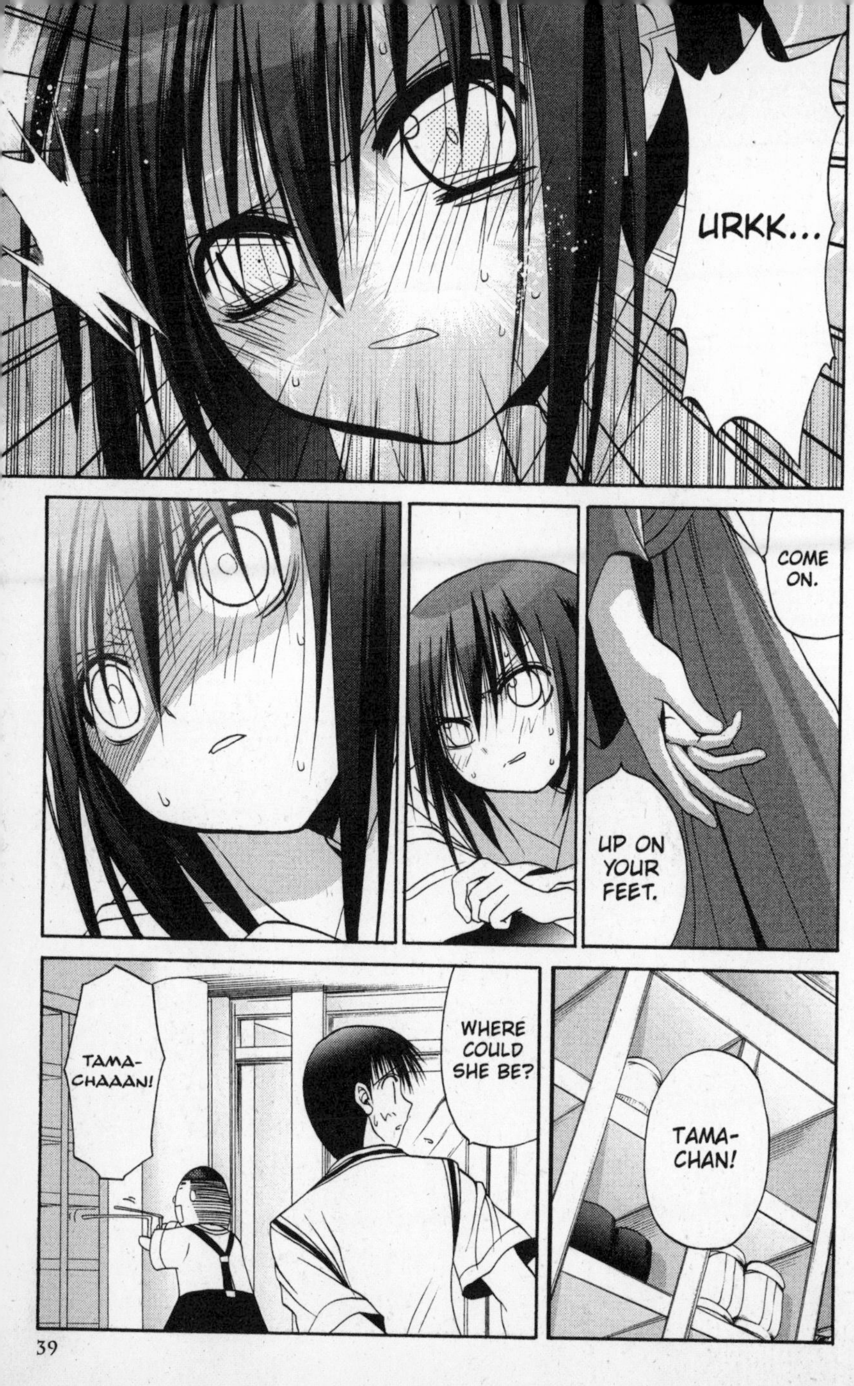
URKK...
COME ON.
UP ON YOUR FEET.
TAMA-CHAN!
WHERE COULD SHE BE?
TAMA-CHAAAN!

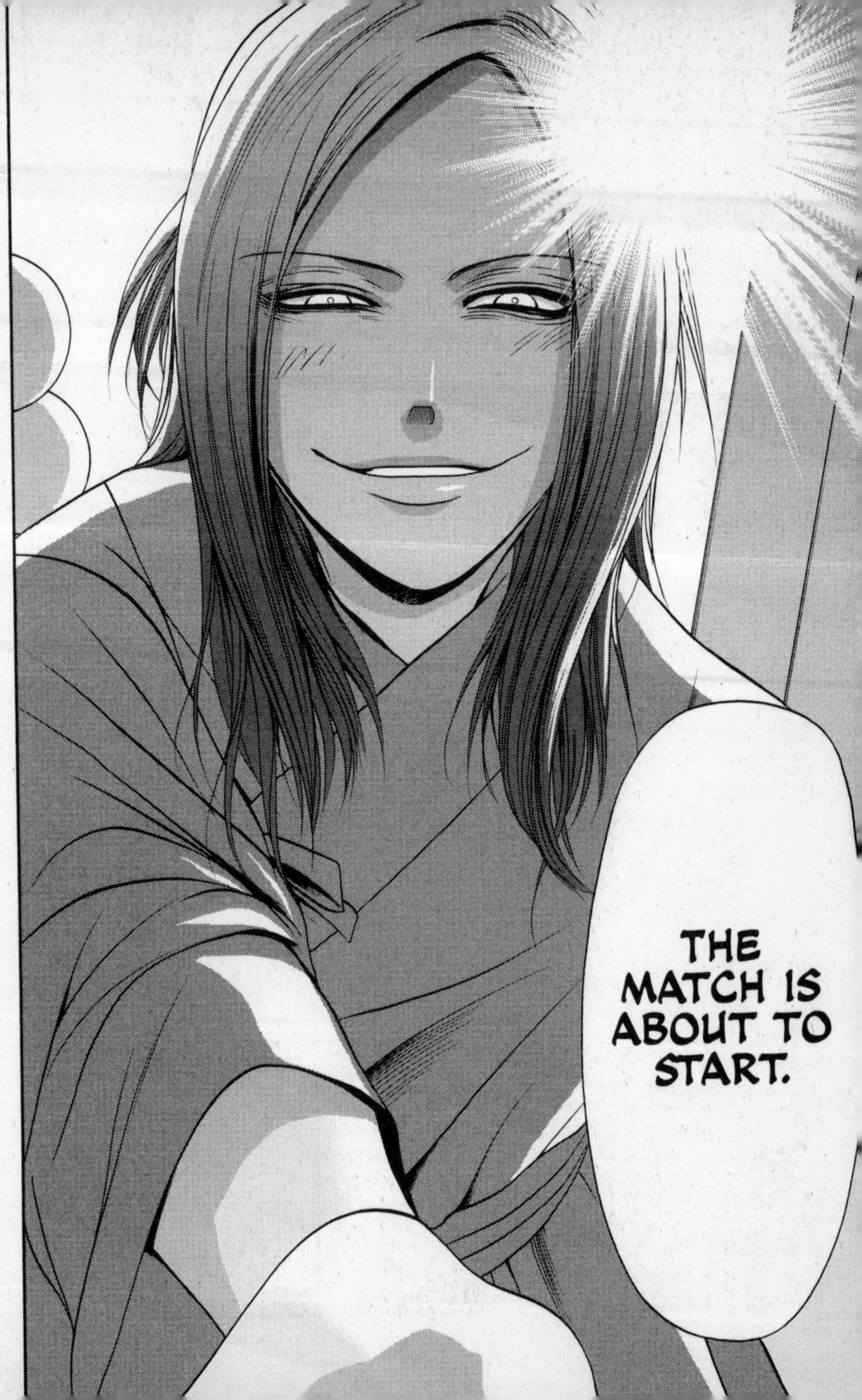
THE MATCH IS ABOUT TO START.

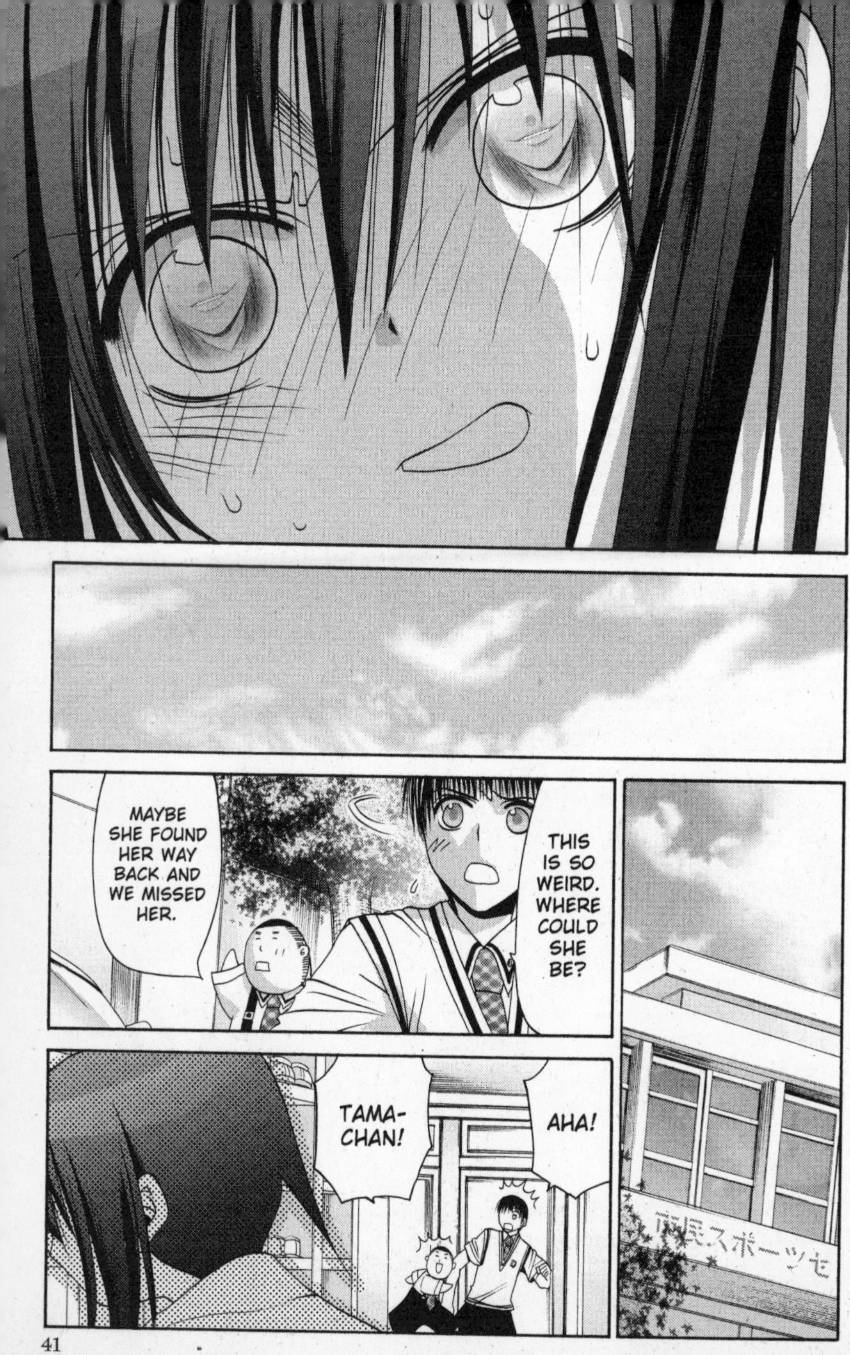
THIS IS SO WEIRD. WHERE COULD SHE BE?
MAYBE SHE FOUND HER WAY BACK AND WE MISSED HER.
AHA!
TAMA-CHAN!

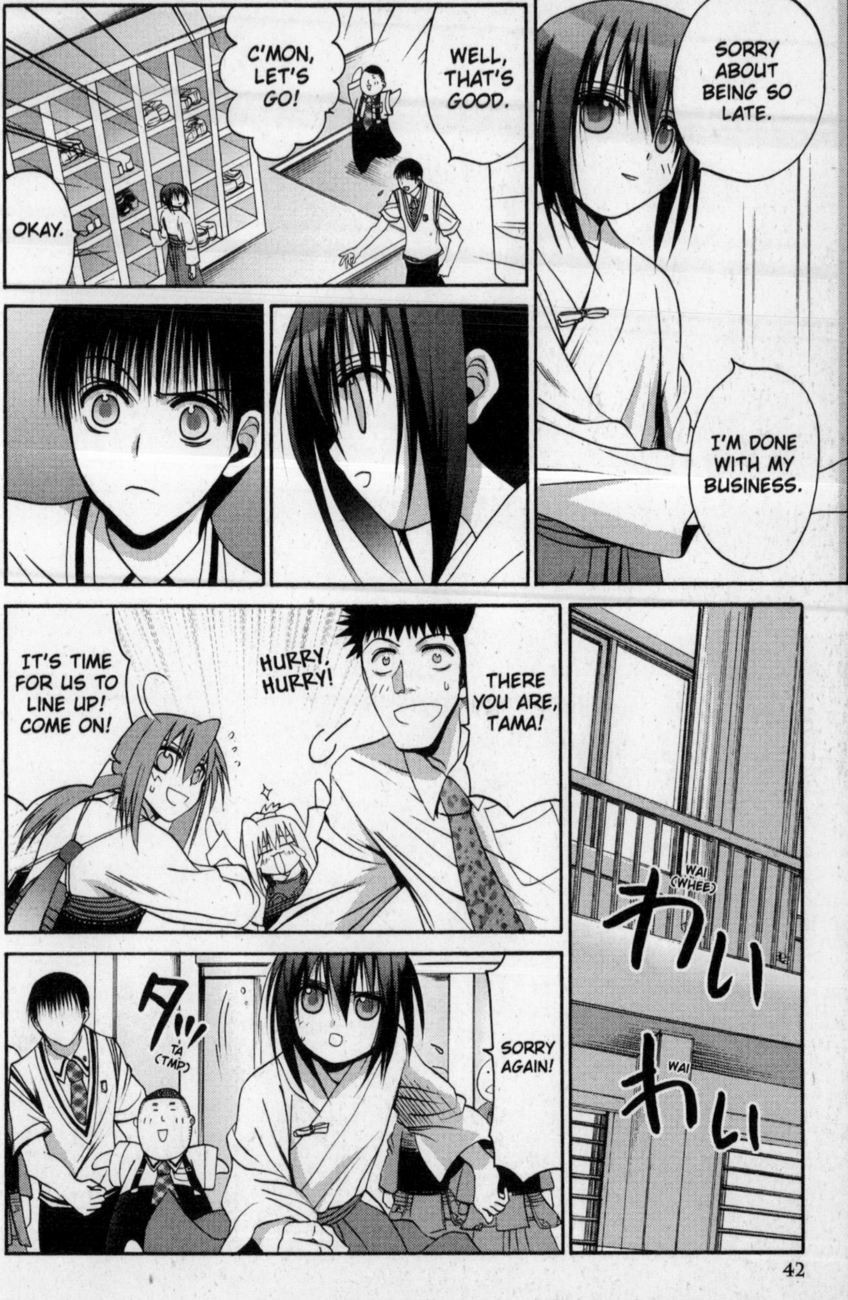
SORRY ABOUT BEING SO LATE.
I'M DONE WITH MY BUSINESS.
WELL, THAT'S GOOD.
C'MON, LET'S GO!
OKAY.
わい
WAI (WHEE)
わい
WAI
THERE YOU ARE, TAMA!
HURRY, HURRY!
IT'S TIME FOR US TO LINE UP! COME ON!
SORRY AGAIN!
タッ
TA (TMP)

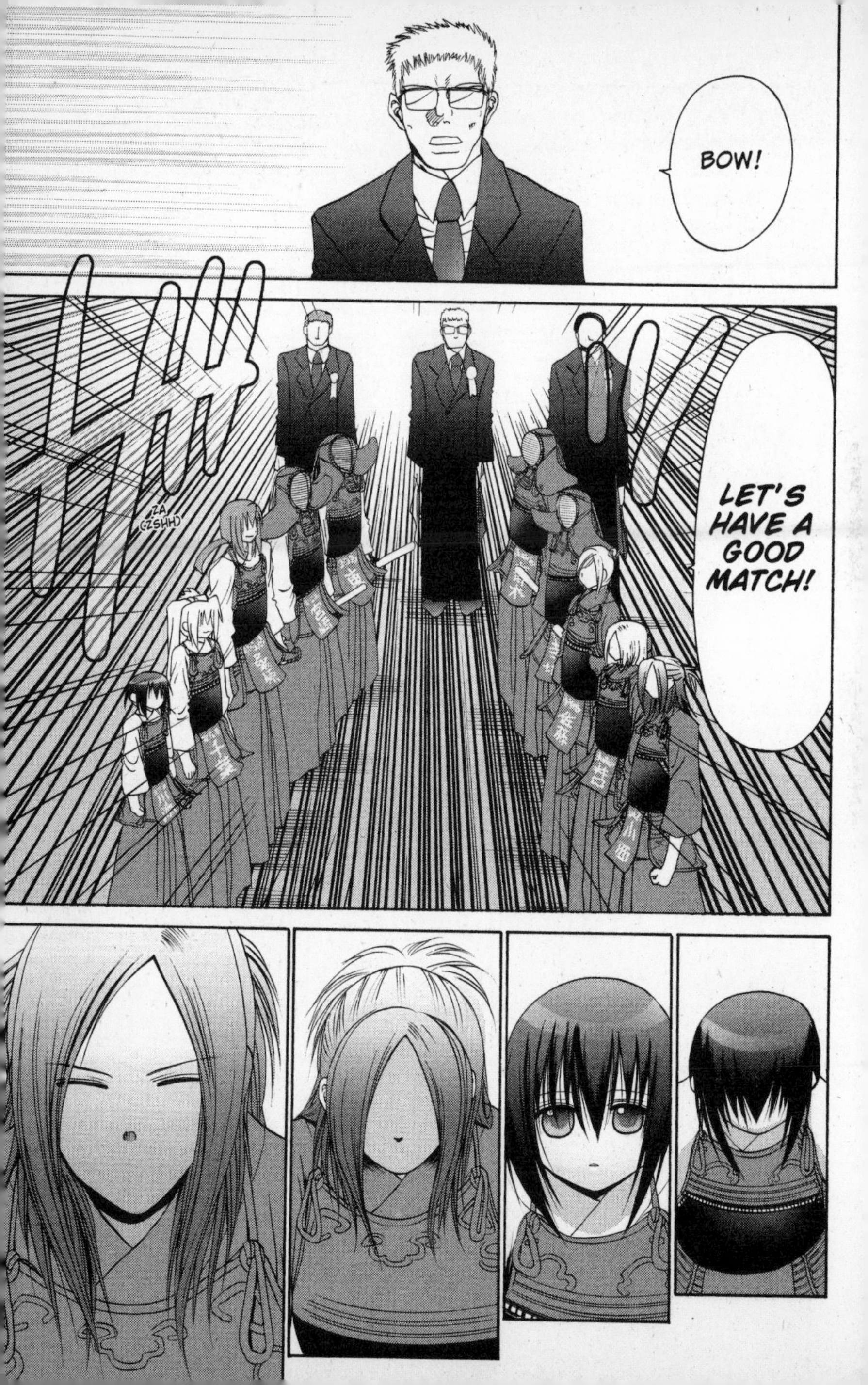
BOW!
LET'S HAVE A GOOD MATCH!
ZA (ZSHH)

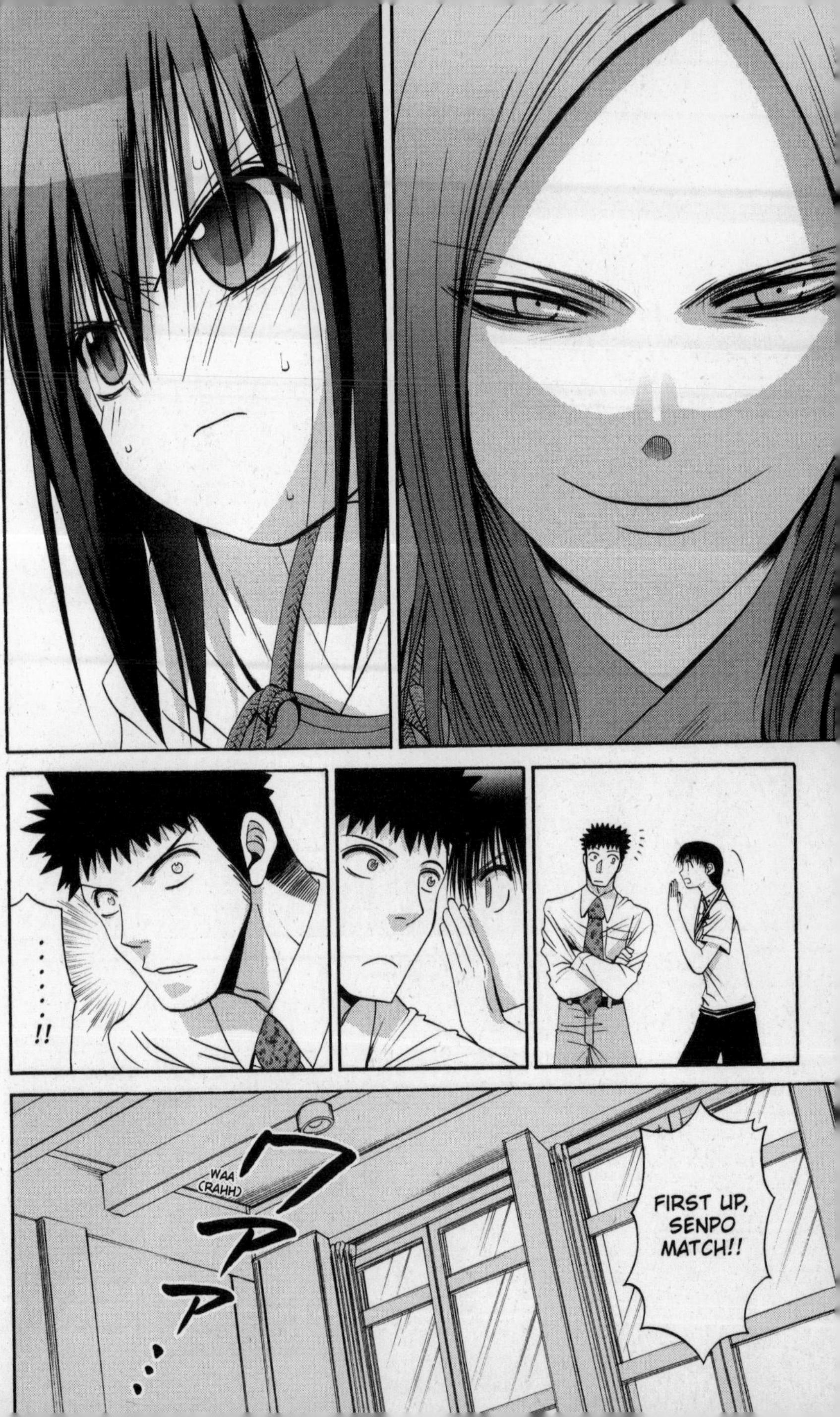
......!!
WAA (RAHH)
FIRST UP, SENPO MATCH!!

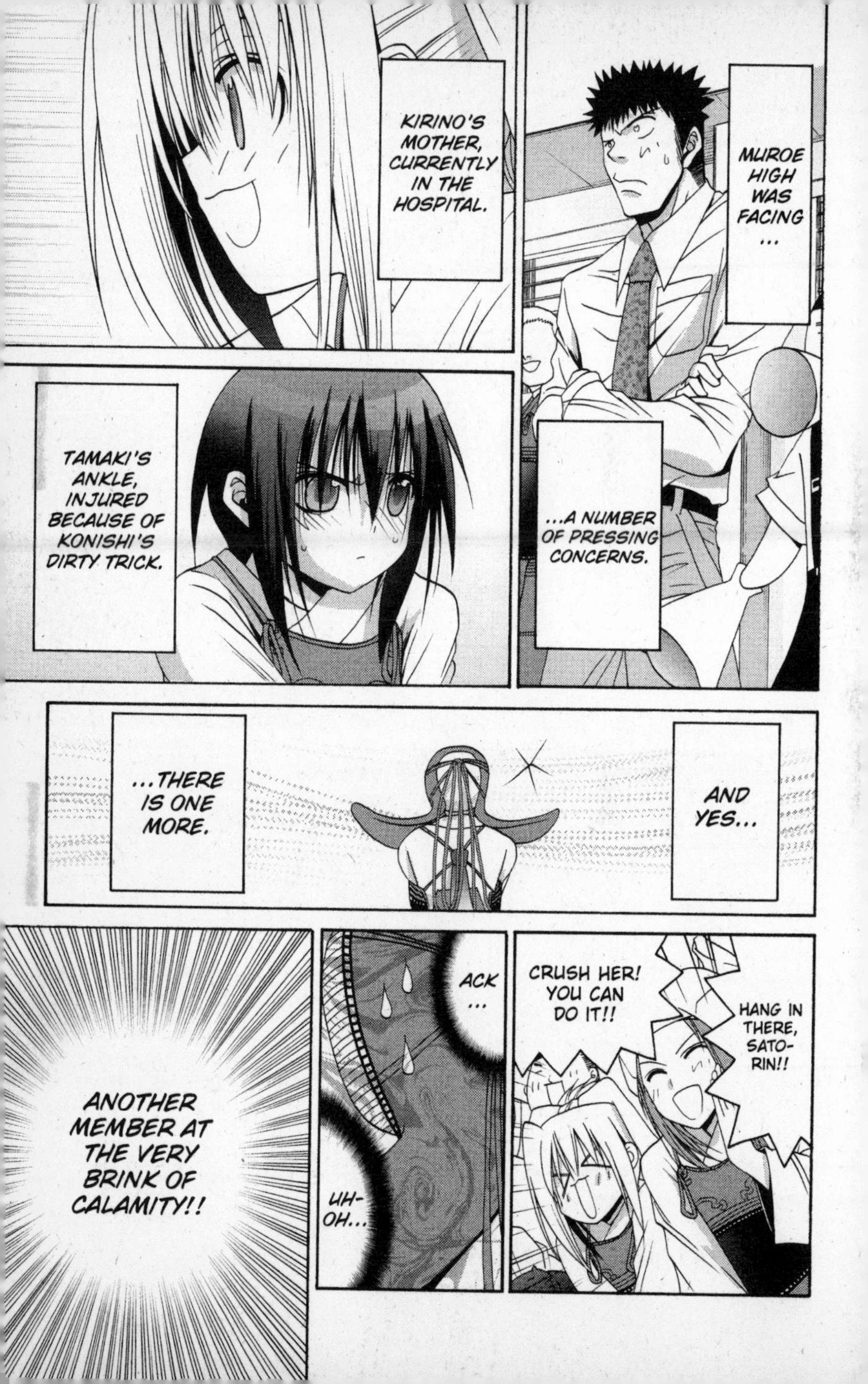
MUROE HIGH WAS FACING ...
...A NUMBER OF PRESSING CONCERNS.
KIRINO'S MOTHER, CURRENTLY IN THE HOSPITAL.
TAMAKI'S ANKLE, INJURED BECAUSE OF KONISHI'S DIRTY TRICK.
AND YES...
...THERE IS ONE MORE.
HANG IN THERE, SATO-RIN!!
CRUSH HER! YOU CAN DO IT!!
ACK ...
UH-OH...
ANOTHER MEMBER AT THE VERY BRINK OF CALAMITY!!

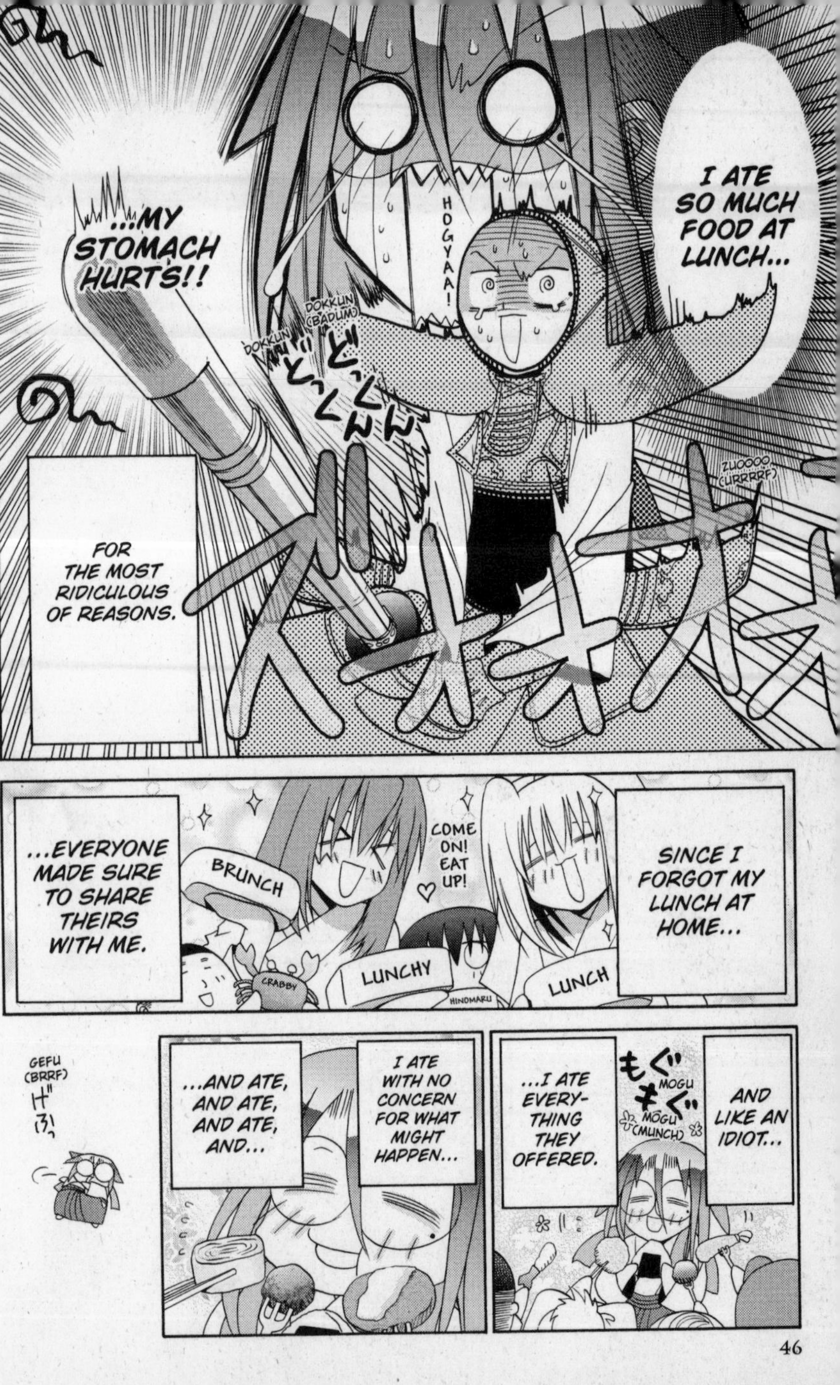
I ATE SO MUCH FOOD AT LUNCH...
HOGYAA!
...MY STOMACH HURTS!!
DOKKUN (BADUM)
DOKKUN
ZUOOOO (URRRRF)
FOR THE MOST RIDICULOUS OF REASONS.
SINCE I FORGOT MY LUNCH AT HOME...
COME ON! EAT UP!
LUNCH
HINOMARU
LUNCHY
BRUNCH
CRABBY
...EVERYONE MADE SURE TO SHARE THEIRS WITH ME.
AND LIKE AN IDIOT...
MOGU
MOGU (MUNCH)
...I ATE EVERYTHING THEY OFFERED.
I ATE WITH NO CONCERN FOR WHAT MIGHT HAPPEN...
...AND ATE, AND ATE, AND ATE, AND...
GEFU (BRRF)

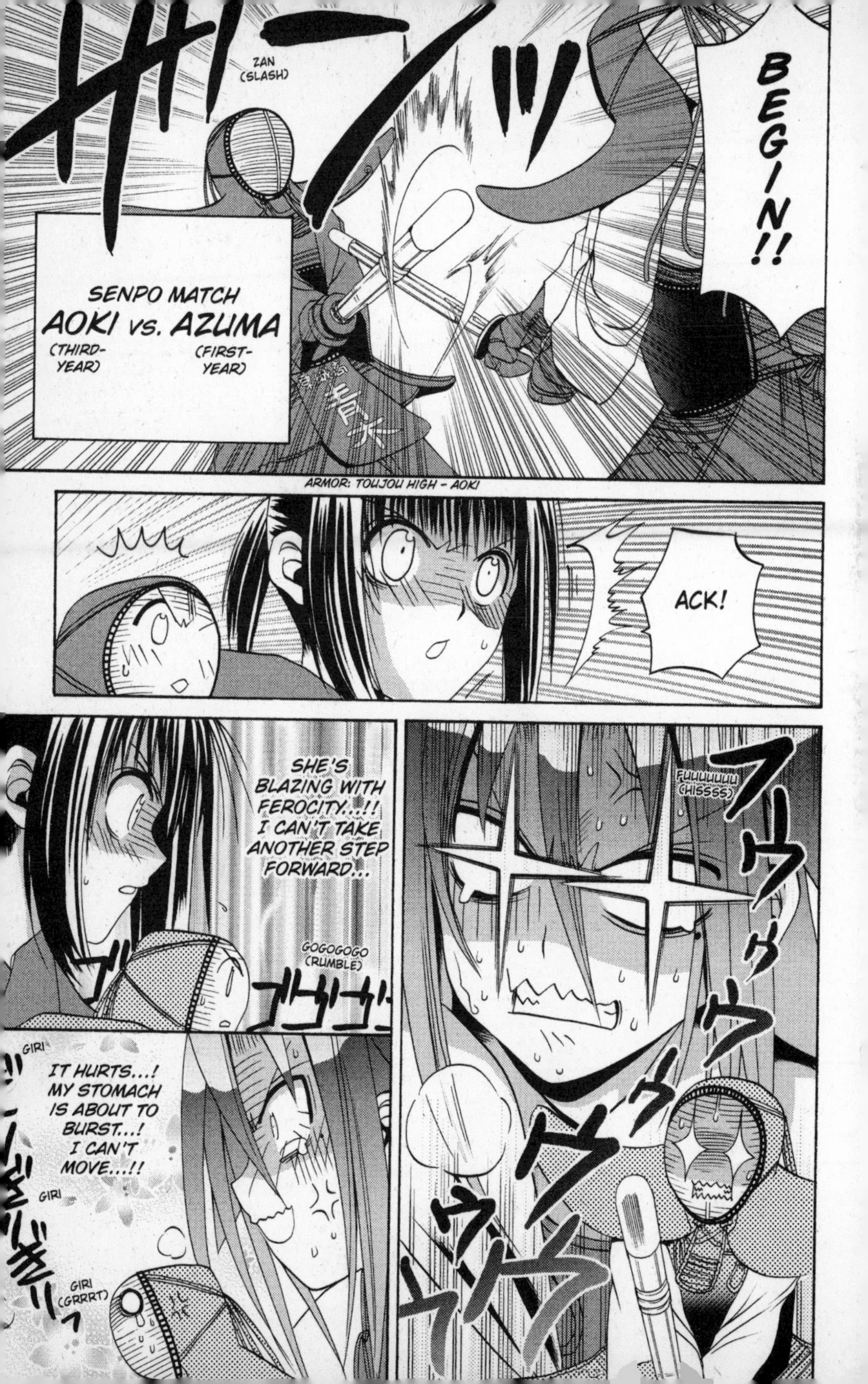
BEGIN!!
ZAN (SLASH)
SENPO MATCH
AOKI vs. AZUMA
(THIRD-YEAR)
(FIRST-YEAR)
ARMOR: TOUJOU HIGH - AOKI
ACK!
FUUUUUUU (HISSSS)
SHE'S BLAZING WITH FEROCITY...!! I CAN'T TAKE ANOTHER STEP FORWARD...
GOGOGOGO (RUMBLE)
GIRI
IT HURTS...! MY STOMACH IS ABOUT TO BURST...! I CAN'T MOVE...!!
GIRI
GIRI (GRRRT)

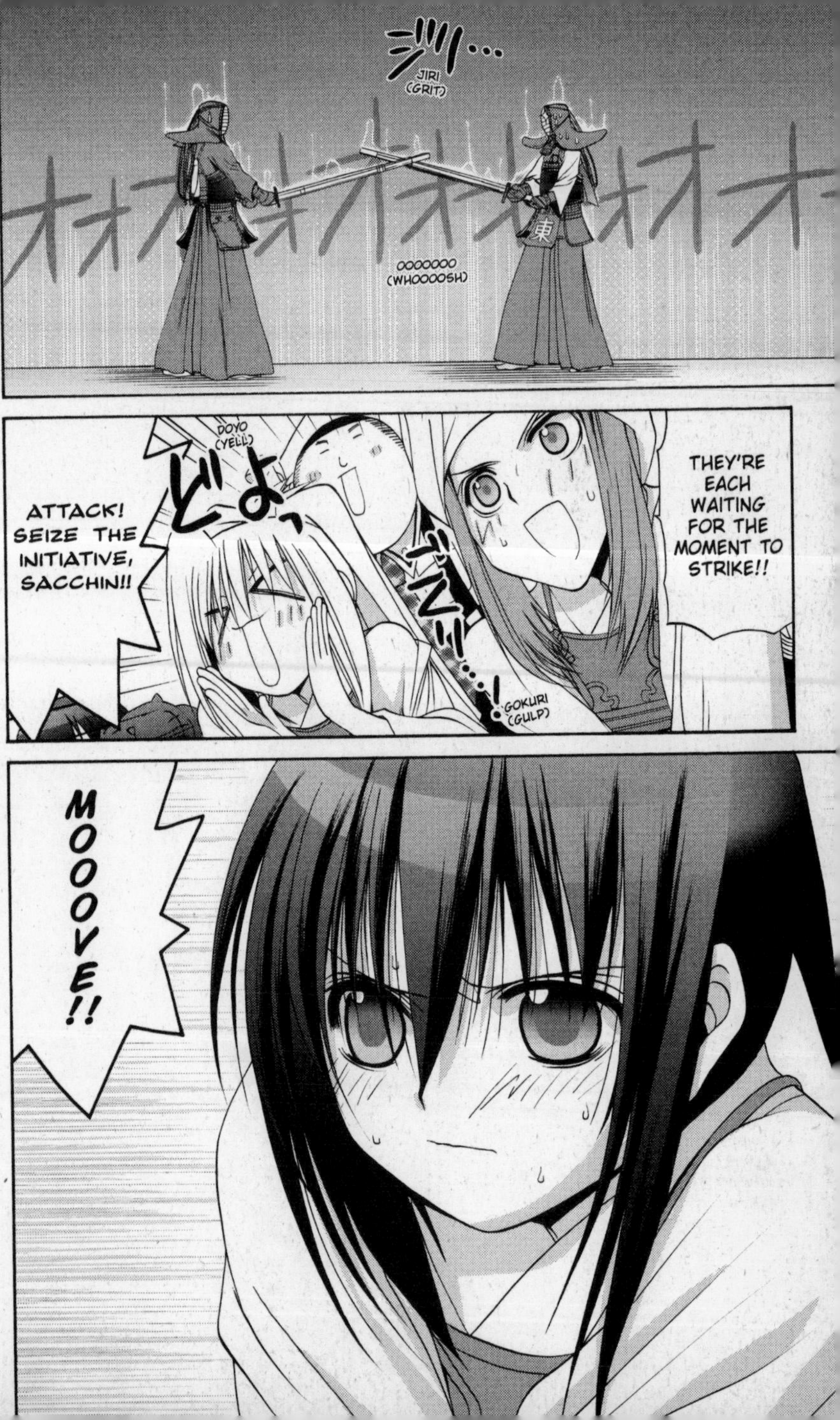
ジリ…
JIRI (GRIT)
OOOOOOO (WHOOOOSH)
THEY'RE EACH WAITING FOR THE MOMENT TO STRIKE!!
ゴクリ…!
GOKURI (GULP)
どよっ
DOYO (YELL)
ATTACK! SEIZE THE INITIATIVE, SACCHIN!!
MOOOOVE!!

BAMBOO BLADE

BAMBOO BLADE

バンブーブレード

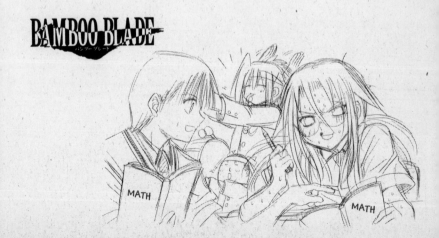

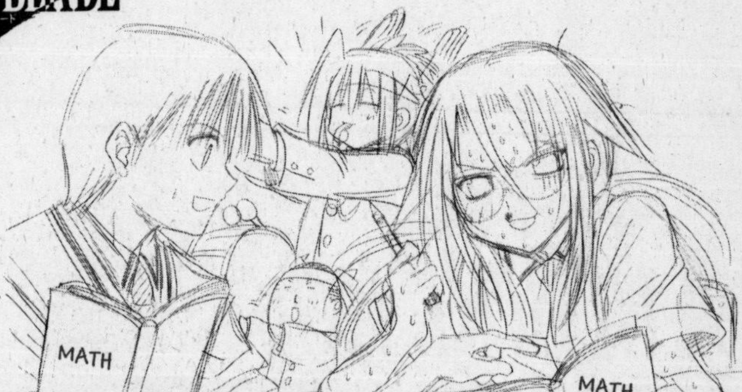
MATH
MATH

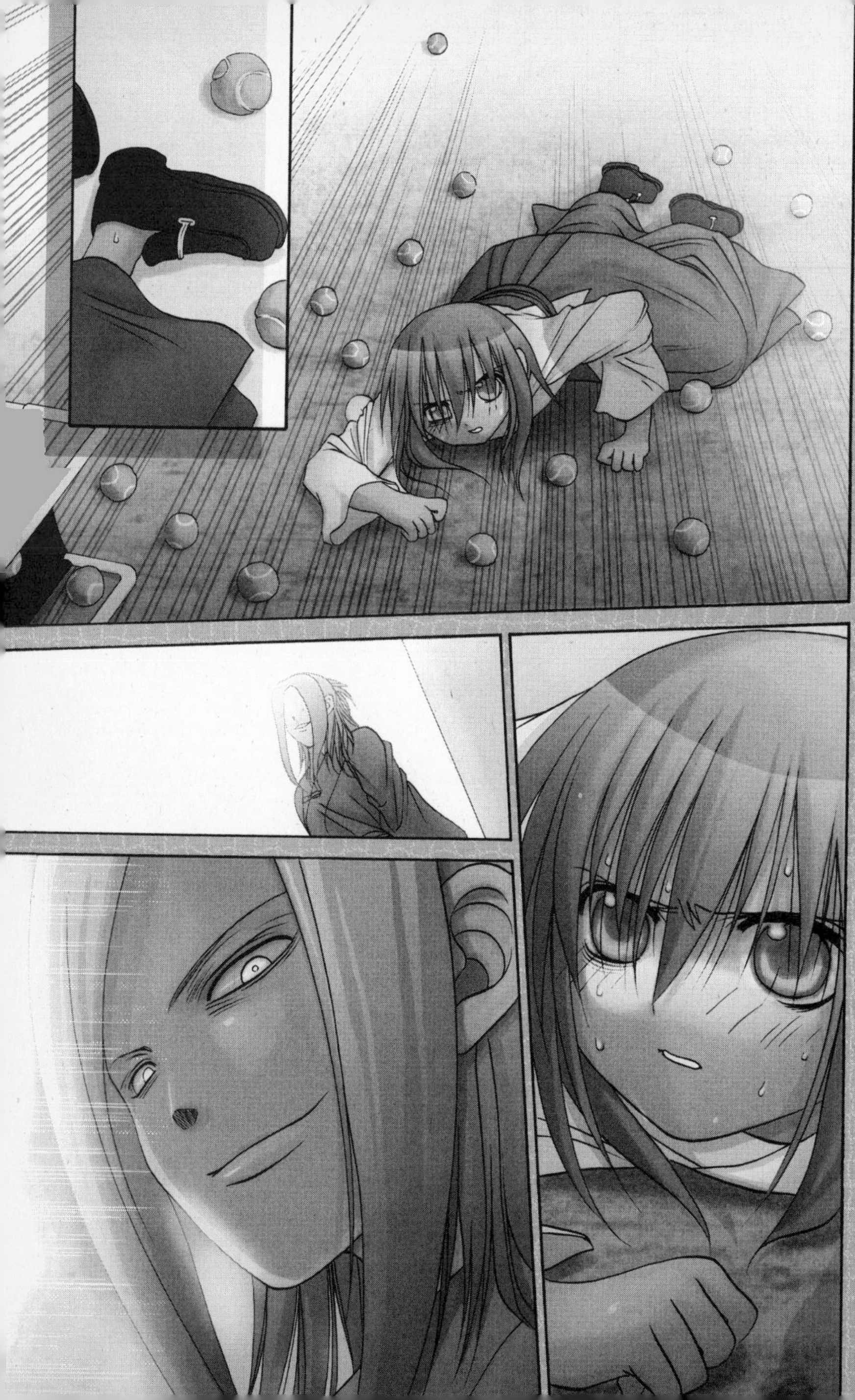

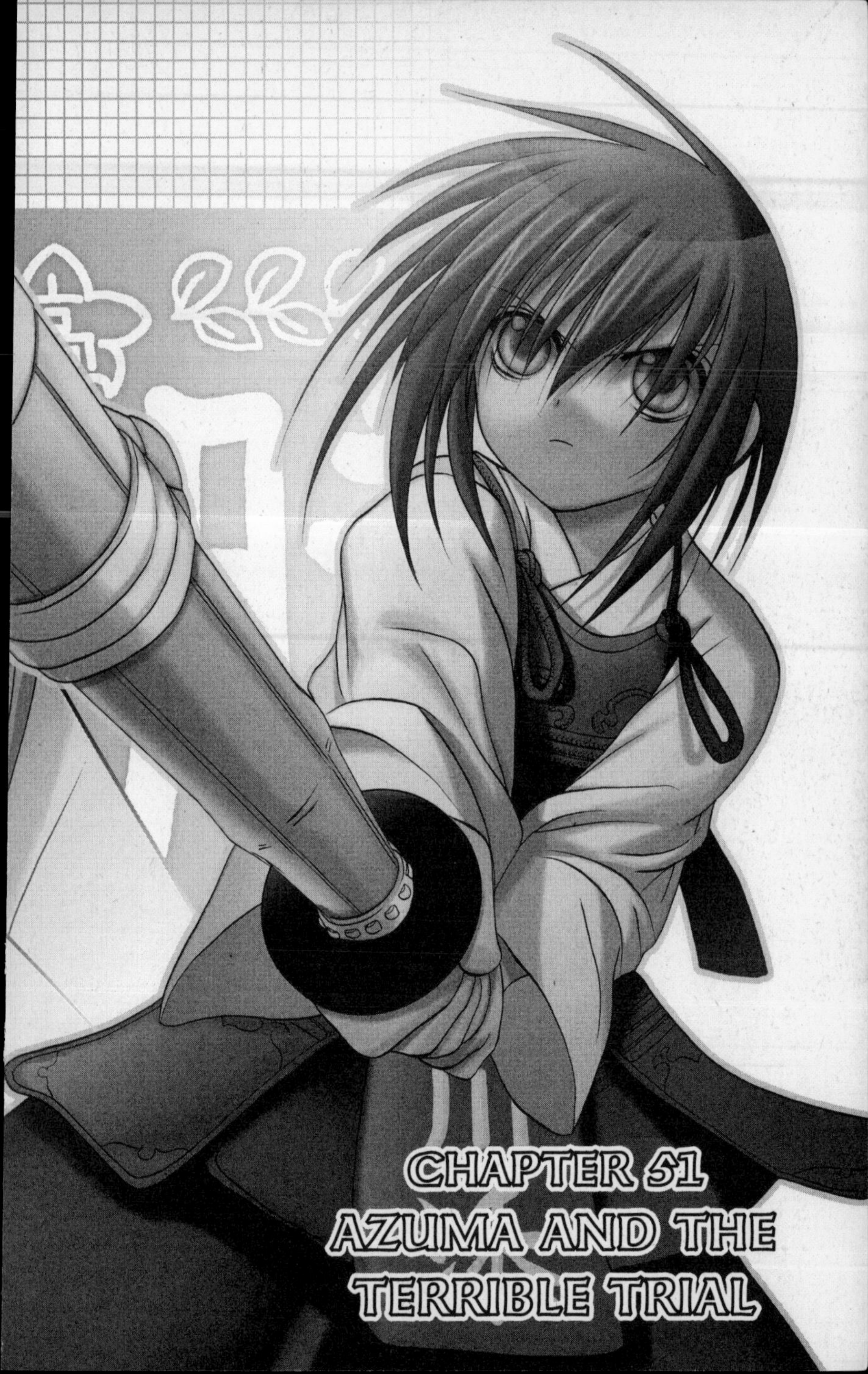
CHAPTER 51
AZUMA AND THE
TERRIBLE TRIAL

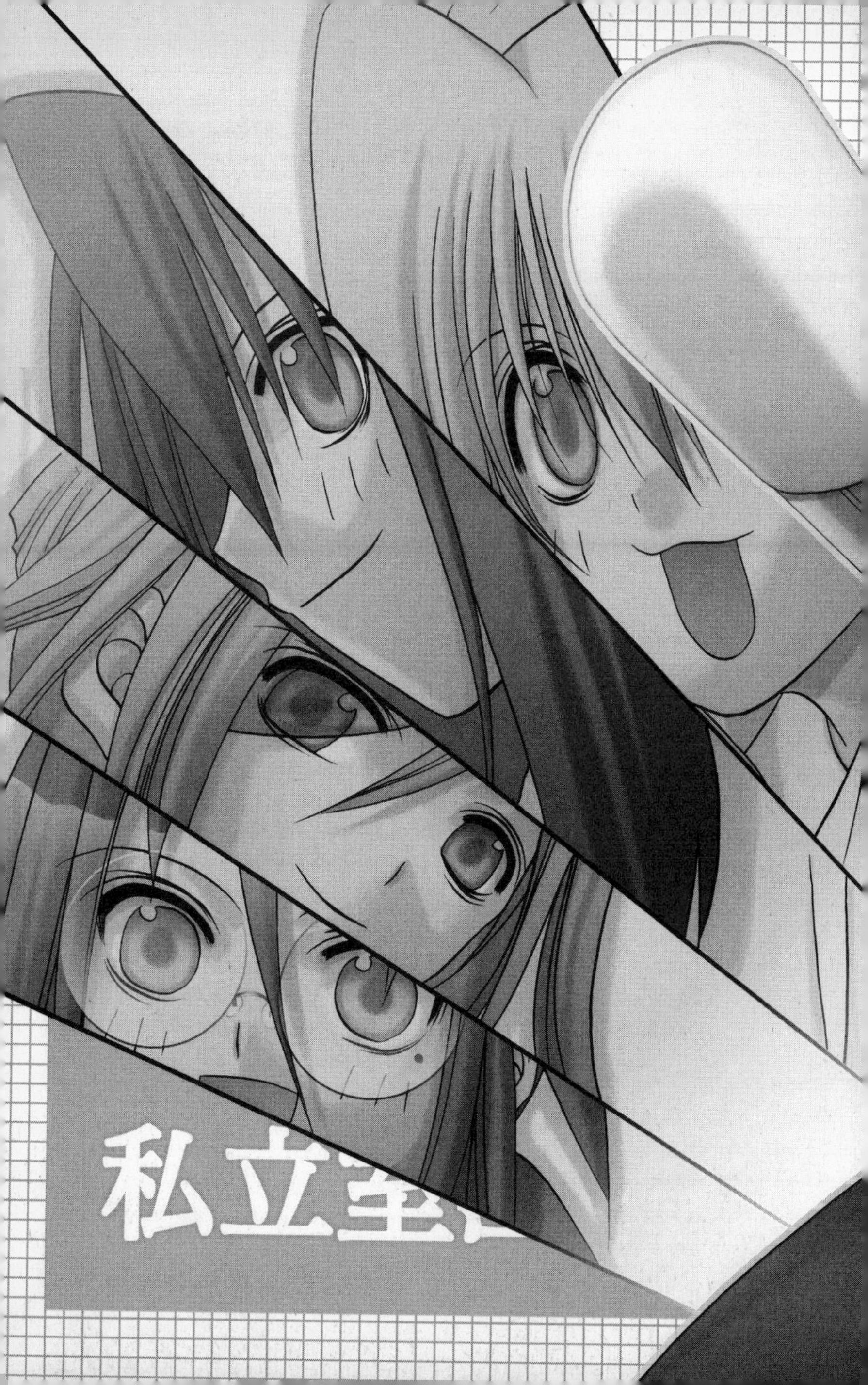

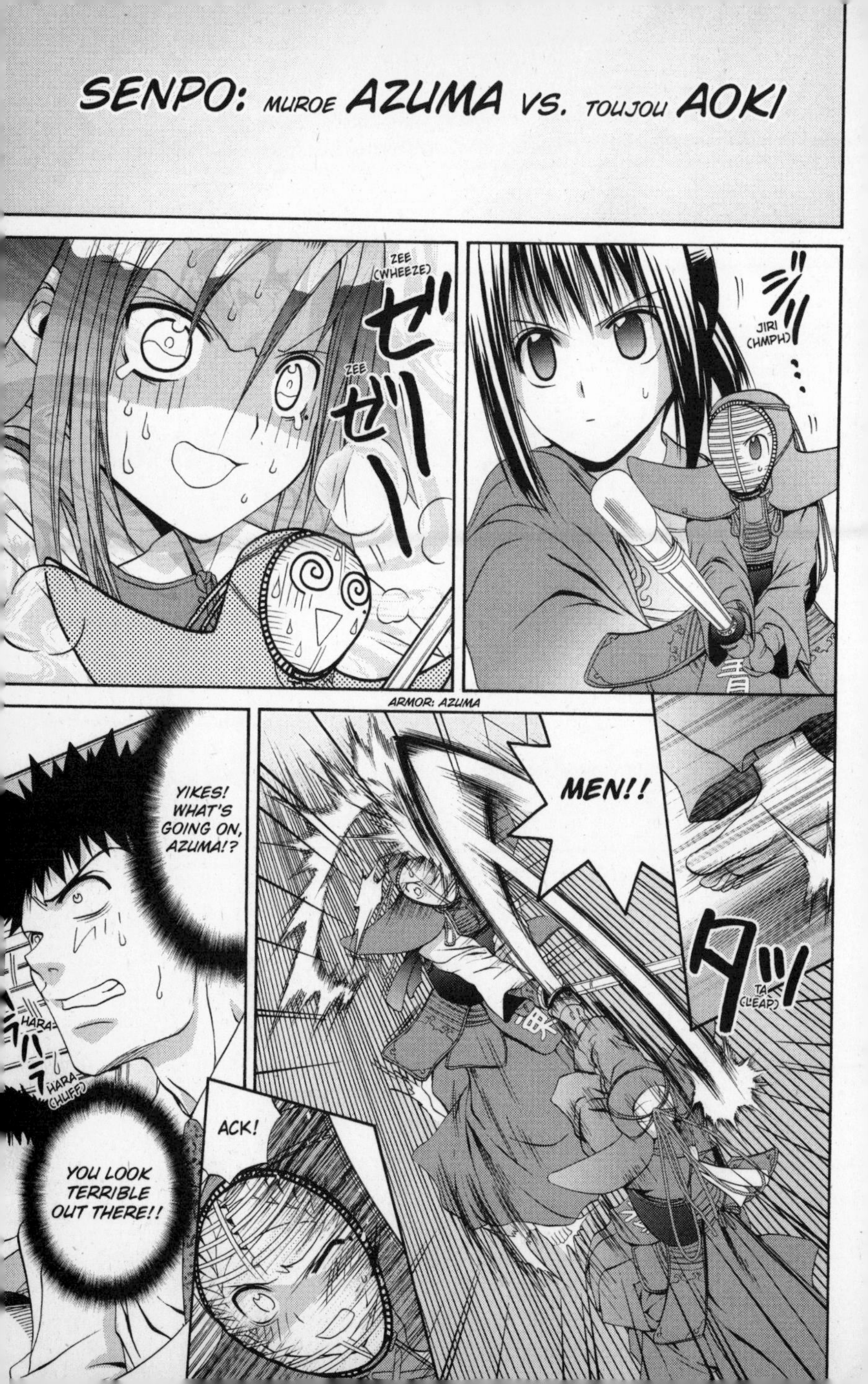
SENPO: MUROE AZUMA VS. TOUJOU AOKI
JIRI (HMPH)
ZEE (WHEEZE)
ZEE
ARMOR: AZUMA
MEN!!
TA (LEAP)
ACK!
YIKES! WHAT'S GOING ON, AZUMA!?
HARA
HARA (HUFF)
YOU LOOK TERRIBLE OUT THERE!!

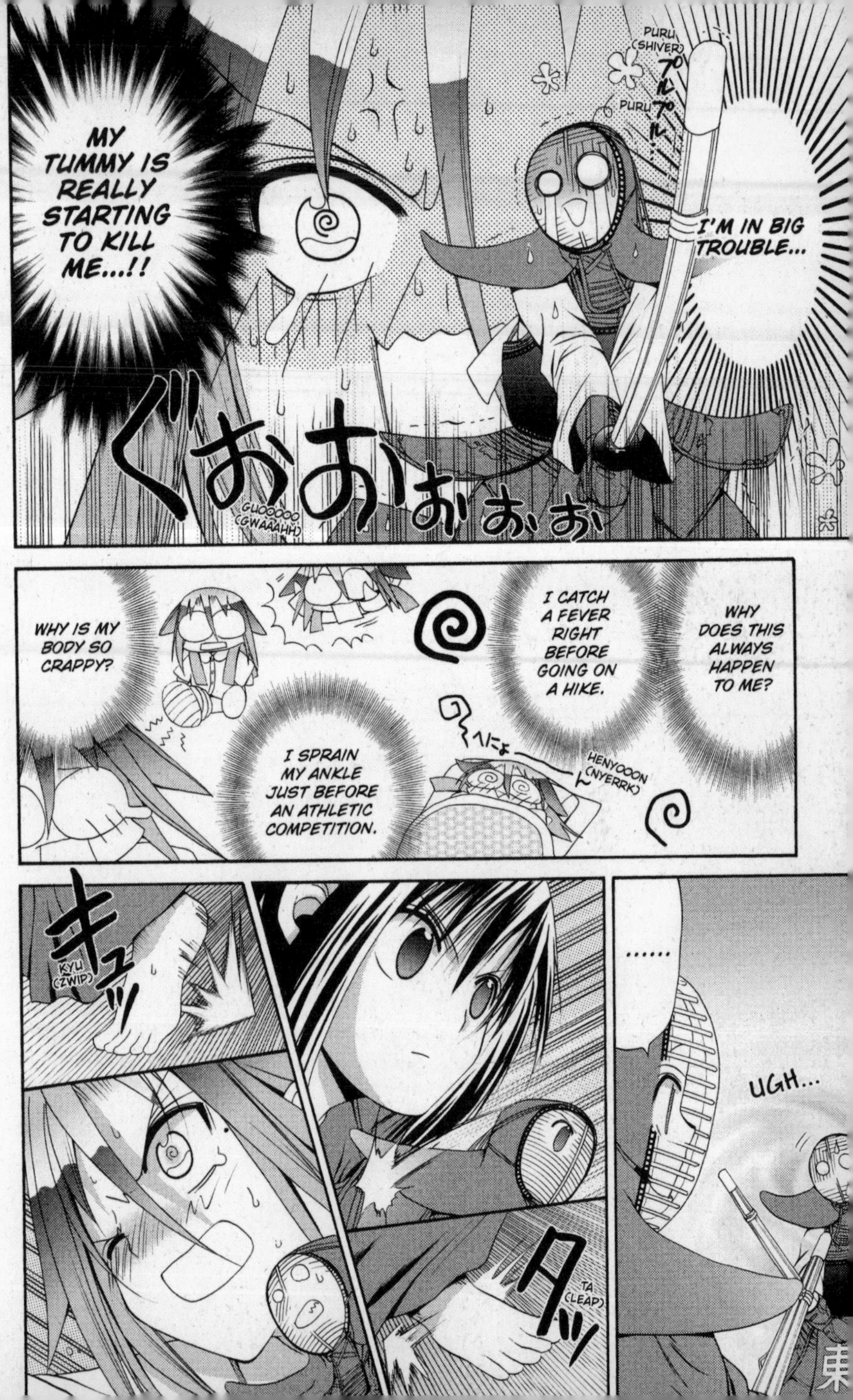
PURU (SHIVER) PURU
I'M IN BIG TROUBLE...
MY TUMMY IS REALLY STARTING TO KILL ME...!!
GUOOOOO (GWAAAHH)
WHY DOES THIS ALWAYS HAPPEN TO ME?
I CATCH A FEVER RIGHT BEFORE GOING ON A HIKE.
HENYOOON (NYERRK)
I SPRAIN MY ANKLE JUST BEFORE AN ATHLETIC COMPETITION.
WHY IS MY BODY SO CRAPPY?
......
UGH...
KYU (ZWIP)
TA (LEAP)

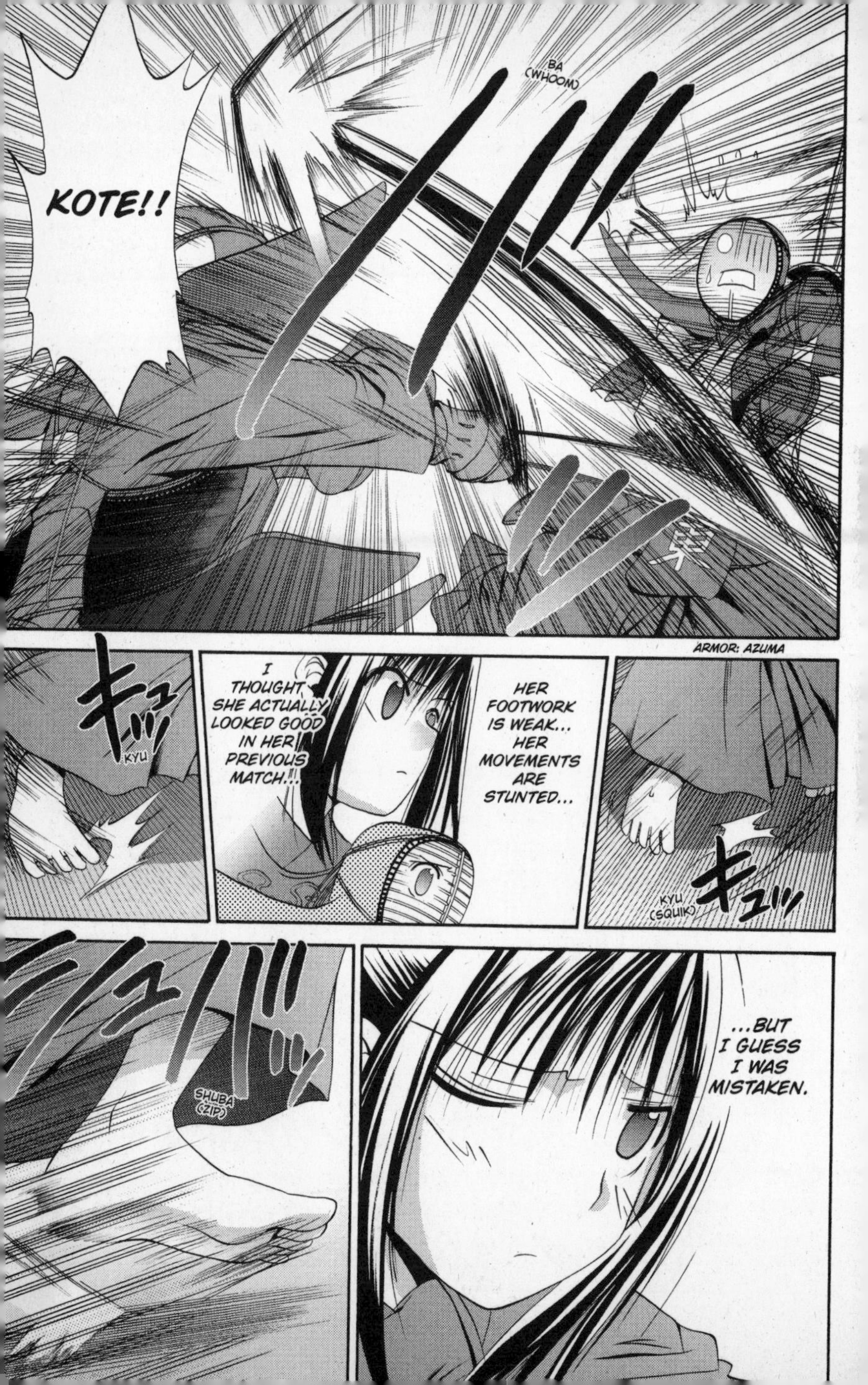
BA
(WHOOM)
KOTE!!
ARMOR: AZUMA
キュッ
KYU
(SQUIK)
HER FOOTWORK IS WEAK... HER MOVEMENTS ARE STUNTED...
I THOUGHT SHE ACTUALLY LOOKED GOOD IN HER PREVIOUS MATCH...
キュッ
KYU
...BUT I GUESS I WAS MISTAKEN.
シュバッ
SHUBA
(ZIP)

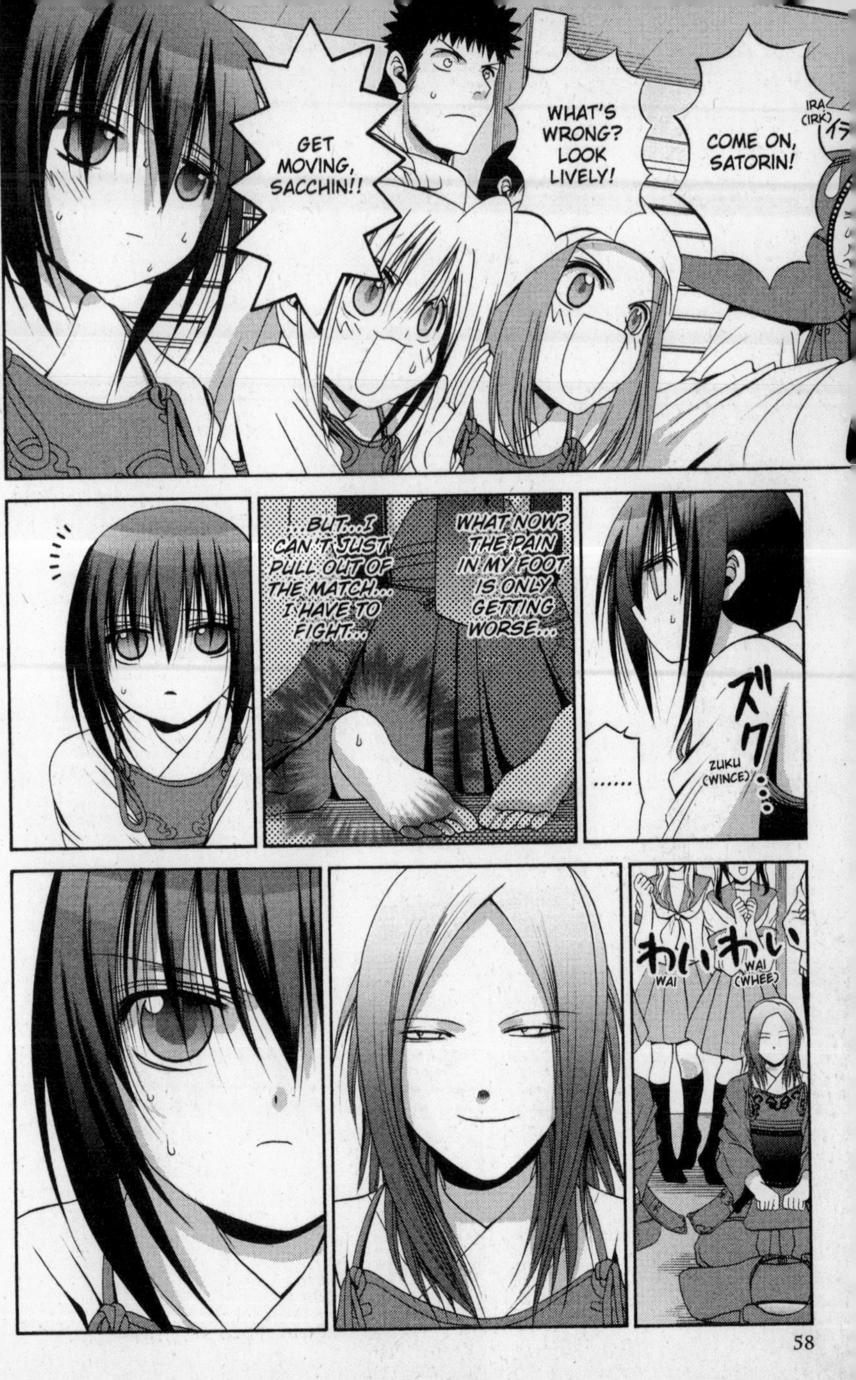
IRA (IRK)
イラ
COME ON, SATORIN!
WHAT'S WRONG? LOOK LIVELY!
GET MOVING, SACCHIN!!
ズク
ZUKU (WINCE)
......
WHAT NOW? THE PAIN IN MY FOOT IS ONLY GETTING WORSE...
...BUT...I CAN'T JUST PULL OUT OF THE MATCH... I HAVE TO FIGHT...
わいわい
WAI WAI (WHEE)

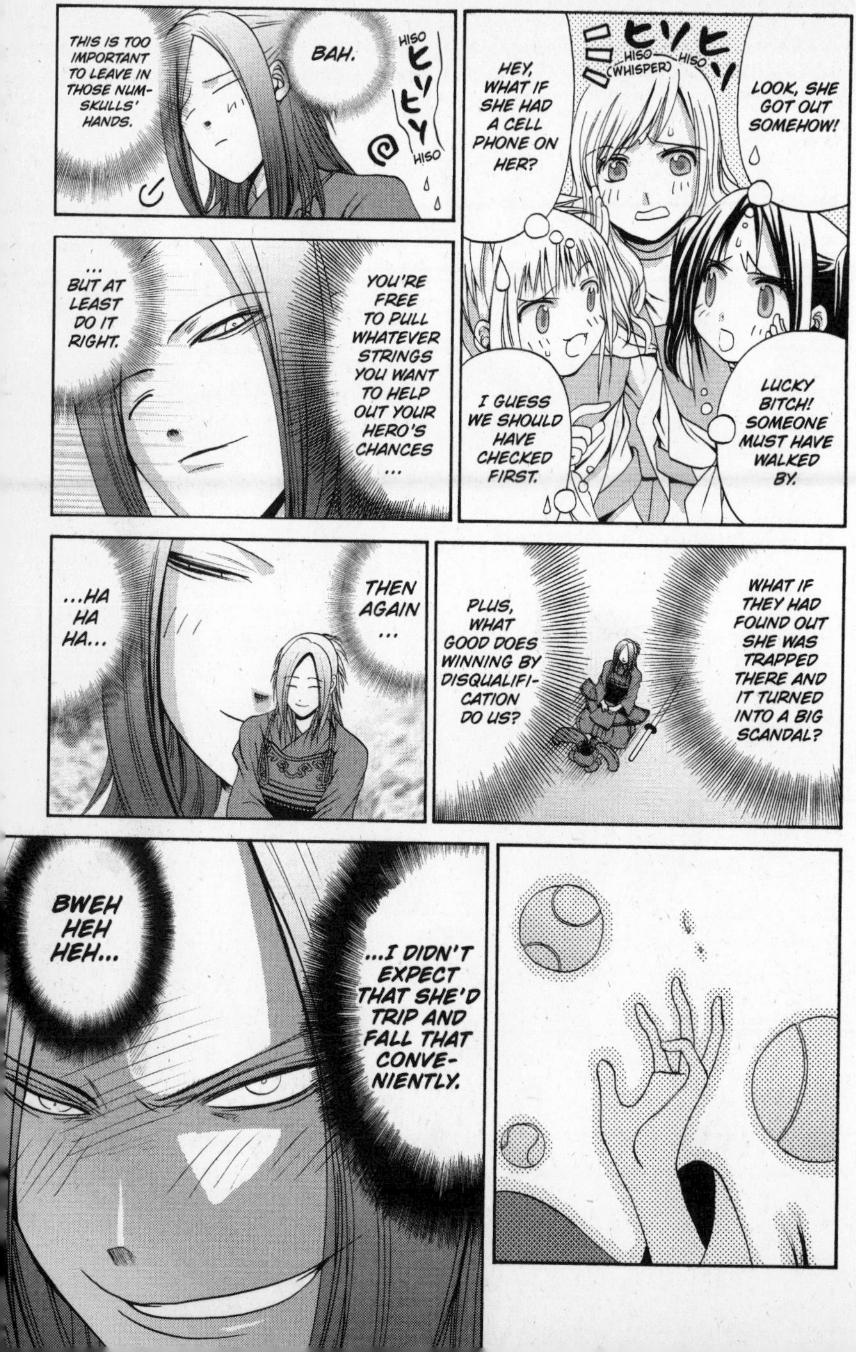
ヒソヒソ
HISO
(WHISPER)
HISO
LOOK, SHE GOT OUT SOMEHOW!
HEY, WHAT IF SHE HAD A CELL PHONE ON HER?
LUCKY BITCH! SOMEONE MUST HAVE WALKED BY.
I GUESS WE SHOULD HAVE CHECKED FIRST.
HISO
ヒソヒソ
HISO
BAH.
THIS IS TOO IMPORTANT TO LEAVE IN THOSE NUMSKULLS' HANDS.
YOU'RE FREE TO PULL WHATEVER STRINGS YOU WANT TO HELP OUT YOUR HERO'S CHANCES ...
... BUT AT LEAST DO IT RIGHT.
WHAT IF THEY HAD FOUND OUT SHE WAS TRAPPED THERE AND IT TURNED INTO A BIG SCANDAL?
PLUS, WHAT GOOD DOES WINNING BY DISQUALIFICATION DO US?
THEN AGAIN ...
...HA HA HA...
...I DIDN'T EXPECT THAT SHE'D TRIP AND FALL THAT CONVENIENTLY.
BWEH HEH HEH...

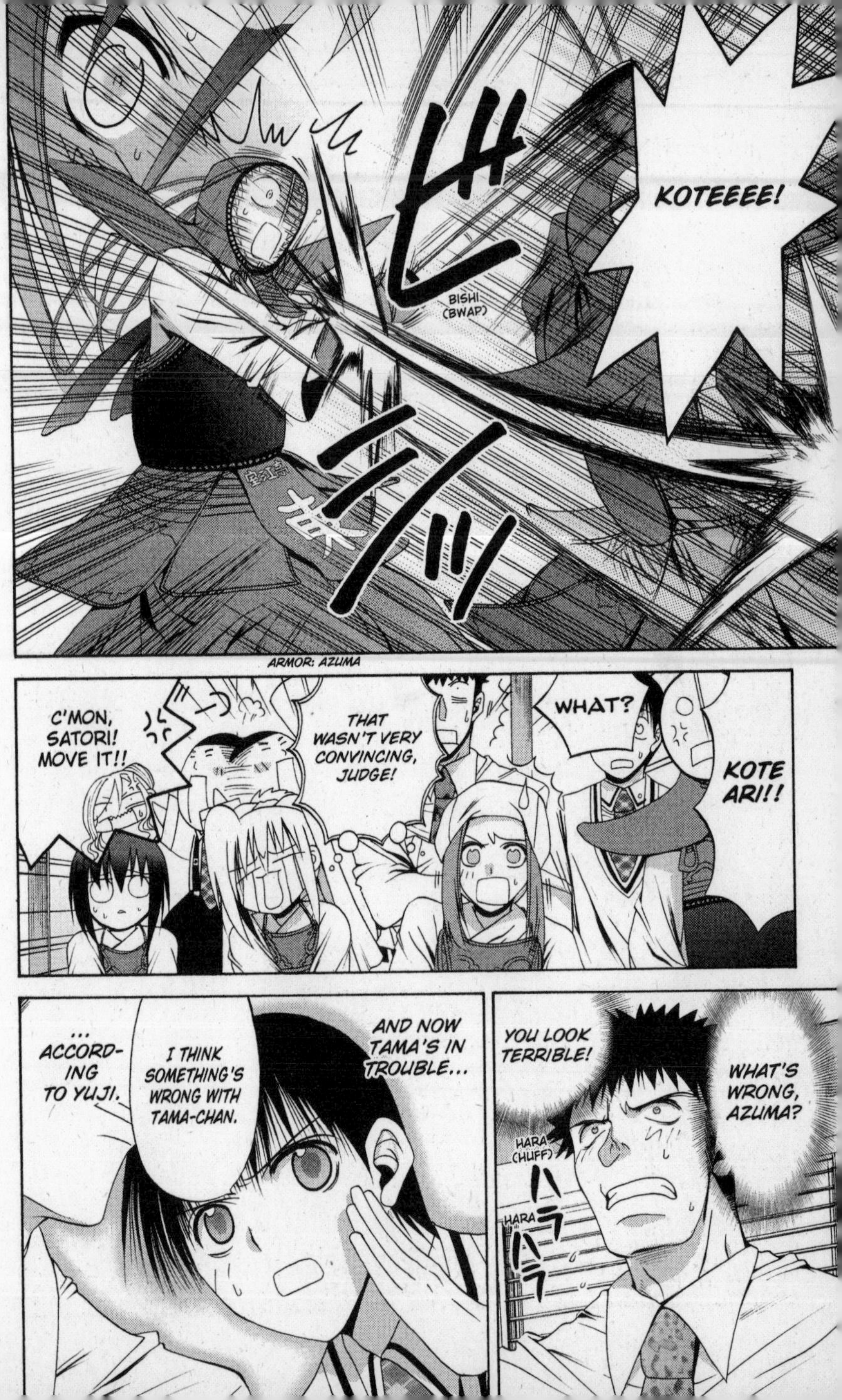
KOTEEEE!
BISHI (BWAP)
ARMOR: AZUMA
KOTE ARI!!
WHAT?
THAT WASN'T VERY CONVINCING, JUDGE!
C'MON, SATORI! MOVE IT!!
WHAT'S WRONG, AZUMA?
YOU LOOK TERRIBLE!
HARA (HUFF)
HARA
AND NOW TAMA'S IN TROUBLE...
I THINK SOMETHING'S WRONG WITH TAMA-CHAN.
... ACCORD-ING TO YUJI.

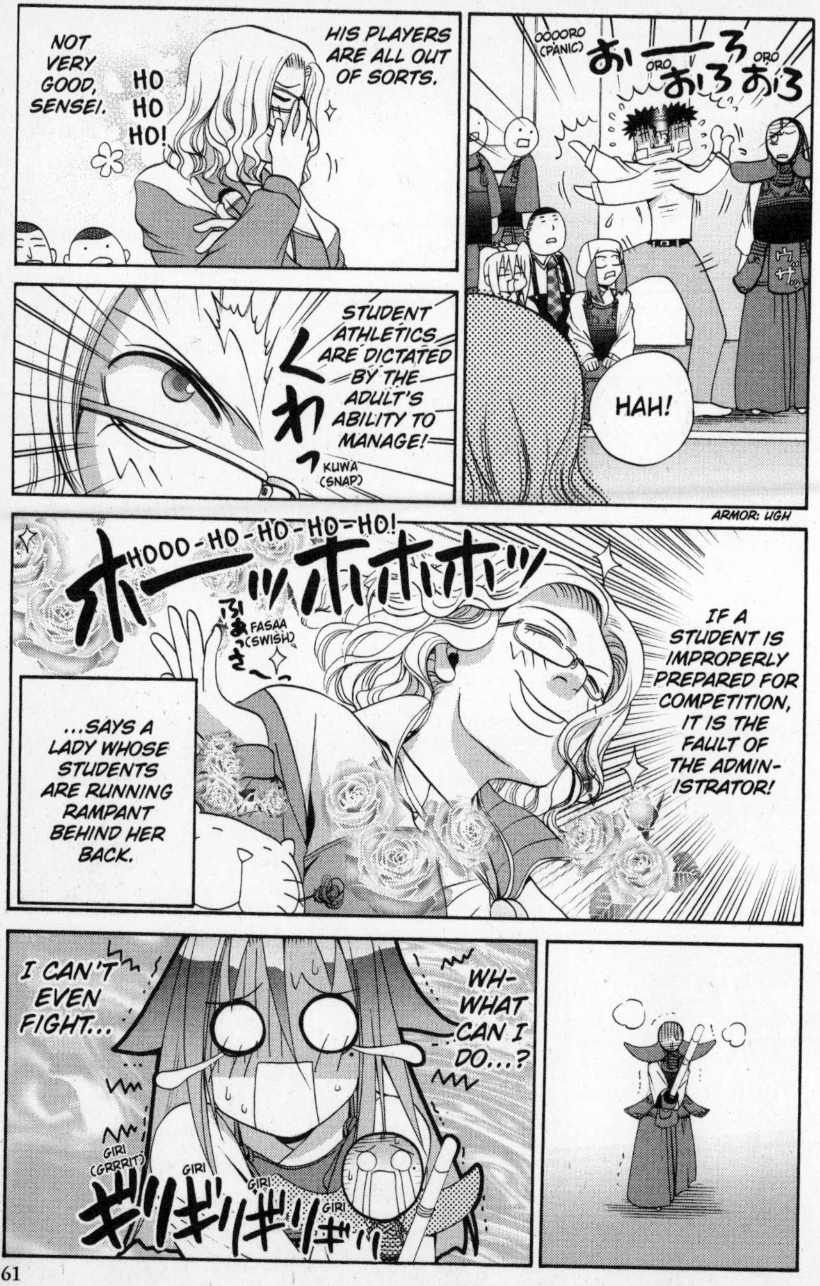
OOOORO (PANIC)
ORO ORO
HIS PLAYERS ARE ALL OUT OF SORTS.
NOT VERY GOOD, SENSEI.
HO HO HO!
HAH!
ARMOR: UGH
STUDENT ATHLETICS ARE DICTATED BY THE ADULT'S ABILITY TO MANAGE!
KUWA (SNAP)
IF A STUDENT IS IMPROPERLY PREPARED FOR COMPETITION, IT IS THE FAULT OF THE ADMIN-ISTRATOR!
HOOO-HO-HO-HO-HO!
FASAA (SWISH)
...SAYS A LADY WHOSE STUDENTS ARE RUNNING RAMPANT BEHIND HER BACK.
WH-WHAT CAN I DO...?
I CAN'T EVEN FIGHT...
GIRI (GRRRIT) GIRI GIRI GIRI

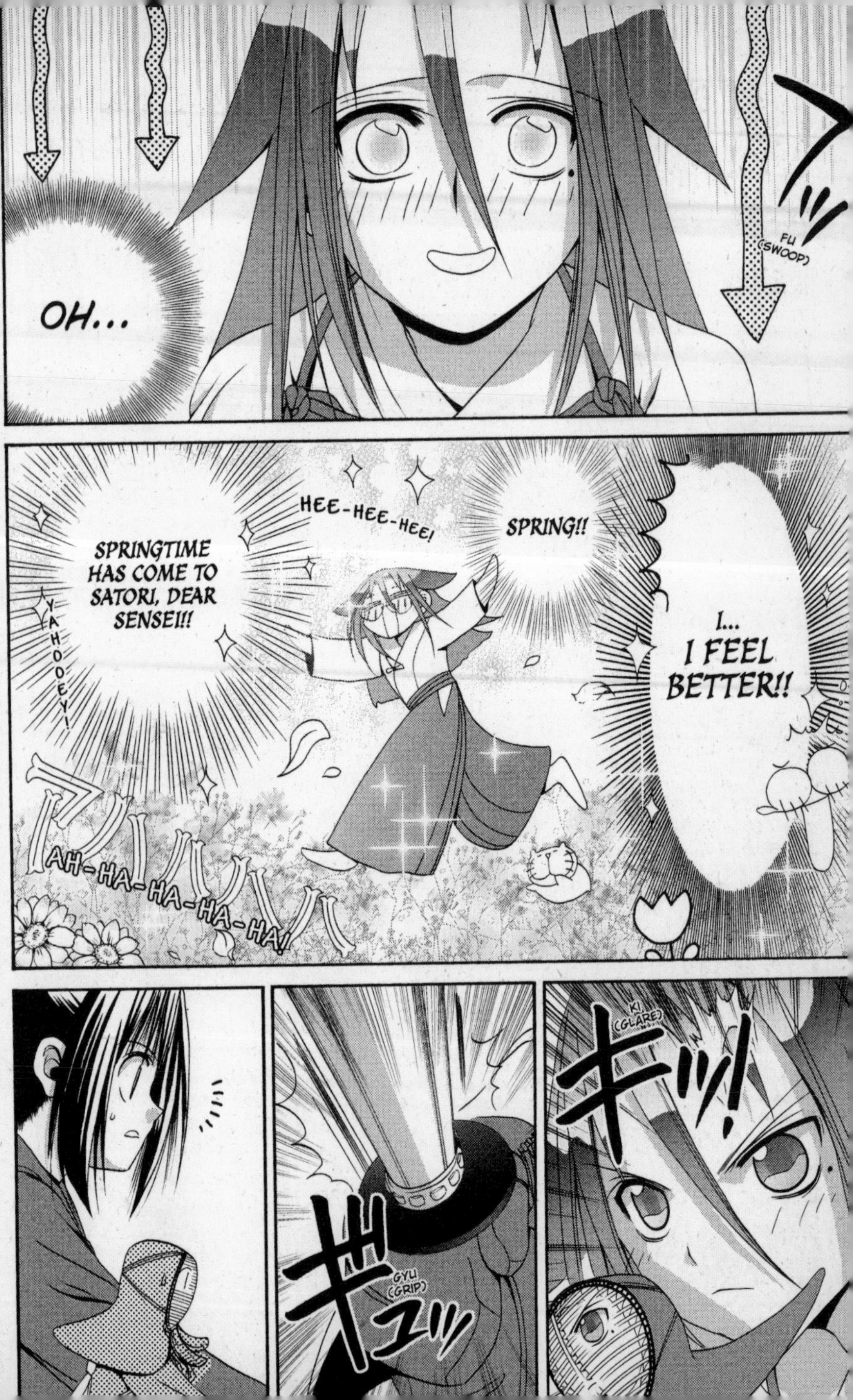
FU
(SWOOP)
OH...
I...
I FEEL BETTER!!
SPRING!!
HEE-HEE-HEE!
SPRINGTIME HAS COME TO SATORI, DEAR SENSEI!!!
YAHOOEY!
AH-HA-HA-HA-HA!
KI
(GLARE)
GYU
(GRIP)

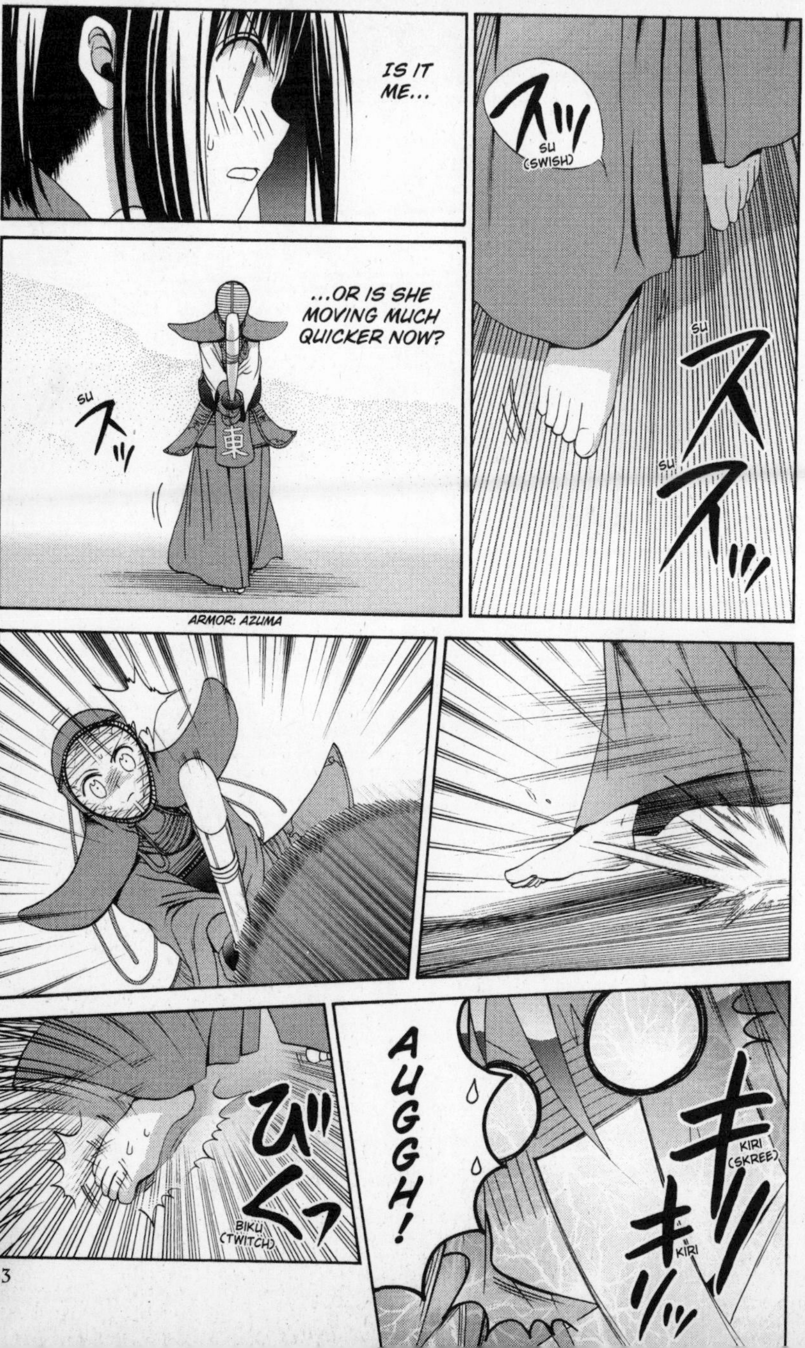
スッ
SU (SWISH)
SU
SU
スス
IS IT ME...
...OR IS SHE MOVING MUCH QUICKER NOW?
SU
スッ
ARMOR: AZUMA
AUGGH!
KIRI (SKREE)
KIRI
キリキリ
BIKU (TWITCH)
びくっ

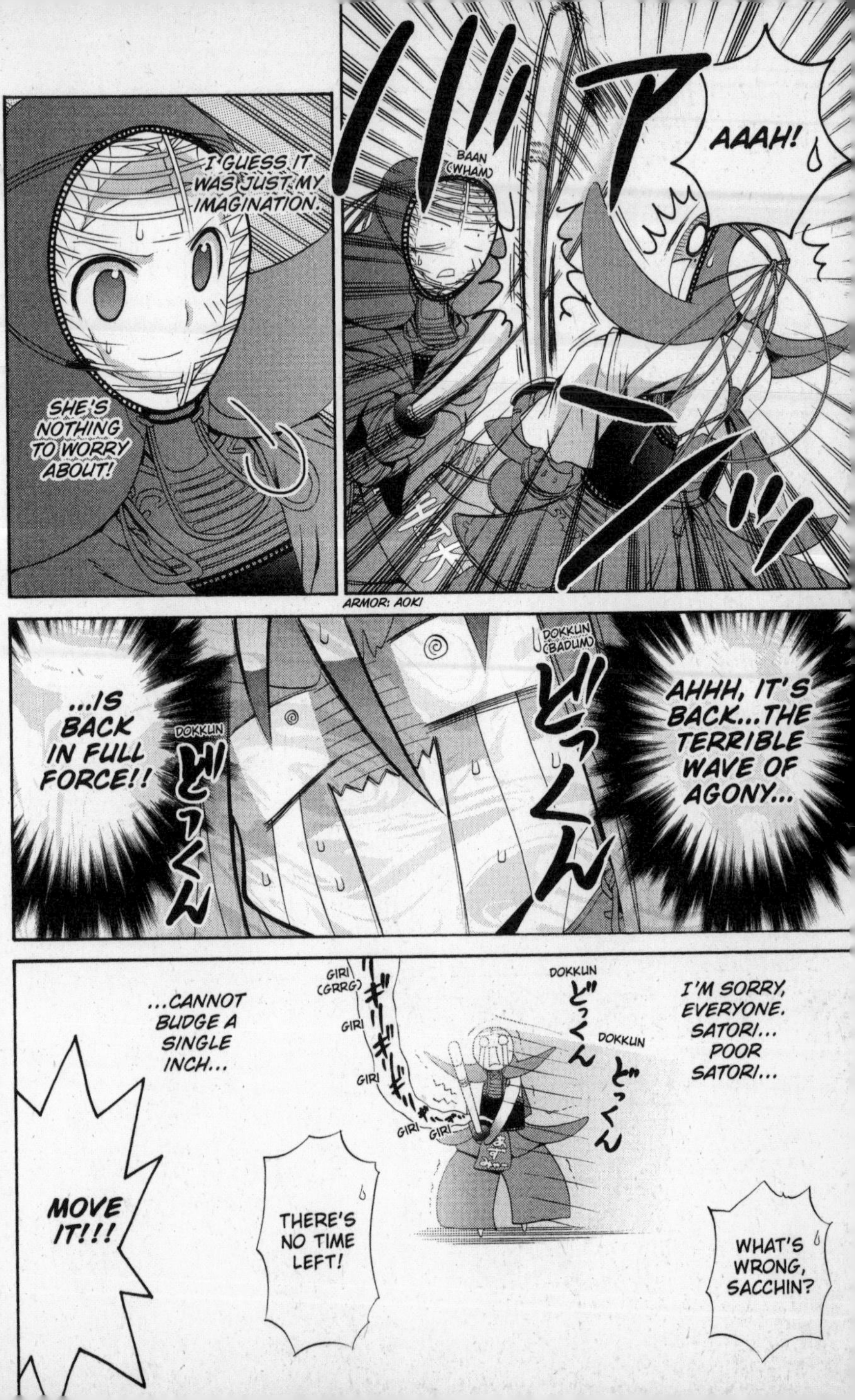

BAAN (WHAM)
AAAH!
ARMOR: AOKI
I GUESS IT WAS JUST MY IMAGINATION.
SHE'S NOTHING TO WORRY ABOUT!
DOKKUN (BADUM)
どっくん
AHHH, IT'S BACK...THE TERRIBLE WAVE OF AGONY...
DOKKUN
どっくん
...IS BACK IN FULL FORCE!!
I'M SORRY, EVERYONE. SATORI... POOR SATORI...
DOKKUN
どっくん
DOKKUN
どっくん
GIRI (GRRG)
GIRI
GIRI
GIRI GIRI
...CANNOT BUDGE A SINGLE INCH...
WHAT'S WRONG, SACCHIN?
THERE'S NO TIME LEFT!
MOVE IT!!!

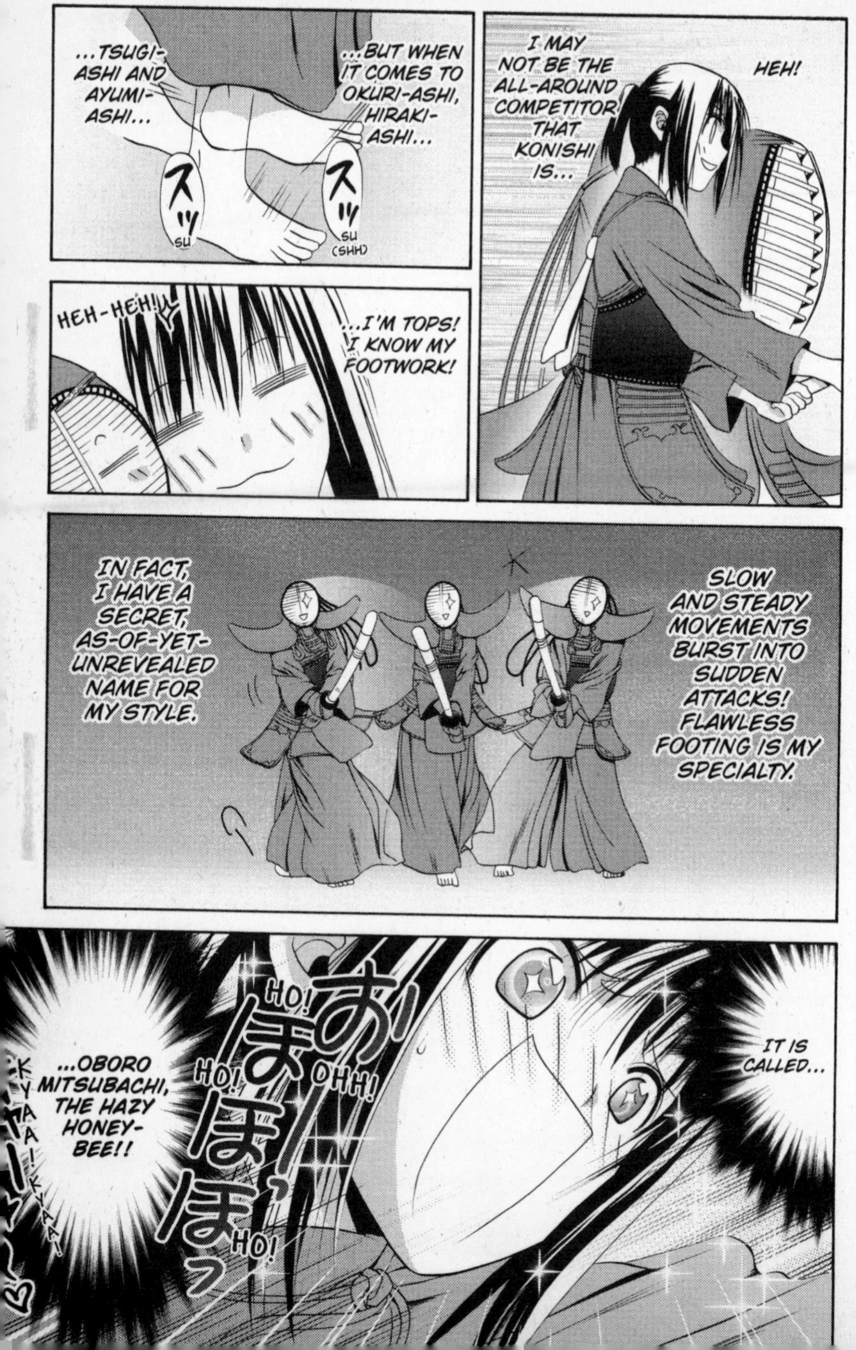
I MAY NOT BE THE ALL-AROUND COMPETITOR THAT KONISHI IS...
HEH!
...BUT WHEN IT COMES TO OKURI-ASHI, HIRAKI-ASHI...
スッ
SU (SHH)
...TSUGI-ASHI AND AYUMI-ASHI...
スッ
SU
...I'M TOPS! I KNOW MY FOOTWORK!
HEH-HEH!
SLOW AND STEADY MOVEMENTS BURST INTO SUDDEN ATTACKS! FLAWLESS FOOTING IS MY SPECIALTY.
IN FACT, I HAVE A SECRET, AS-OF-YET-UNREVEALED NAME FOR MY STYLE.
IT IS CALLED...
おほほほっ
HO! OHH! HO! HO!
...OBORO MITSUBACHI, THE HAZY HONEY-BEE!!
キャ～♡
KYAA! KYAA!

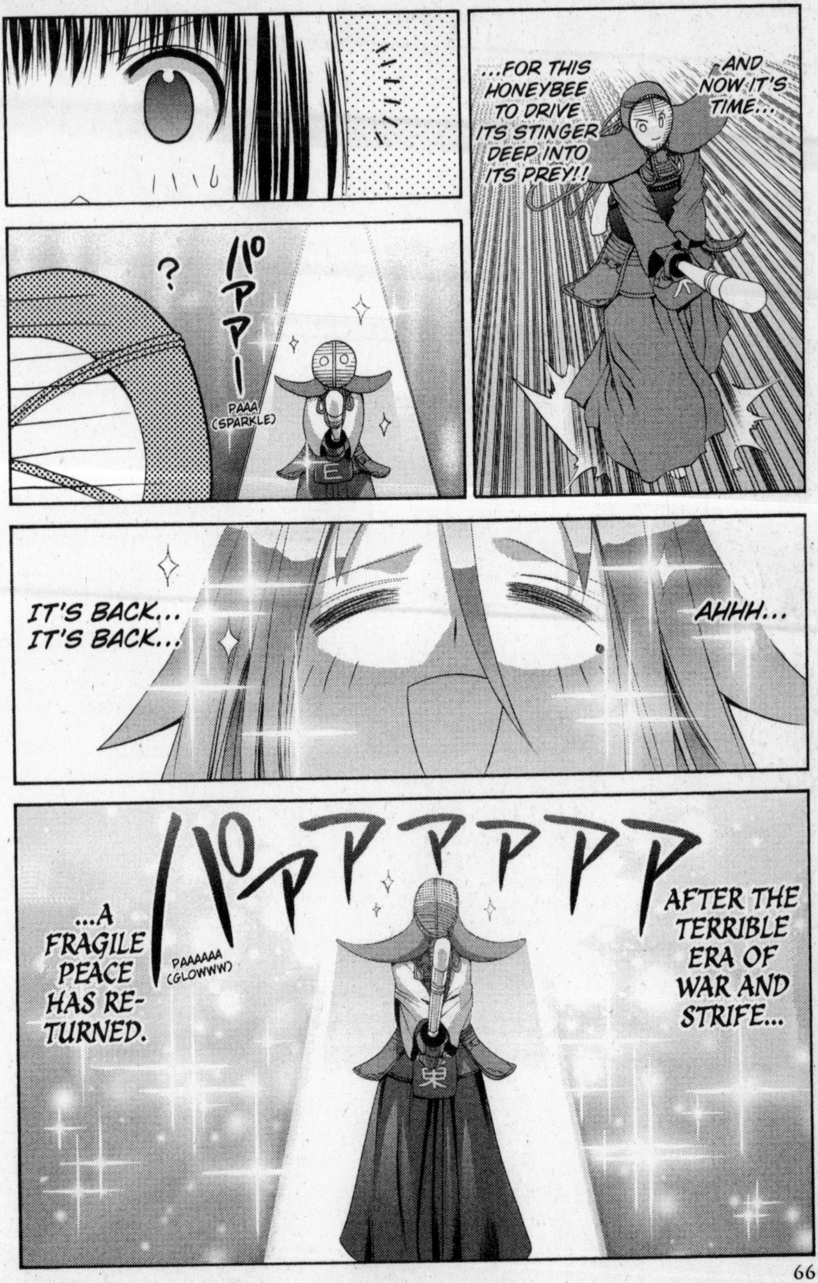
-AND NOW IT'S TIME...
...FOR THIS HONEYBEE TO DRIVE ITS STINGER DEEP INTO ITS PREY!!
パァアー
?
PAAA (SPARKLE)
AHHH...
IT'S BACK... IT'S BACK...
パァアアアア
AFTER THE TERRIBLE ERA OF WAR AND STRIFE...
...A FRAGILE PEACE HAS RE-TURNED.
PAAAAAA (GLOWWW)

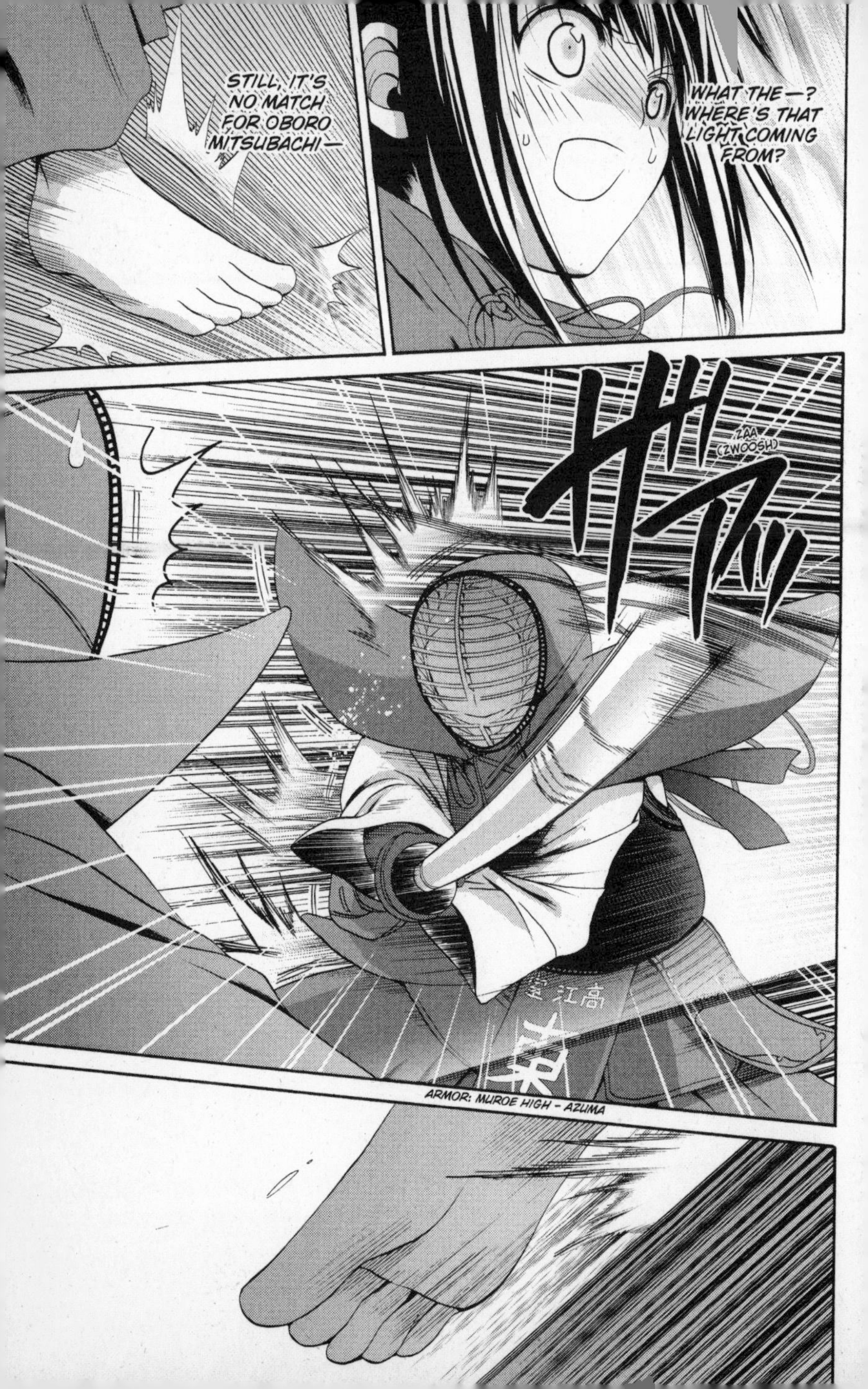
WHAT THE—? WHERE'S THAT LIGHT COMING FROM?
STILL, IT'S NO MATCH FOR OBORO MITSUBACHI—
ザァッ
ZAA (ZWOOSH)
室江高
ARMOR: MUROE HIGH - AZUMA

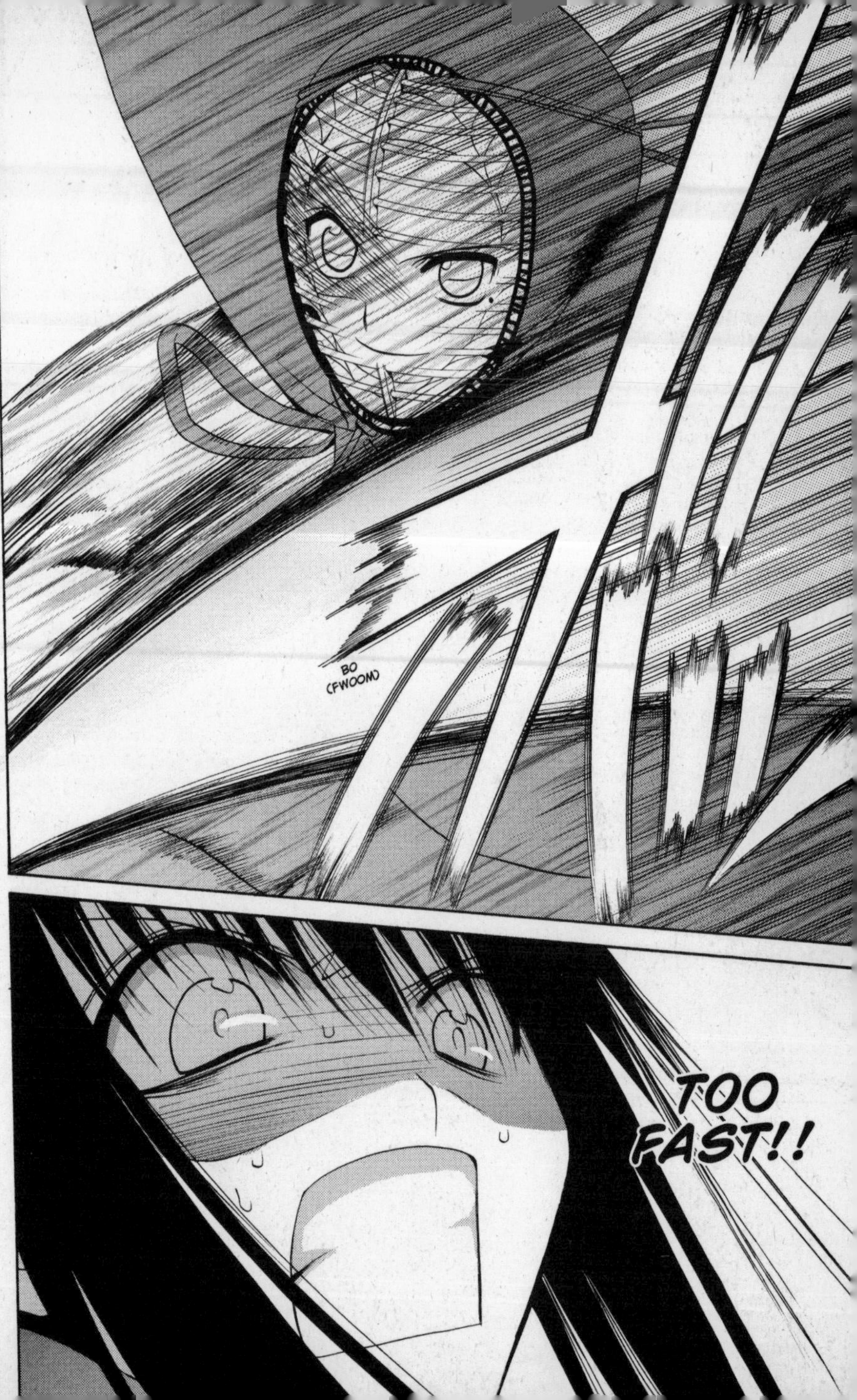
BO
(FWOOM)
TOO FAST!!

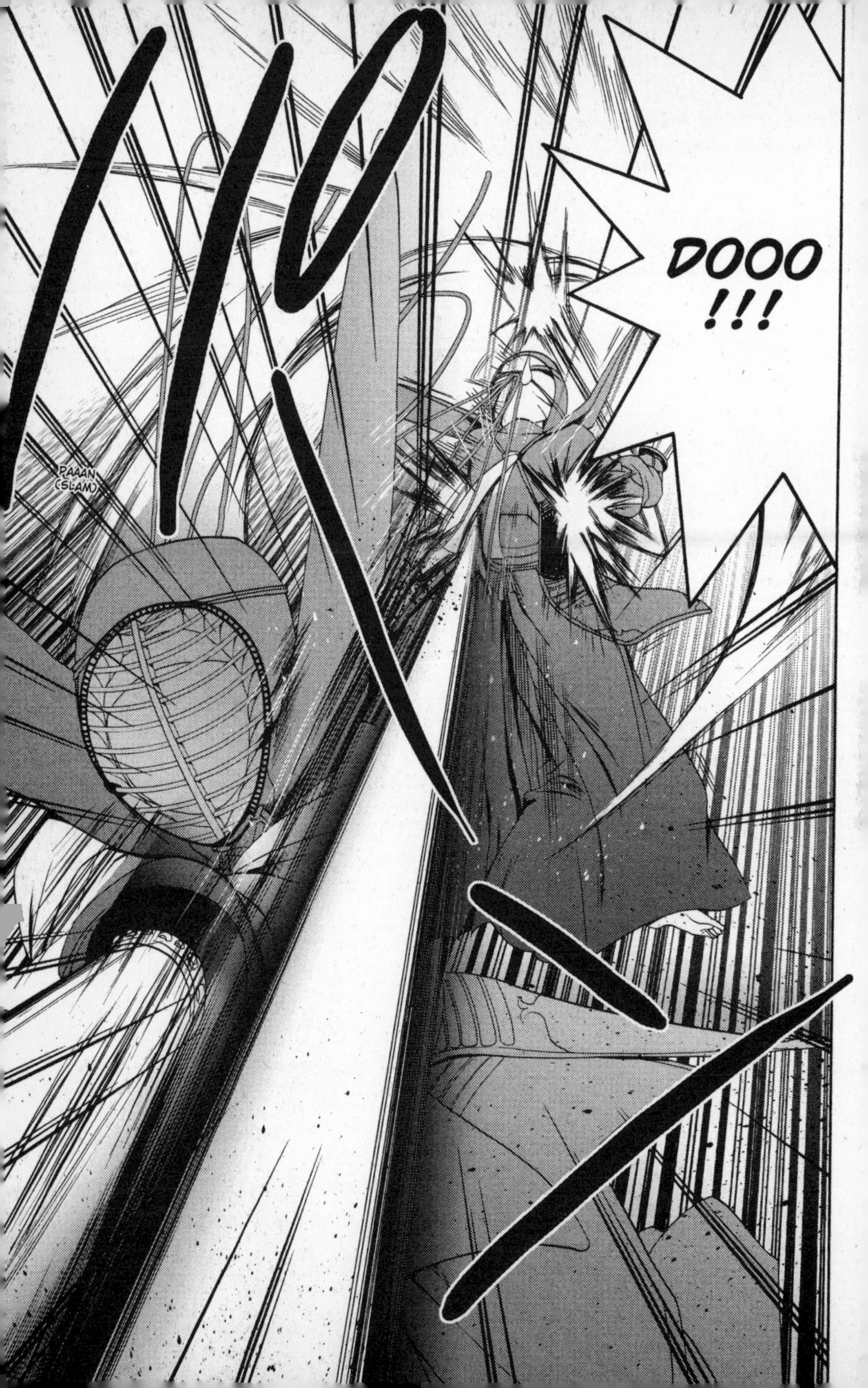
DOOO
!!!
PAAAN
(SLAM)

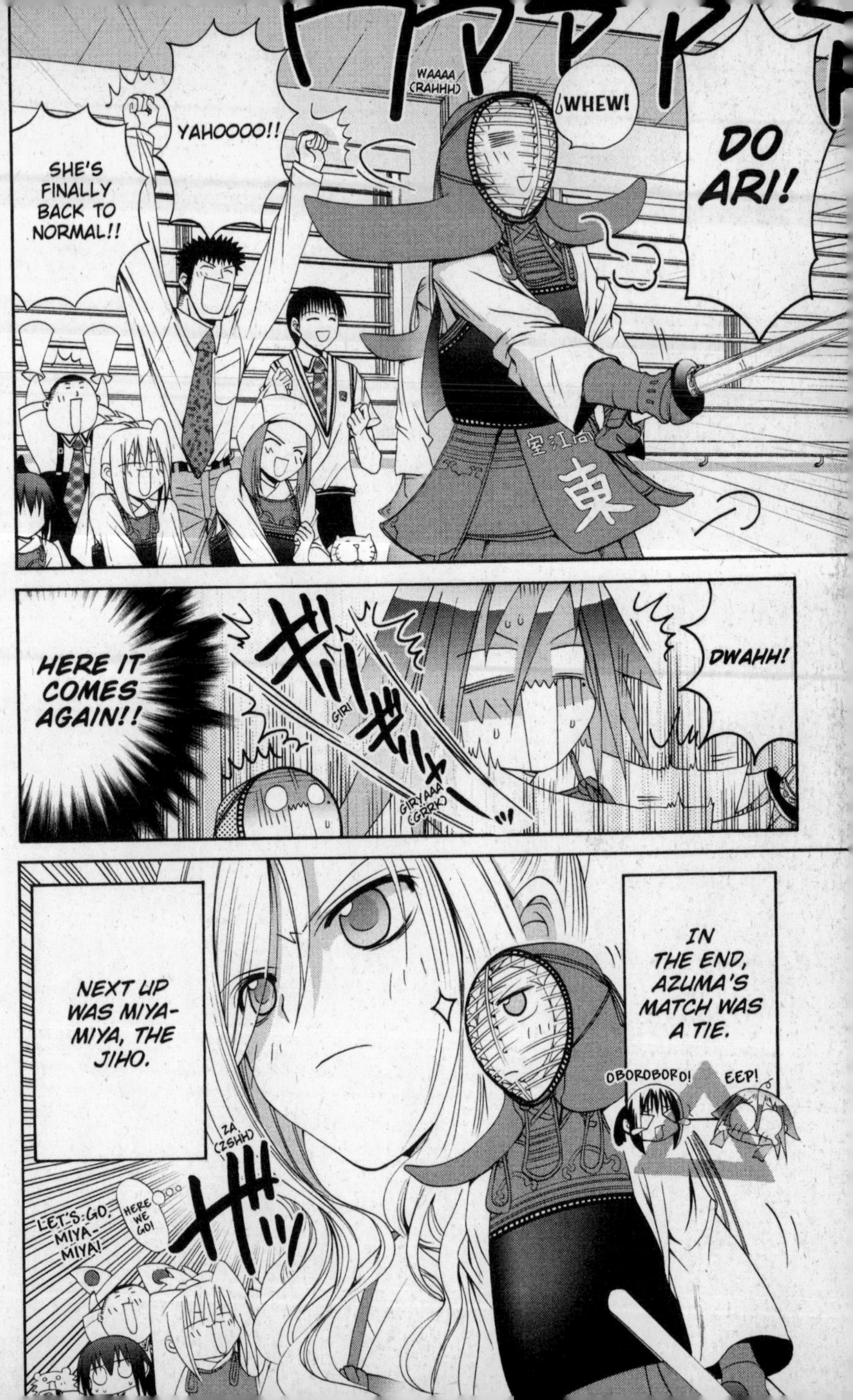
DO ARI!
WHEW!
WAAAA (RAHHH)
YAHOOOO!!
SHE'S FINALLY BACK TO NORMAL!!
DWAHH!
GIRYAAA (GRRK)
GIRI
HERE IT COMES AGAIN!!
IN THE END, AZUMA'S MATCH WAS A TIE.
EEP!
OBOROBORO!
NEXT UP WAS MIYA-MIYA, THE JIHO.
ZA (ZSHH)
HERE WE GO!
LET'S GO, MIYA-MIYA!

BAMBOO BLADE

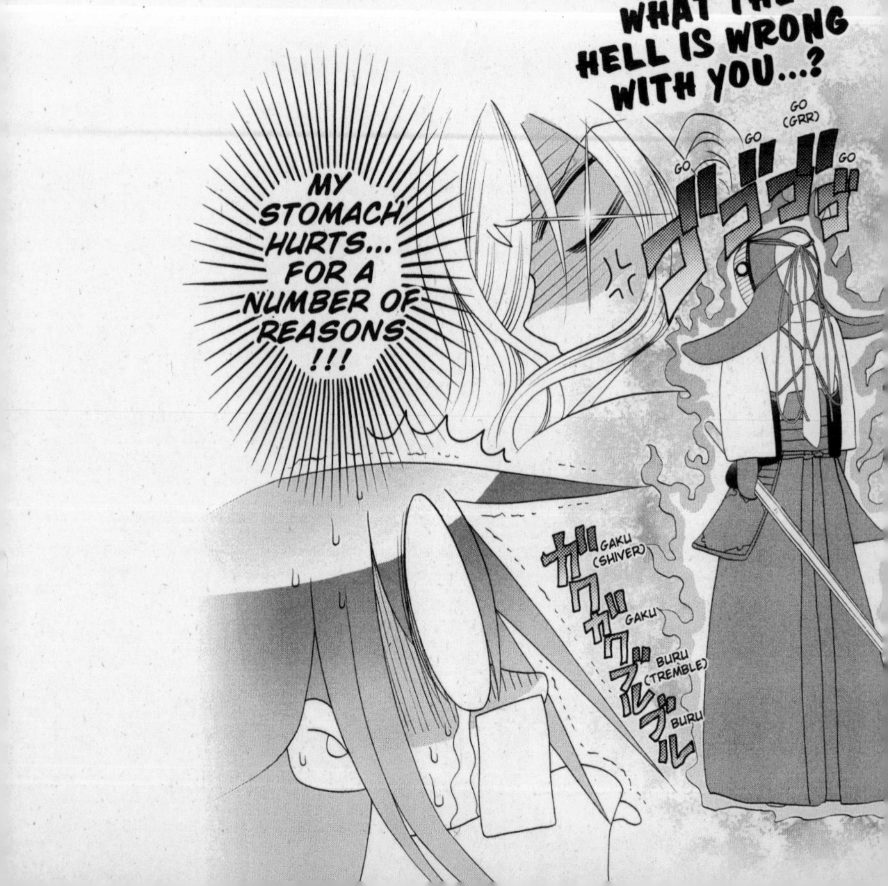
WHAT THE HELL IS WRONG WITH YOU...?
GO (GRR)
GO
GO
GO
MY STOMACH HURTS... FOR A NUMBER OF REASONS!!!
GAKU (SHIVER)
GAKU
BURU (TREMBLE)
BURU

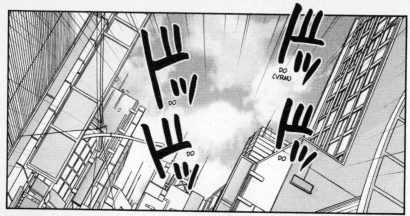

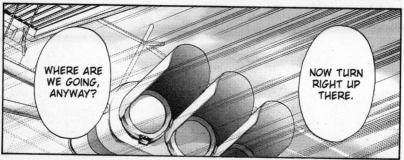

DO
(VRM)
DO
DO
DO
NOW TURN RIGHT UP THERE.
WHERE ARE WE GOING, ANYWAY?
DO
DO
DO
DO
DO

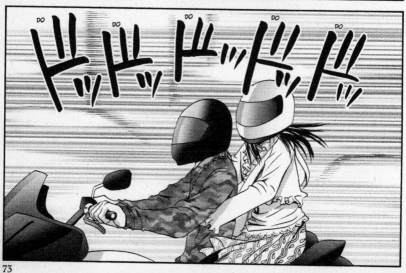

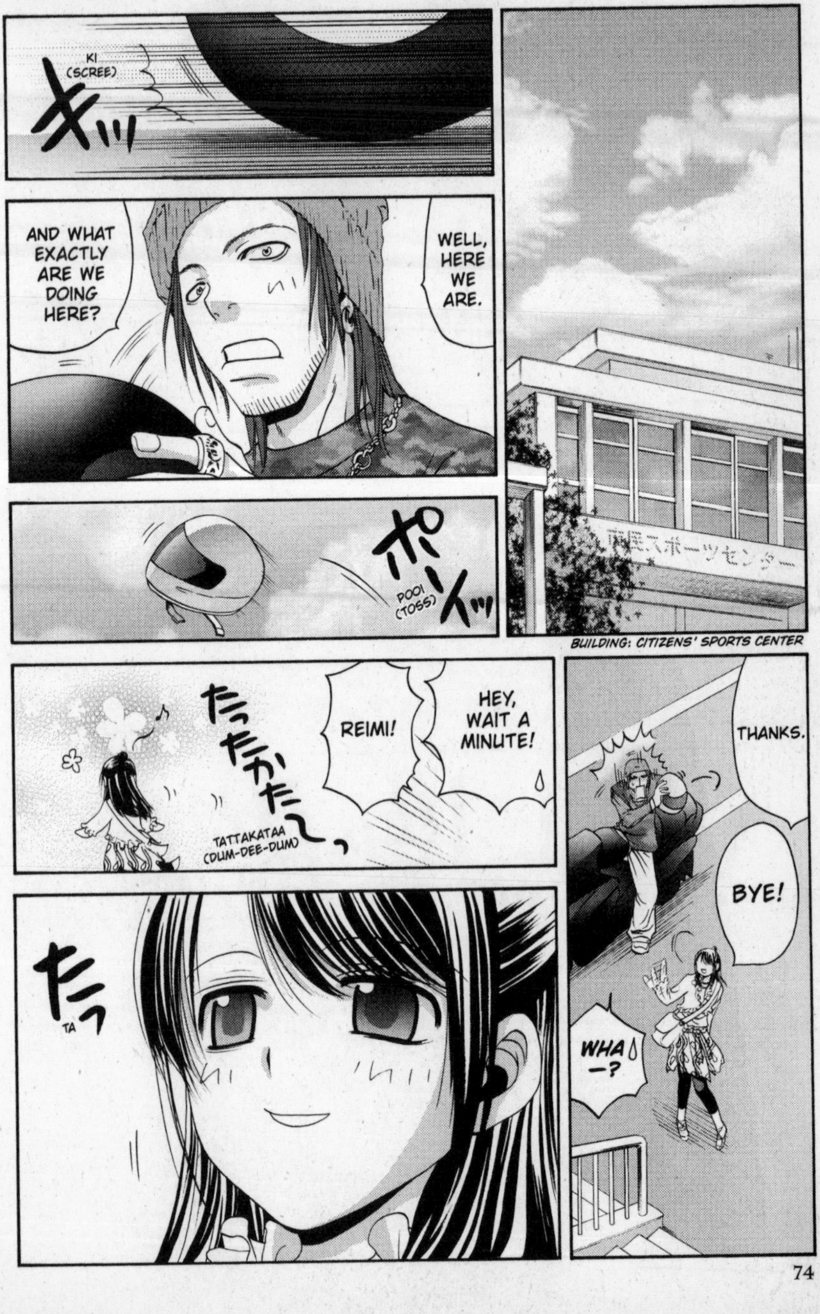
BUILDING: CITIZENS' SPORTS CENTER
KI (SCREE)
WELL, HERE WE ARE.
AND WHAT EXACTLY ARE WE DOING HERE?
POOI (TOSS)
THANKS.
BYE!
WHA—?
HEY, WAIT A MINUTE!
REIMI!
TATTAKATAA (DUM-DEE-DUM)
TA

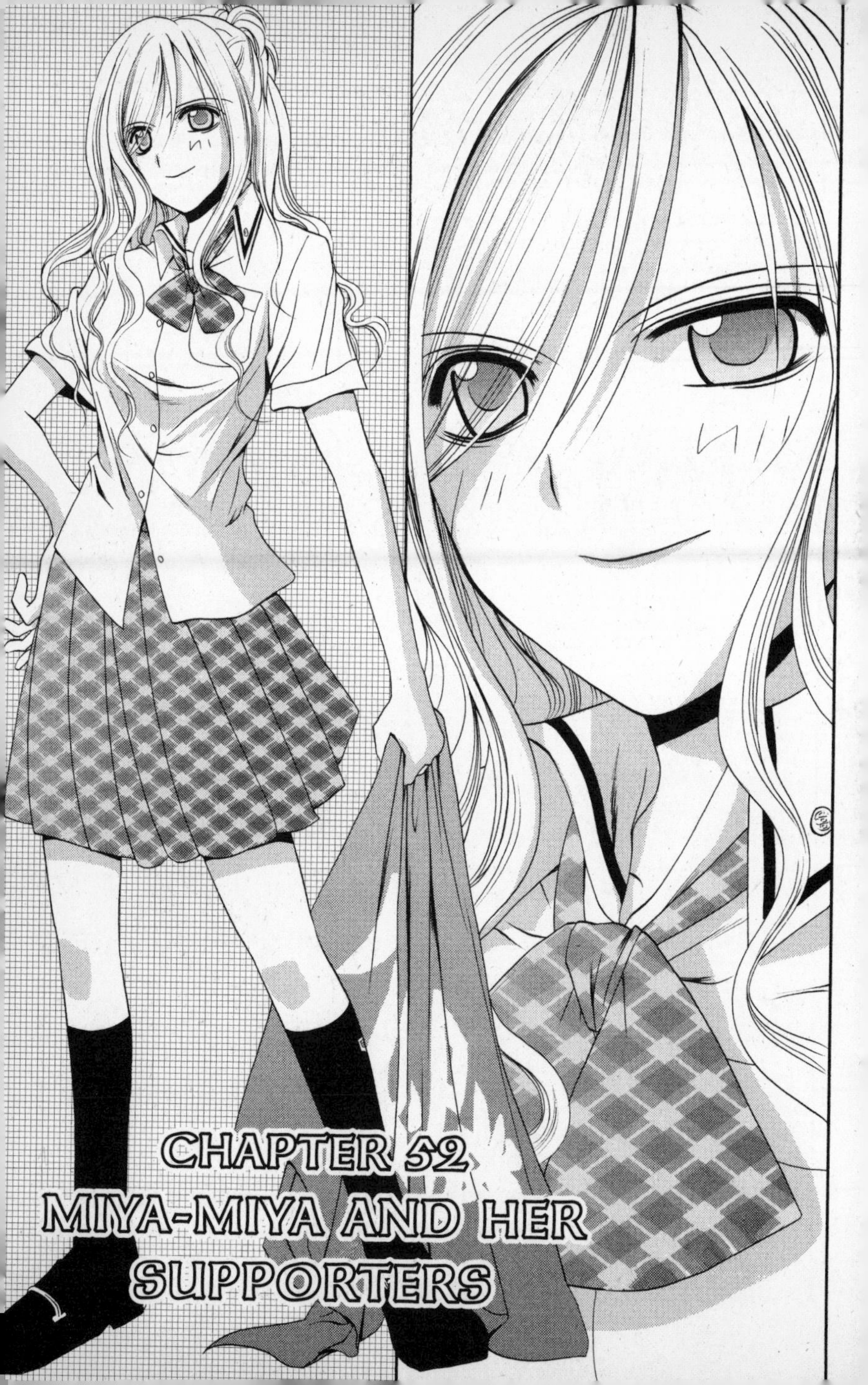
CHAPTER 52
MIYA-MIYA AND HER SUPPORTERS

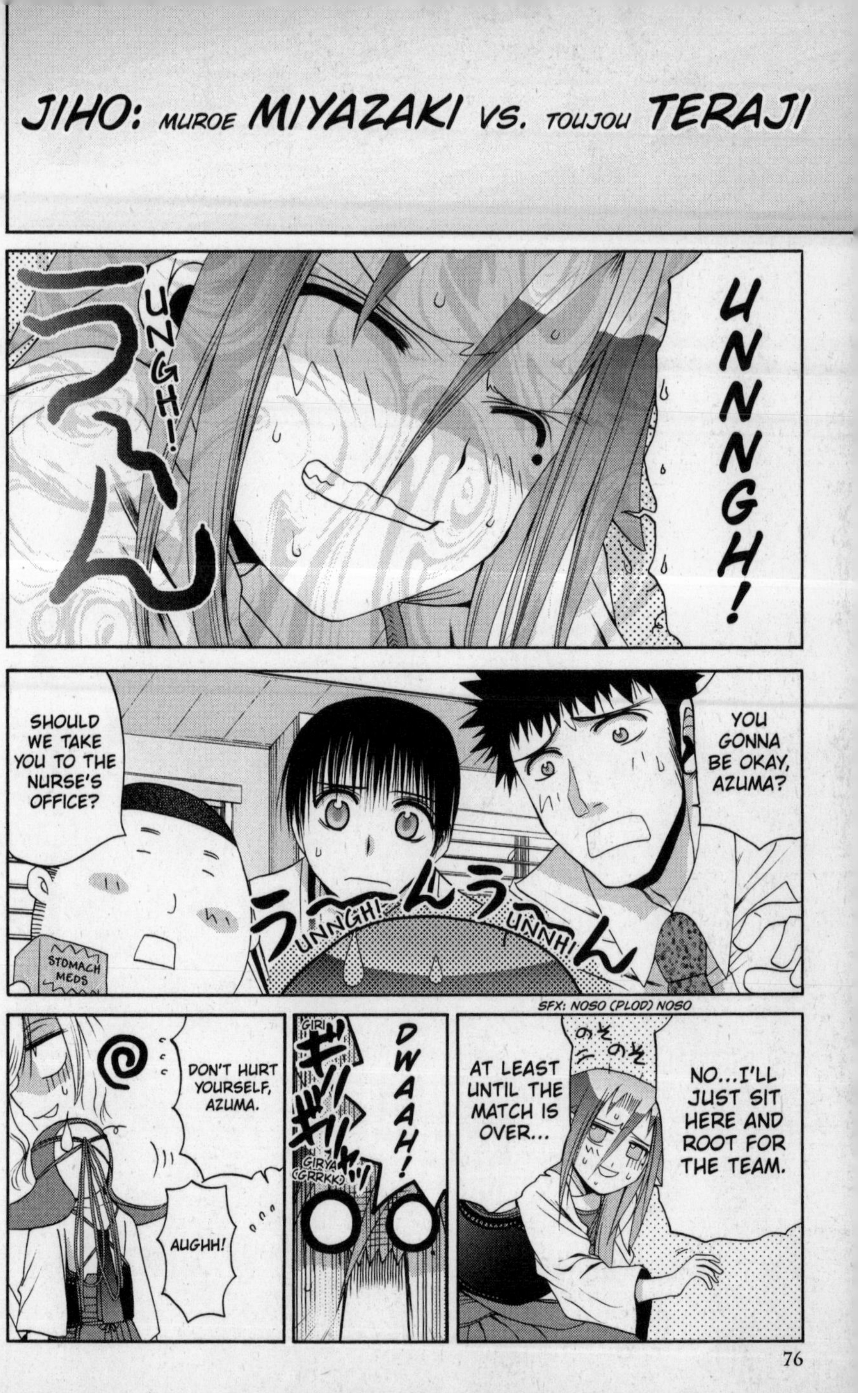
JIHO: MUROE MIYAZAKI VS. TOUJOU TERAJI
UNNNGH!
UNGH!
YOU GONNA BE OKAY, AZUMA?
SHOULD WE TAKE YOU TO THE NURSE'S OFFICE?
UNNHH
UNNNGH!
STOMACH MEDS
SFX: NOSO (PLOD) NOSO
NO...I'LL JUST SIT HERE AND ROOT FOR THE TEAM.
AT LEAST UNTIL THE MATCH IS OVER...
DWAAH!
GIRI
GIRYA (GRRKK)
DON'T HURT YOURSELF, AZUMA.
AUGHH!

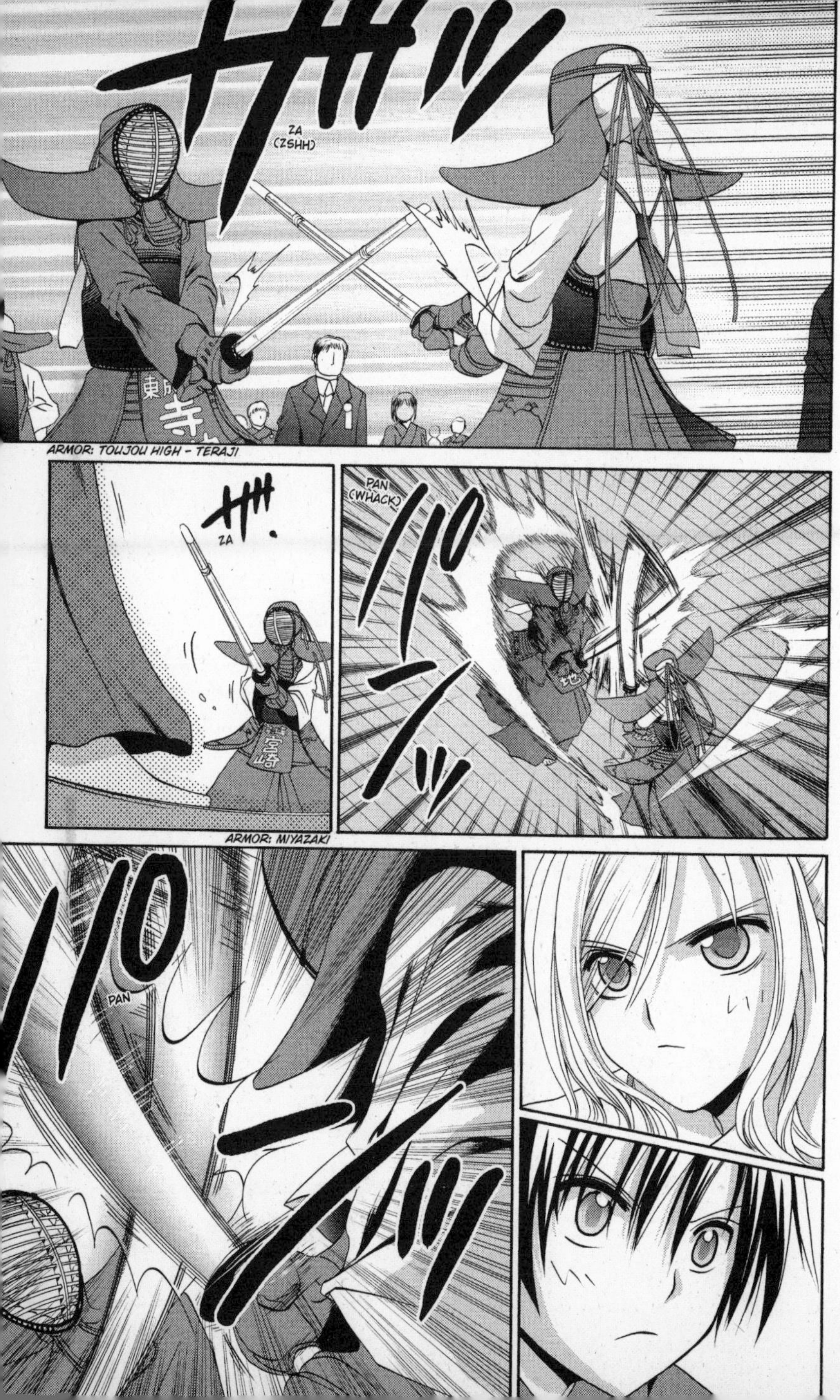
ZA
(ZSHH)
ARMOR: TOUJOU HIGH - TERAJI
PAN
(WHACK)
ZA
ARMOR: MIYAZAKI
PAN

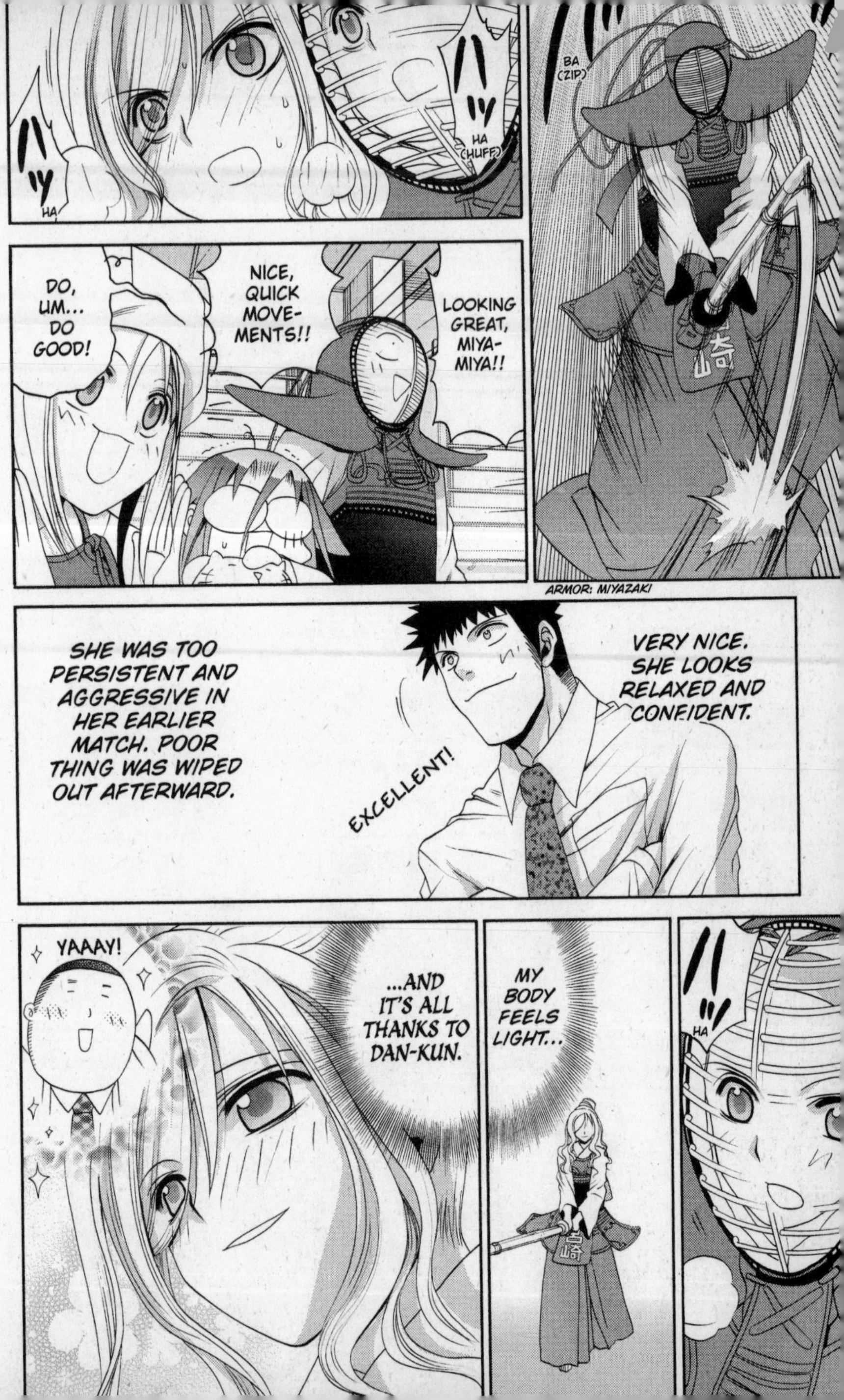
バッ
BA (ZIP)
崎
ARMOR: MIYAZAKI
ハッ
HA (HUFF?)
ハッ
HA
LOOKING GREAT, MIYA-MIYA!!
NICE, QUICK MOVEMENTS!!
DO, UM... DO GOOD!
VERY NICE. SHE LOOKS RELAXED AND CONFIDENT.
EXCELLENT!
SHE WAS TOO PERSISTENT AND AGGRESSIVE IN HER EARLIER MATCH. POOR THING WAS WIPED OUT AFTERWARD.
ハッ
HA
MY BODY FEELS LIGHT...
...AND IT'S ALL THANKS TO DAN-KUN.
YAAAY!

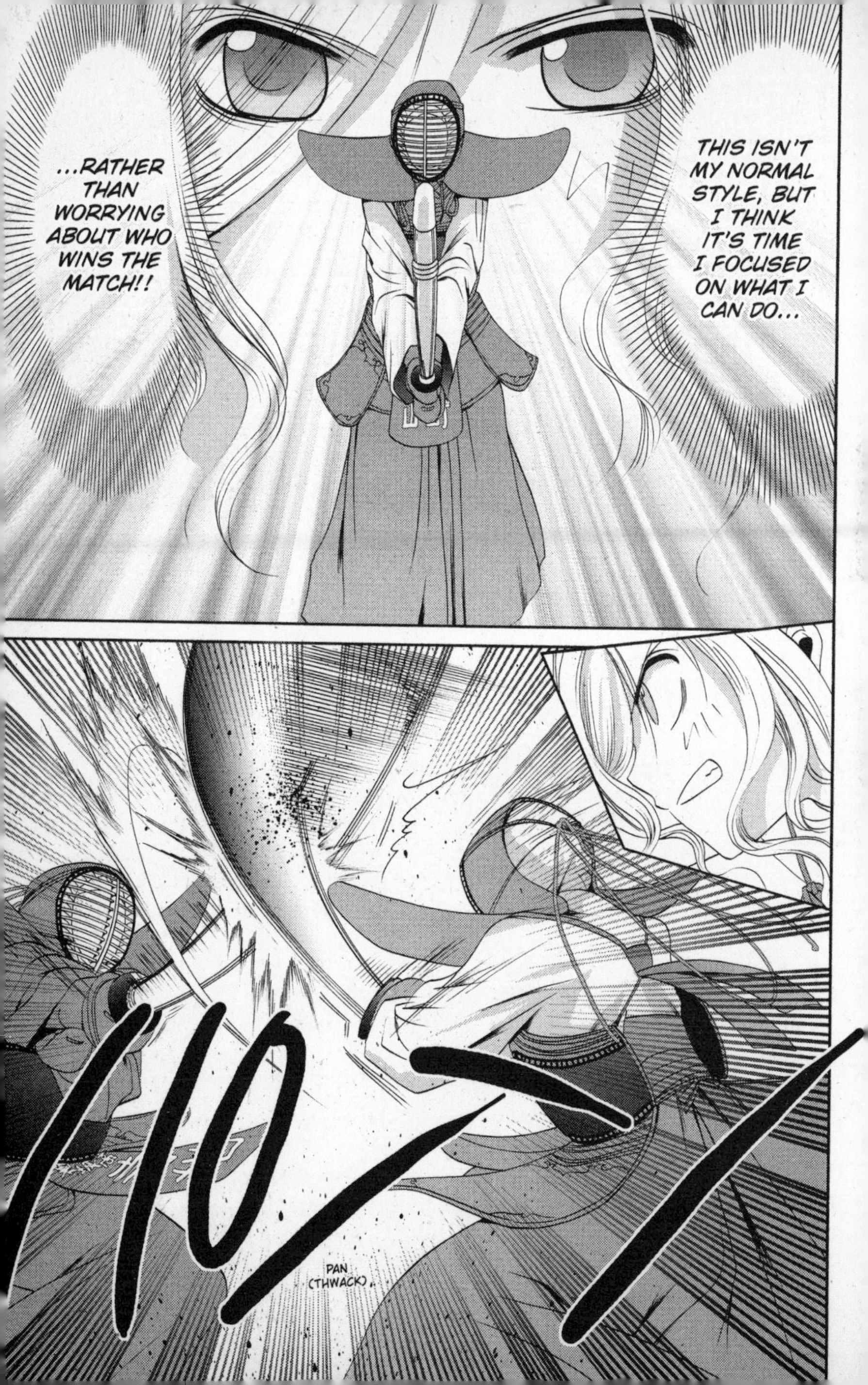
THIS ISN'T MY NORMAL STYLE, BUT I THINK IT'S TIME I FOCUSED ON WHAT I CAN DO...
...RATHER THAN WORRYING ABOUT WHO WINS THE MATCH!!
PAN (THWACK)

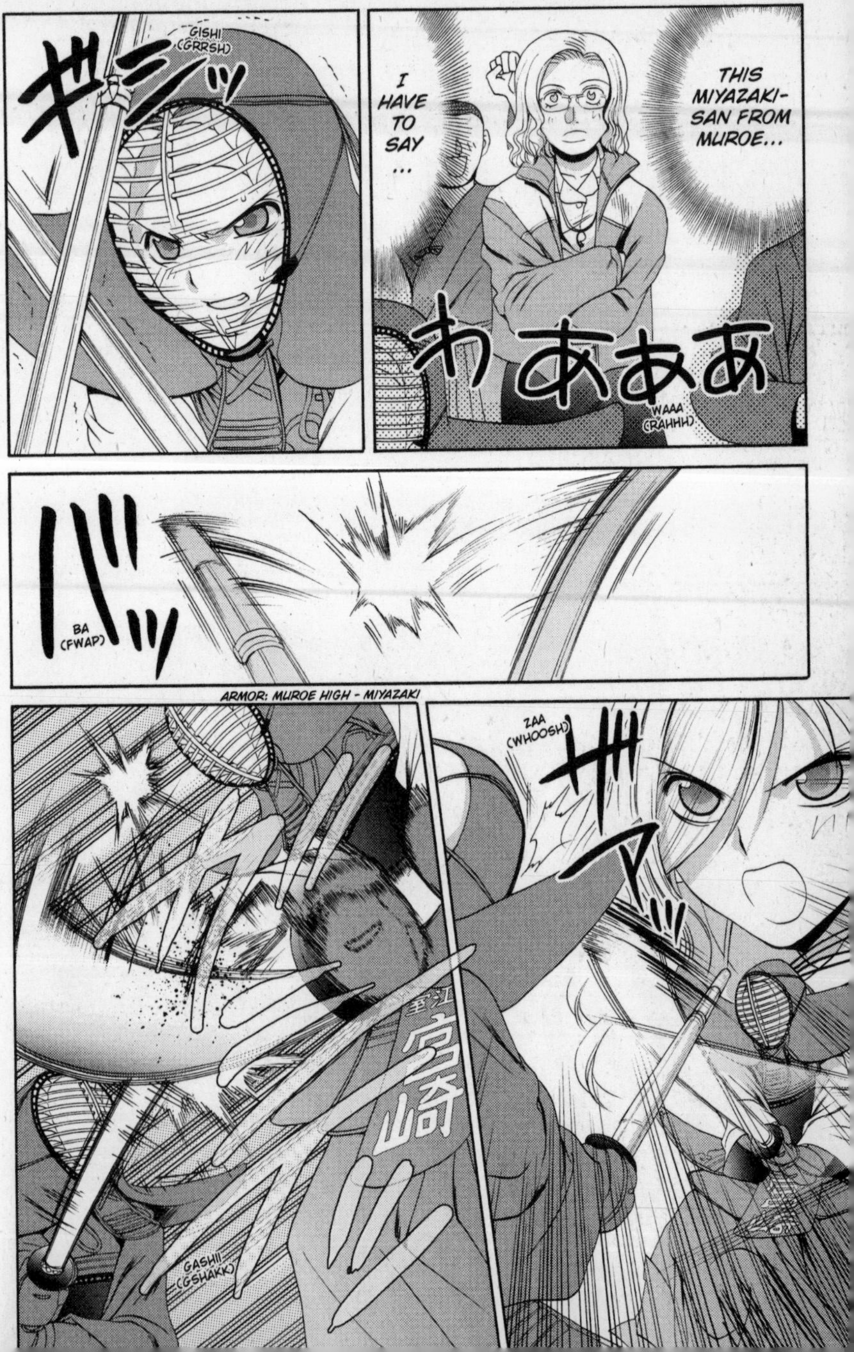

THIS MIYAZAKI-SAN FROM MUROE...
I HAVE TO SAY ...
わあああ
WAAA (RAHHH)
ギシッ
GISHI (GRRSH)
バッ
BA (FWAP)
ザァッ
ZAA (WHOOSH)
ARMOR: MUROE HIGH - MIYAZAKI
室江
宮崎
GASHII (GSHAKK)

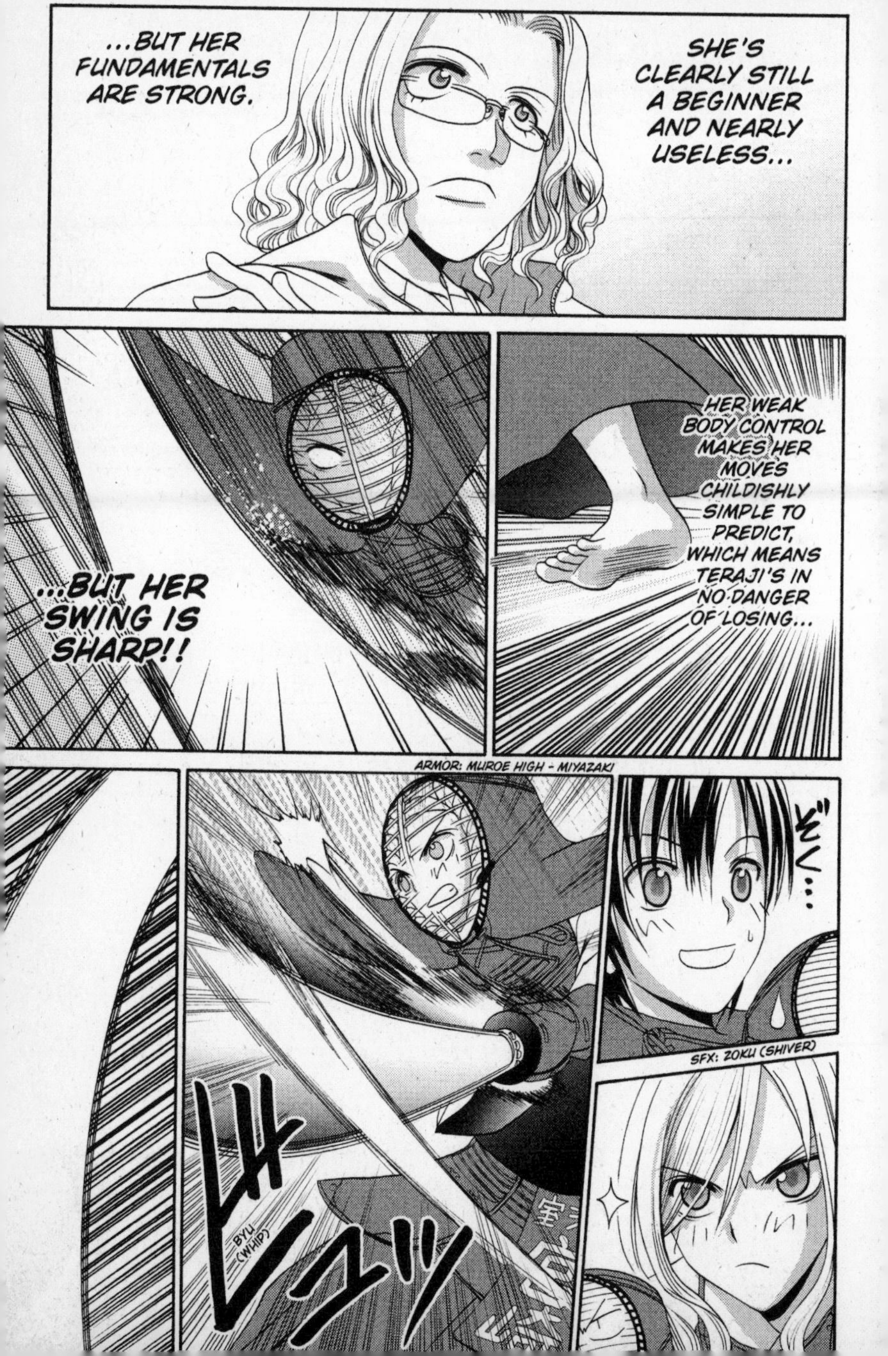
SHE'S CLEARLY STILL A BEGINNER AND NEARLY USELESS...
...BUT HER FUNDAMENTALS ARE STRONG.
HER WEAK BODY CONTROL MAKES HER MOVES CHILDISHLY SIMPLE TO PREDICT, WHICH MEANS TERAJI'S IN NO DANGER OF LOSING...
...BUT HER SWING IS SHARP!!
ARMOR: MUROE HIGH - MIYAZAKI
ぞく…
SFX: ZOKU (SHIVER)
ビュッ
BYU (WHIP)

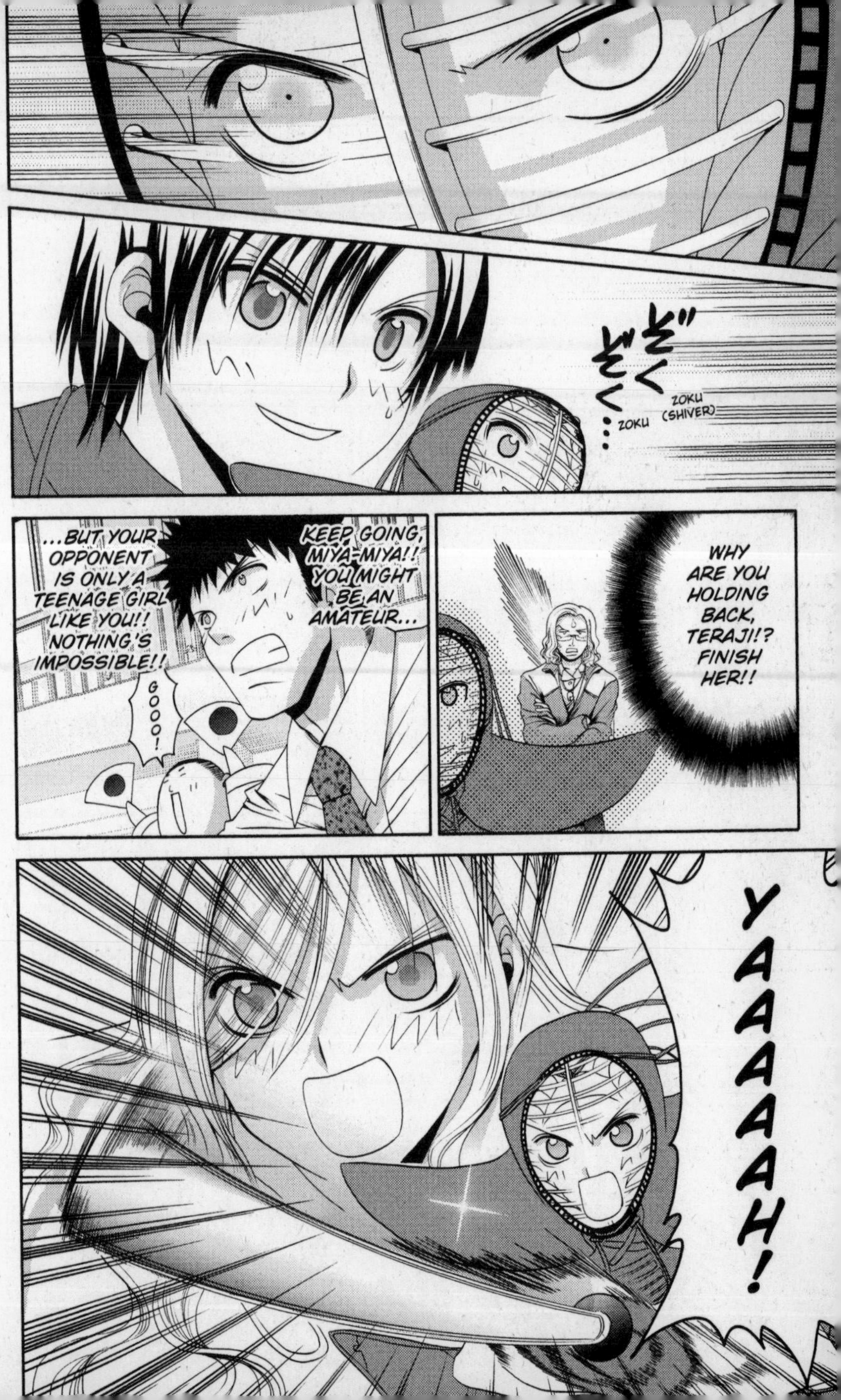
ぞく
ぞく…
ZOKU (SHIVER)
ZOKU
WHY ARE YOU HOLDING BACK, TERAJI!? FINISH HER!!
KEEP GOING, MIYA-MIYA!! YOU MIGHT BE AN AMATEUR...
...BUT YOUR OPPONENT IS ONLY A TEENAGE GIRL LIKE YOU!! NOTHING'S IMPOSSIBLE!!
GOOOO!
YAAAAAH!

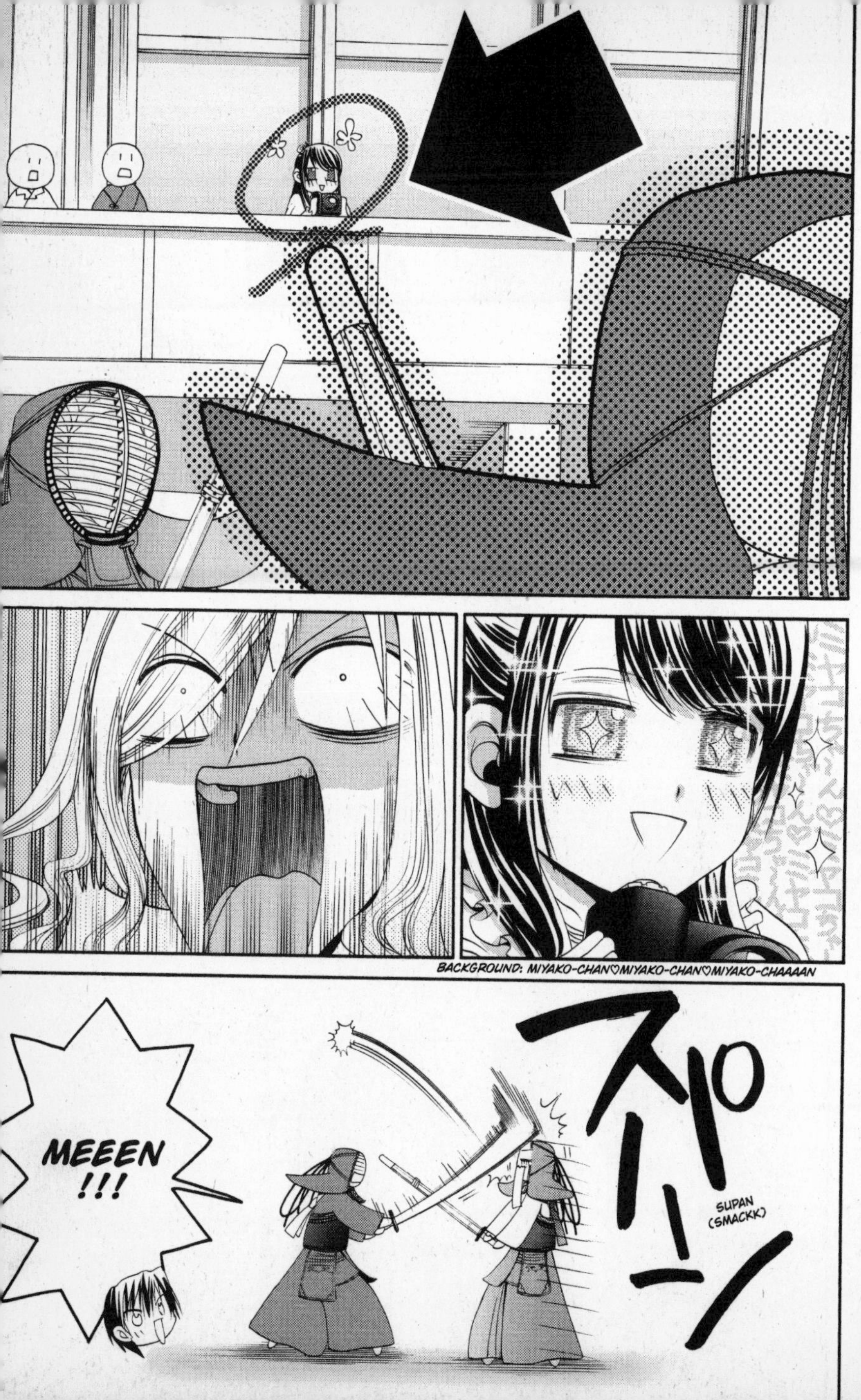
BACKGROUND: MIYAKO-CHAN♡MIYAKO-CHAN♡MIYAKO-CHAAAAN
スパーン
SUPAN (SMACKK)
MEEEN !!!

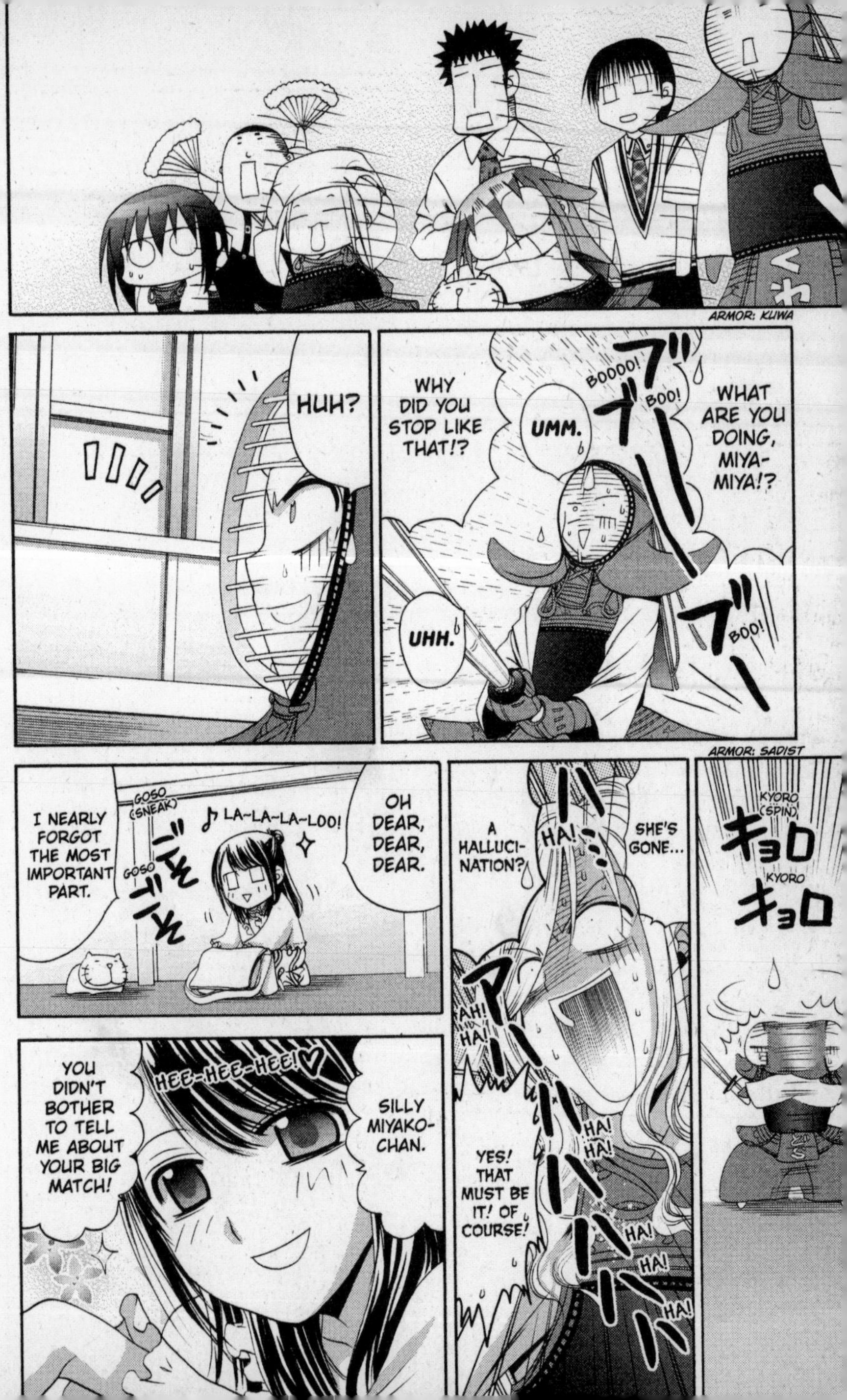
ARMOR: KUWA
WHAT ARE YOU DOING, MIYA-MIYA!?
BOOOO!
BOO!
WHY DID YOU STOP LIKE THAT!?
UMM.
UHH.
BOO!
ARMOR: SADIST
HUH?
KYORO (SPIN)
KYORO
SHE'S GONE...
A HALLUCI-NATION?
HA!
AH! HA!
HA! HA!
HA!
HA!
HA!
YES! THAT MUST BE IT! OF COURSE!
OH DEAR, DEAR, DEAR.
♪ LA-LA-LA-LOO!
GOSO (SNEAK)
GOSO
I NEARLY FORGOT THE MOST IMPORTANT PART.
SILLY MIYAKO-CHAN.
HEE-HEE-HEE!♥
YOU DIDN'T BOTHER TO TELL ME ABOUT YOUR BIG MATCH!

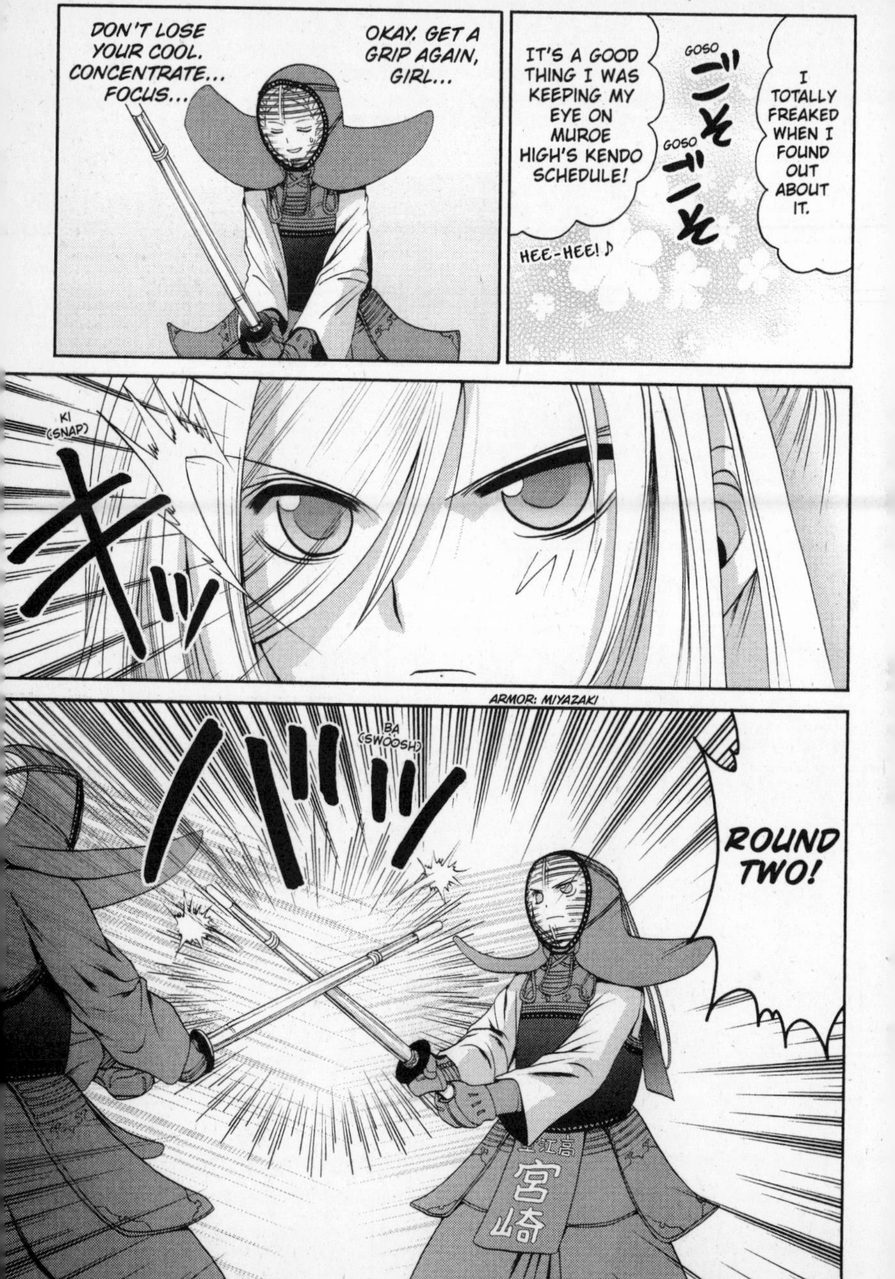
I TOTALLY FREAKED WHEN I FOUND OUT ABOUT IT.
GOSO
GOSO
IT'S A GOOD THING I WAS KEEPING MY EYE ON MUROE HIGH'S KENDO SCHEDULE!
HEE-HEE!♪
OKAY. GET A GRIP AGAIN, GIRL...
DON'T LOSE YOUR COOL. CONCENTRATE... FOCUS...
KI (SNAP)
ARMOR: MIYAZAKI
ROUND TWO!
BA (SWOOSH)
宮崎

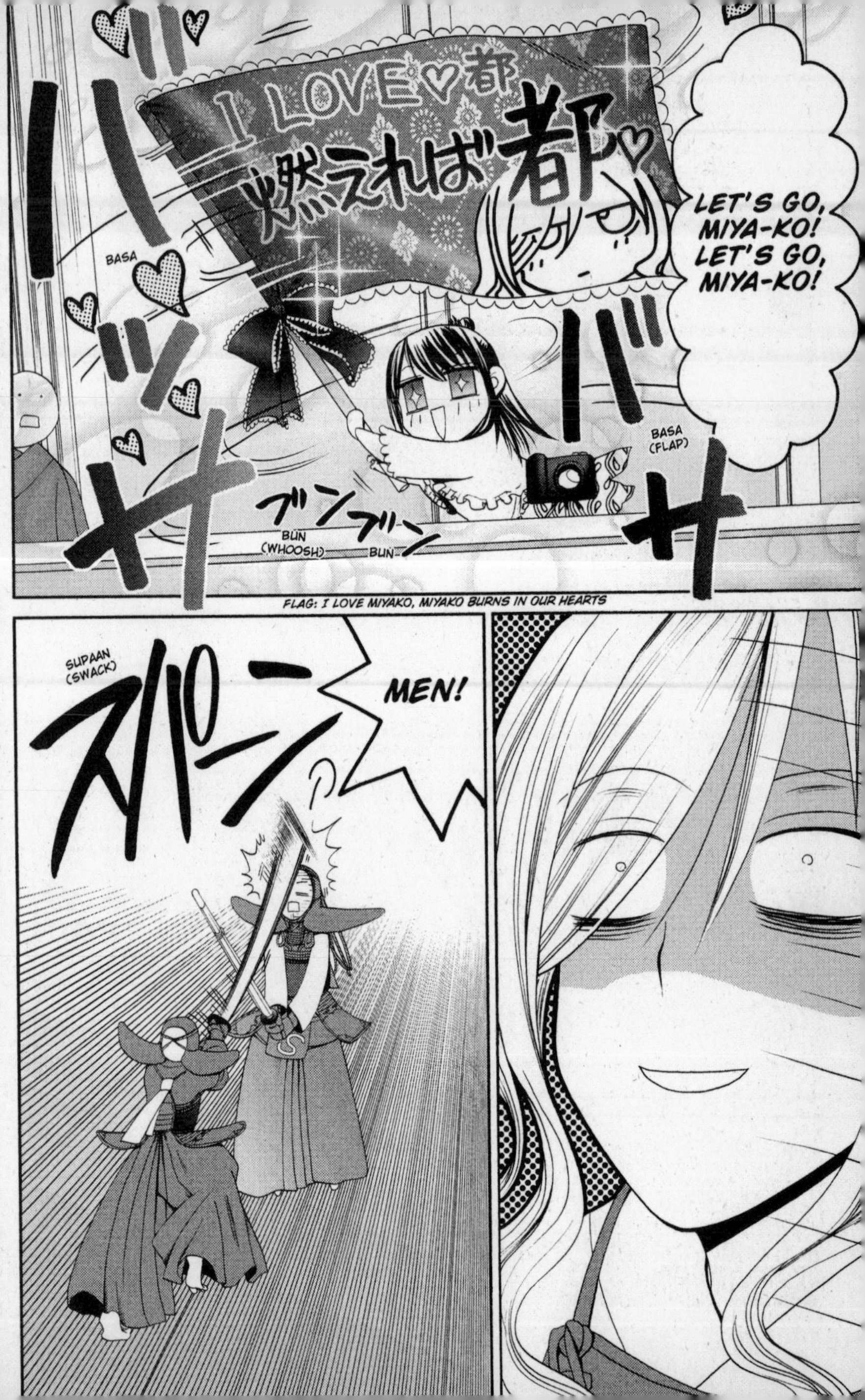
LET'S GO, MIYA-KO! LET'S GO, MIYA-KO!
I LOVE♡都
燃えれば都♡
バサッ
BASA (FLAP)
バサッ
BASA
ブン
BUN (WHOOSH)
ブン
BUN
FLAG: I LOVE MIYAKO, MIYAKO BURNS IN OUR HEARTS
MEN!
スパーン
SUPAAN (SWACK)

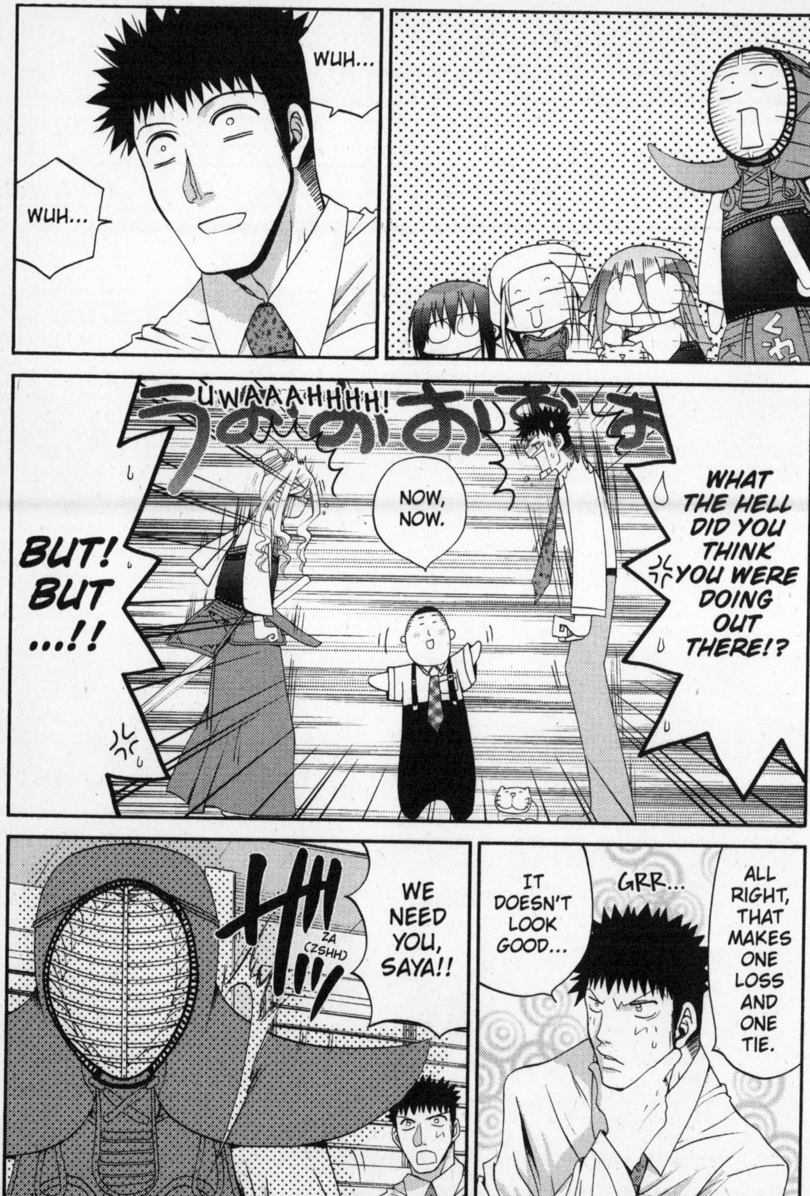
WUH...
WUH...
UWAAAHHHH!
WHAT THE HELL DID YOU THINK YOU WERE DOING OUT THERE!?
NOW, NOW.
BUT! BUT ...!!
ALL RIGHT, THAT MAKES ONE LOSS AND ONE TIE.
GRR...
IT DOESN'T LOOK GOOD...
WE NEED YOU, SAYA!!
ZA (ZSHH)

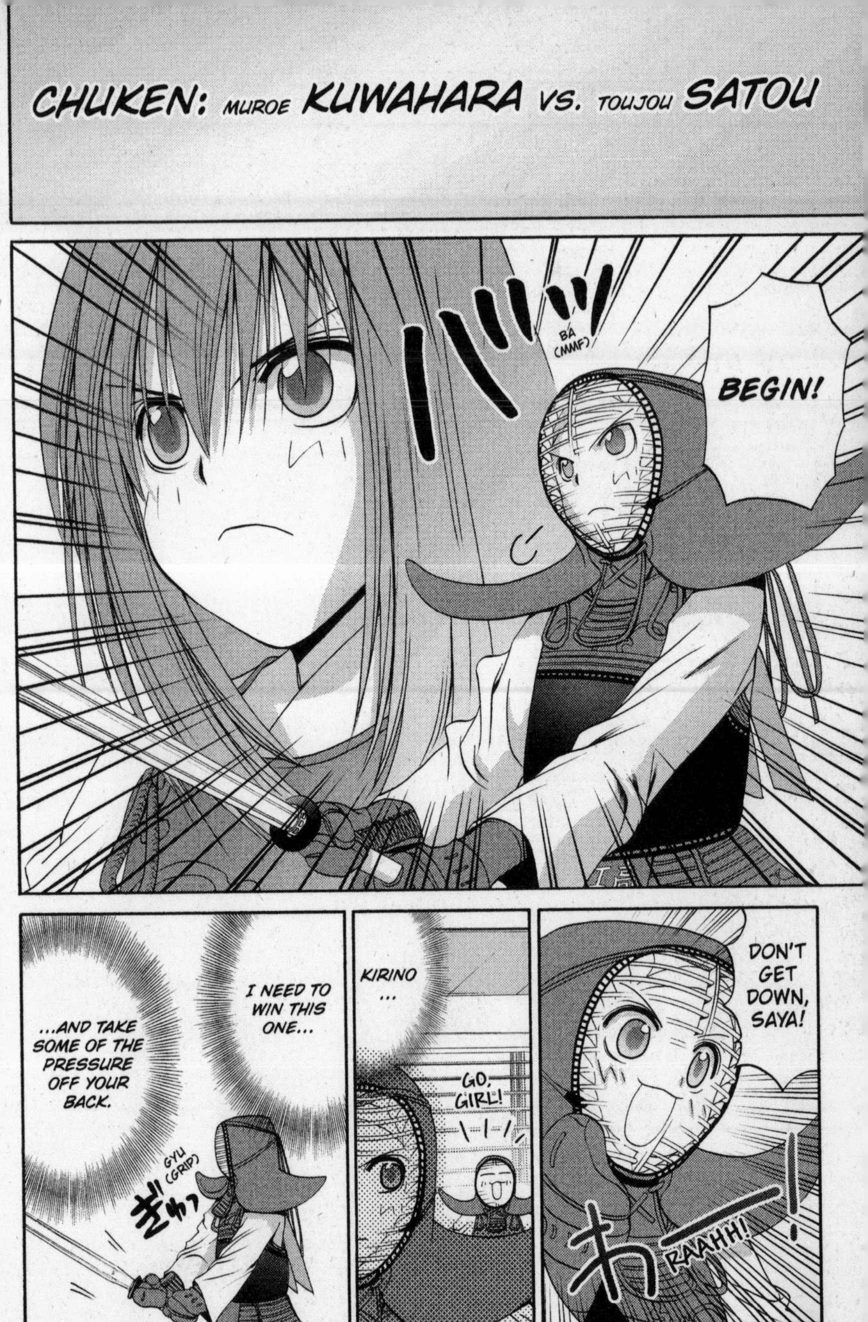
CHUKEN: MUROE KUWAHARA VS. TOUJOU SATOU
BEGIN!
BA (MMF)
DON'T GET DOWN, SAYA!
RAAHH!
KIRINO ...
GO, GIRL!
I NEED TO WIN THIS ONE...
...AND TAKE SOME OF THE PRESSURE OFF YOUR BACK.
GYU (GRIP)

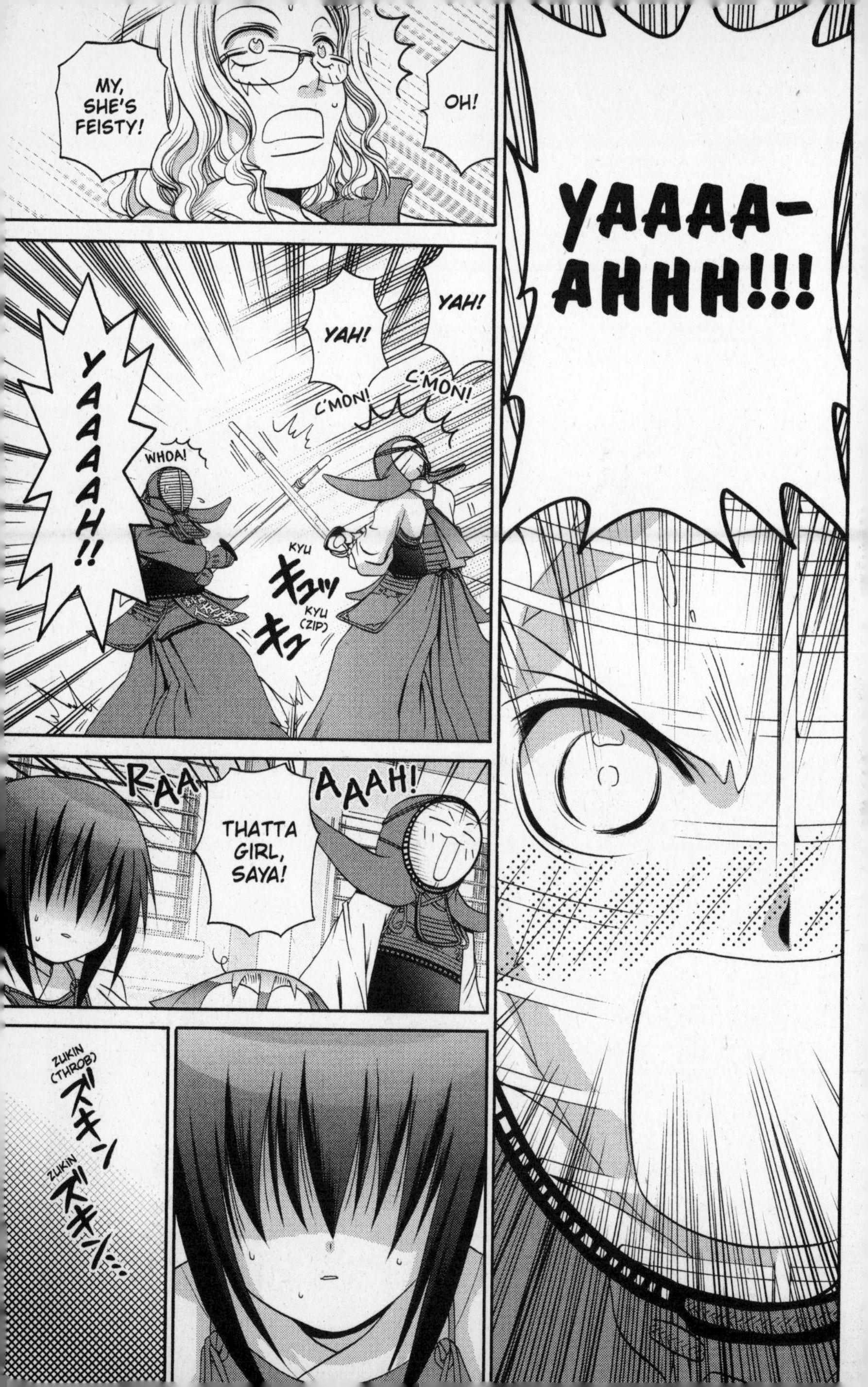

YAAAA-AHHH!!!
OH!
MY, SHE'S FEISTY!
YAH!
YAH!
C'MON!
C'MON!
YAAAAAH!!
WHOA!
KYU
キュッ
KYU (ZIP)
キュ
RAA
AAAH!
THATTA GIRL, SAYA!
ZUKIN (THROB)
ズキン
ZUKIN
ズキン…

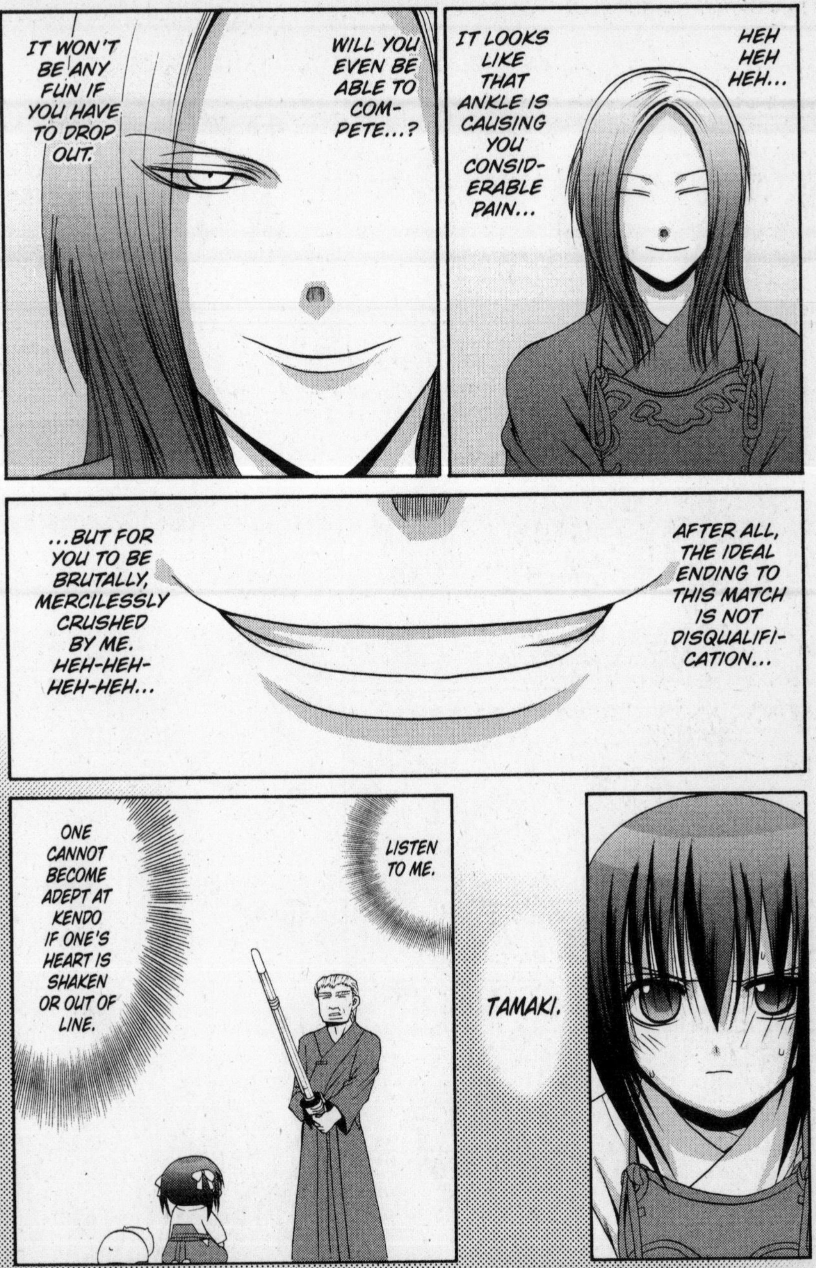
HEH HEH HEH...
IT LOOKS LIKE THAT ANKLE IS CAUSING YOU CONSID-ERABLE PAIN...
WILL YOU EVEN BE ABLE TO COM-PETE...?
IT WON'T BE ANY FUN IF YOU HAVE TO DROP OUT.
AFTER ALL, THE IDEAL ENDING TO THIS MATCH IS NOT DISQUALIFI-CATION...
...BUT FOR YOU TO BE BRUTALLY, MERCILESSLY CRUSHED BY ME. HEH-HEH-HEH-HEH...
TAMAKI.
LISTEN TO ME.
ONE CANNOT BECOME ADEPT AT KENDO IF ONE'S HEART IS SHAKEN OR OUT OF LINE.

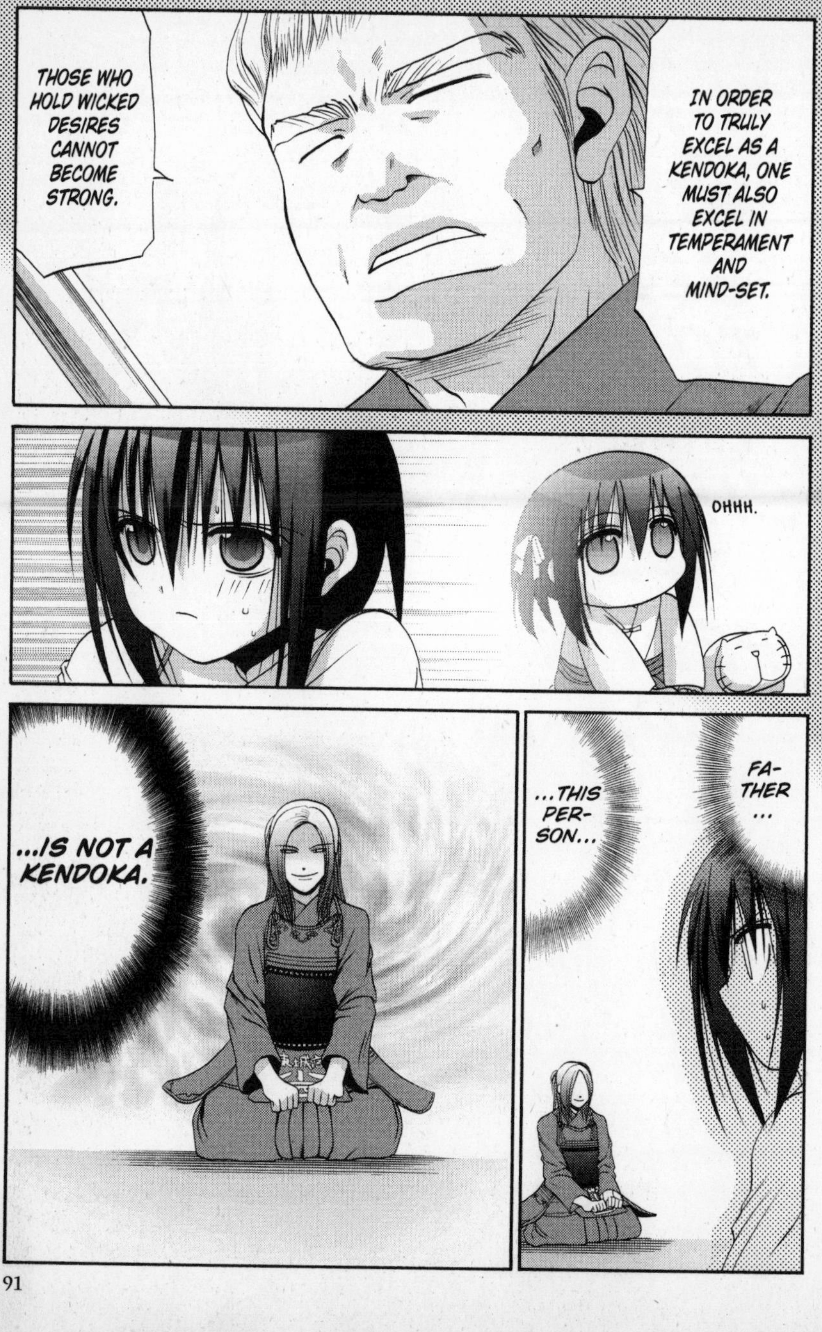
IN ORDER TO TRULY EXCEL AS A KENDOKA, ONE MUST ALSO EXCEL IN TEMPERAMENT AND MIND-SET.
THOSE WHO HOLD WICKED DESIRES CANNOT BECOME STRONG.
OHHH.
FA-THER...
...THIS PER-SON...
...IS NOT A KENDOKA.

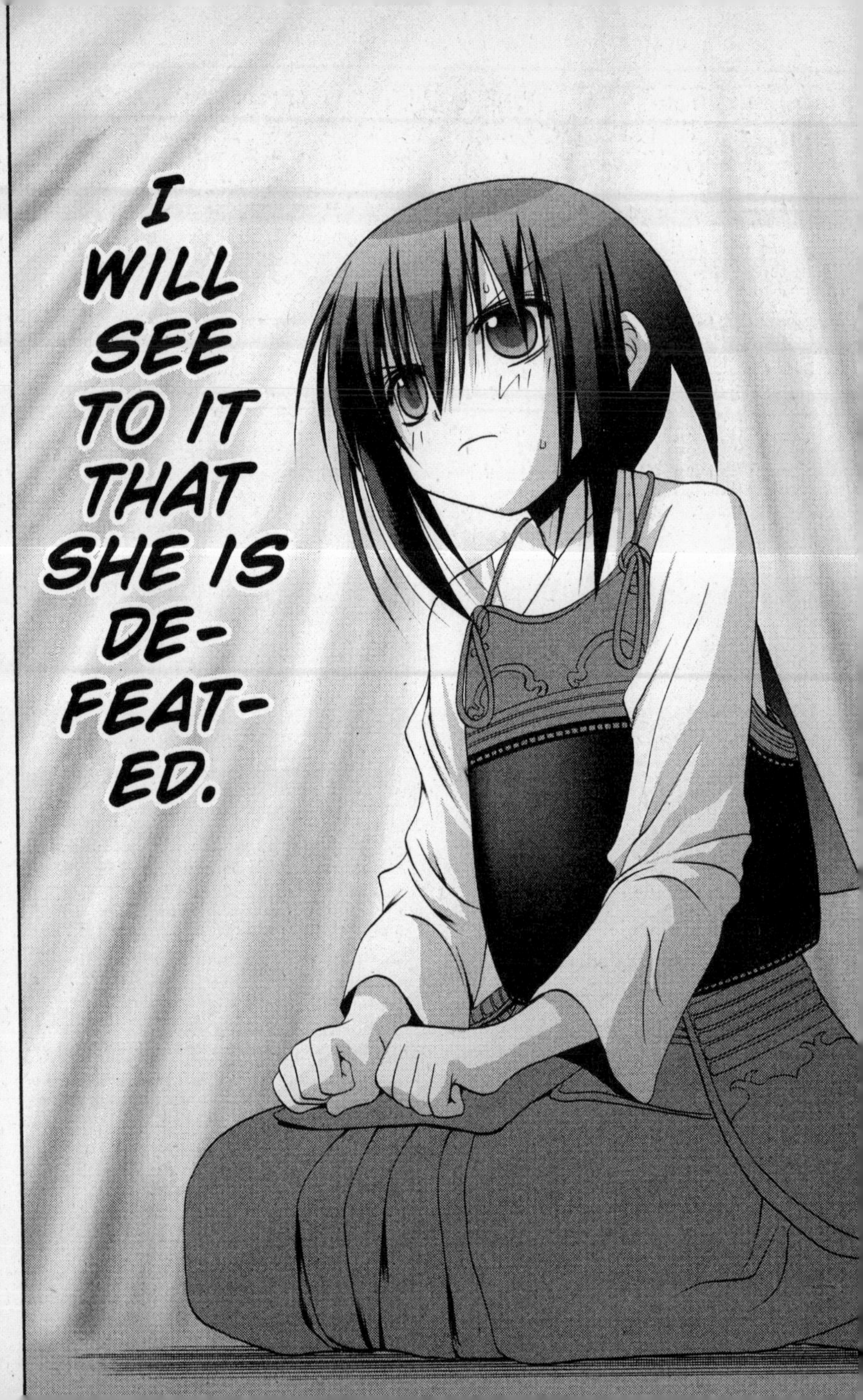
I WILL SEE TO IT THAT SHE IS DE-FEAT-ED.

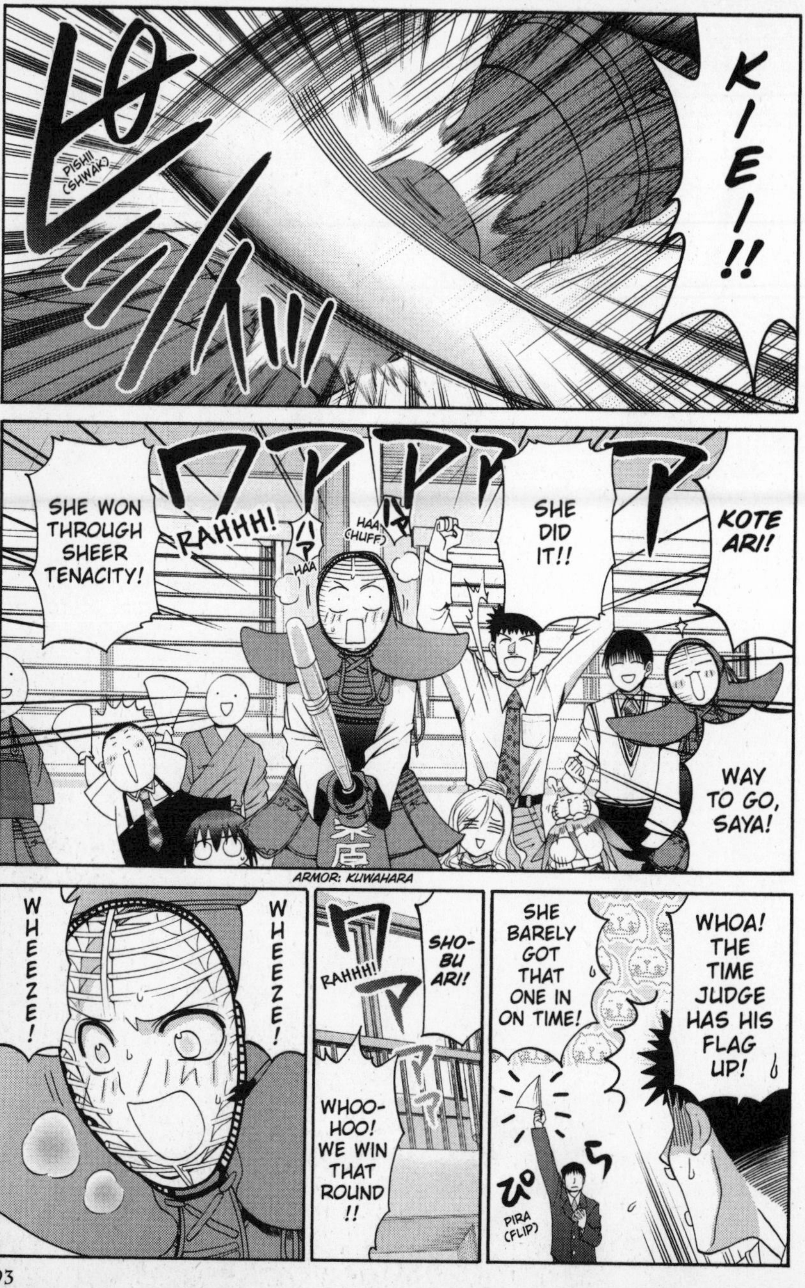
KIEI!!
PISHII (SHWAK)
KOTE ARI!
SHE DID IT!!
HAA (HUFF)
HAA
RAHHH!
SHE WON THROUGH SHEER TENACITY!
WAY TO GO, SAYA!
ARMOR: KUWAHARA
WHOA! THE TIME JUDGE HAS HIS FLAG UP!
SHE BARELY GOT THAT ONE IN ON TIME!
PIRA (FLIP)
SHOBU ARI!
RAHHH!
WHOO-HOO! WE WIN THAT ROUND!!
WHEEZE!
WHEEZE!

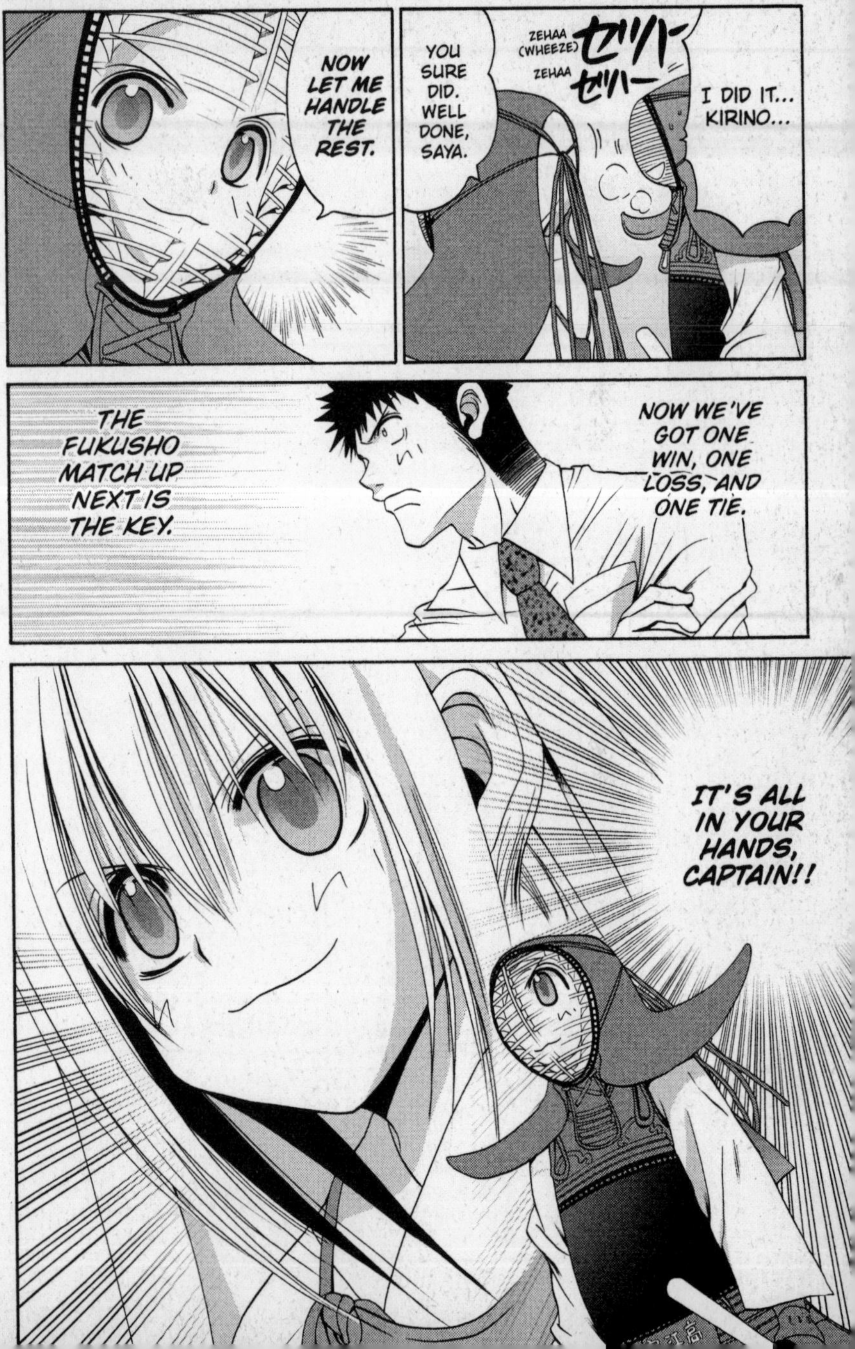
I DID IT... KIRINO...
ゼハー ゼハー
ZEHAA (WHEEZE) ZEHAA
YOU SURE DID. WELL DONE, SAYA.
NOW LET ME HANDLE THE REST.
NOW WE'VE GOT ONE WIN, ONE LOSS, AND ONE TIE.
THE FUKUSHO MATCH UP NEXT IS THE KEY.
IT'S ALL IN YOUR HANDS, CAPTAIN!!

BAMBOO BLADE

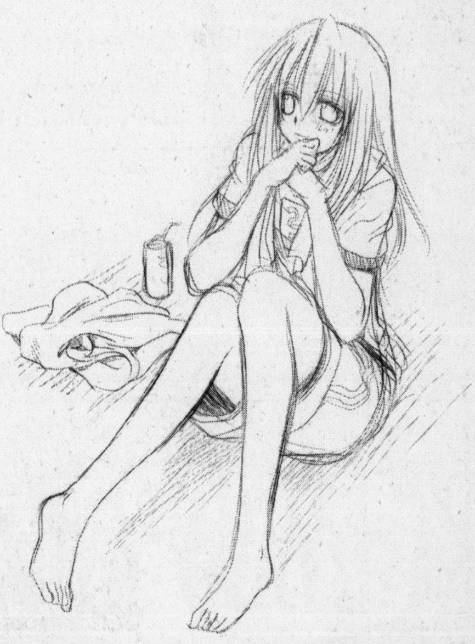

BAMBOO BLADE
バンブーブレード

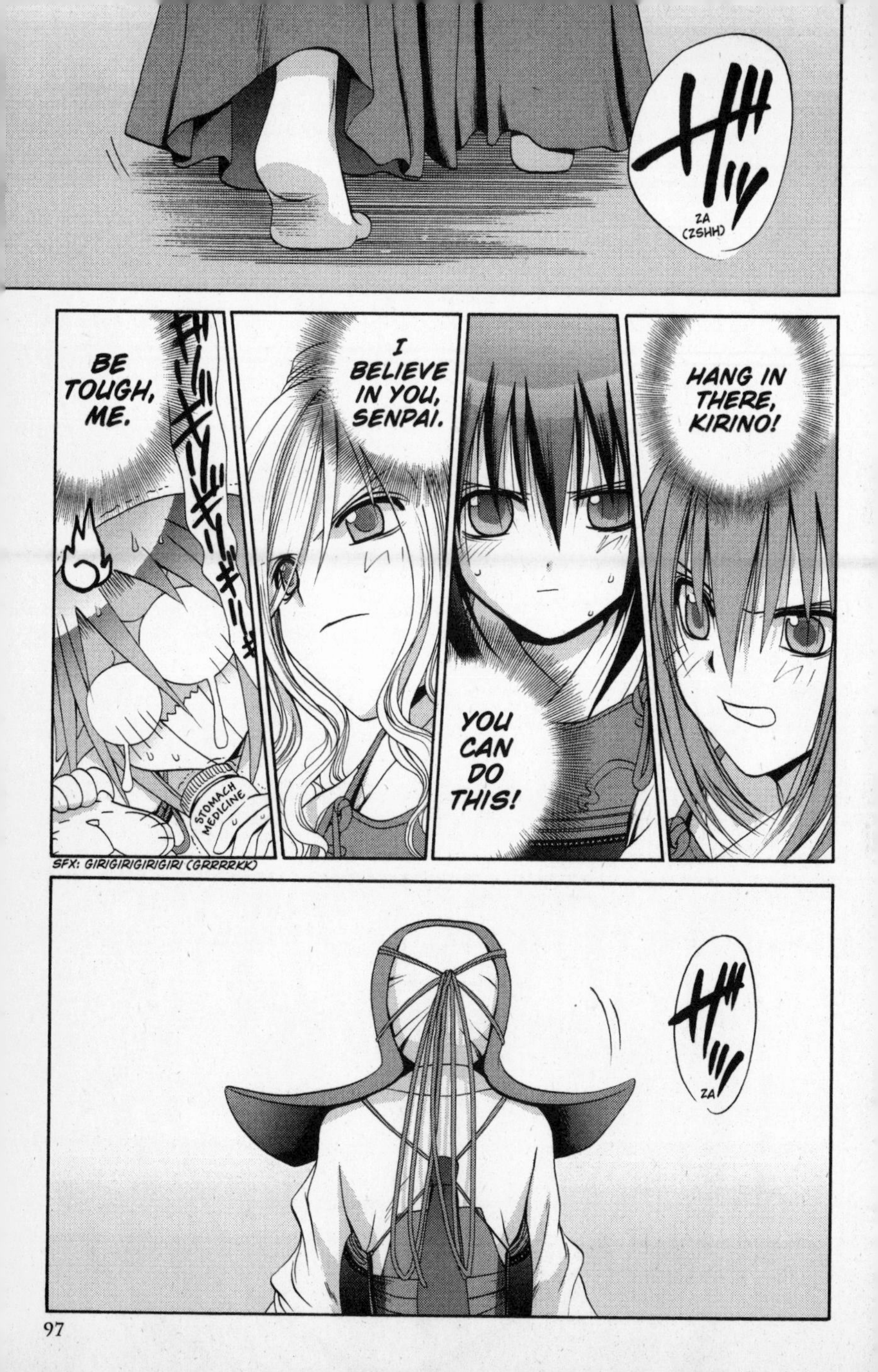
ZA (ZSHH)
HANG IN THERE, KIRINO!
YOU CAN DO THIS!
I BELIEVE IN YOU, SENPAI.
BE TOUGH, ME.
STOMACH MEDICINE
SFX: GIRIGIRIGIRIGIRI (GRRRRKK)
ZA

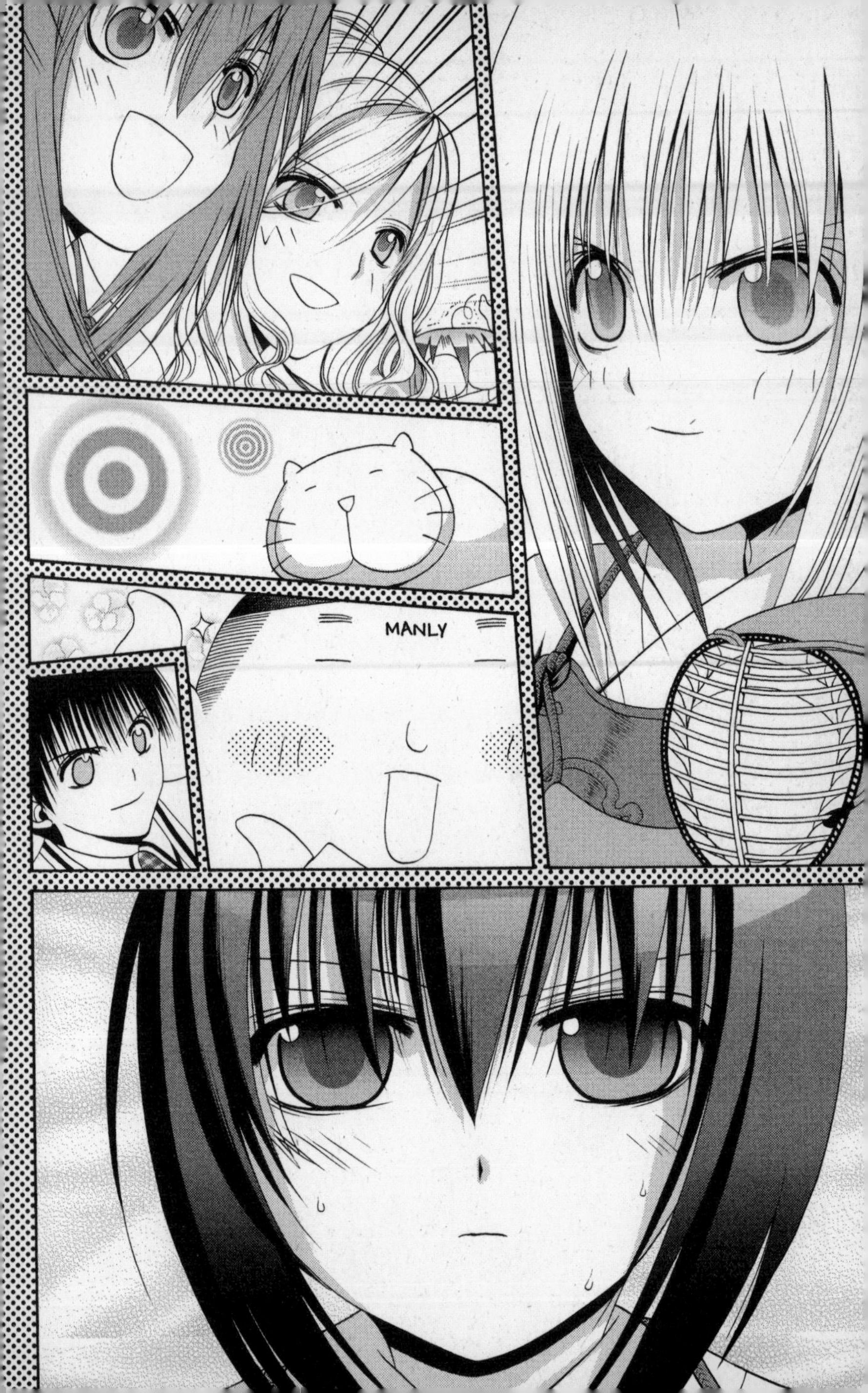
MANLY

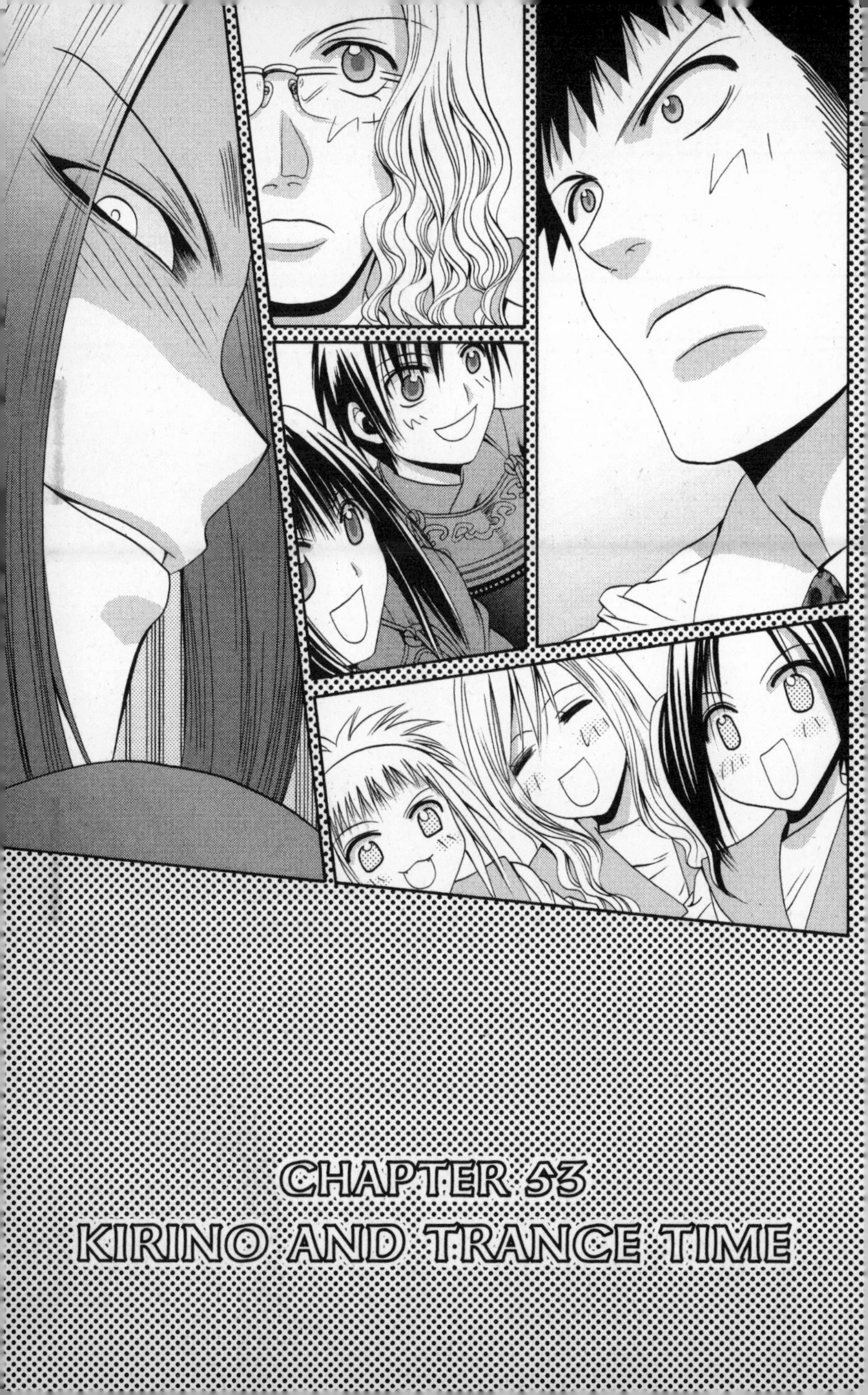

CHAPTER 53
KIRINO AND TRANCE TIME

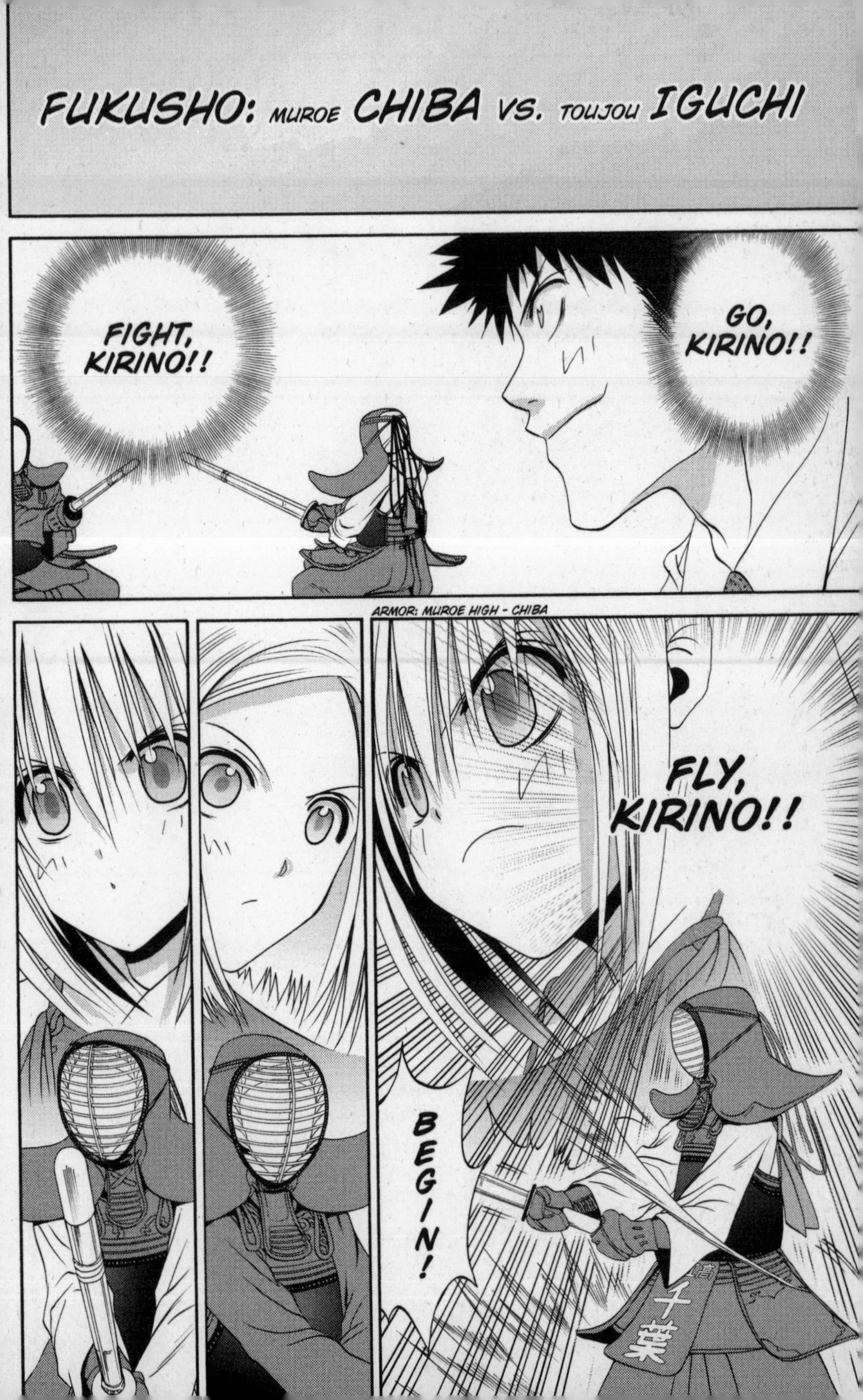
FUKUSHO: MUROE CHIBA VS. TOUJOU IGUCHI
GO, KIRINO!!
FIGHT, KIRINO!!
ARMOR: MUROE HIGH - CHIBA
FLY, KIRINO!!
BEGIN!

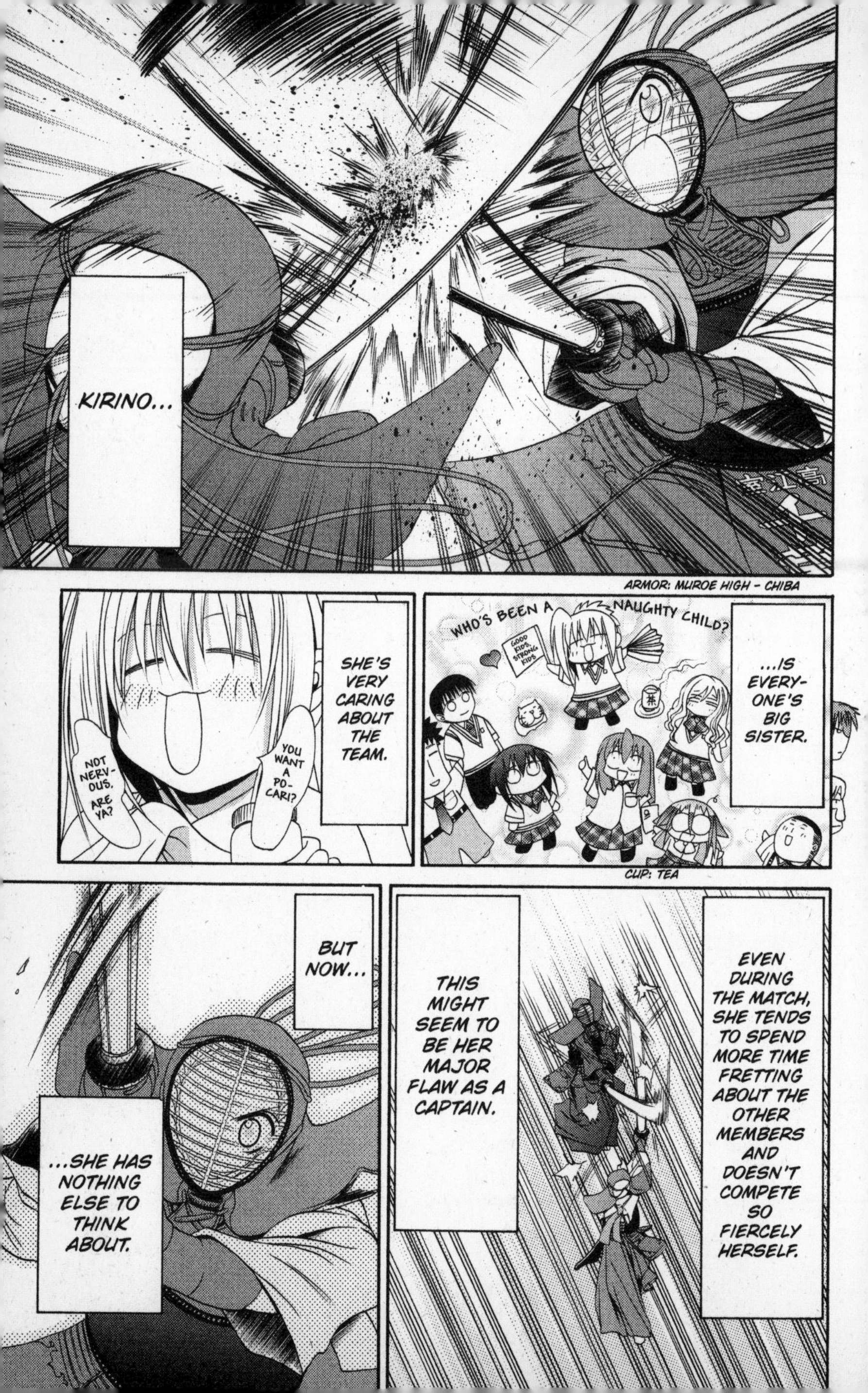
KIRINO...
ARMOR: MUROE HIGH - CHIBA
WHO'S BEEN A NAUGHTY CHILD?
GOOD KIDS, STRONG KIDS
...IS EVERY-ONE'S BIG SISTER.
CUP: TEA
SHE'S VERY CARING ABOUT THE TEAM.
YOU WANT A PO-CARI?
NOT NERV-OUS, ARE YA?
EVEN DURING THE MATCH, SHE TENDS TO SPEND MORE TIME FRETTING ABOUT THE OTHER MEMBERS AND DOESN'T COMPETE SO FIERCELY HERSELF.
THIS MIGHT SEEM TO BE HER MAJOR FLAW AS A CAPTAIN.
BUT NOW...
...SHE HAS NOTHING ELSE TO THINK ABOUT.

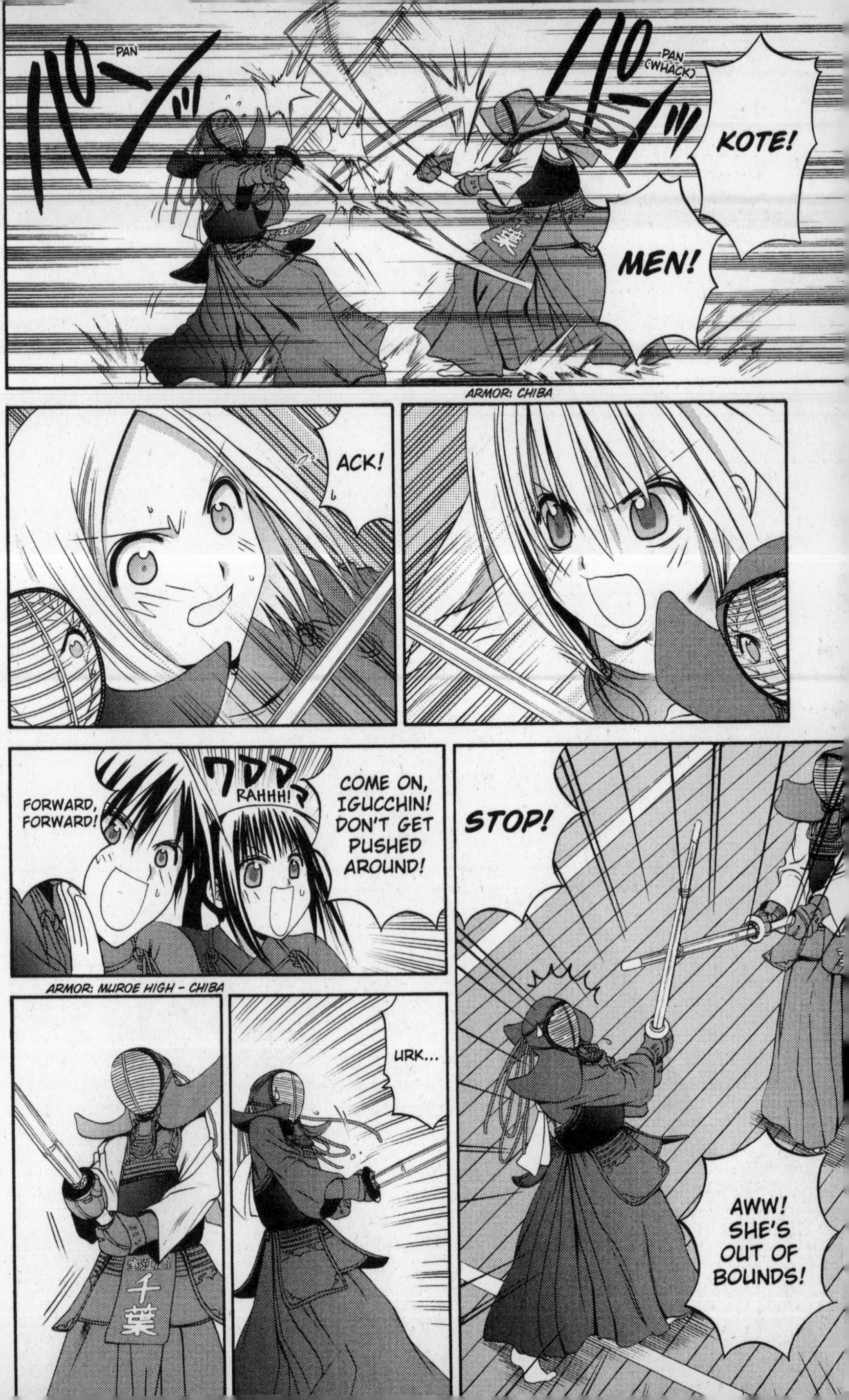
KOTE!
PAN (WHACK)
MEN!
PAN
ARMOR: CHIBA
ACK!
STOP!
AWW! SHE'S OUT OF BOUNDS!
COME ON, IGUCCHIN! DON'T GET PUSHED AROUND!
RAHHH!
FORWARD, FORWARD!
ARMOR: MUROE HIGH - CHIBA
URK...

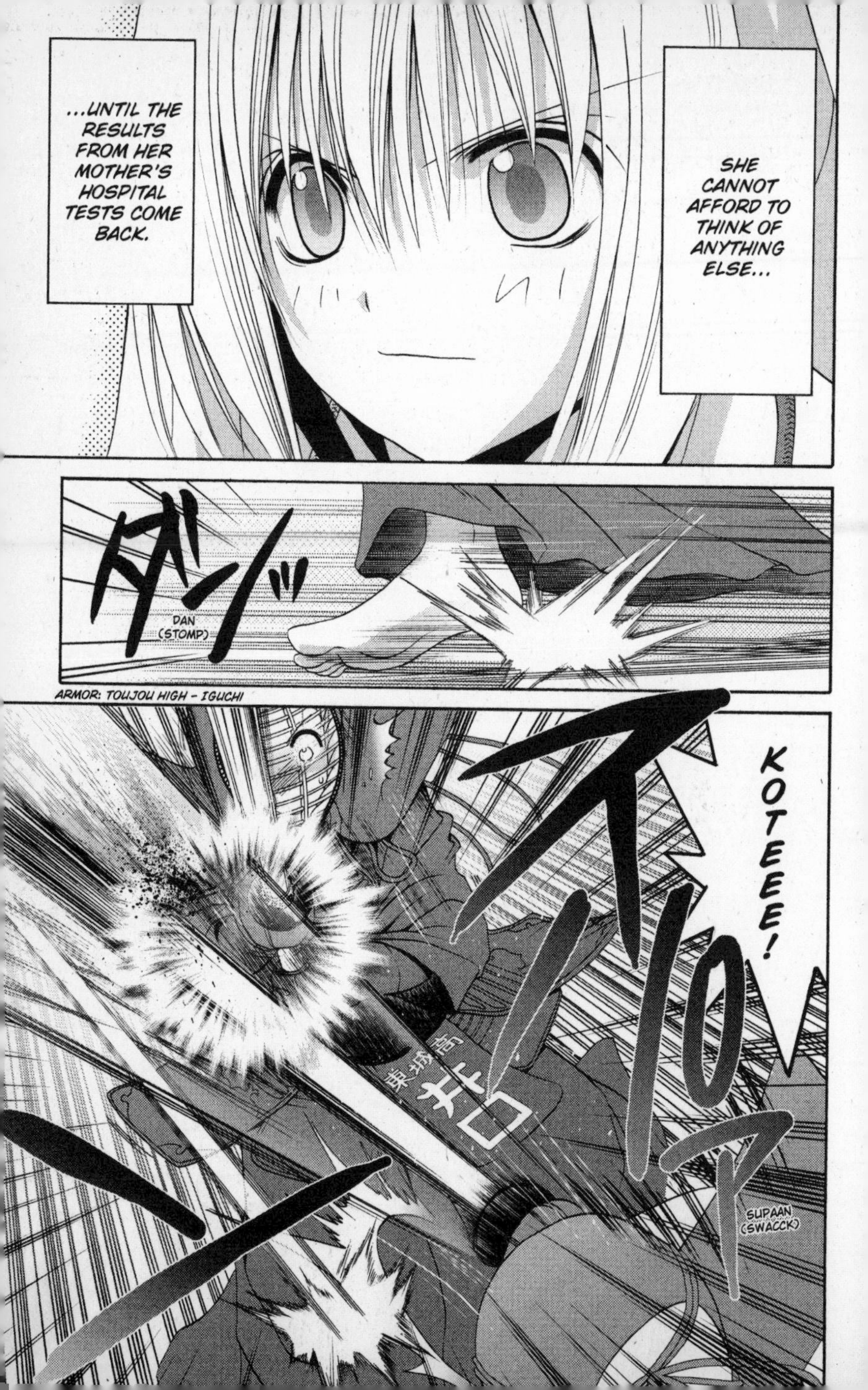
SHE CANNOT AFFORD TO THINK OF ANYTHING ELSE...
...UNTIL THE RESULTS FROM HER MOTHER'S HOSPITAL TESTS COME BACK.
DAN (STOMP)
ARMOR: TOUJOU HIGH - IGUCHI
KOTEEE!
SUPAAN (SWACCK)

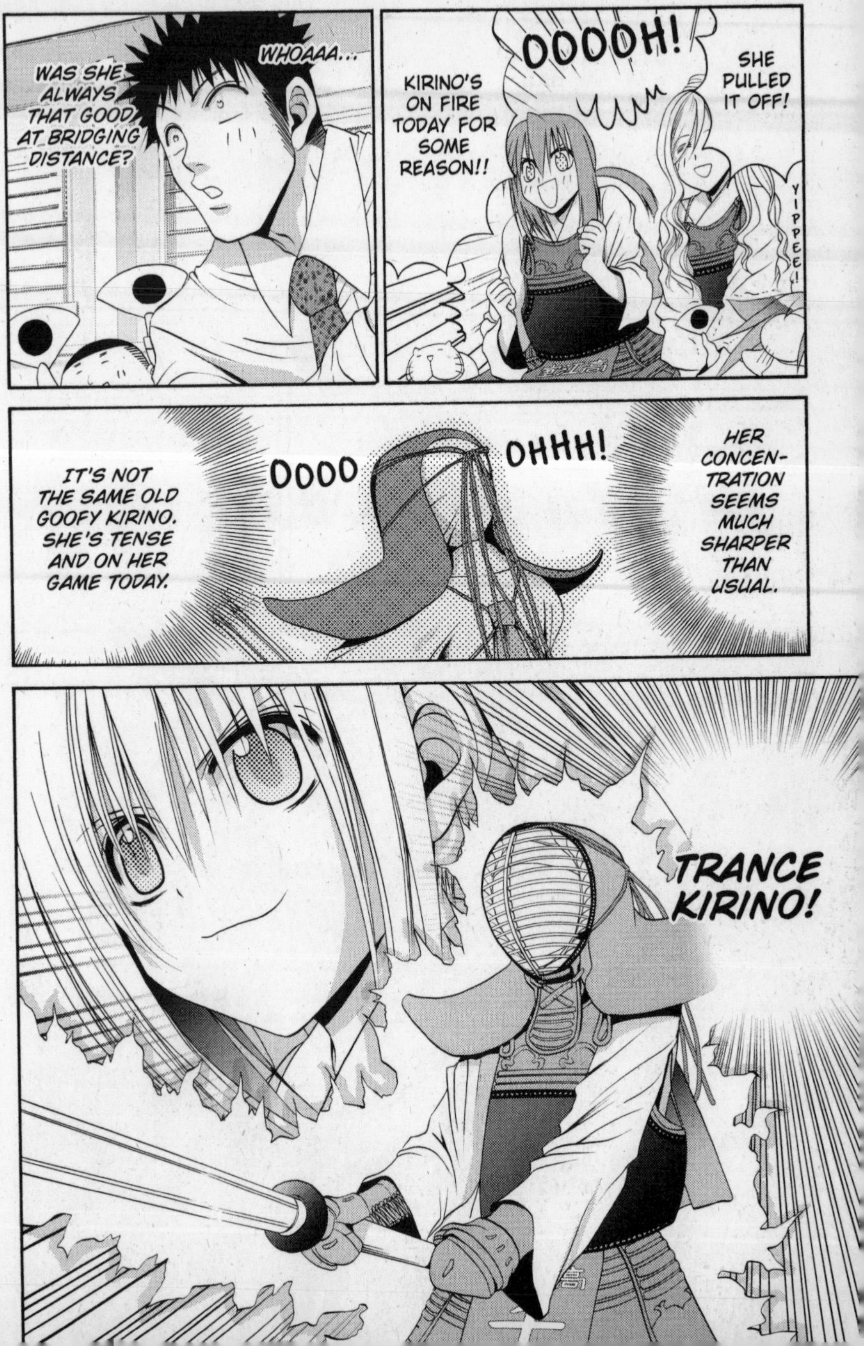

OOOOH!
SHE PULLED IT OFF!
KIRINO'S ON FIRE TODAY FOR SOME REASON!!
YIPPEE!
WHOAAA...
WAS SHE ALWAYS THAT GOOD AT BRIDGING DISTANCE?
HER CONCENTRATION SEEMS MUCH SHARPER THAN USUAL.
OOOO OHHH!
IT'S NOT THE SAME OLD GOOFY KIRINO. SHE'S TENSE AND ON HER GAME TODAY.
TRANCE KIRINO!

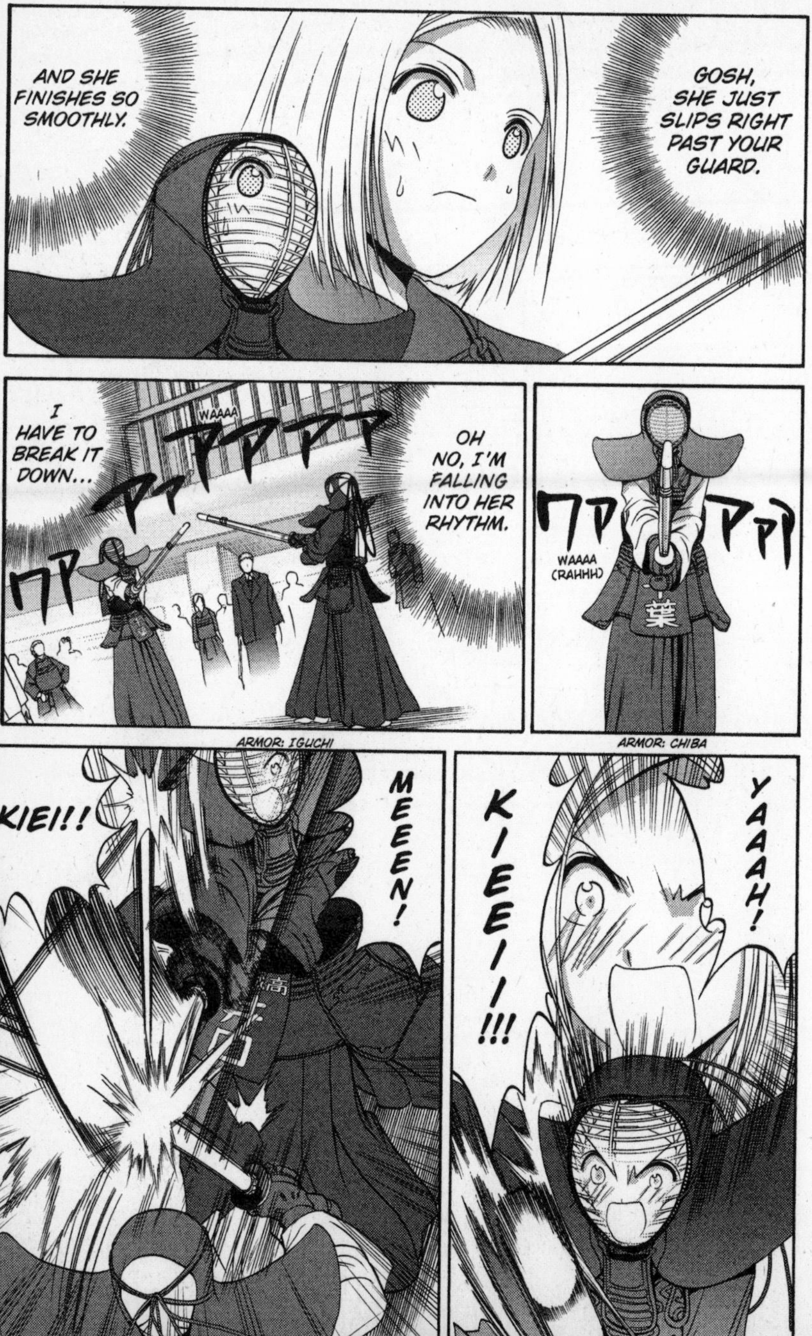
GOSH, SHE JUST SLIPS RIGHT PAST YOUR GUARD.
AND SHE FINISHES SO SMOOTHLY.
WAAAA (RAHHH)
ARMOR: CHIBA
OH NO, I'M FALLING INTO HER RHYTHM.
I HAVE TO BREAK IT DOWN...
WAAAA
ARMOR: IGUCHI
YAAAAH!
KIEEII!!!
MEEEEN!
KIEI!!

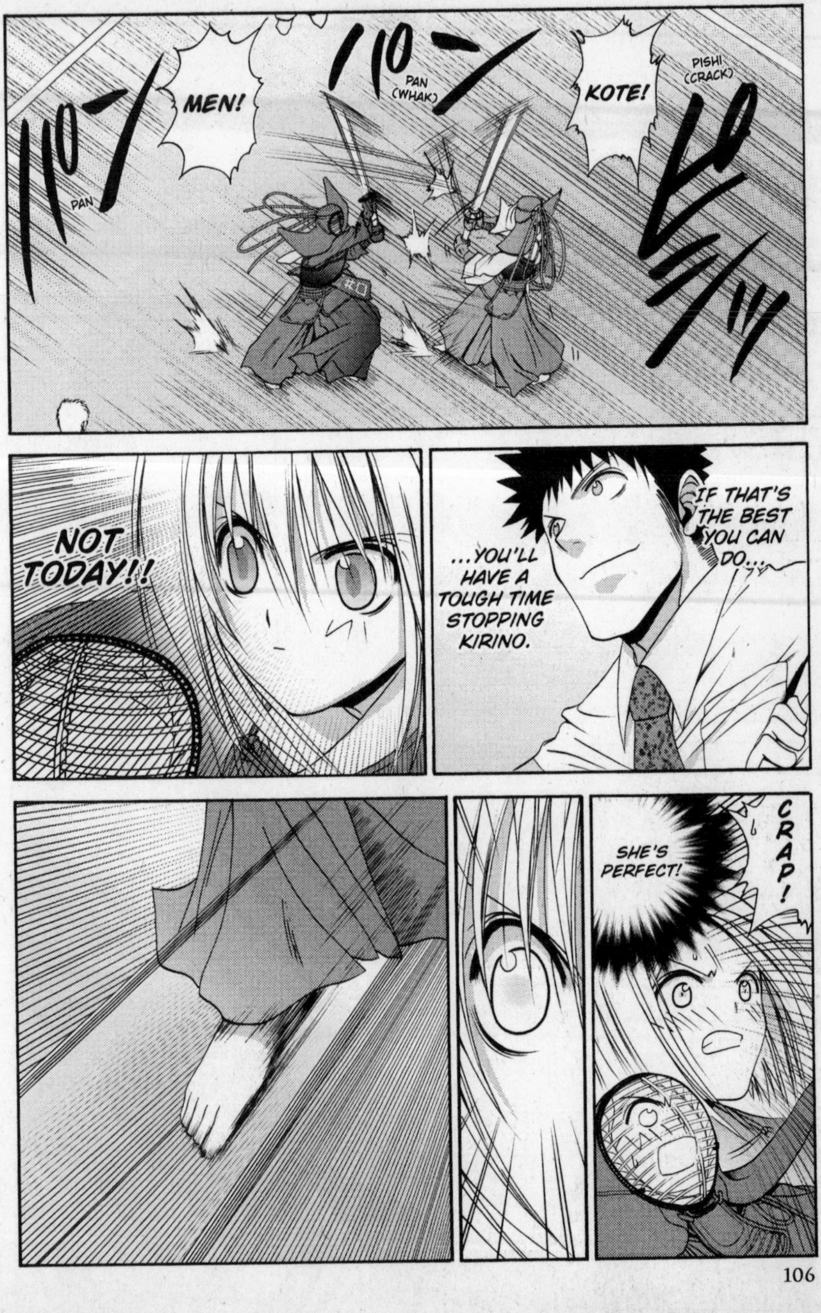
PISHI (CRACK)
KOTE!
PAN (WHAK)
MEN!
PAN
IF THAT'S THE BEST YOU CAN DO...
...YOU'LL HAVE A TOUGH TIME STOPPING KIRINO.
NOT TODAY!!
CRAP!
SHE'S PERFECT!

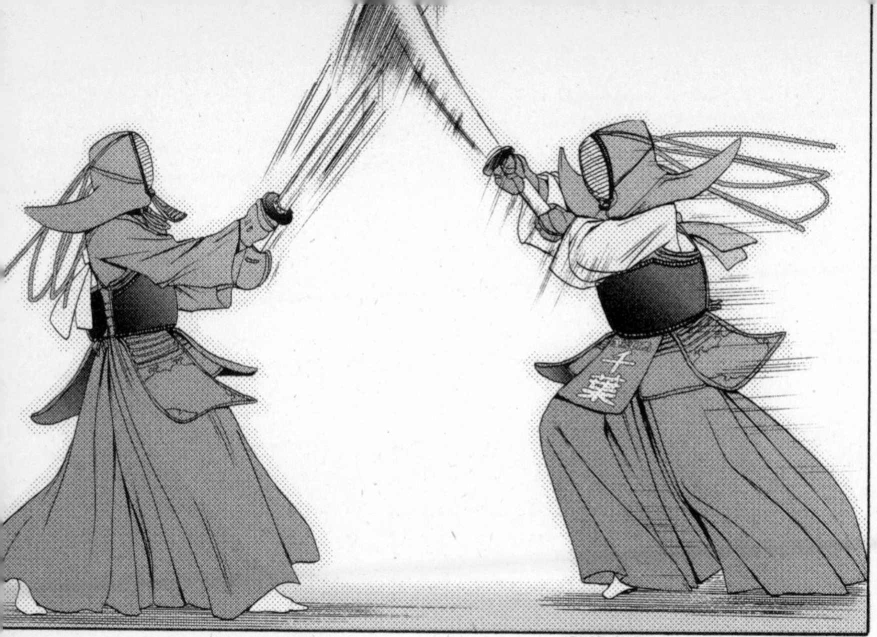
千葉
ARMOR: CHIBA

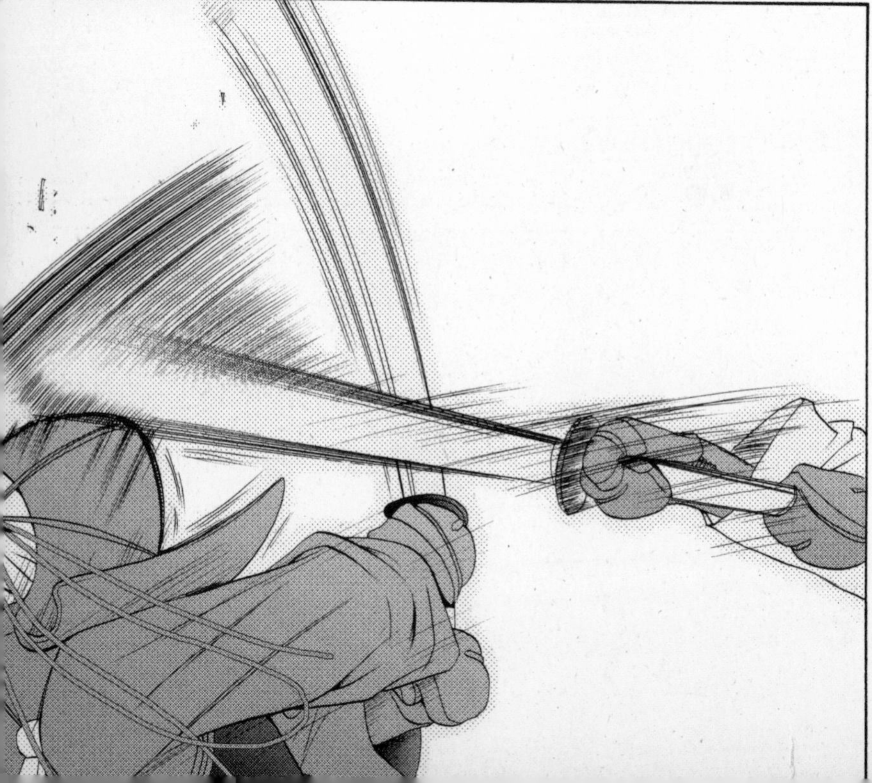

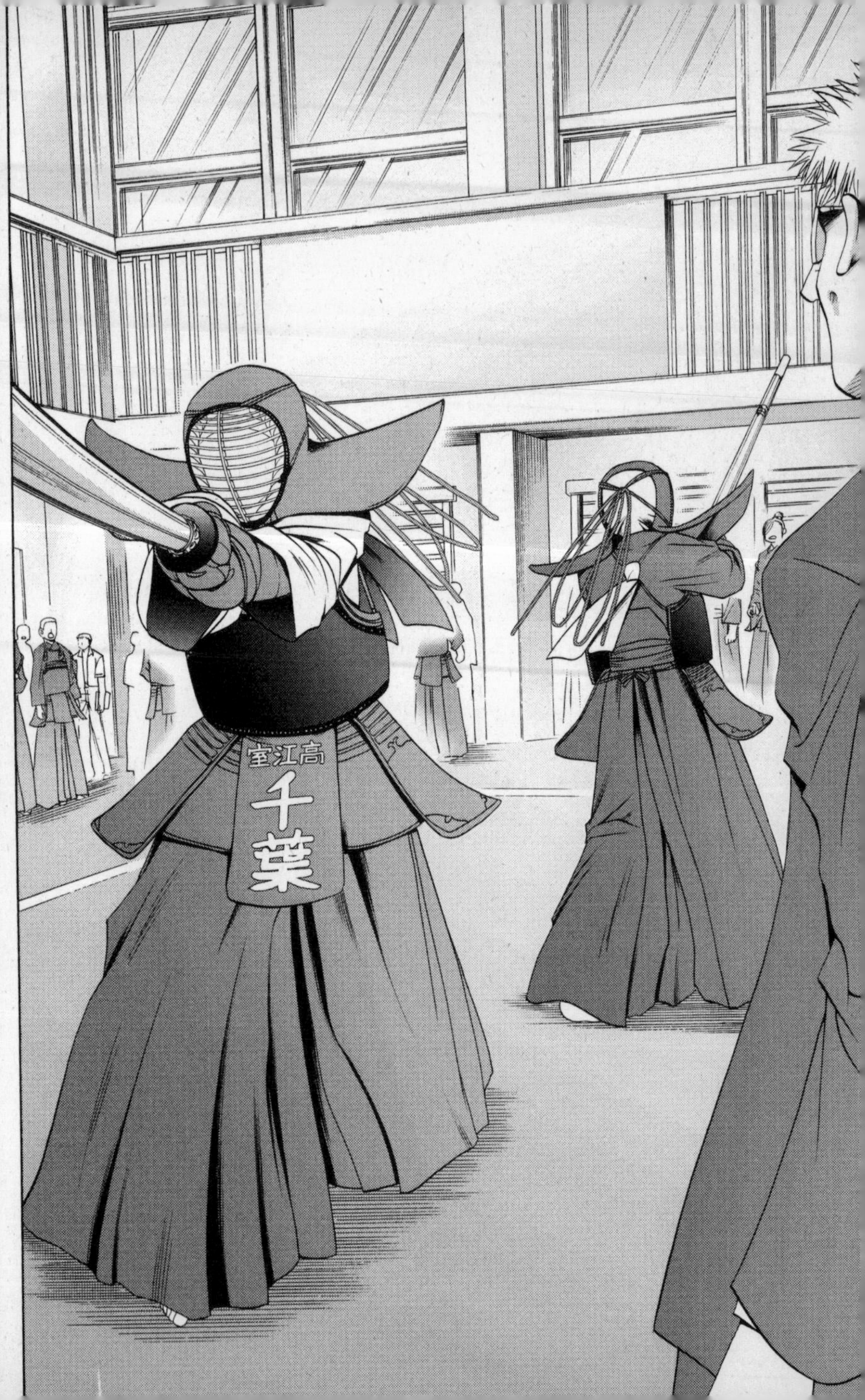
室江高
千葉

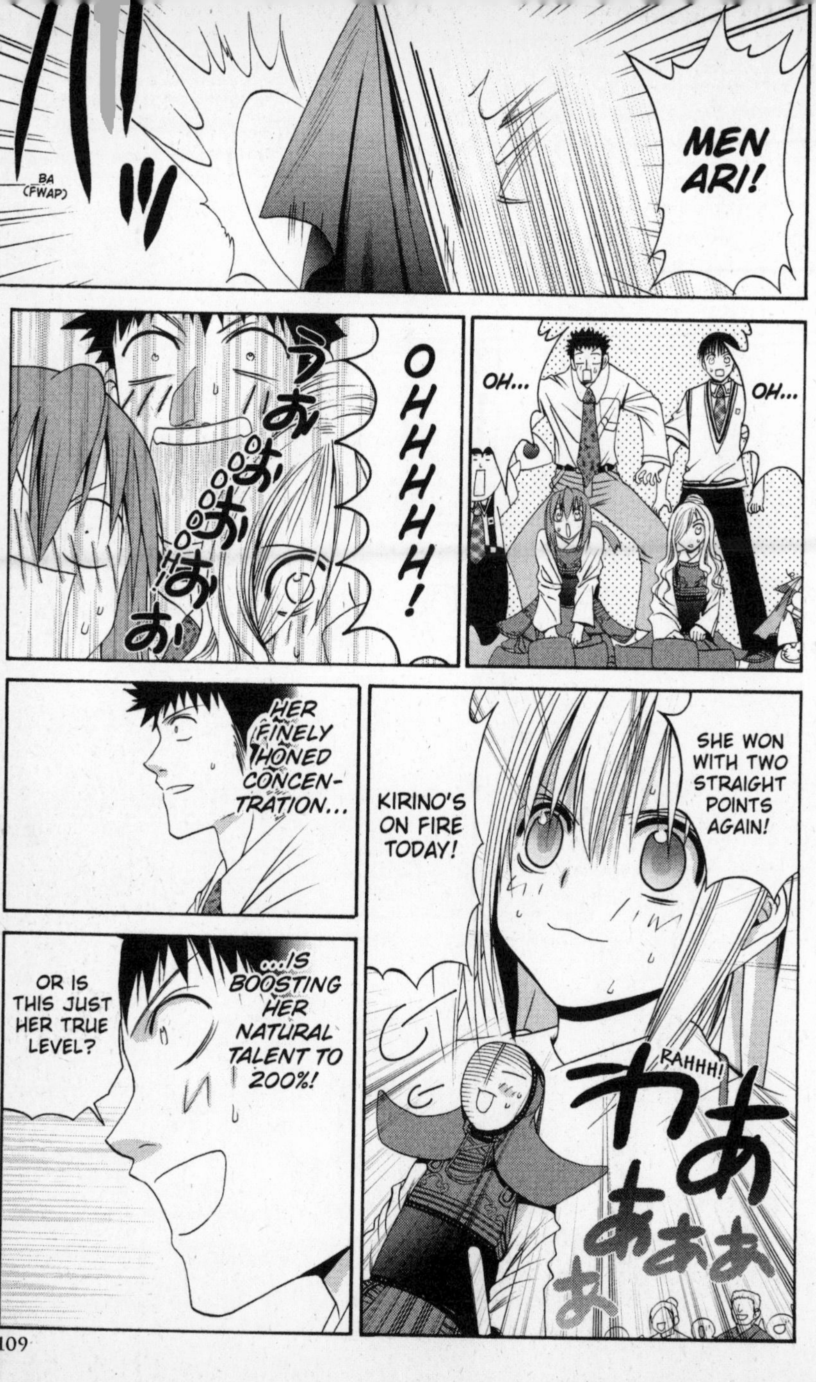
MEN ARI!
BA (FWAP)
OH...
OH...
OHHHHHH!
SHE WON WITH TWO STRAIGHT POINTS AGAIN!
KIRINO'S ON FIRE TODAY!
RAHHHH!
HER FINELY HONED CONCENTRATION...
...IS BOOSTING HER NATURAL TALENT TO 200%!
OR IS THIS JUST HER TRUE LEVEL?

	SENPO	JIHO	CHUKEN	FUKUSHO	TAISHO		
TOUJOU	AOKI	TERAJI	SATOU	IGUCHI	KONISHI		
	(K)	(M) M					
	×						
MUROE	D		(K)	(K) M			
	AZUMA	MIYAZAKI	KUWAHARA	CHIBA	KAWAZOE		

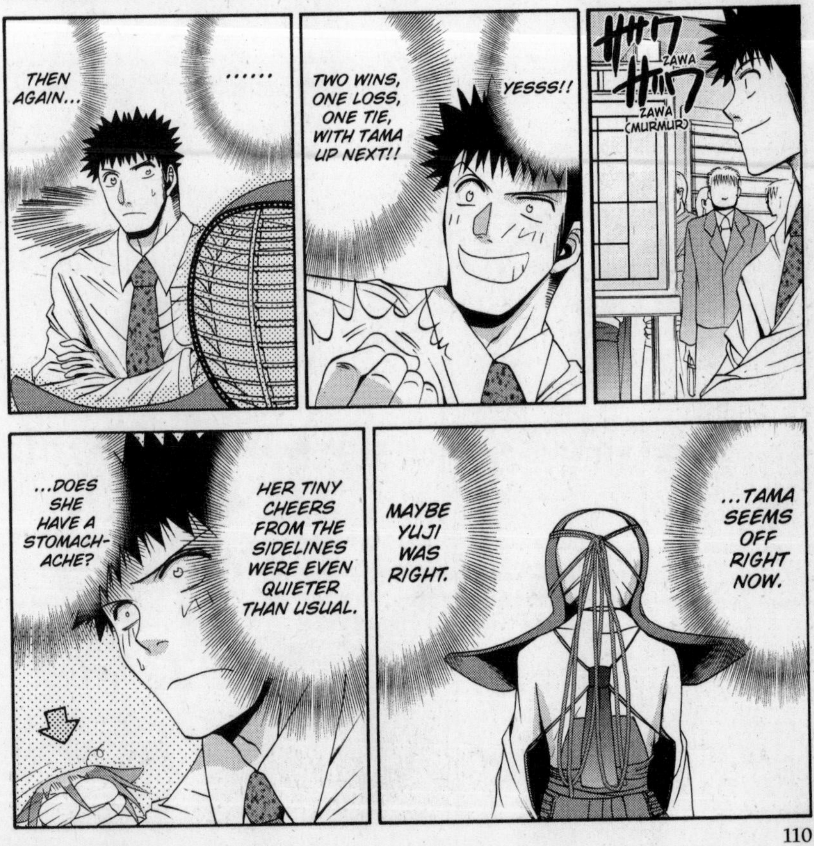
ザワ
ZAWA
ザワ
ZAWA
(MURMUR)
YESSS!!
TWO WINS, ONE LOSS, ONE TIE, WITH TAMA UP NEXT!!
......
THEN AGAIN...
...TAMA SEEMS OFF RIGHT NOW.
MAYBE YUJI WAS RIGHT.
HER TINY CHEERS FROM THE SIDELINES WERE EVEN QUIETER THAN USUAL.
...DOES SHE HAVE A STOMACH-ACHE?

IF KONISHI SCORES TWO POINTS WITHOUT GIVING UP ONE...

BUT WE STILL HAVE A CHANCE TO WIN.

THIS IS NOT A GOOD SITUATION.

HMMM.

ONE WIN, TWO LOSSES, ONE TIE.

THEN WE'LL BE THE ONES TO ADVANCE!!

...WE'LL BE EVEN AT TWO WINS APIECE, BUT OUR TEAM WILL HAVE THE ADVANTAGE IN TOTAL POINTS SCORED.

		SENPO		
T O U J O U		AOKI		
	(K)		(M)	
M U R O E		✱		
	D			

ワアァァ

RAHHHH!

DO IT FOR US, TAISHO!!

TAMA-CHAN!!

UKYAAA!

KYAAA!

KYAAA!

キャァ

COME ON, KONISHI-SAN!

ｱｱｱｱ

KYAAAAA!

111

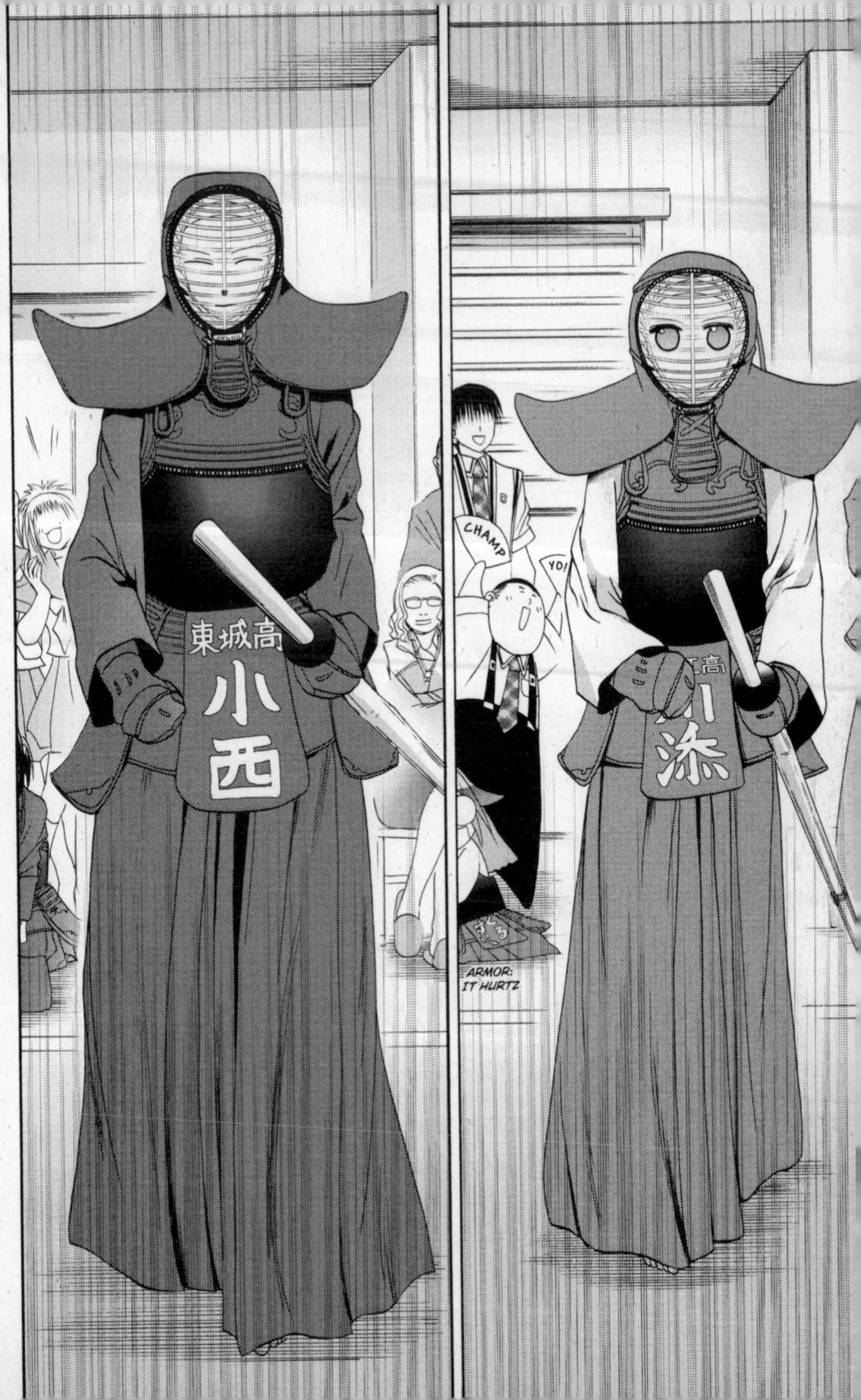
CHAMP
YO!
ARMOR: IT HURTZ
東城高
小西

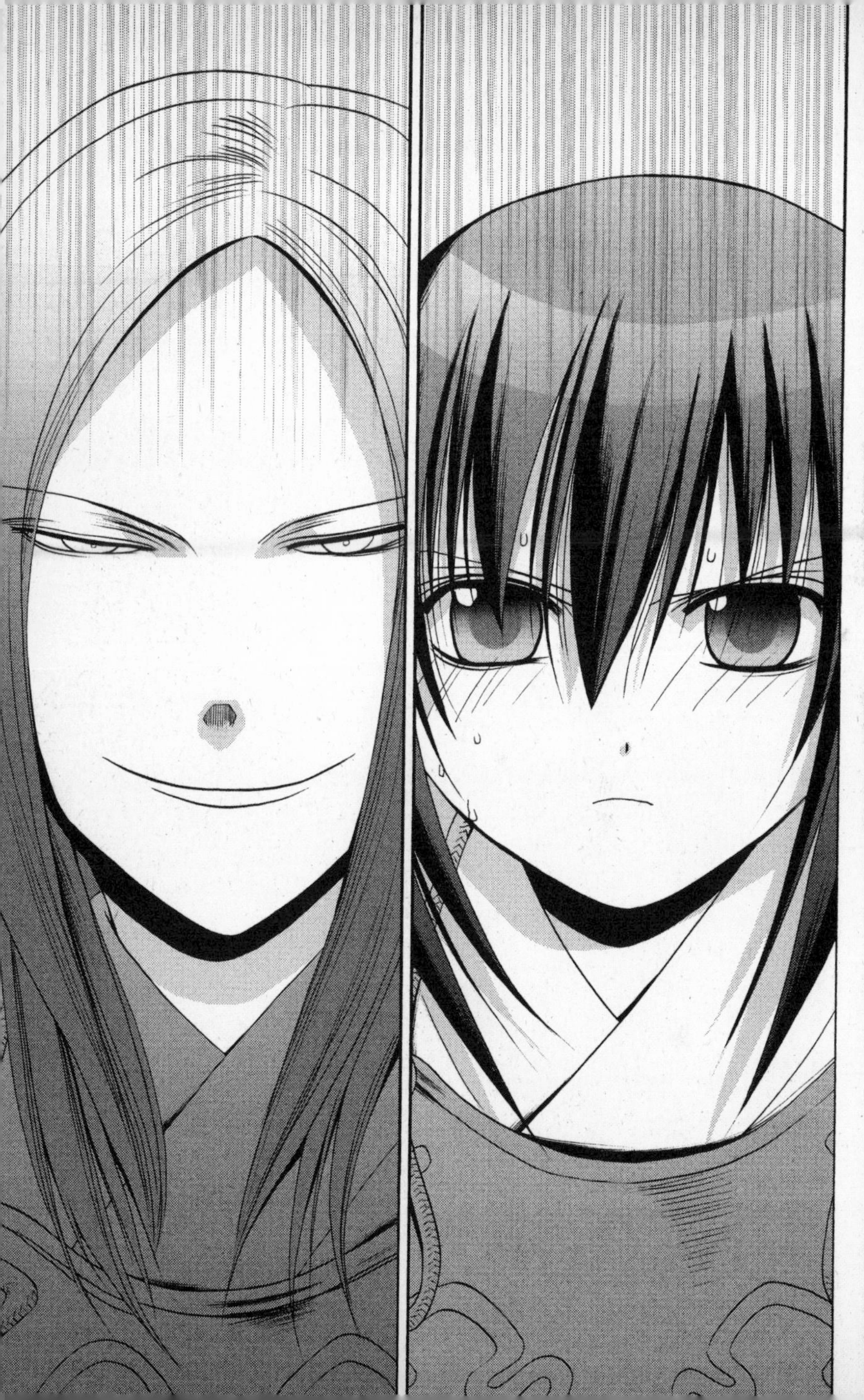

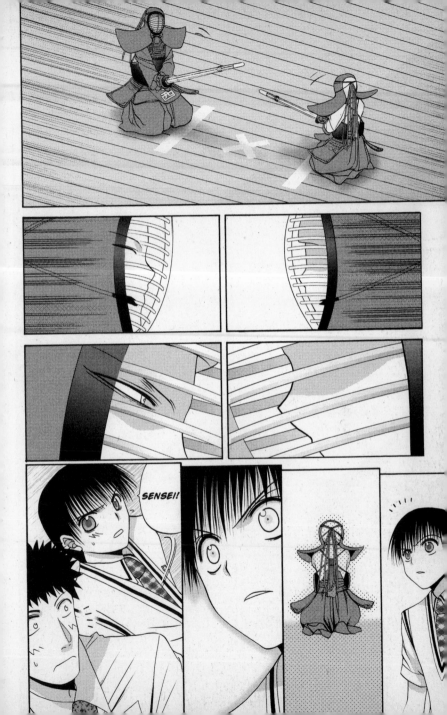

SENSEI!!

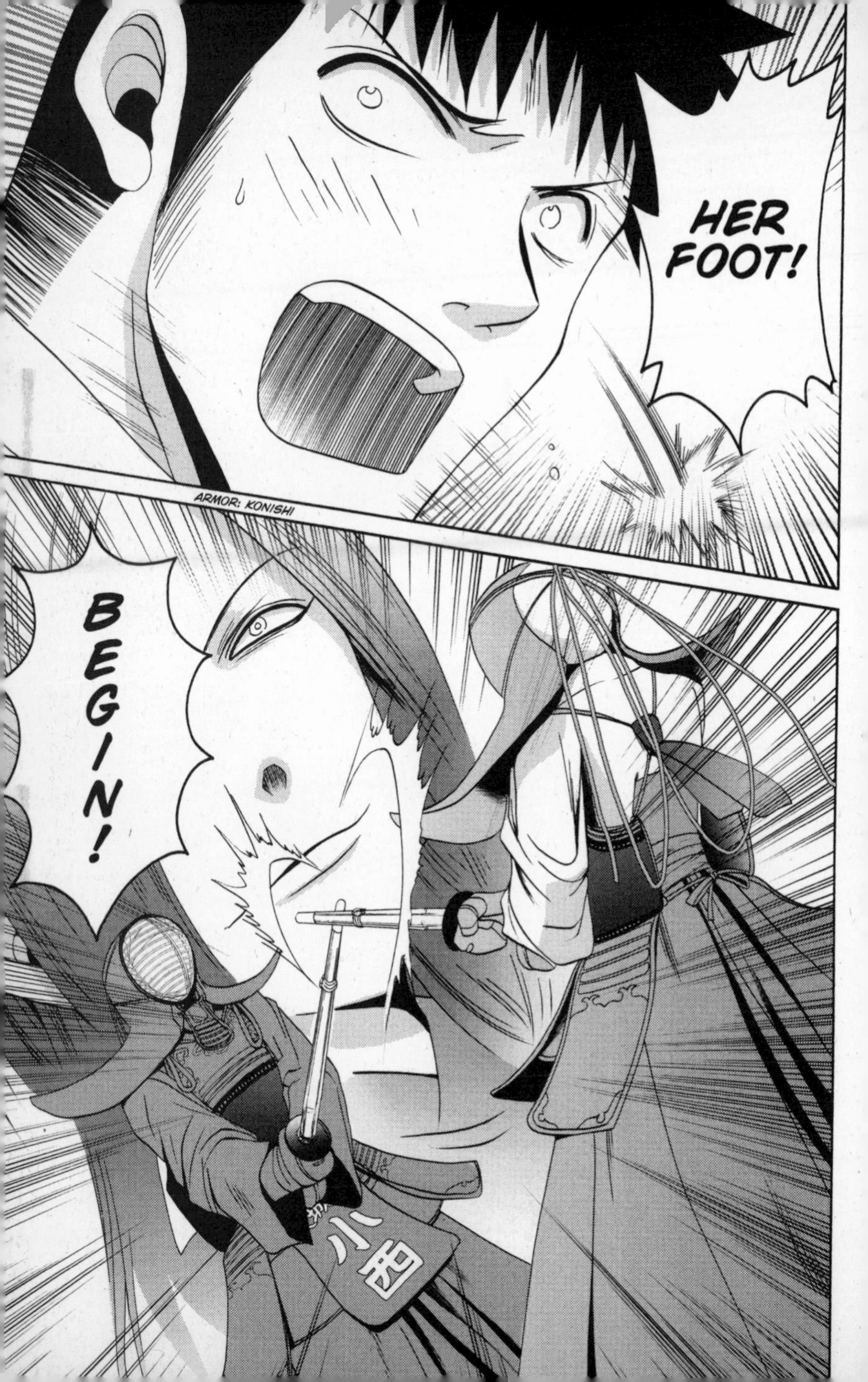
HER FOOT!
ARMOR: KONISHI
BEGIN!

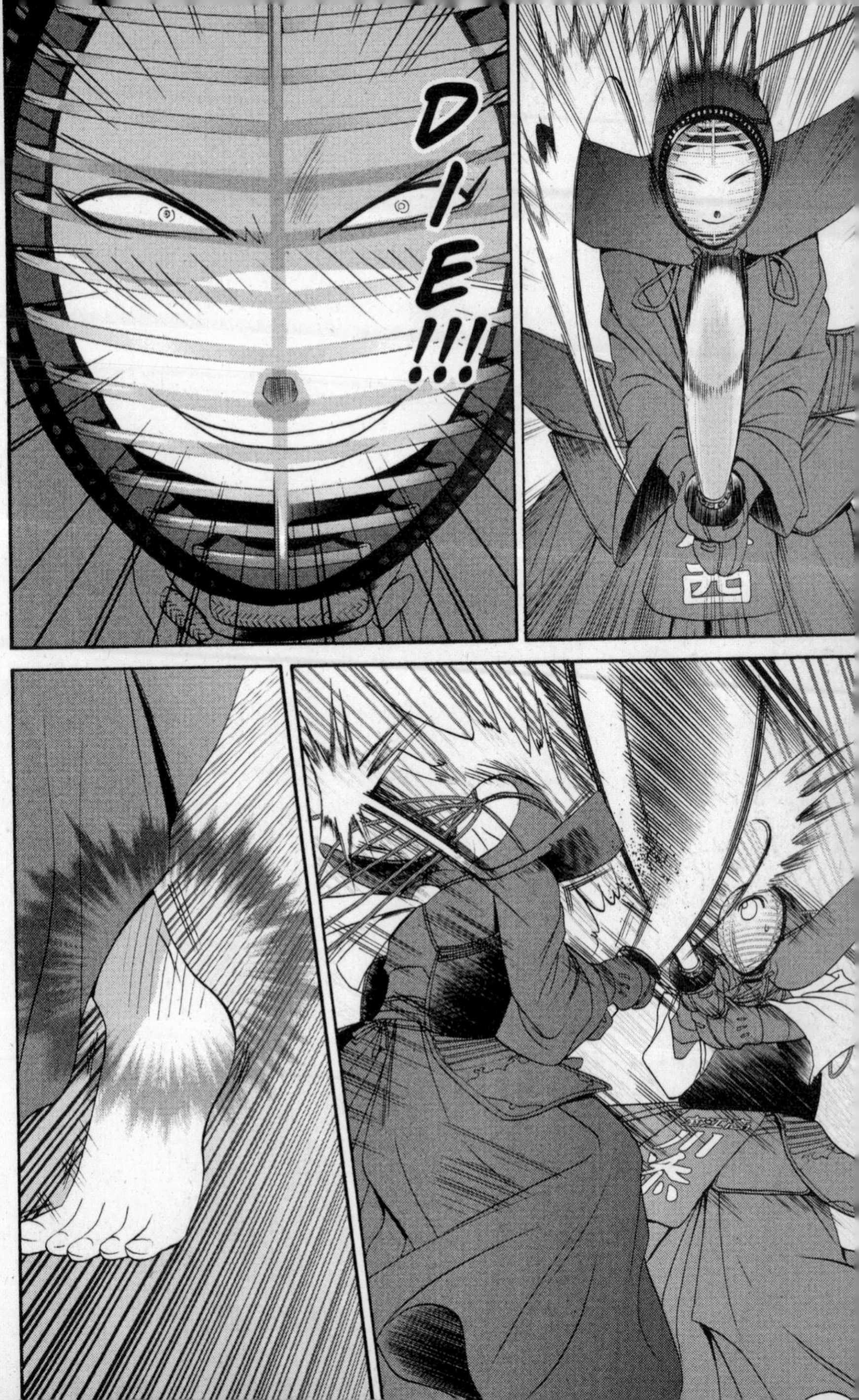
DIE!!!

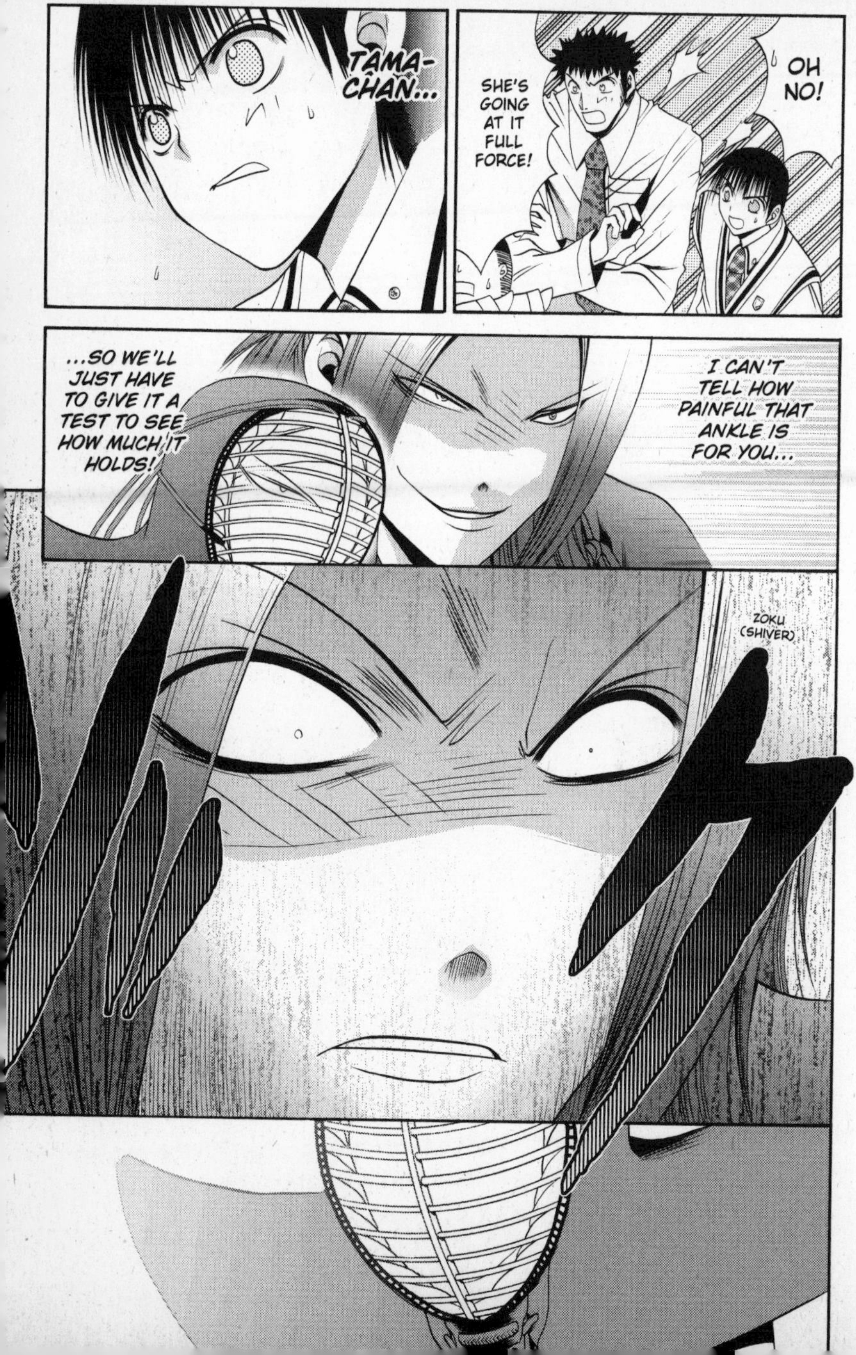
OH NO!
SHE'S GOING AT IT FULL FORCE!
TAMA-CHAN...
I CAN'T TELL HOW PAINFUL THAT ANKLE IS FOR YOU...
...SO WE'LL JUST HAVE TO GIVE IT A TEST TO SEE HOW MUCH IT HOLDS!
ZOKU (SHIVER)

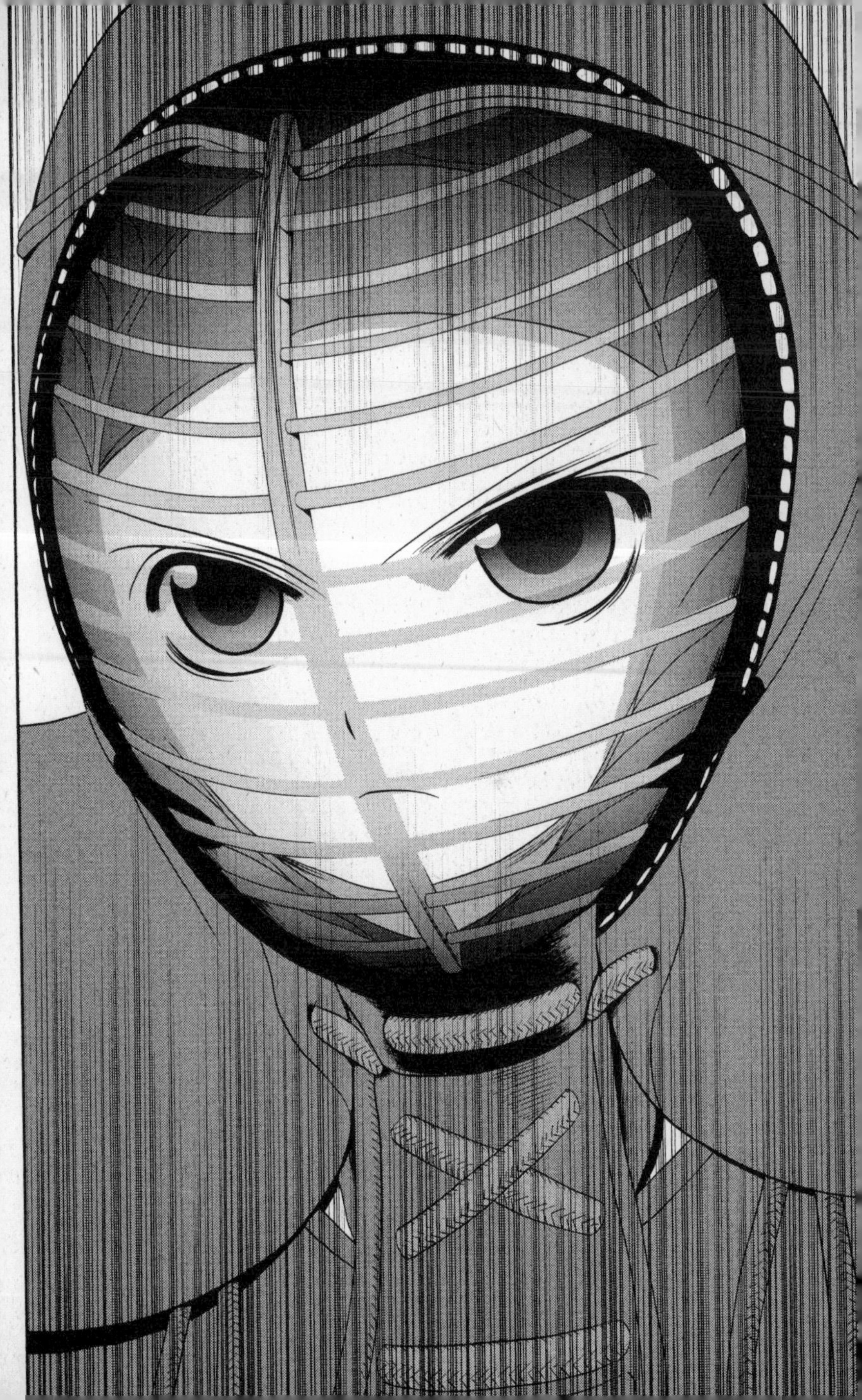

BAMBOO BLADE

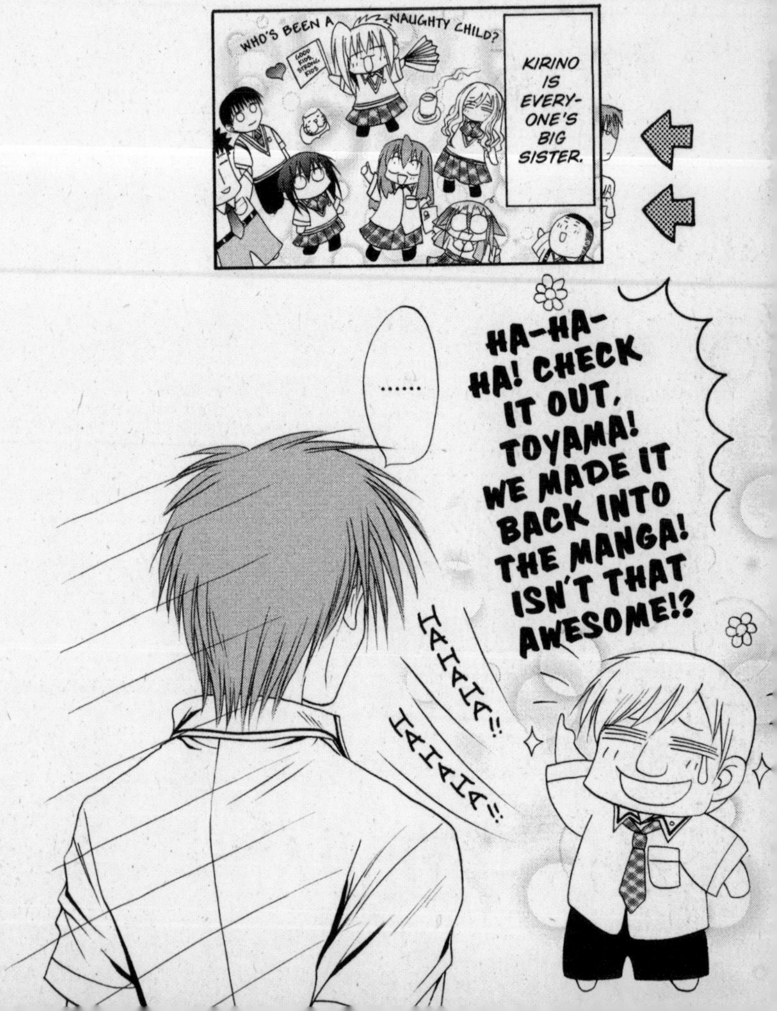
KIRINO IS EVERYONE'S BIG SISTER.
WHO'S BEEN A NAUGHTY CHILD?
GOOD KIDS, STRONG KIDS
HA-HA-HA! CHECK IT OUT, TOYAMA! WE MADE IT BACK INTO THE MANGA! ISN'T THAT AWESOME!?
......
IAIAIA!!
IAIAIA!!

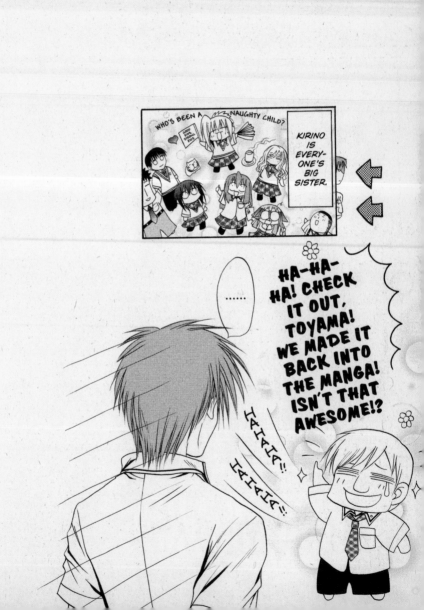

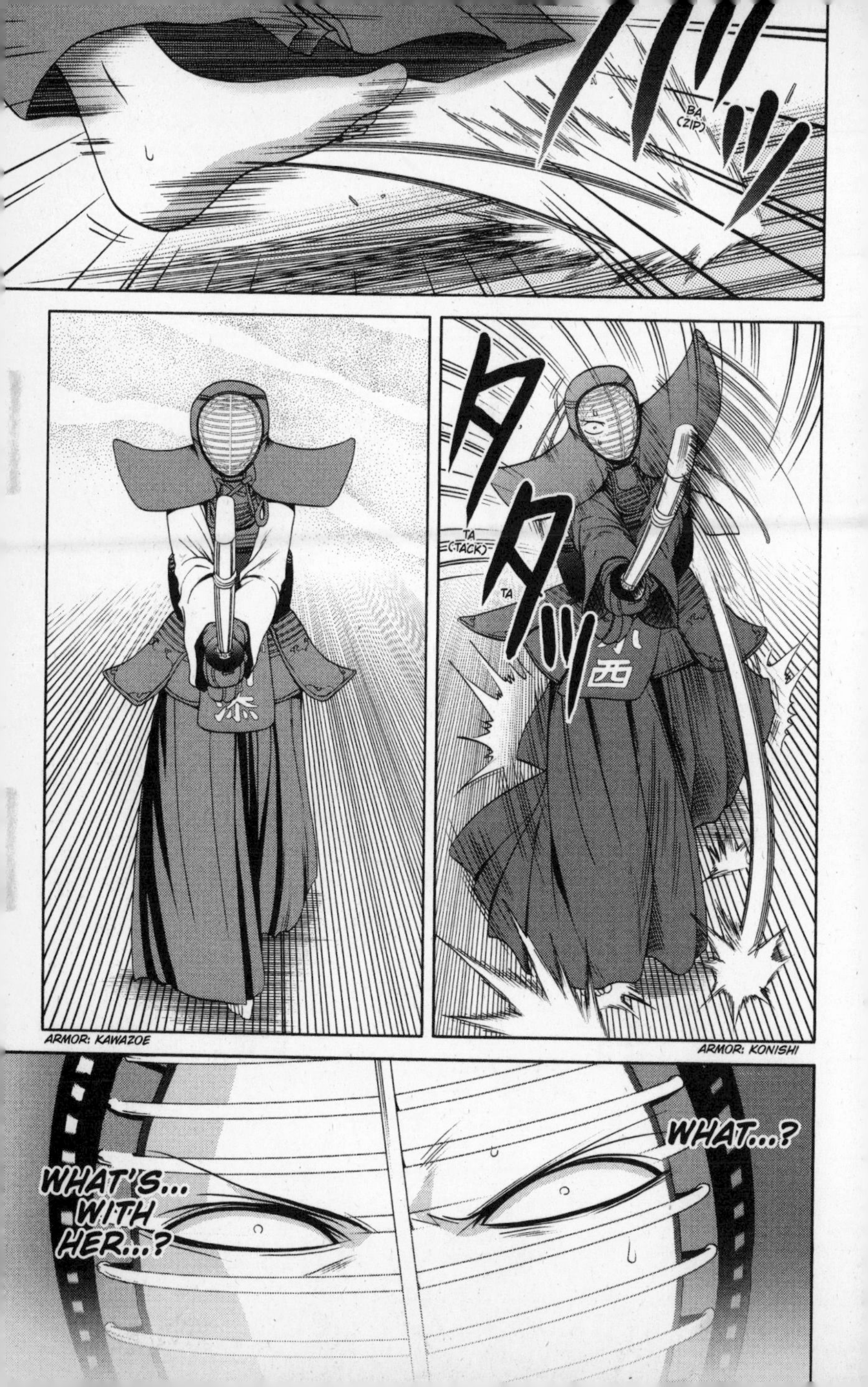

BA
(ZIP)
TA
(TACK)
TA
ARMOR: KONISHI
ARMOR: KAWAZOE
WHAT...?
WHAT'S... WITH HER...?

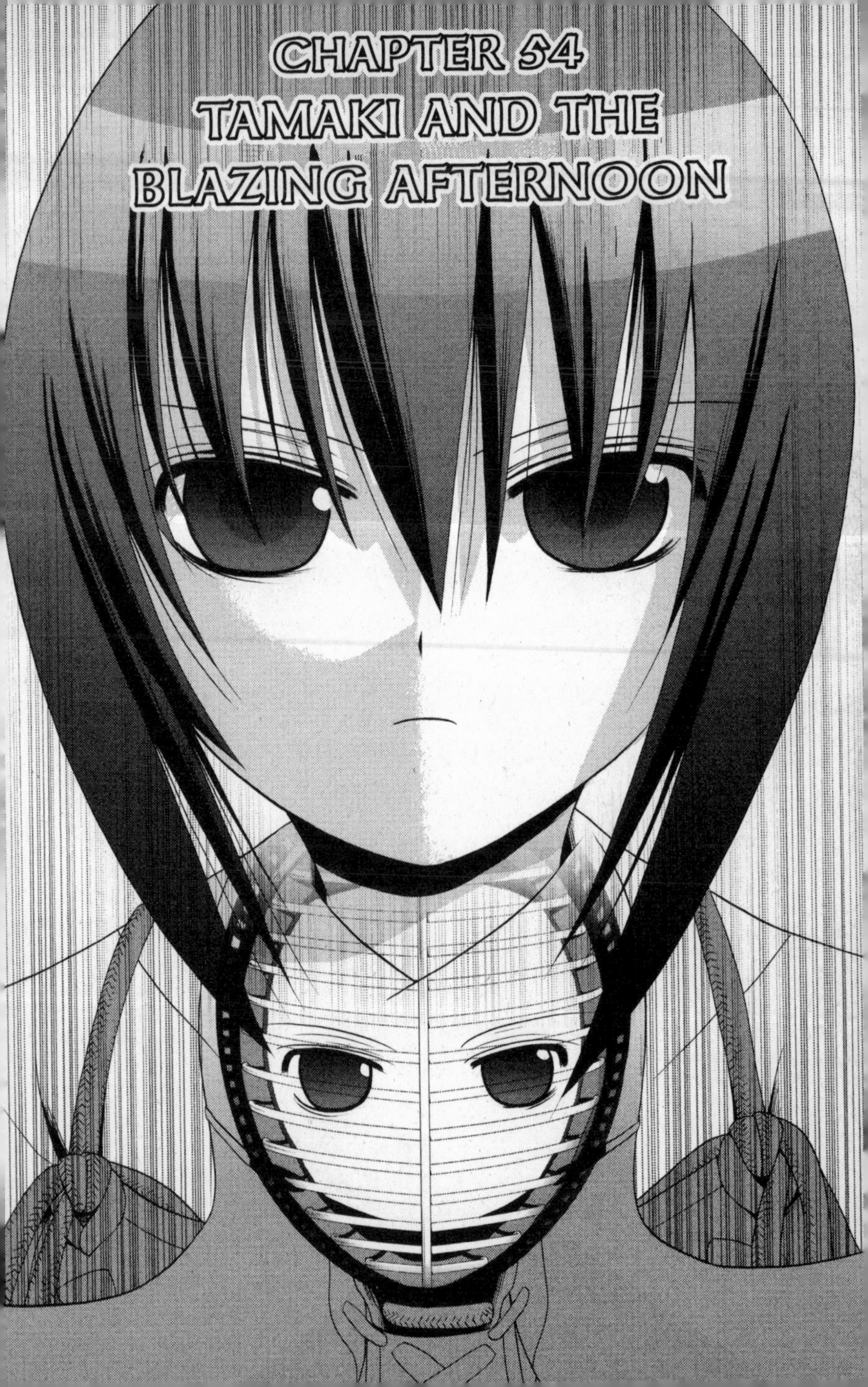
CHAPTER 54
TAMAKI AND THE BLAZING AFTERNOON

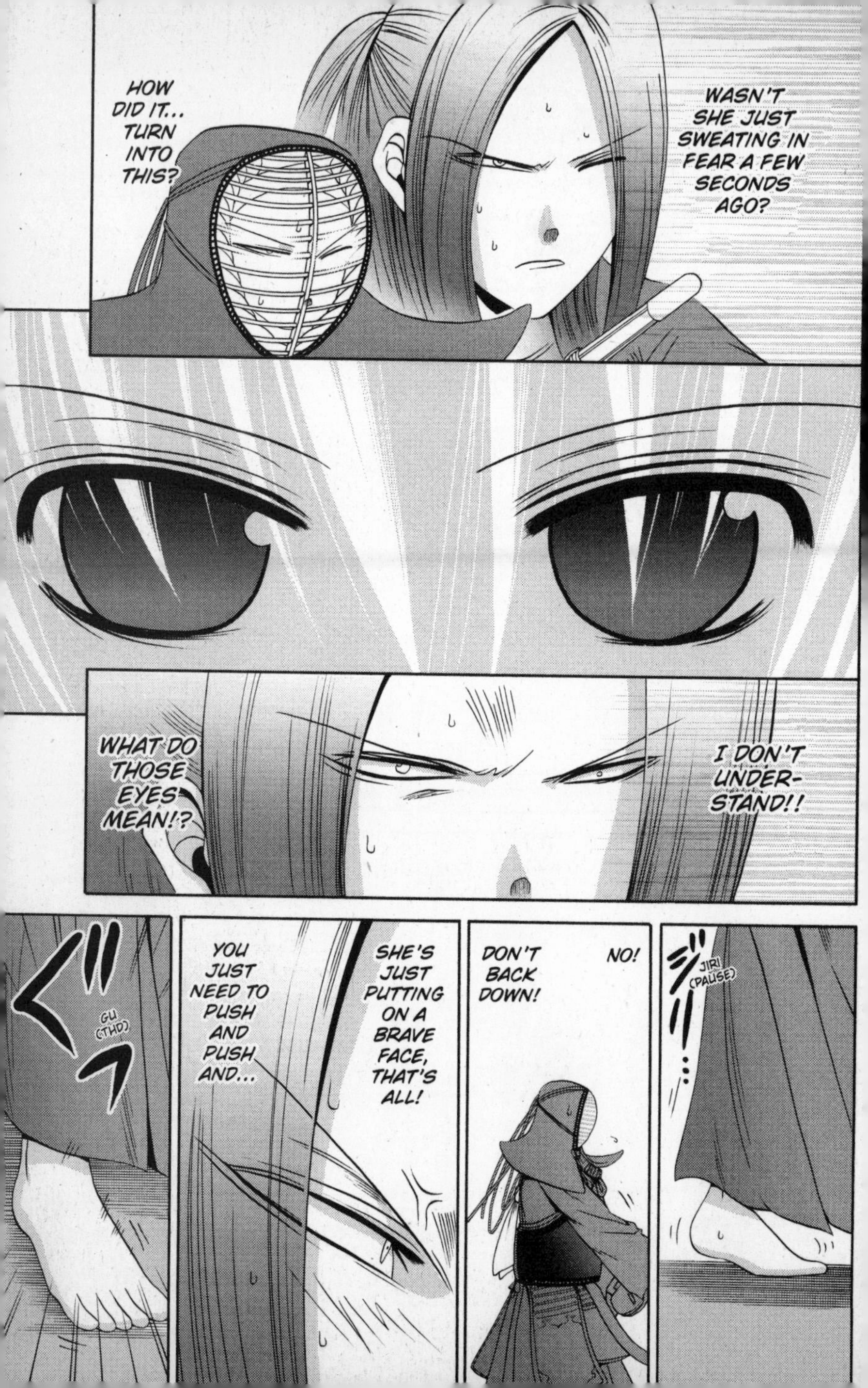
WASN'T SHE JUST SWEATING IN FEAR A FEW SECONDS AGO?
HOW DID IT... TURN INTO THIS?
I DON'T UNDER-STAND!!
WHAT DO THOSE EYES MEAN!?
JIRI (PAUSE)
...
NO!
DON'T BACK DOWN!
SHE'S JUST PUTTING ON A BRAVE FACE, THAT'S ALL!
YOU JUST NEED TO PUSH AND PUSH AND...
GU (THD)

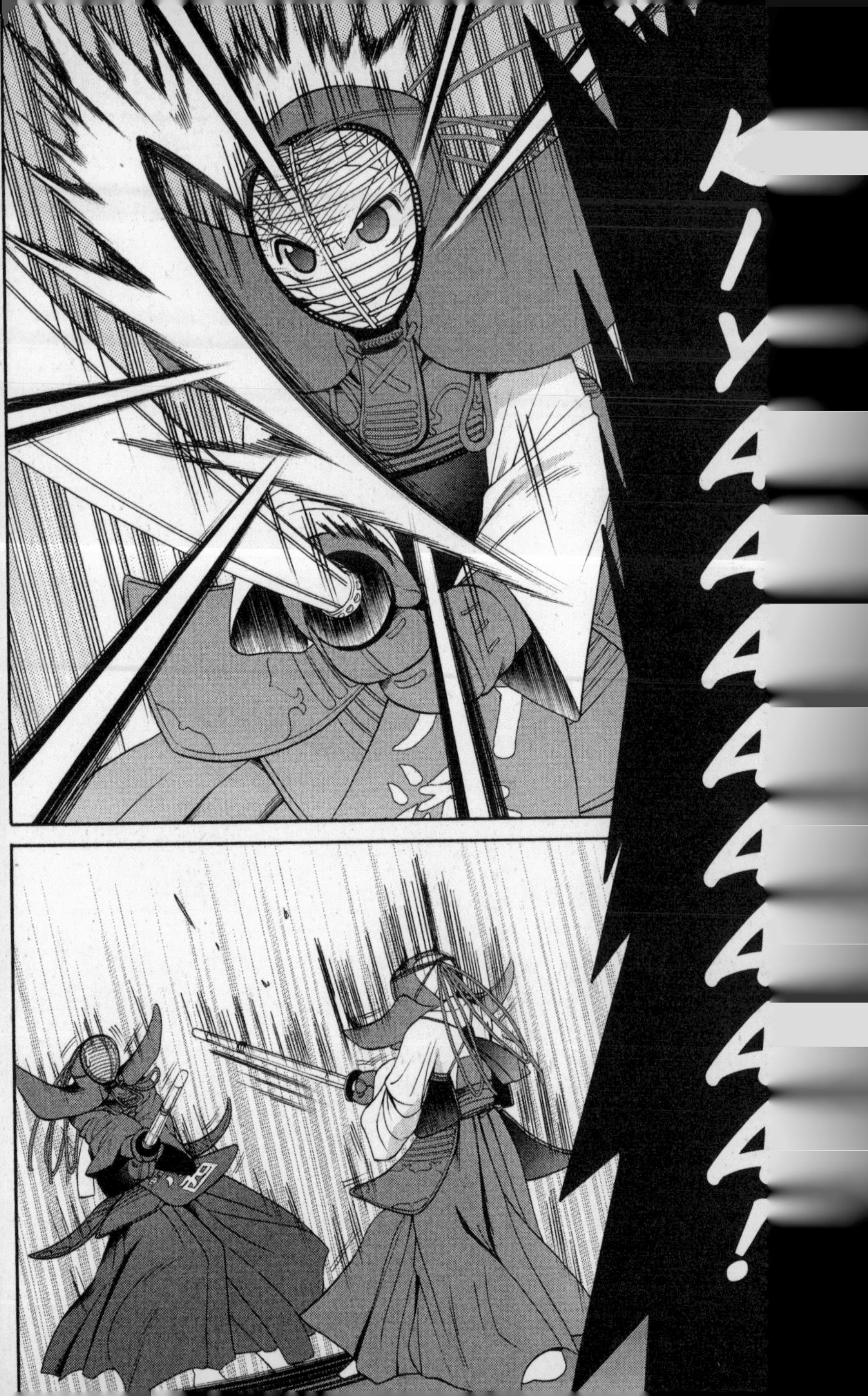
KIYAAAAAAAAAA!

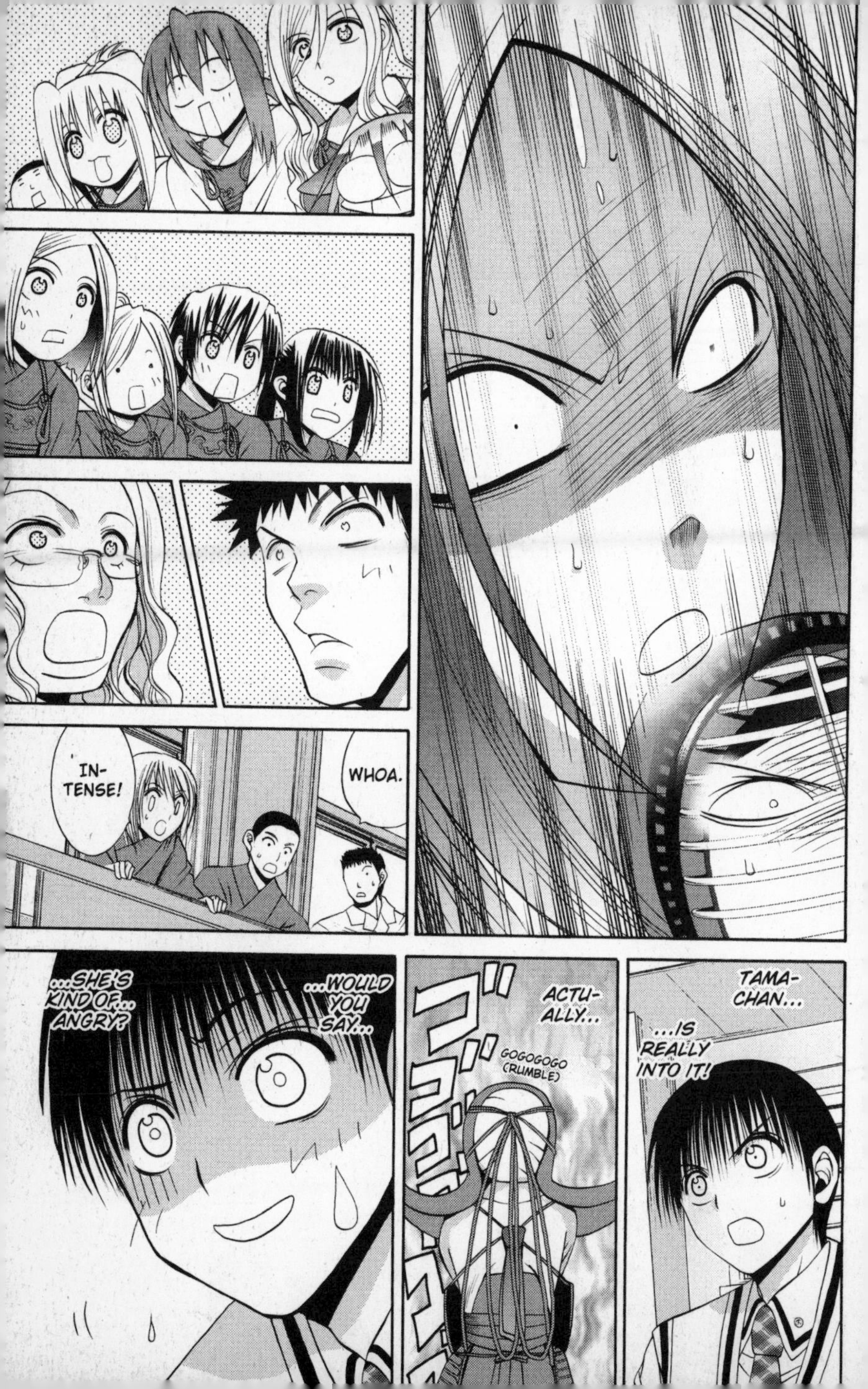
WHOA.
IN-TENSE!
TAMA-CHAN...
...IS REALLY INTO IT!
ACTU-ALLY...
GOGOGOGO (RUMBLE)
...WOULD YOU SAY...
...SHE'S KIND OF... ANGRY?

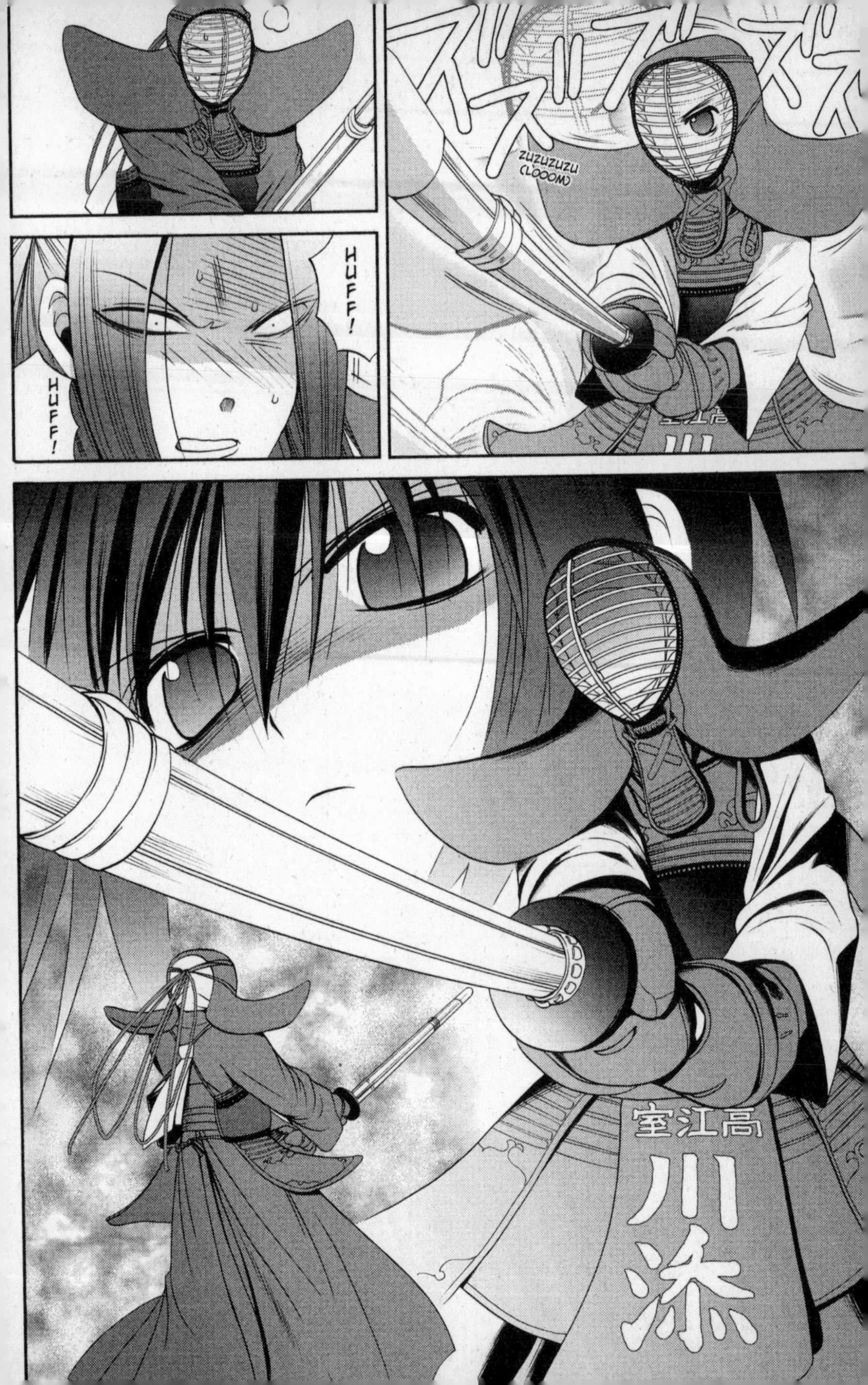
ズズズズ
ZUZUZUZU (LOOOM)
HUFF!
HUFF!
室江高
川添

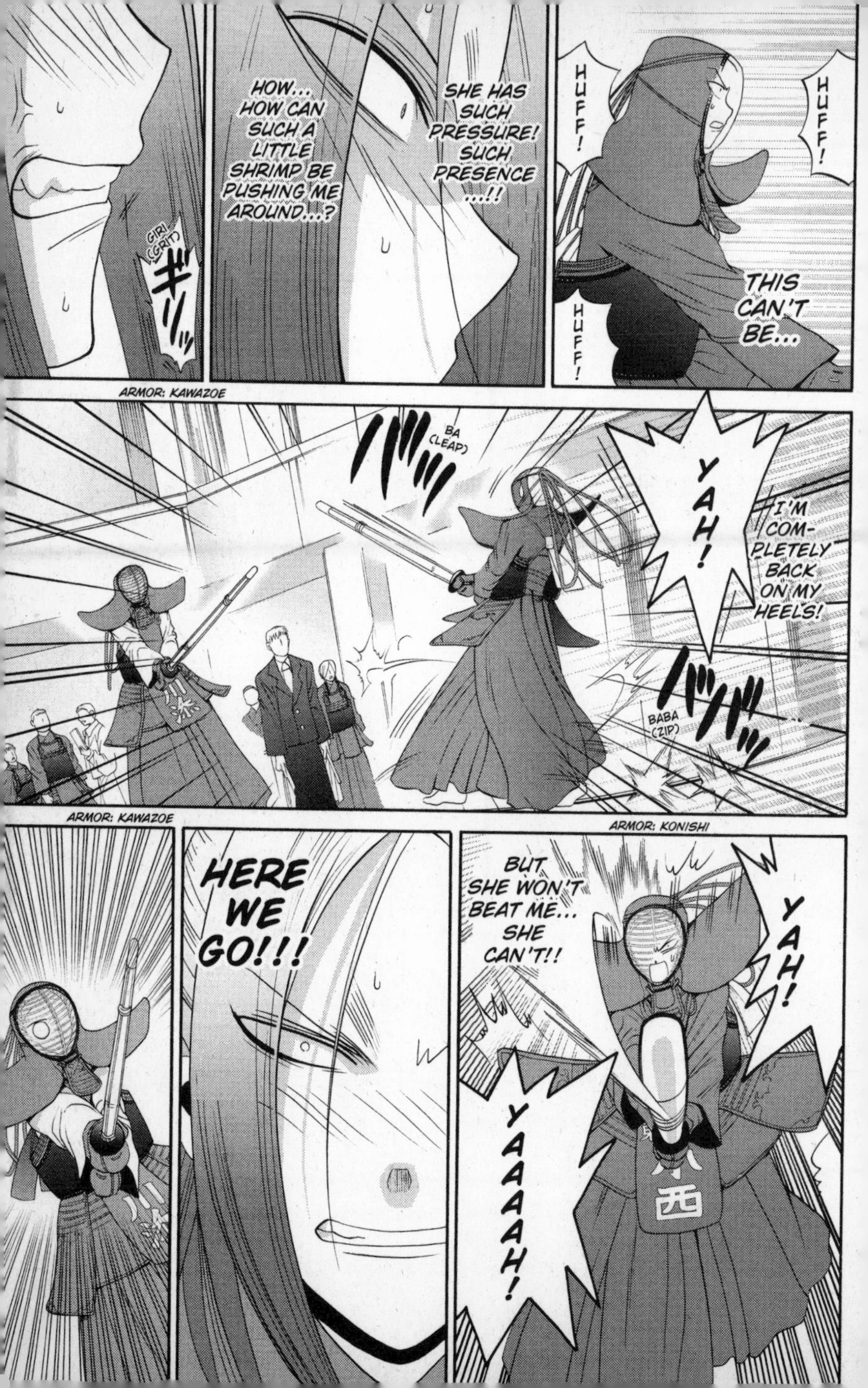
HUFF!
HUFF!
HUFF!
THIS CAN'T BE...
SHE HAS SUCH PRESSURE! SUCH PRESENCE...!!
HOW... HOW CAN SUCH A LITTLE SHRIMP BE PUSHING ME AROUND...?
GIRI (GRIT)
ARMOR: KAWAZOE
YAH!
I'M COM-PLETELY BACK ON MY HEELS!
BA (LEAP)
BABA (ZIP)
ARMOR: KAWAZOE
ARMOR: KONISHI
BUT SHE WON'T BEAT ME... SHE CAN'T!!
YAH!
YAAAAAH!
HERE WE GO!!!

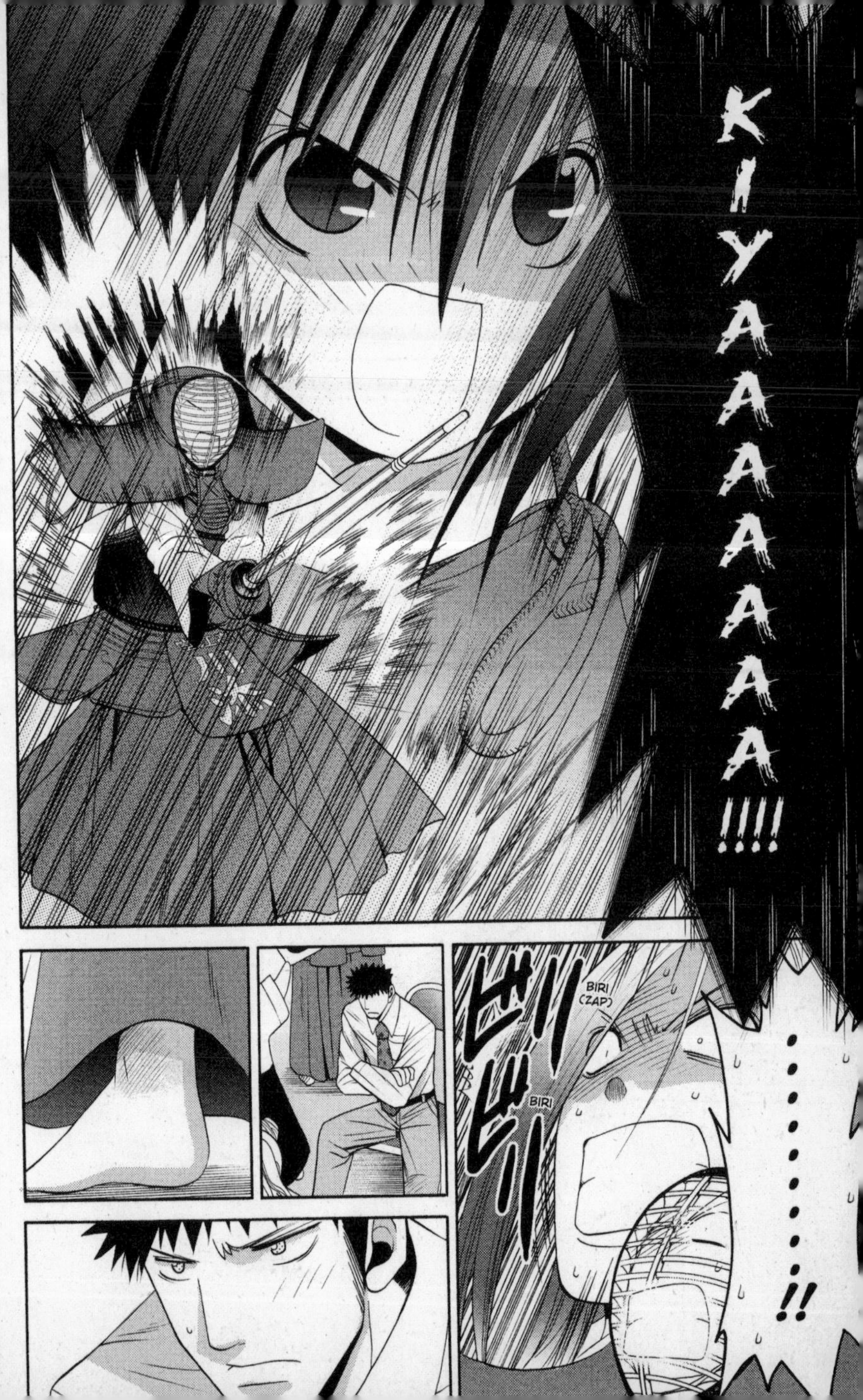
KIYAAAAAAA!!!!
.........!!
BIRI (ZAP)
BIRI

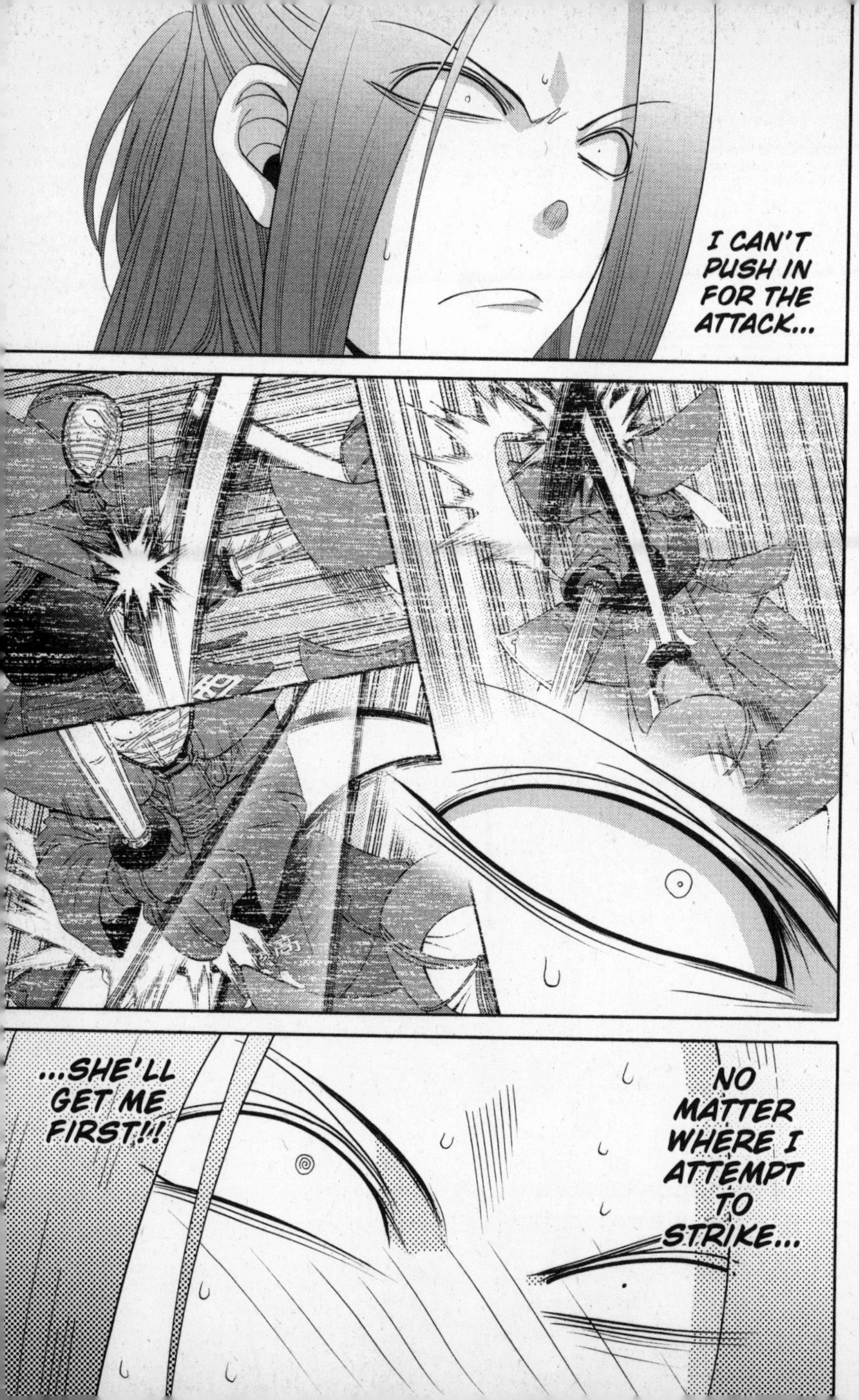
I CAN'T PUSH IN FOR THE ATTACK...
NO MATTER WHERE I ATTEMPT TO STRIKE...
...SHE'LL GET ME FIRST!!

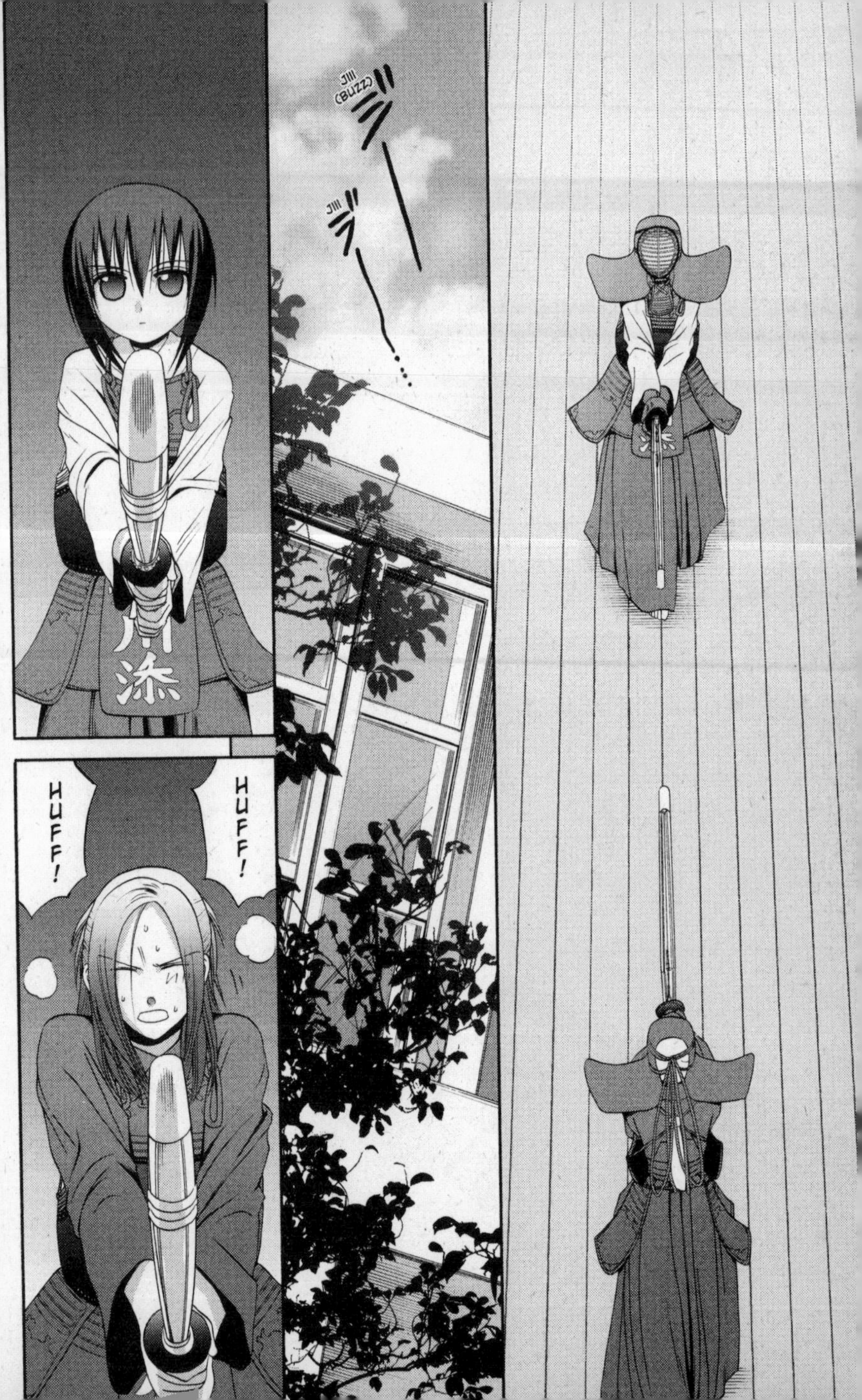
JIII (BUZZ)
JIII
HUFF!
HUFF!

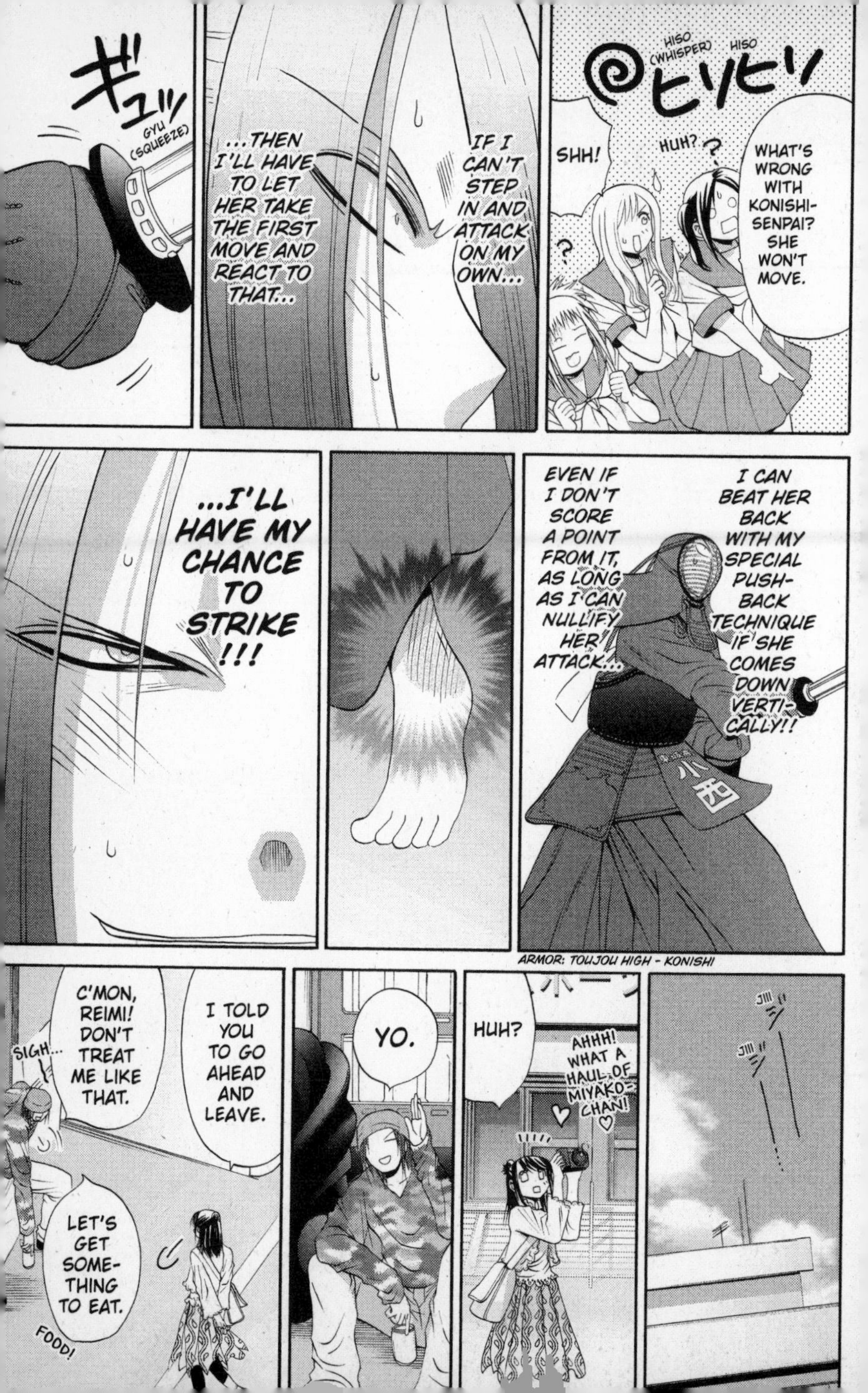
HISO (WHISPER) HISO
ヒソヒソ
WHAT'S WRONG WITH KONISHI-SENPAI? SHE WON'T MOVE.
HUH?
SHH!
IF I CAN'T STEP IN AND ATTACK ON MY OWN...
...THEN I'LL HAVE TO LET HER TAKE THE FIRST MOVE AND REACT TO THAT...
ギュッ
GYU (SQUEEZE)
I CAN BEAT HER BACK WITH MY SPECIAL PUSH-BACK TECHNIQUE IF SHE COMES DOWN VERTICALLY!!
EVEN IF I DON'T SCORE A POINT FROM IT, AS LONG AS I CAN NULLIFY HER ATTACK...
ARMOR: TOUJOU HIGH - KONISHI
...I'LL HAVE MY CHANCE TO STRIKE!!!
JIII
JIII
HUH?
AHHH! WHAT A HAUL OF MIYAKO-CHAN! ♡
YO.
I TOLD YOU TO GO AHEAD AND LEAVE.
C'MON, REIMI! DON'T TREAT ME LIKE THAT.
SIGH...
LET'S GET SOMETHING TO EAT.
FOOD!

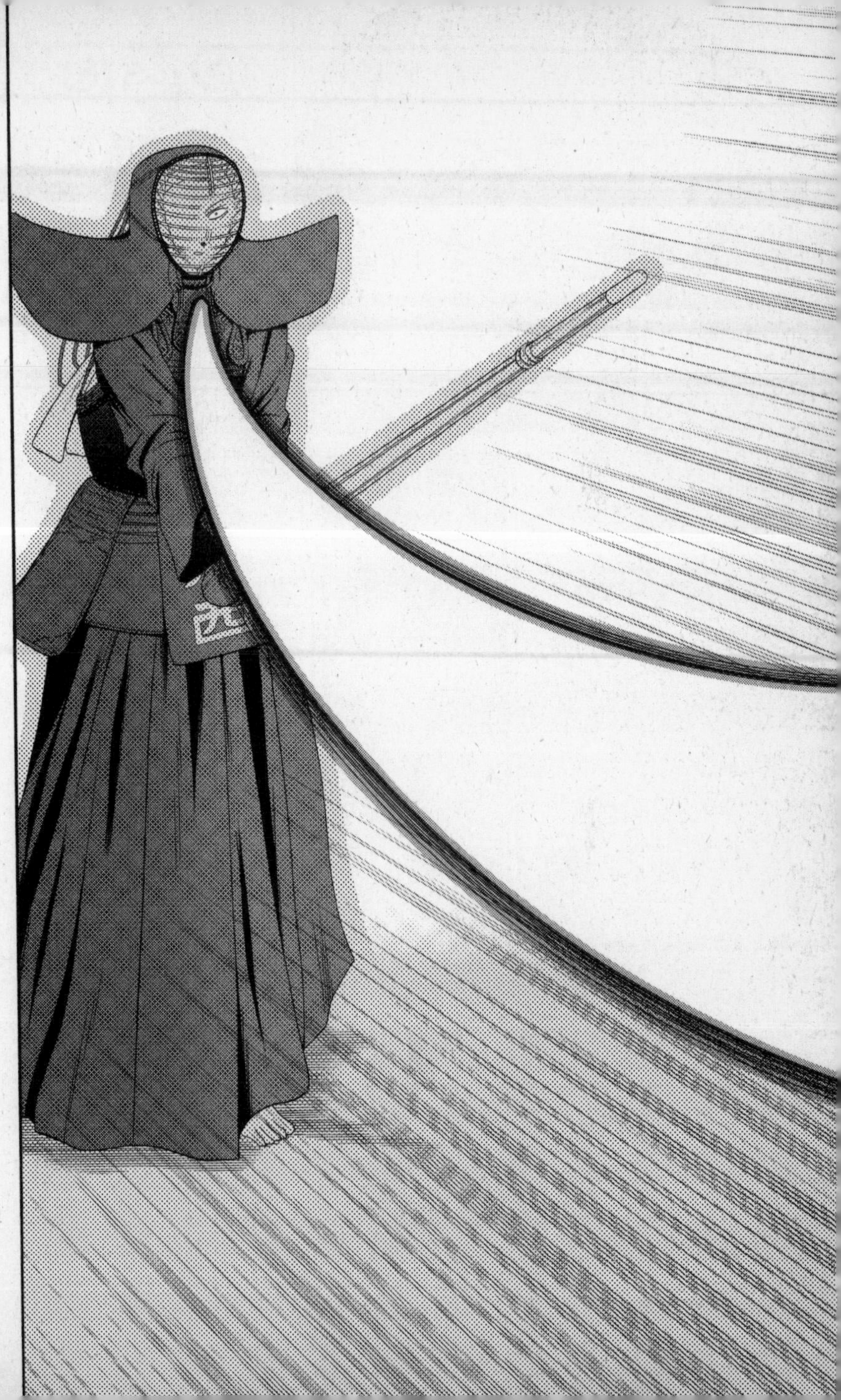

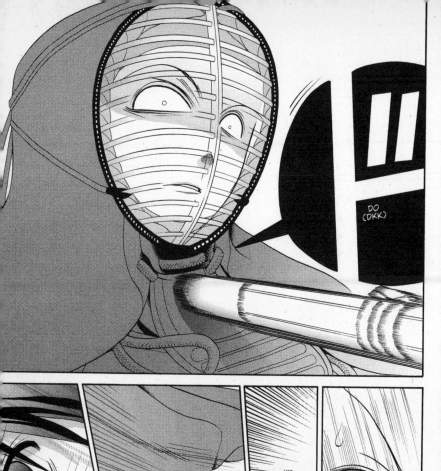

DO
(DKK)

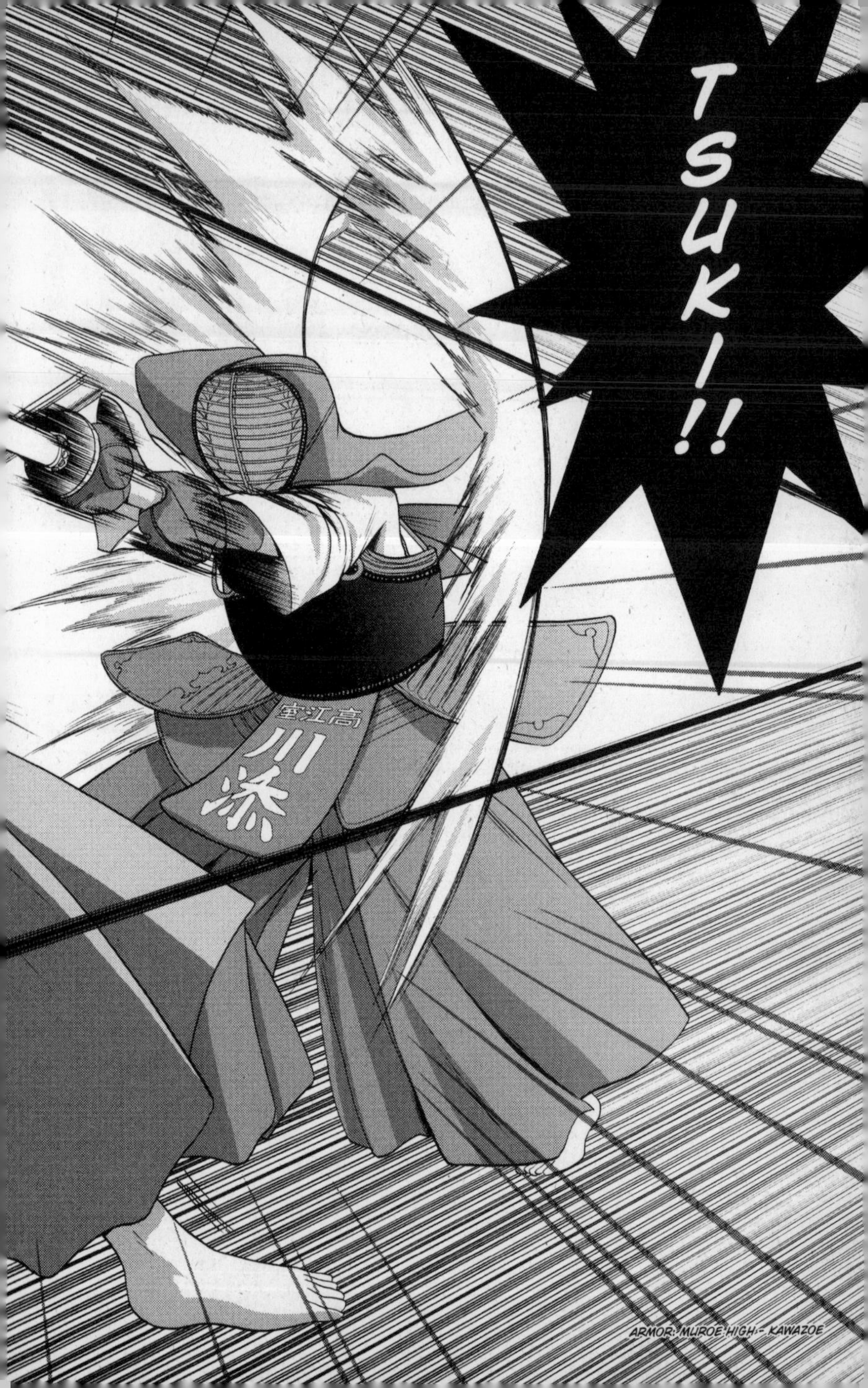
TSUKI!!
室江高
川添
ARMOR: MUROE HIGH - KAWAZOE

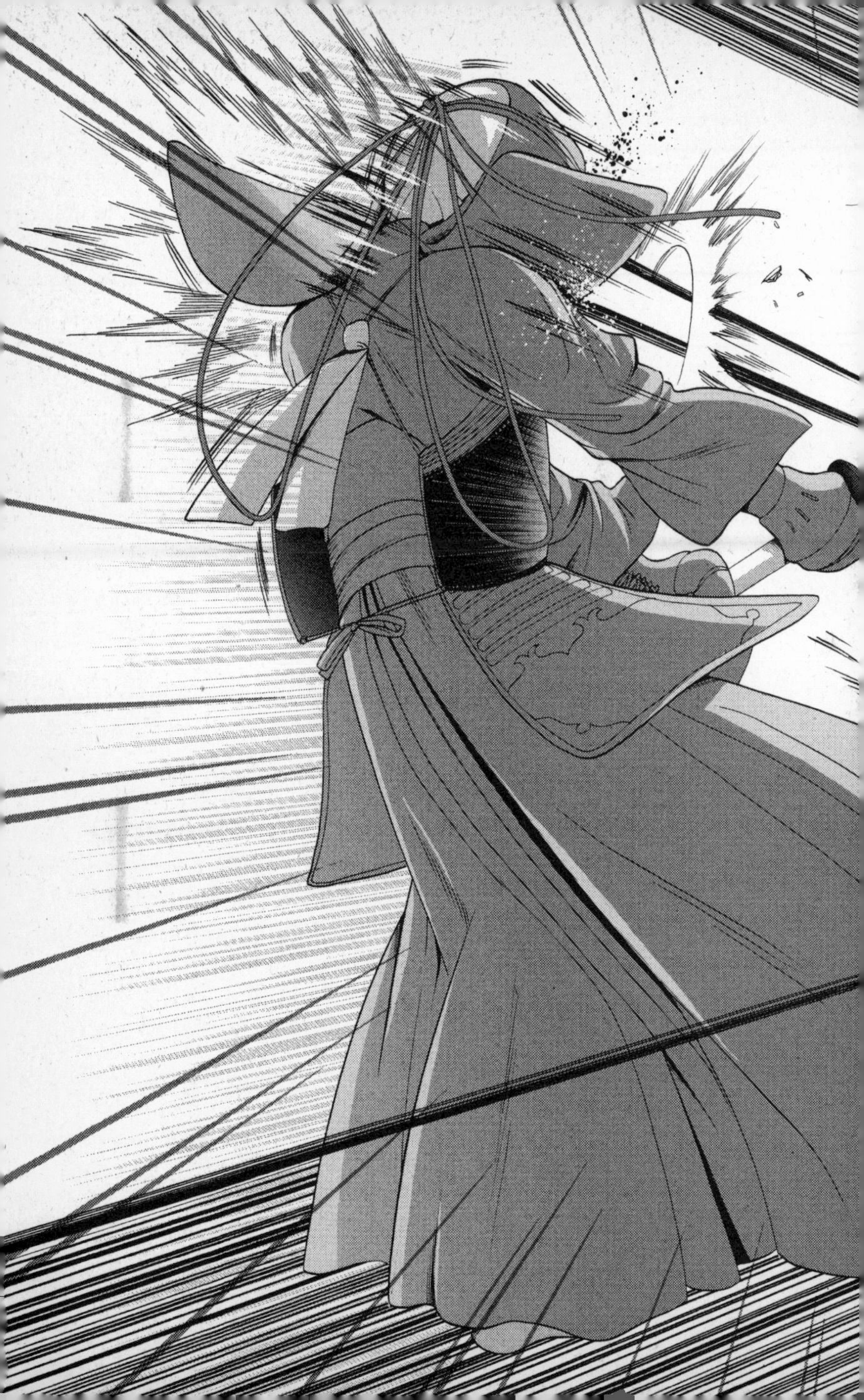

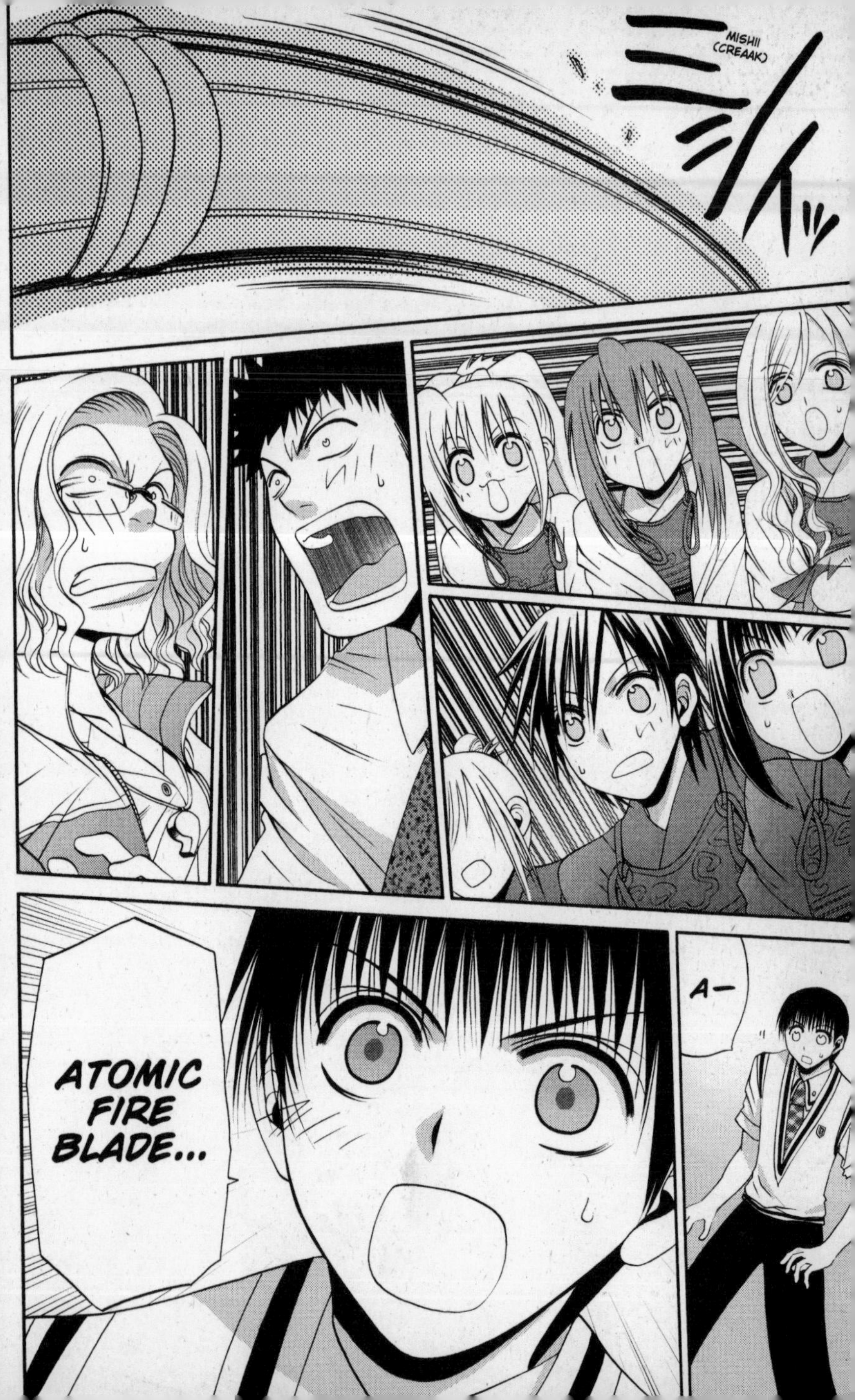
MISHII (CREAAK)
A—
ATOMIC FIRE BLADE...

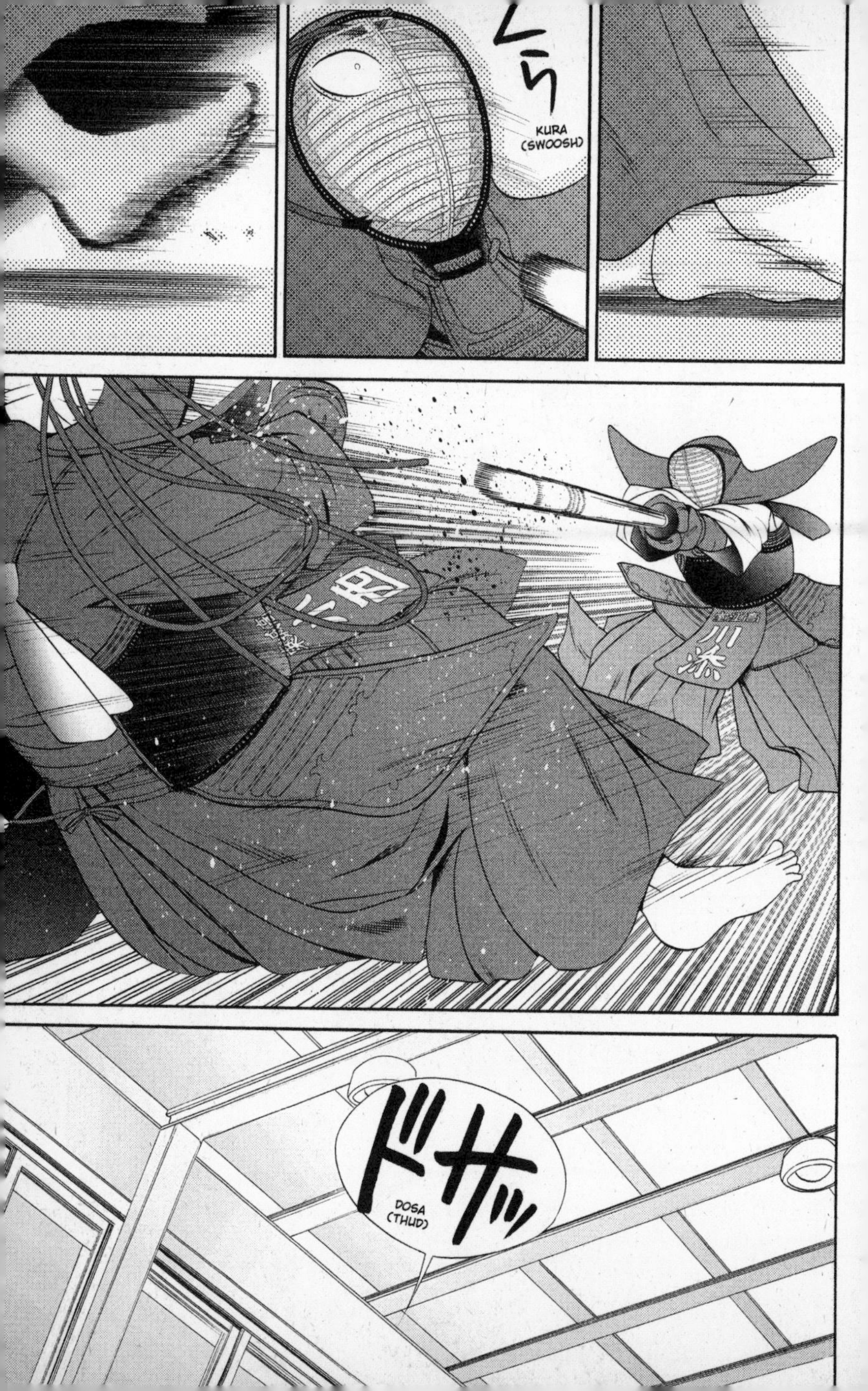
くら
KURA
(SWOOSH)
川添
ドサッ
DOSA
(THUD)

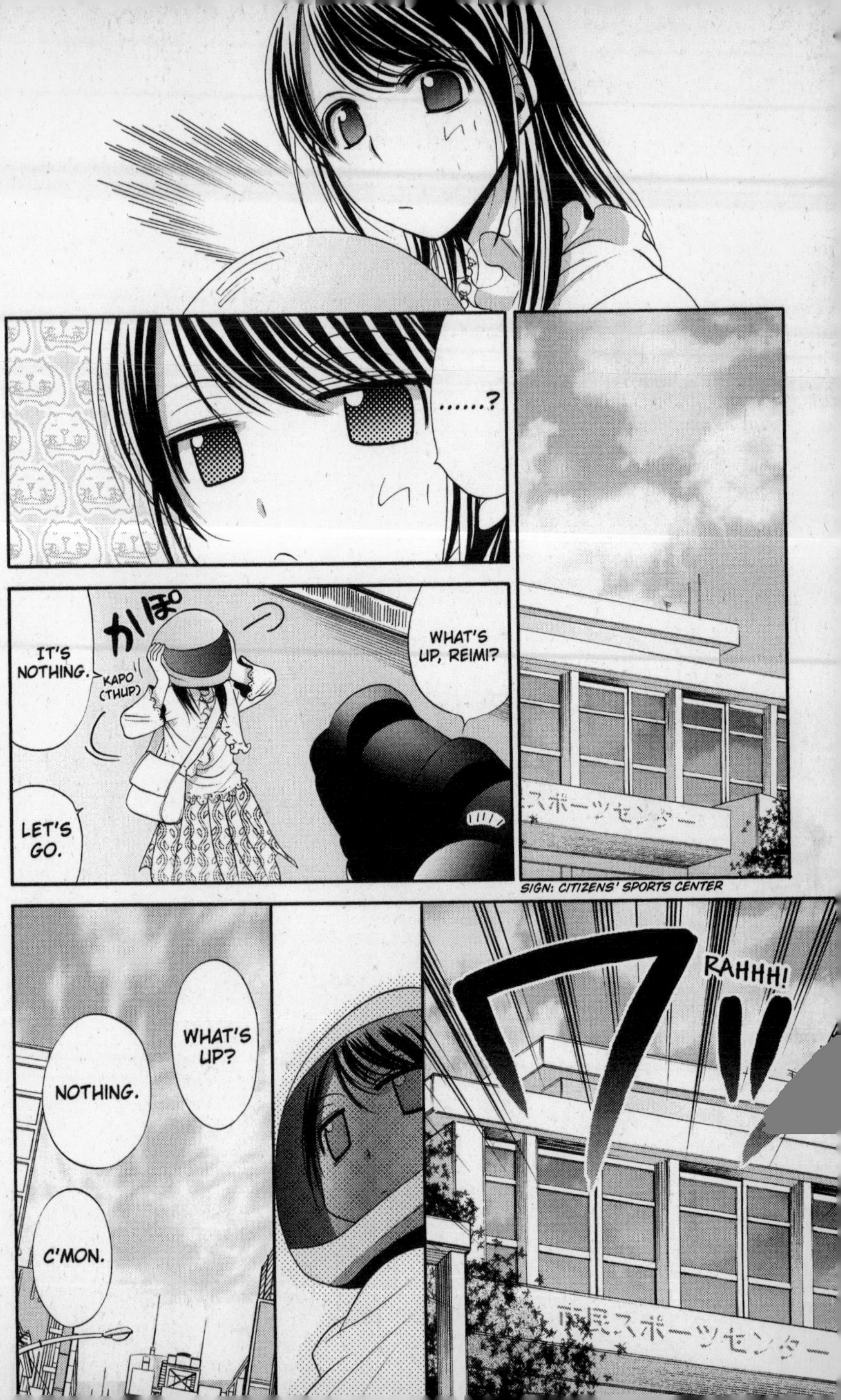
SIGN: CITIZENS' SPORTS CENTER
......?
WHAT'S UP, REIMI?
かぽ
KAPO (THUP)
IT'S NOTHING.
LET'S GO.
RAHHH!
WHAT'S UP?
NOTHING.
C'MON.

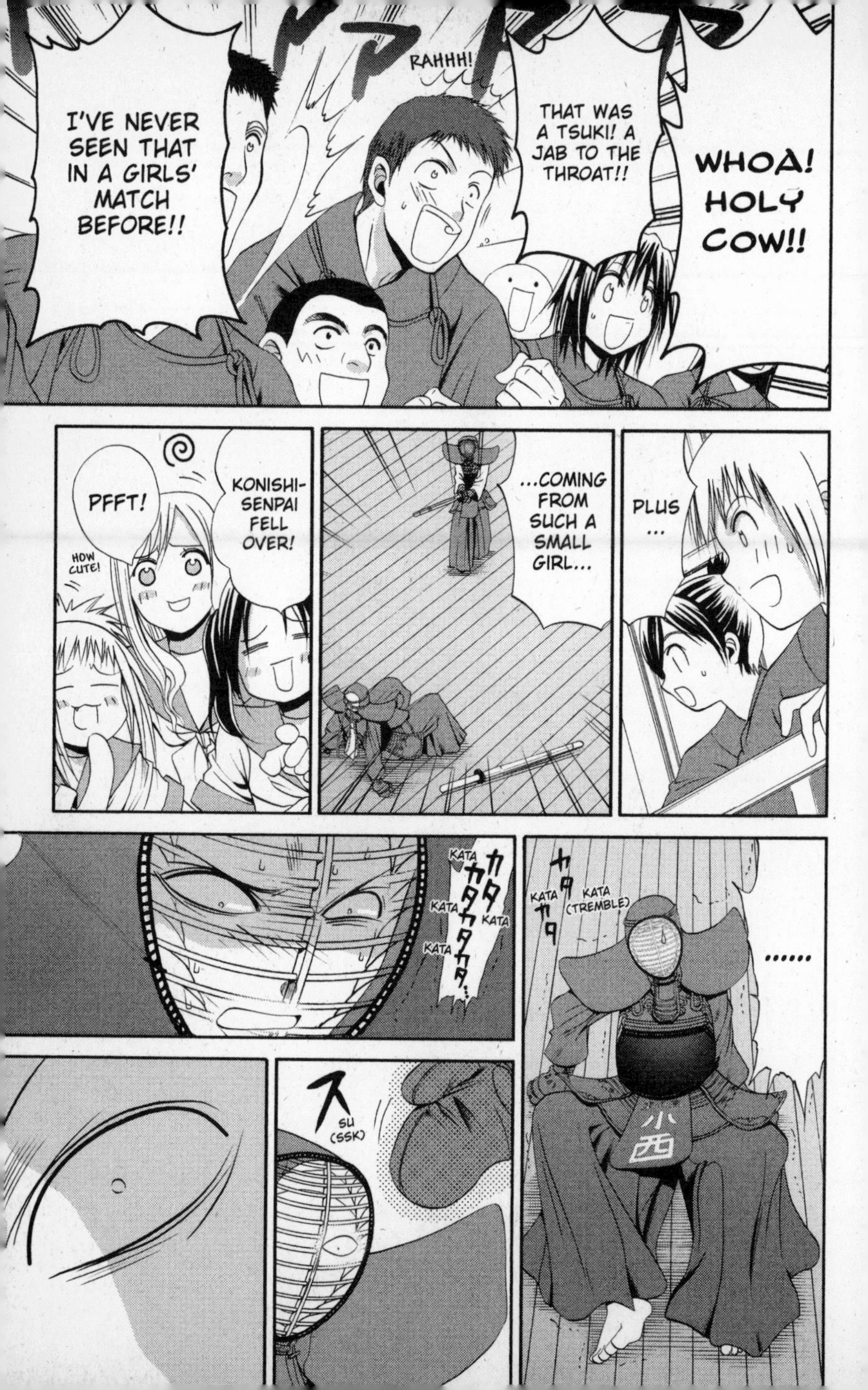
RAHHH!
WHOA! HOLY COW!!
THAT WAS A TSUKI! A JAB TO THE THROAT!!
I'VE NEVER SEEN THAT IN A GIRLS' MATCH BEFORE!!
PLUS ...
...COMING FROM SUCH A SMALL GIRL...
KONISHI-SENPAI FELL OVER!
PFFT!
HOW CUTE!
......
KATA
KATA (TREMBLE)
KATA
KATA
KATA
KATA
SU (SSK)

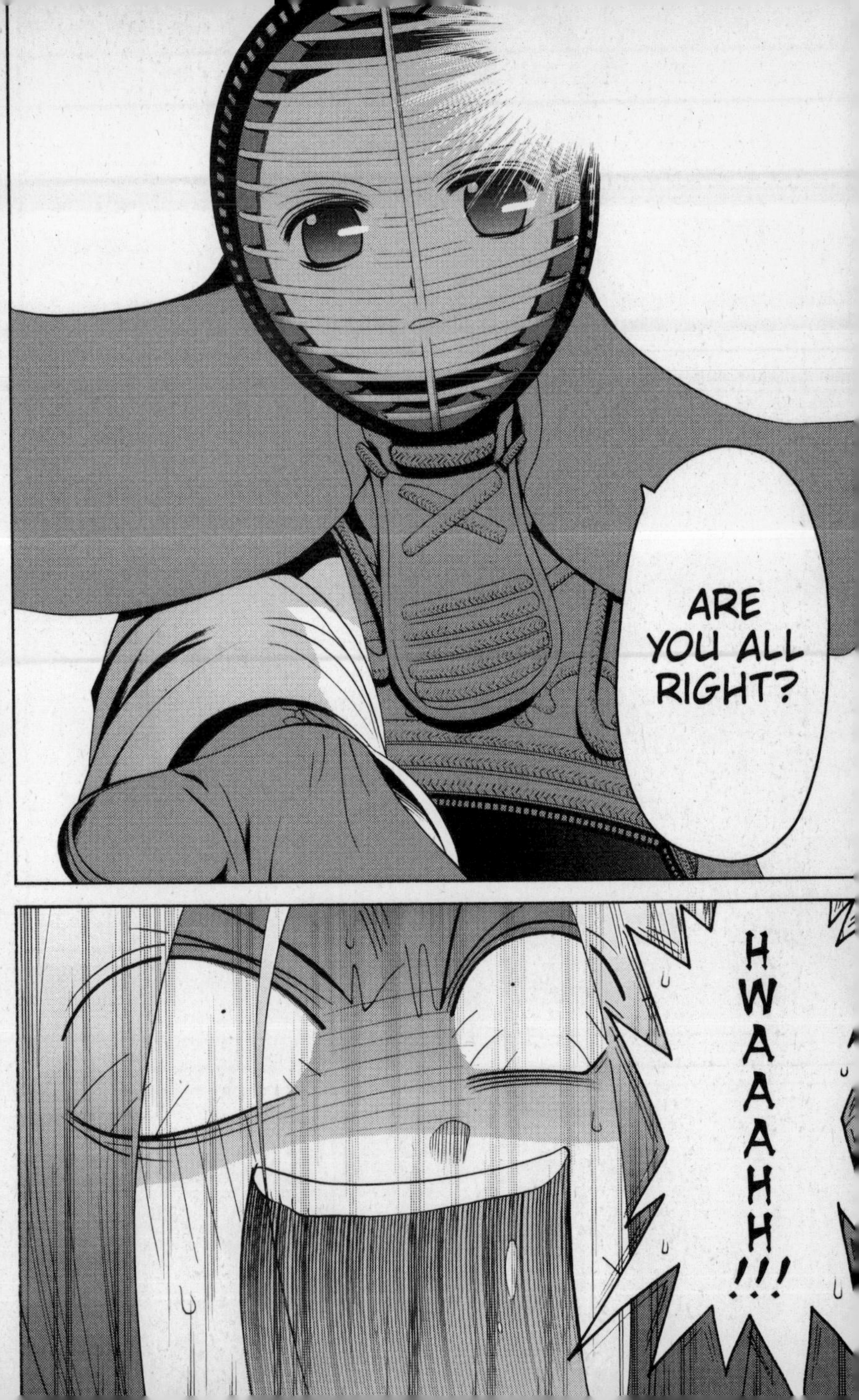
ARE YOU ALL RIGHT?
HWAAAHH!!!

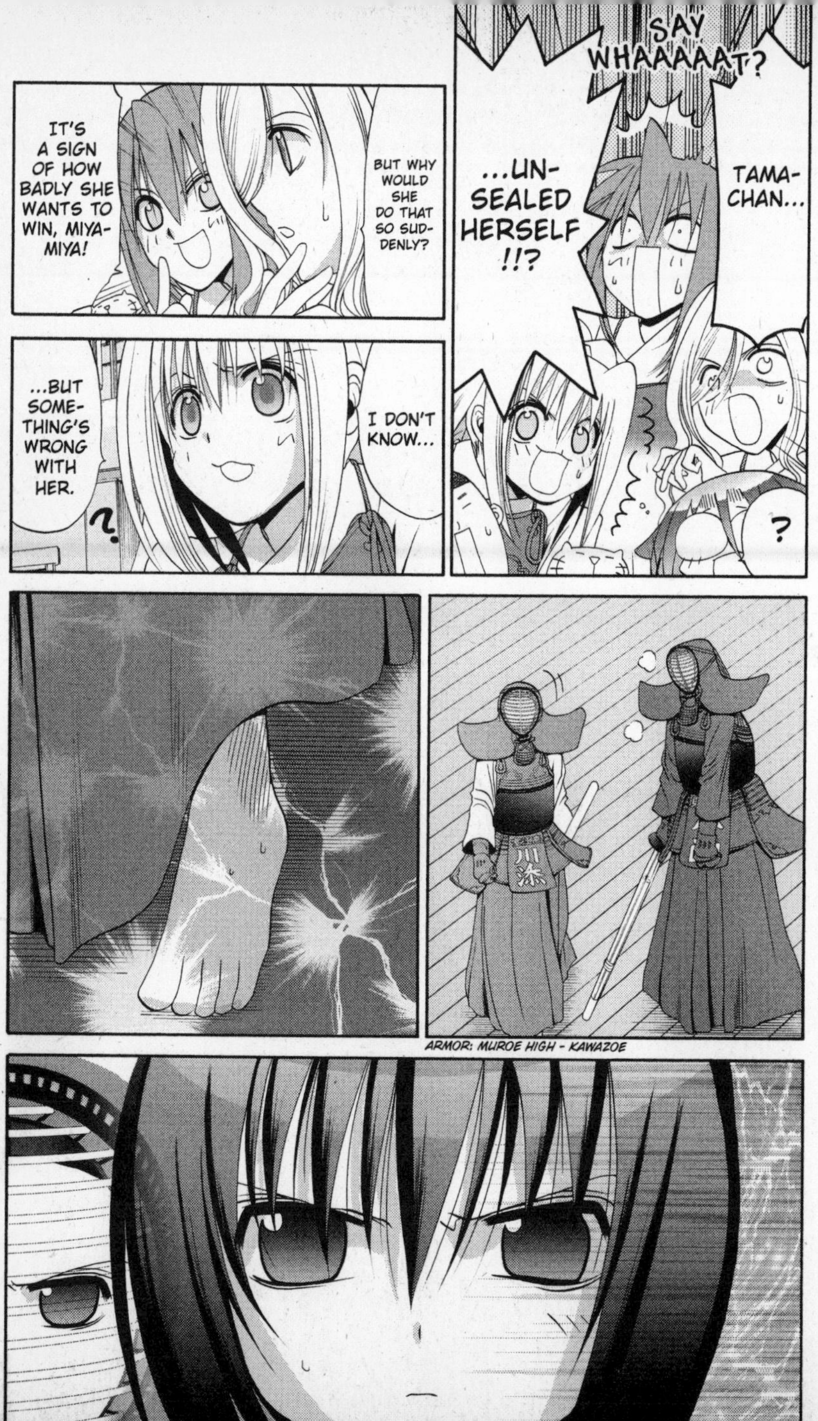
SAY WHAAAAAT?
TAMA-CHAN...
...UN-SEALED HERSELF!!?
?
BUT WHY WOULD SHE DO THAT SO SUD-DENLY?
IT'S A SIGN OF HOW BADLY SHE WANTS TO WIN, MIYA-MIYA!
I DON'T KNOW...
...BUT SOME-THING'S WRONG WITH HER.
?
川添
ARMOR: MUROE HIGH - KAWAZOE

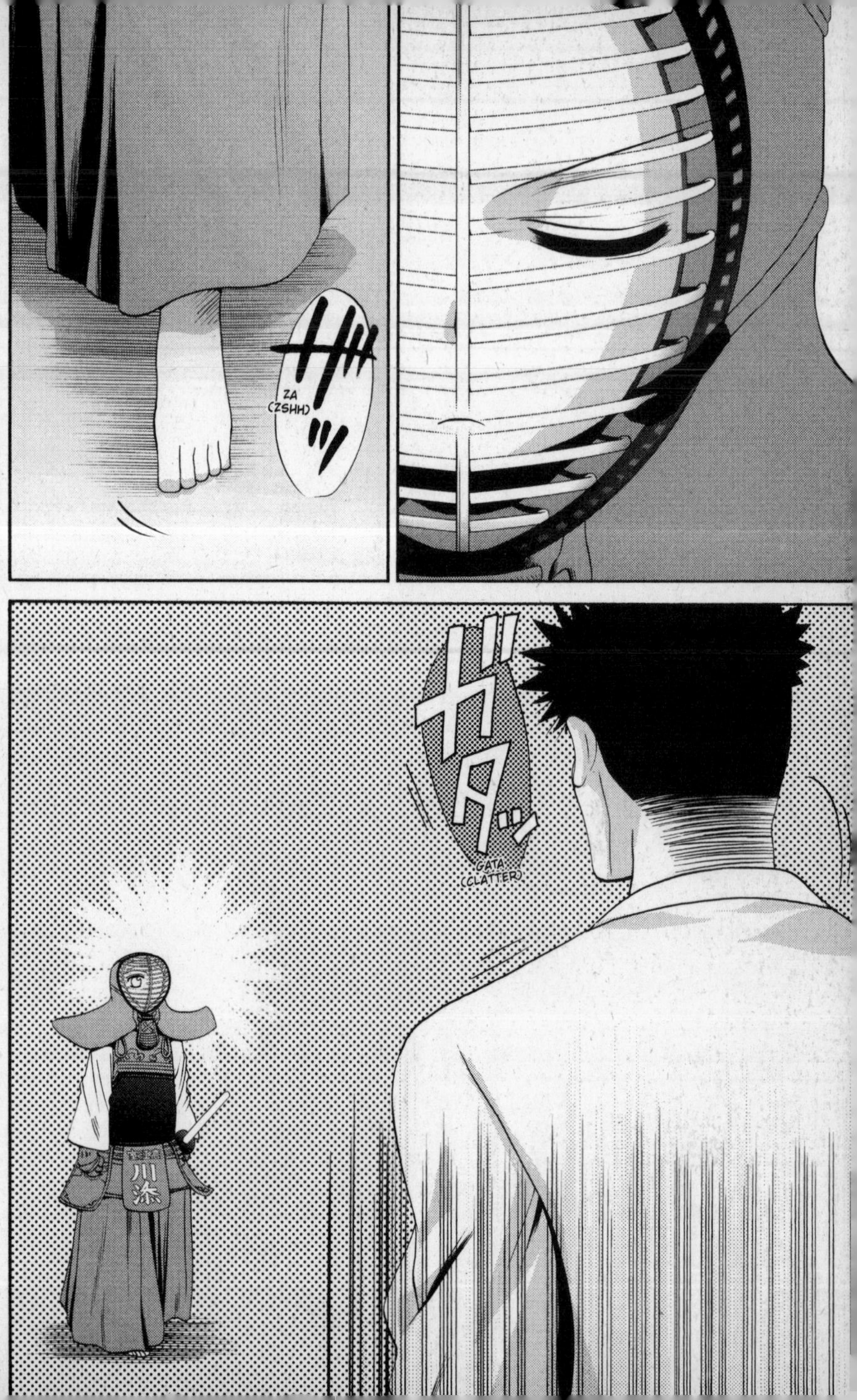
ZA
(ZSHH)
GATA
(CLATTER)
川添

BAMBOO BLADE

BAMBOO BLADE
バンブーブレード

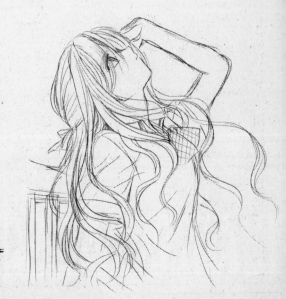

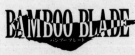

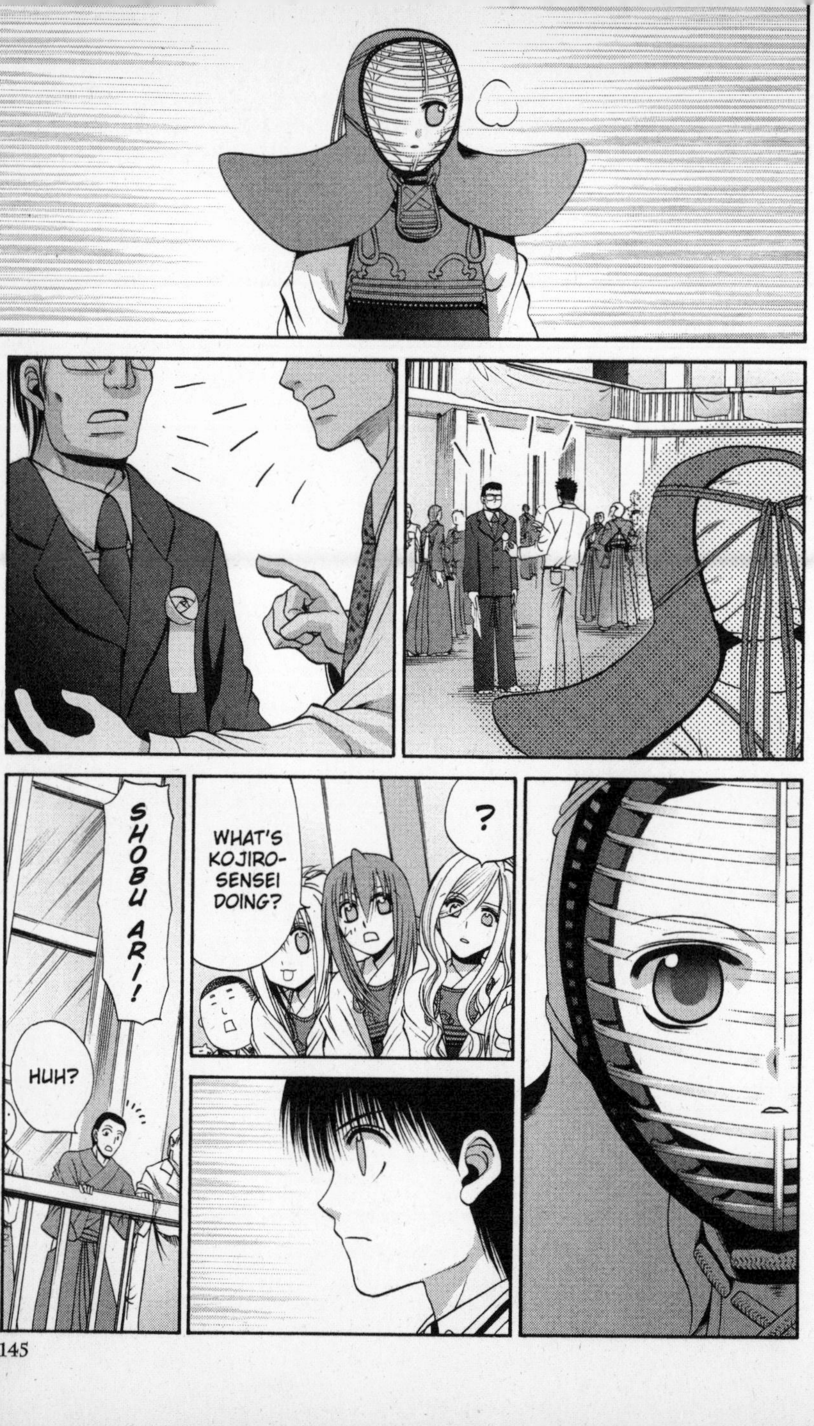
?
WHAT'S KOJIRO-SENSEI DOING?
SHOBU ARI!
HUH?

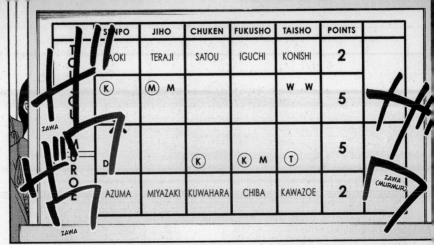

	SENPO	JIHO	CHUKEN	FUKUSHO	TAISHO	POINTS
	AOKI	TERAJI	SATOU	IGUCHI	KONISHI	2
	(K)	(M) M			W W	5
						5
	D		(K)	(K) M	(T)	
	AZUMA	MIYAZAKI	KUWAHARA	CHIBA	KAWAZOE	2

I THINK THAT GIRL MUST BE HURT.

THAT'S WHY THEIR COACH WENT AHEAD AND WITHDREW HER FROM THE MATCH.

I THINK?

WHY DID YOU STOP ME!?

I CAN STILL FIGHT!

WHY DIDN'T YOU TELL ME!?

SETTLE DOWN!

BECAUSE I'M JUST FINE!

YOU'VE GOT TO SUPPORT YOUR LEGS!

HANG ON, KONISHI-SAN!

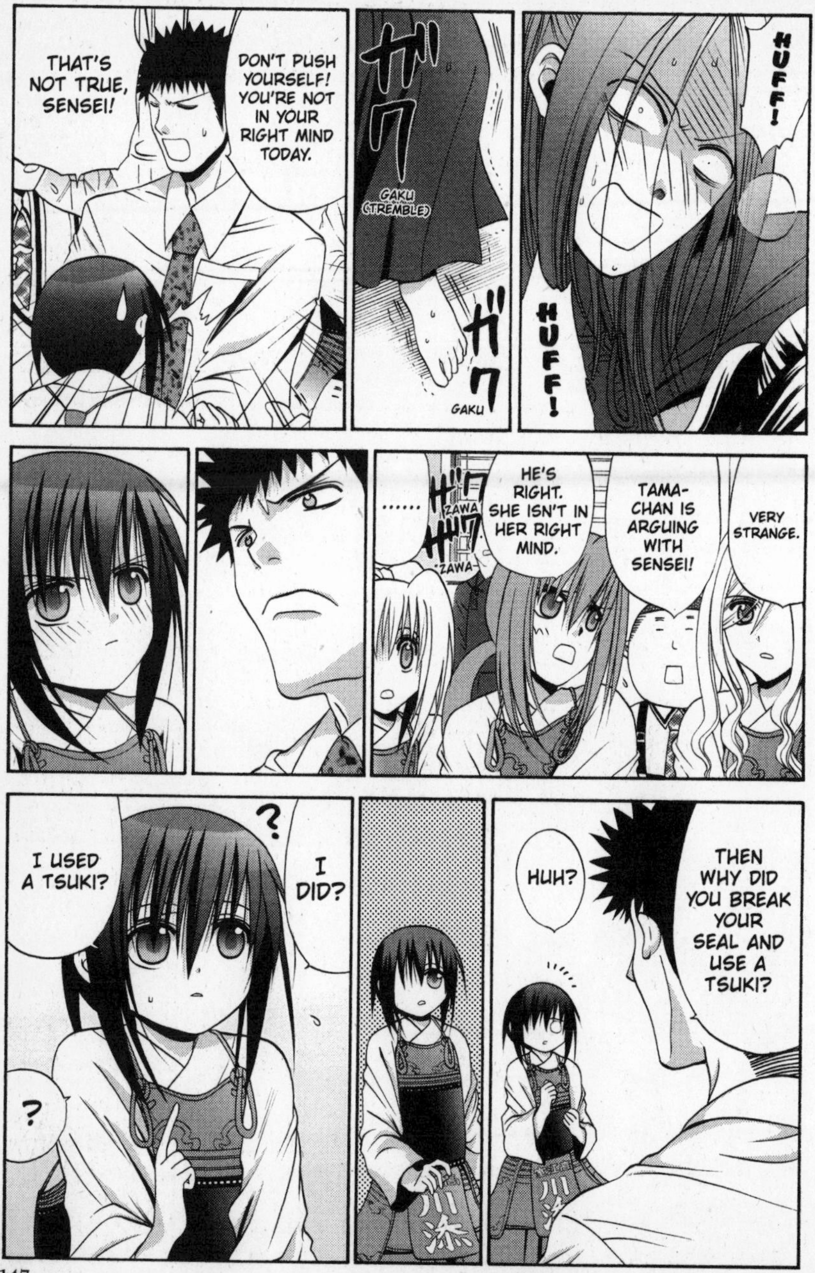
HUFF!
HUFF!
GAKU (TREMBLE)
GAKU
DON'T PUSH YOURSELF! YOU'RE NOT IN YOUR RIGHT MIND TODAY.
THAT'S NOT TRUE, SENSEI!
VERY STRANGE.
TAMA-CHAN IS ARGUING WITH SENSEI!
HE'S RIGHT. SHE ISN'T IN HER RIGHT MIND.
ZAWA
ZAWA
......
THEN WHY DID YOU BREAK YOUR SEAL AND USE A TSUKI?
HUH?
?
I DID?
I USED A TSUKI?
?

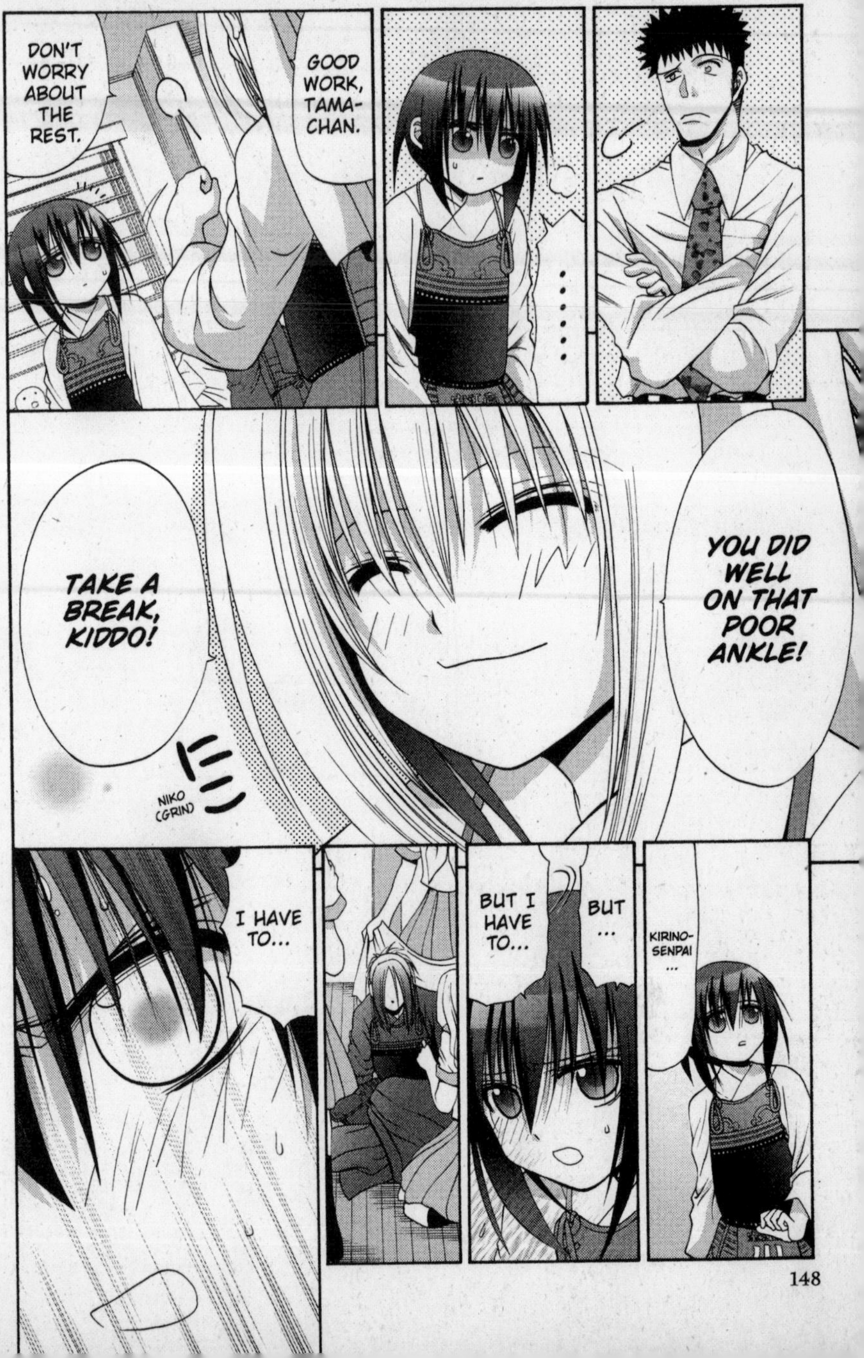
......
GOOD WORK, TAMA-CHAN.
DON'T WORRY ABOUT THE REST.
YOU DID WELL ON THAT POOR ANKLE!
TAKE A BREAK, KIDDO!
NIKO (GRIN)
KIRINO-SENPAI ...
BUT ...
BUT I HAVE TO...
I HAVE TO...

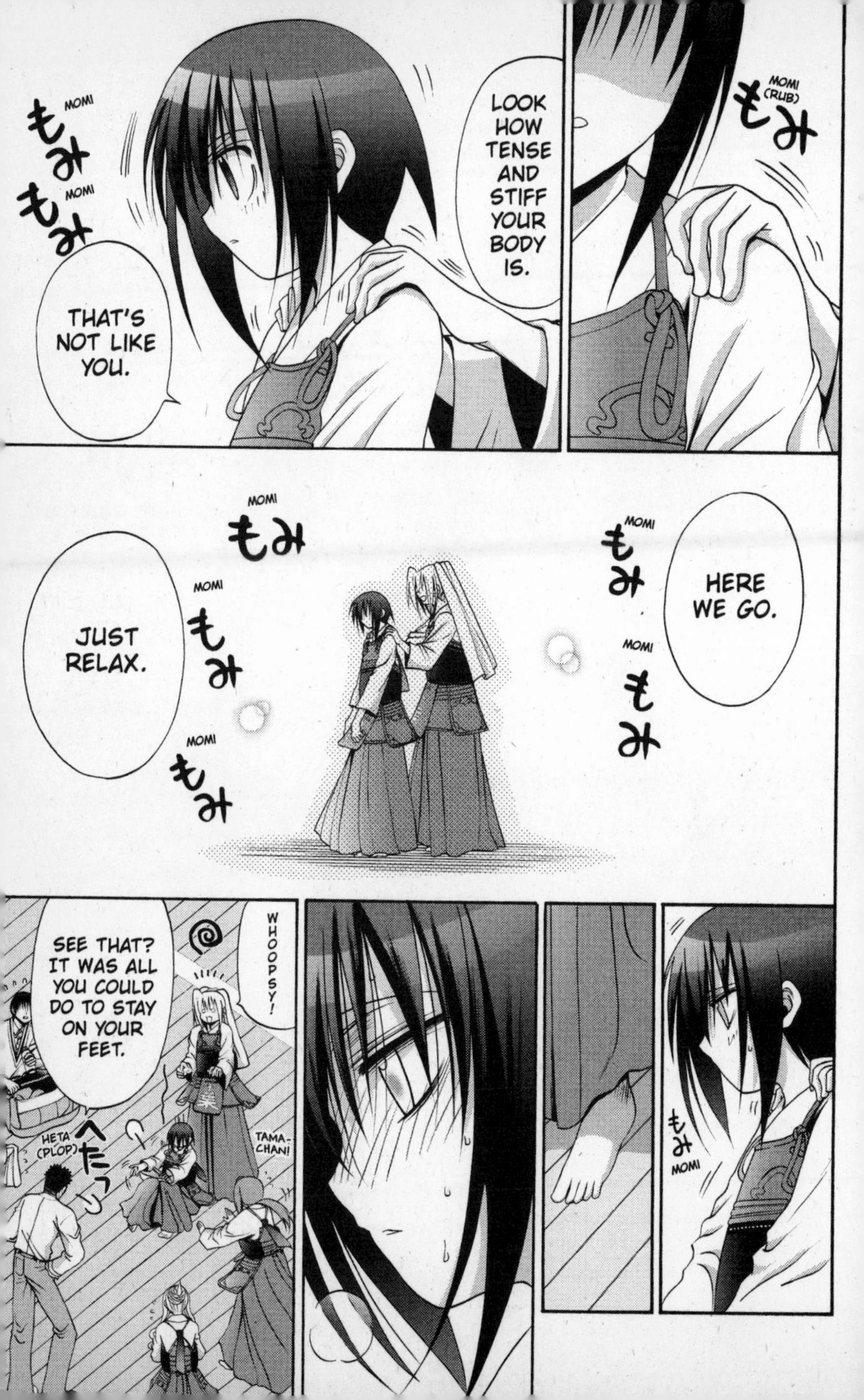
MOMI (RUB)
もみ
LOOK HOW TENSE AND STIFF YOUR BODY IS.
MOMI
もみ
MOMI
もみ
THAT'S NOT LIKE YOU.
HERE WE GO.
MOMI
もみ
MOMI
もみ
MOMI
もみ
JUST RELAX.
MOMI
もみ
MOMI
もみ
もみ
MOMI
WHOOPSY!
SEE THAT? IT WAS ALL YOU COULD DO TO STAY ON YOUR FEET.
TAMA-CHAN!
HETA (PLOP)
へたっ

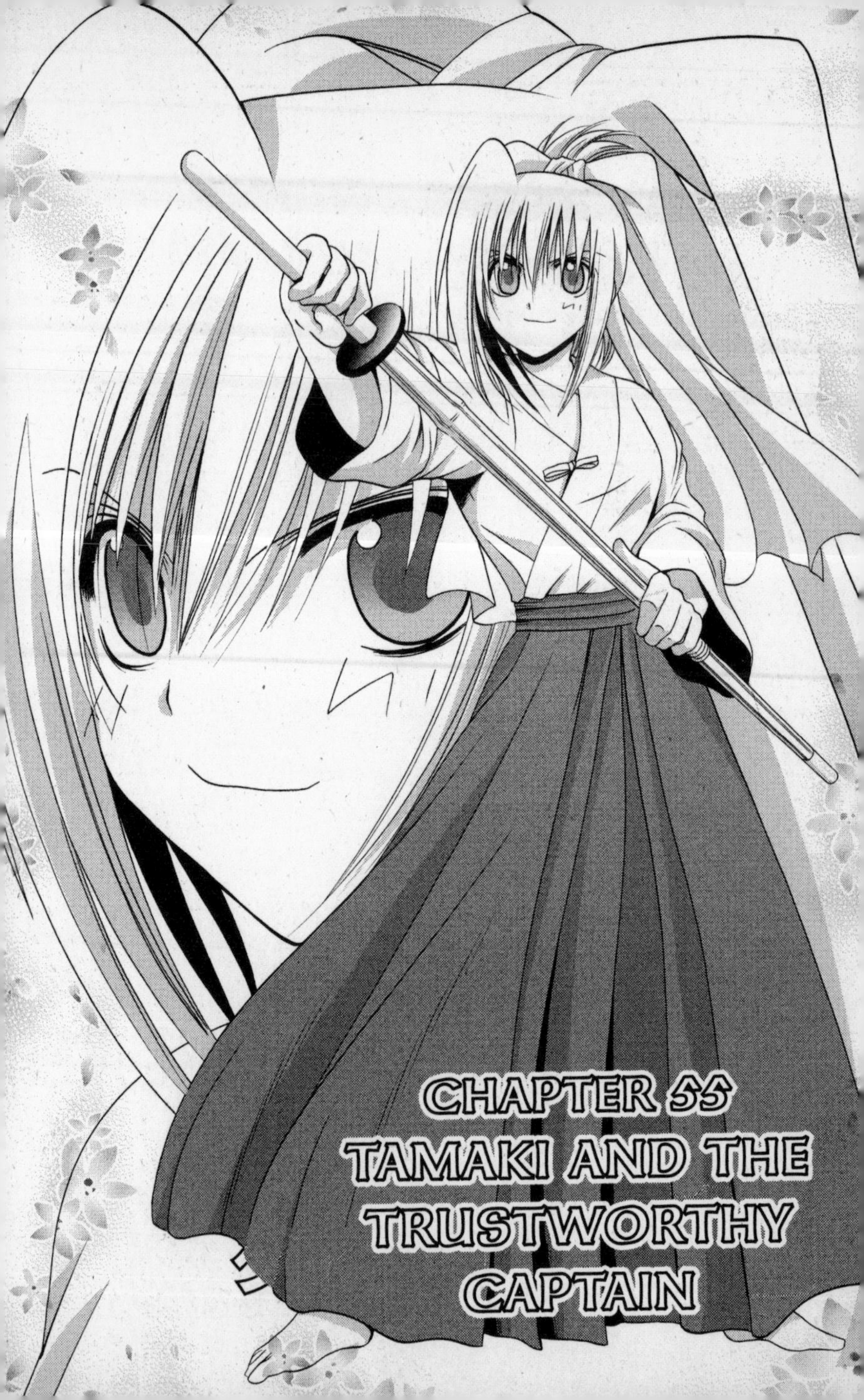
CHAPTER 55
TAMAKI AND THE TRUSTWORTHY CAPTAIN

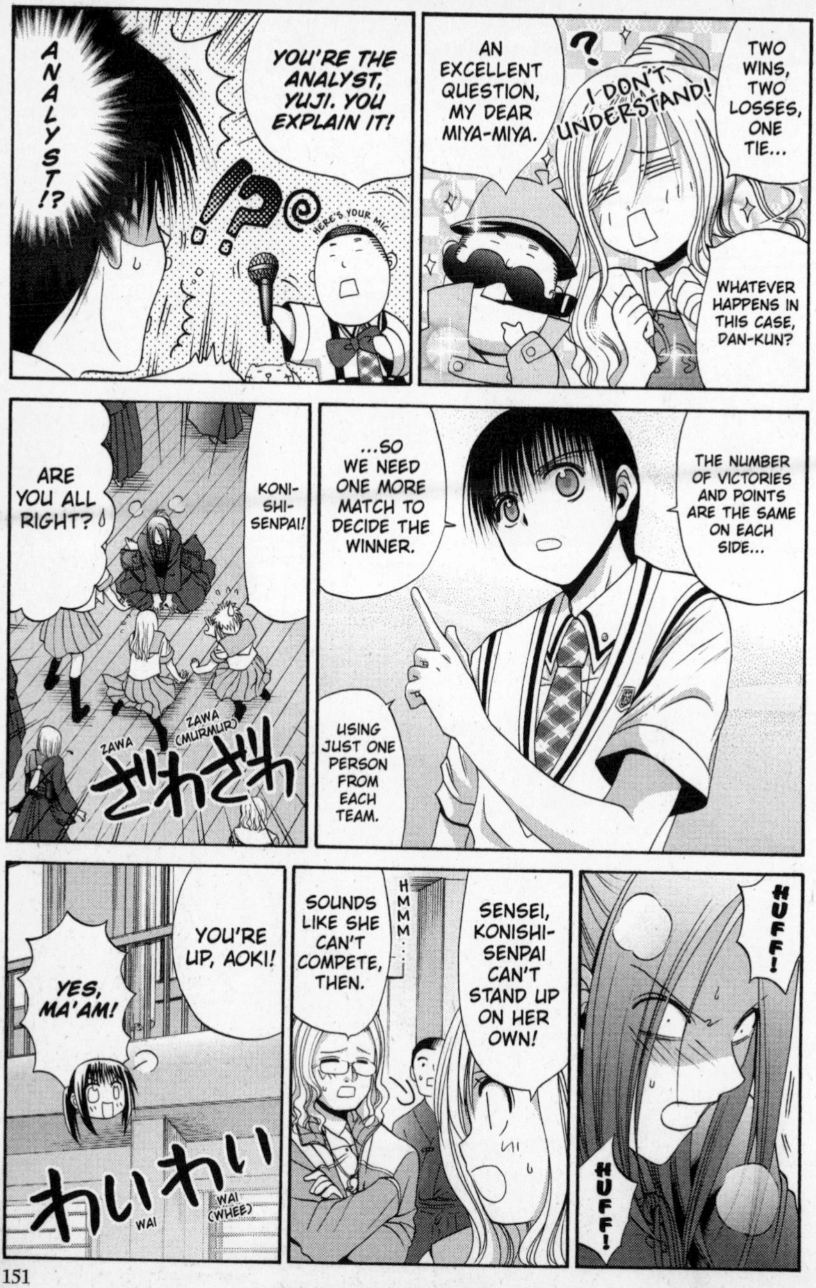
TWO WINS, TWO LOSSES, ONE TIE...
I DON'T UNDERSTAND!
?
WHATEVER HAPPENS IN THIS CASE, DAN-KUN?
AN EXCELLENT QUESTION, MY DEAR MIYA-MIYA.
YOU'RE THE ANALYST, YUJI. YOU EXPLAIN IT!
HERE'S YOUR MIC.
!?
ANALYST!?
THE NUMBER OF VICTORIES AND POINTS ARE THE SAME ON EACH SIDE...
...SO WE NEED ONE MORE MATCH TO DECIDE THE WINNER.
USING JUST ONE PERSON FROM EACH TEAM.
KONI-SHI-SENPAI!
ARE YOU ALL RIGHT?
ZAWA ZAWA (MURMUR)
ざわざわ
HUFF!
HUFF!
SENSEI, KONISHI-SENPAI CAN'T STAND UP ON HER OWN!
HMMM...
SOUNDS LIKE SHE CAN'T COMPETE, THEN.
YOU'RE UP, AOKI!
YES, MA'AM!
わいわい
WAI WAI (WHEE)

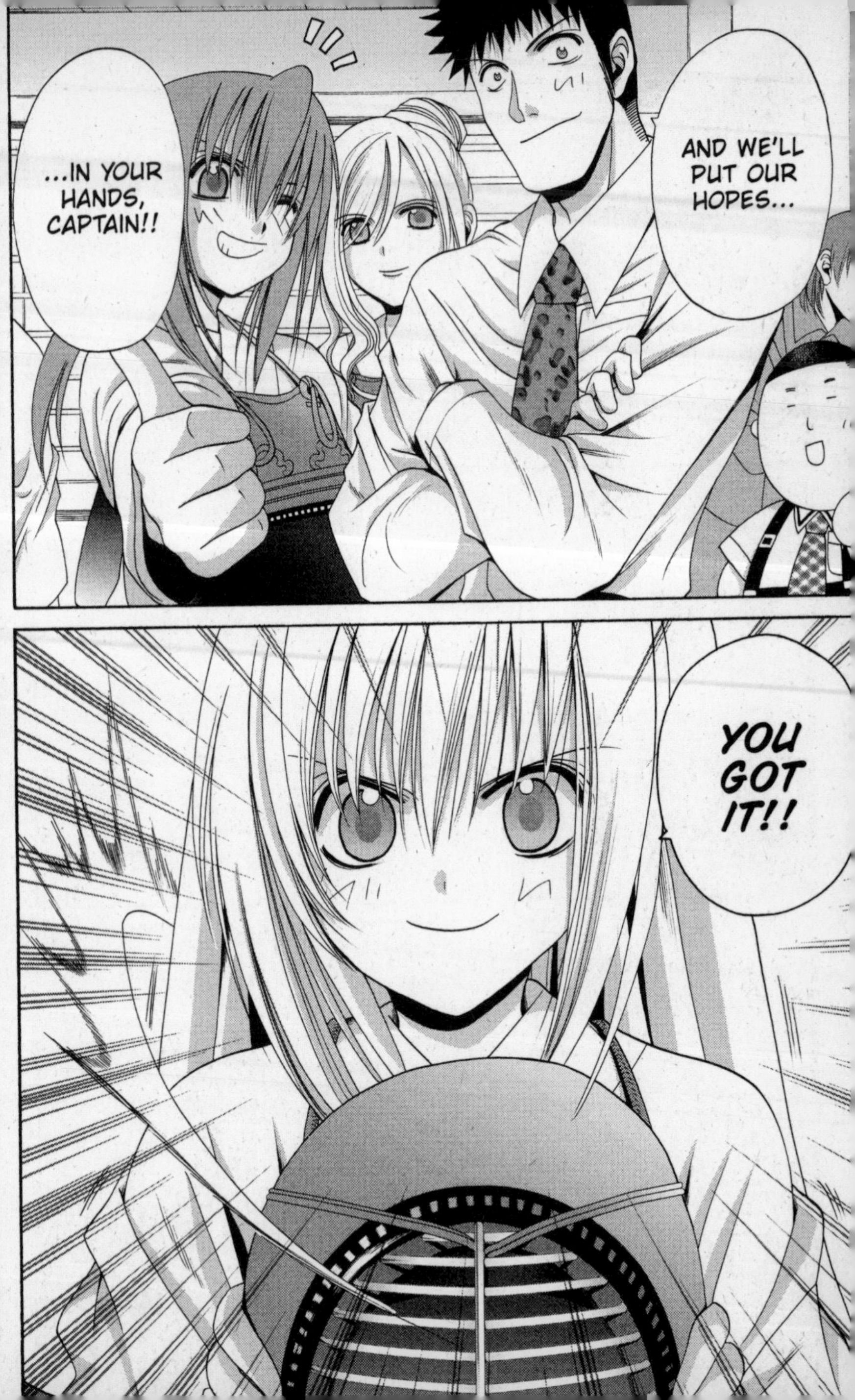
AND WE'LL PUT OUR HOPES...
...IN YOUR HANDS, CAPTAIN!!
YOU GOT IT!!

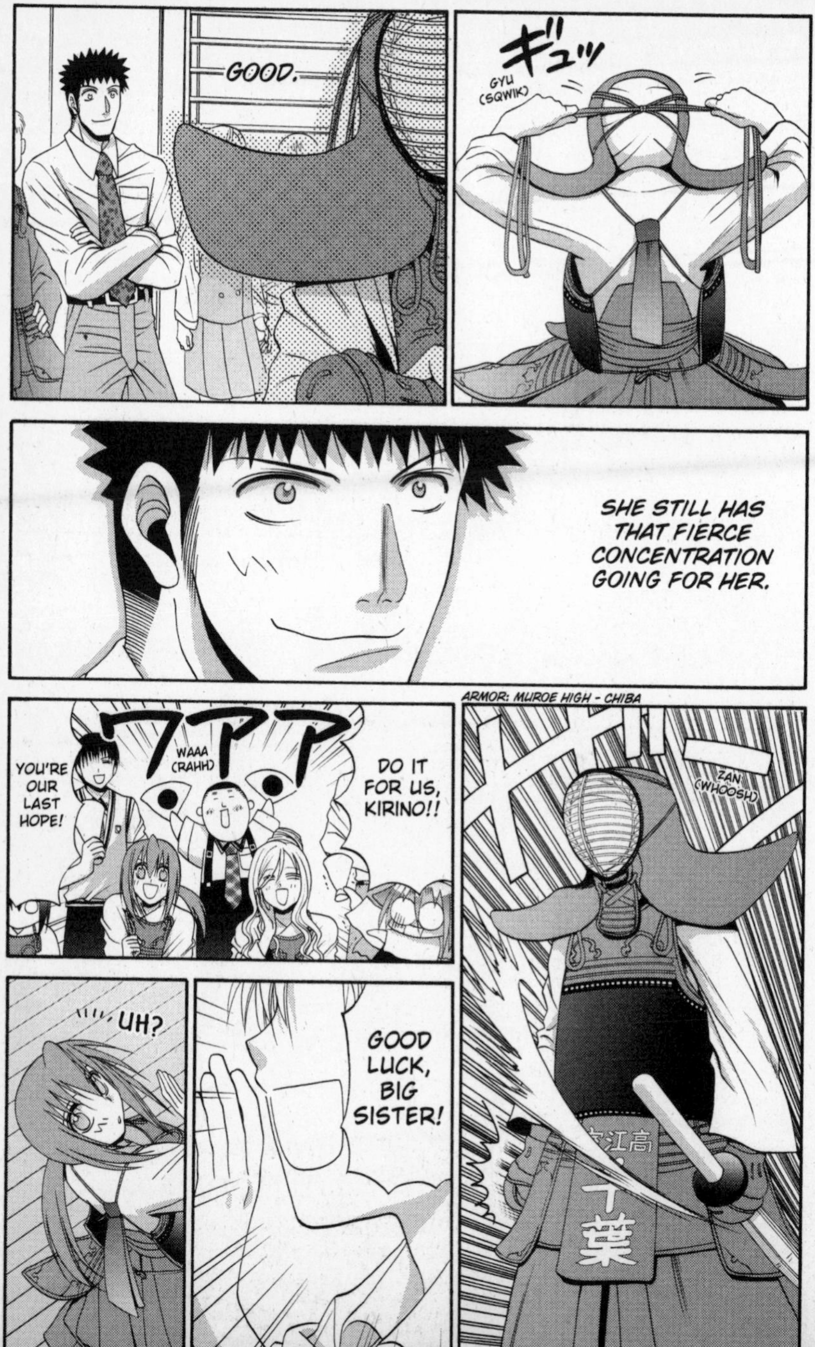
ギュッ
GYU (SQWIK)
GOOD.
SHE STILL HAS THAT FIERCE CONCENTRATION GOING FOR HER.
ARMOR: MUROE HIGH - CHIBA
ZAN (WHOOSH)
江高
千葉
DO IT FOR US, KIRINO!!
ワアア
WAAA (RAHH)
YOU'RE OUR LAST HOPE!
GOOD LUCK, BIG SISTER!
UH?

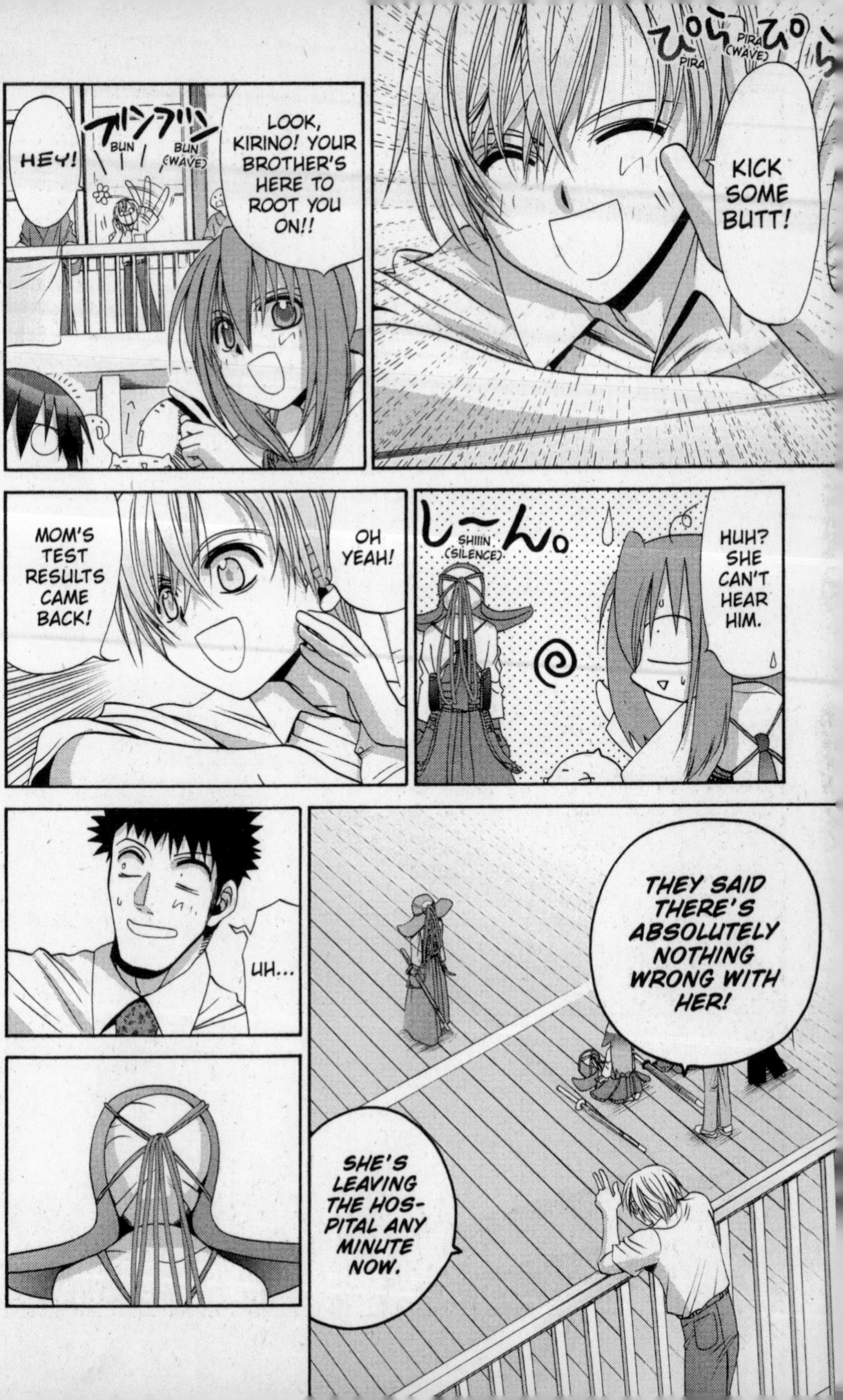
ぴらぴら
PIRA PIRA (WAVE)
KICK SOME BUTT!
LOOK, KIRINO! YOUR BROTHER'S HERE TO ROOT YOU ON!!
ブンブン
BUN BUN (WAVE)
HEY!
HUH? SHE CAN'T HEAR HIM.
しーん。
SHIIIN (SILENCE)
OH YEAH!
MOM'S TEST RESULTS CAME BACK!
THEY SAID THERE'S ABSOLUTELY NOTHING WRONG WITH HER!
SHE'S LEAVING THE HOSPITAL ANY MINUTE NOW.
UH...

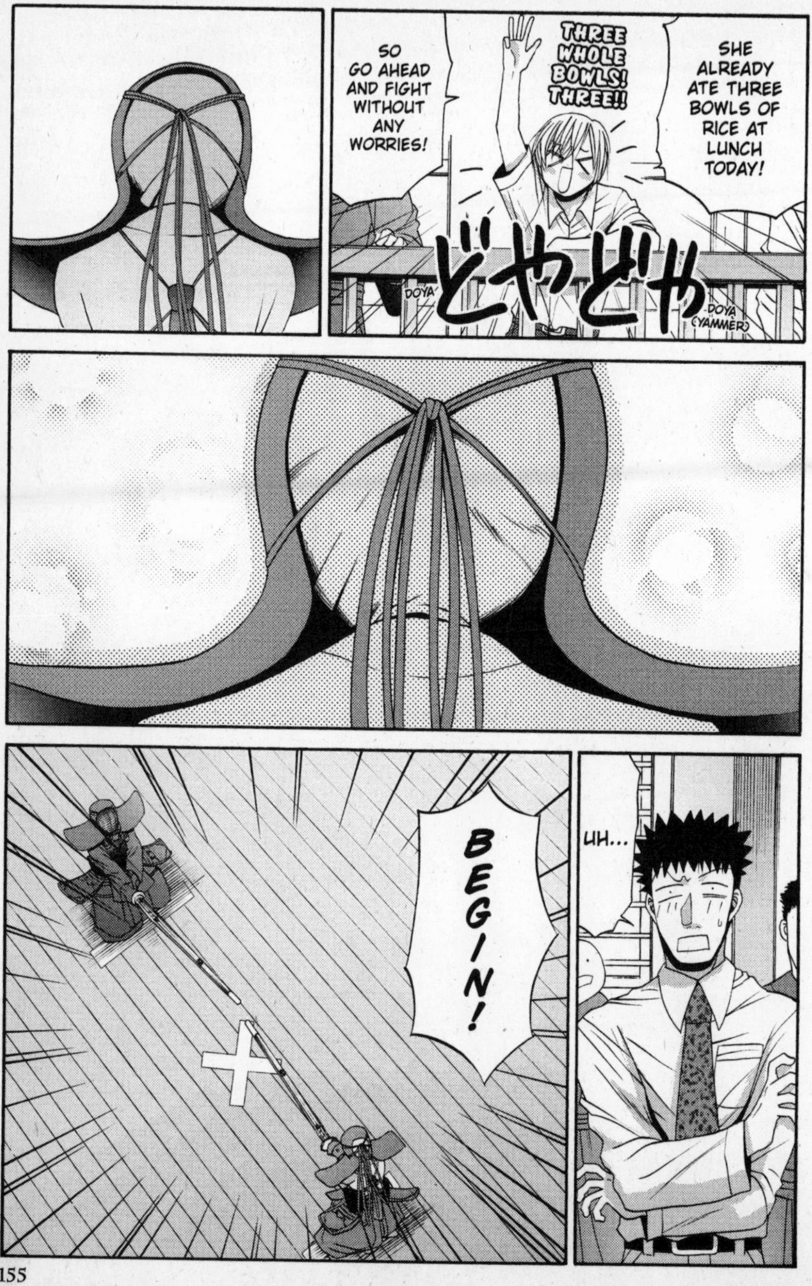
SHE ALREADY ATE THREE BOWLS OF RICE AT LUNCH TODAY!
THREE WHOLE BOWLS! THREE!!
SO GO AHEAD AND FIGHT WITHOUT ANY WORRIES!
どやどや
DOYA DOYA (YAMMER)
UH...
BEGIN!

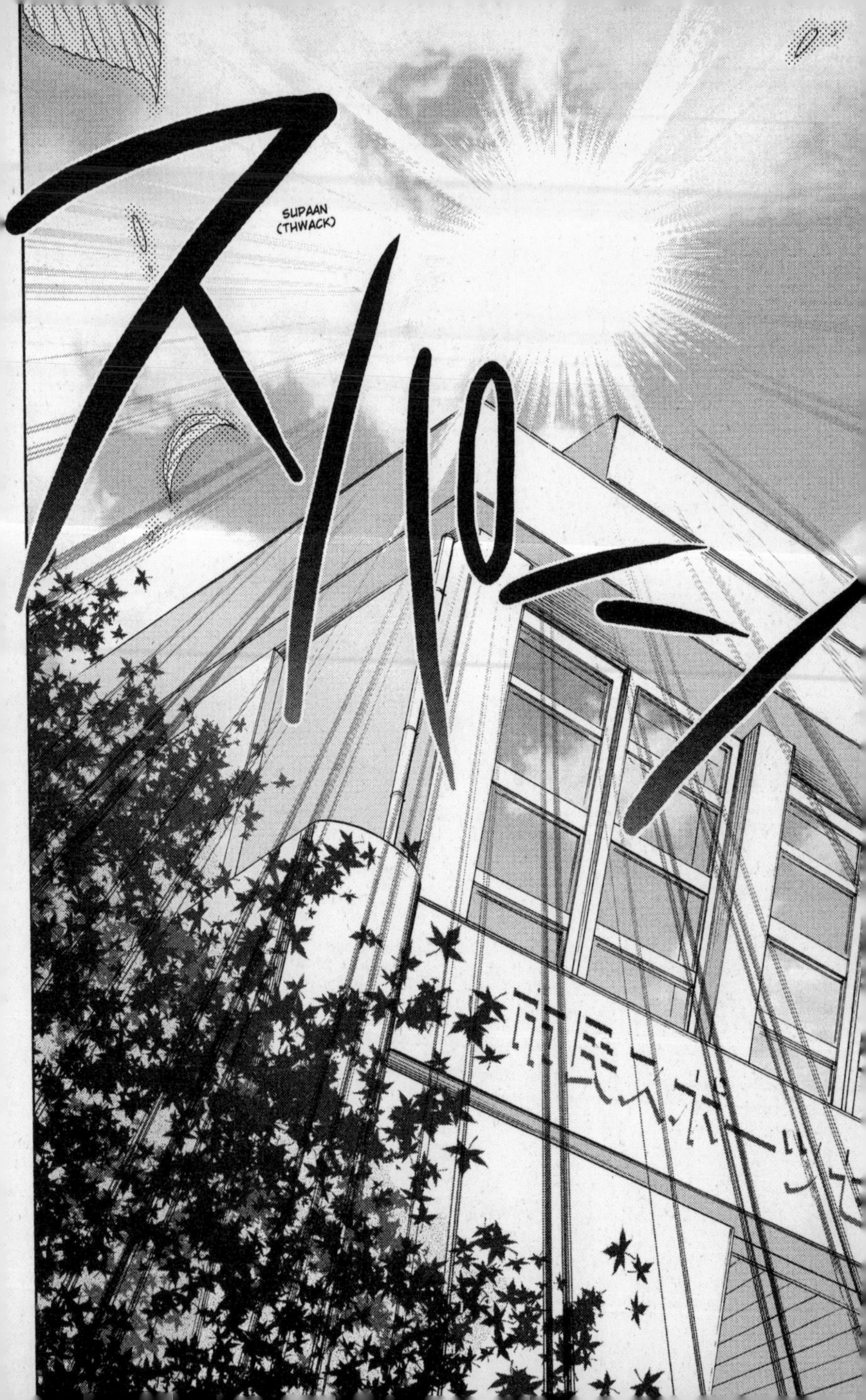
スパーン
SUPAAN
(THWACK)
市民スポーツセ

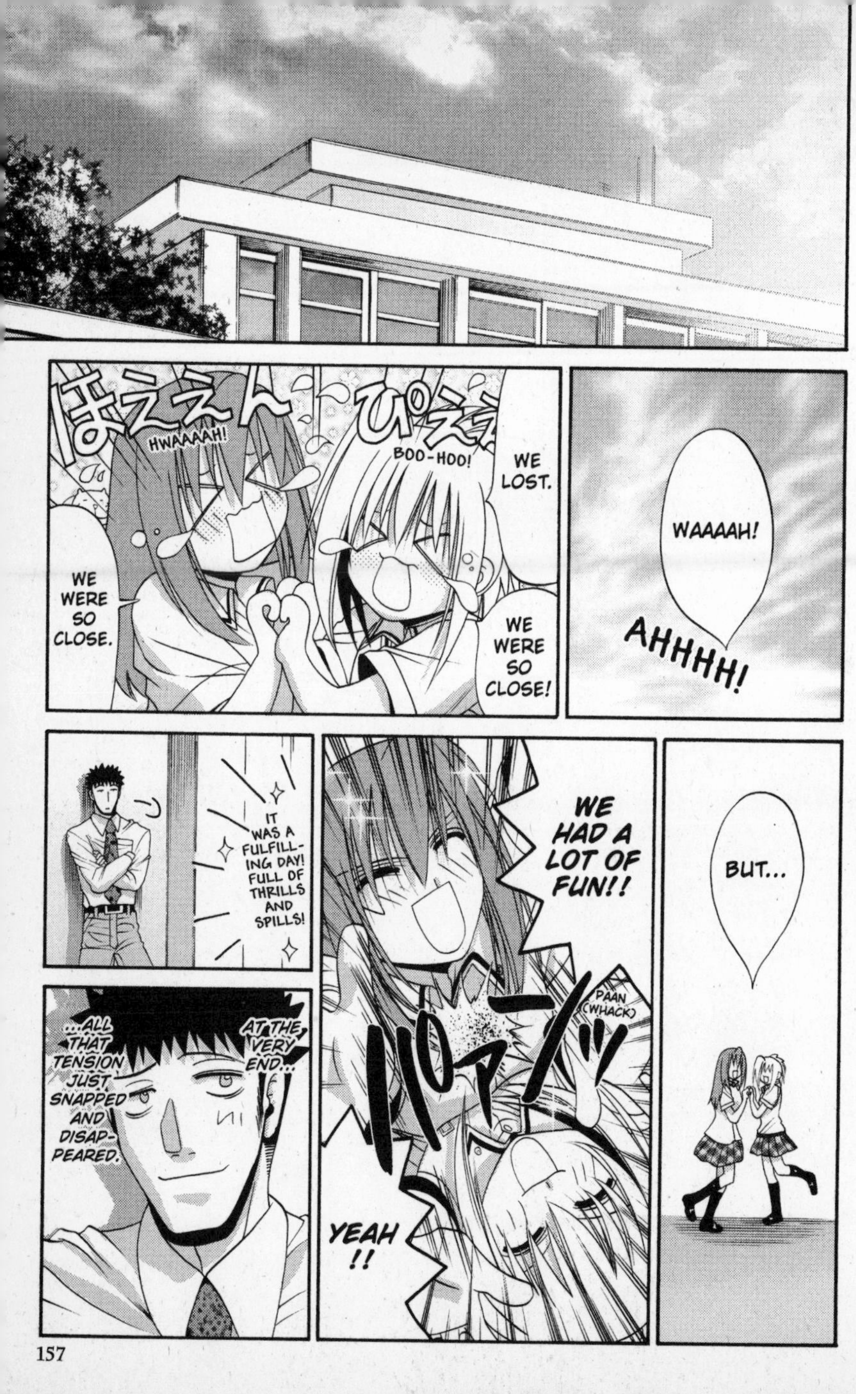
WAAAAH!
AHHHHH!
ぴえぇ
BOO-HOO!
WE LOST.
ほえぇん
HWAAAAH!
WE WERE SO CLOSE!
WE WERE SO CLOSE.
BUT...
WE HAD A LOT OF FUN!!
パァーンッ
PAAN (WHACK)
YEAH!!
IT WAS A FULFILLING DAY! FULL OF THRILLS AND SPILLS!
AT THE VERY END...
...ALL THAT TENSION JUST SNAPPED AND DISAPPEARED.

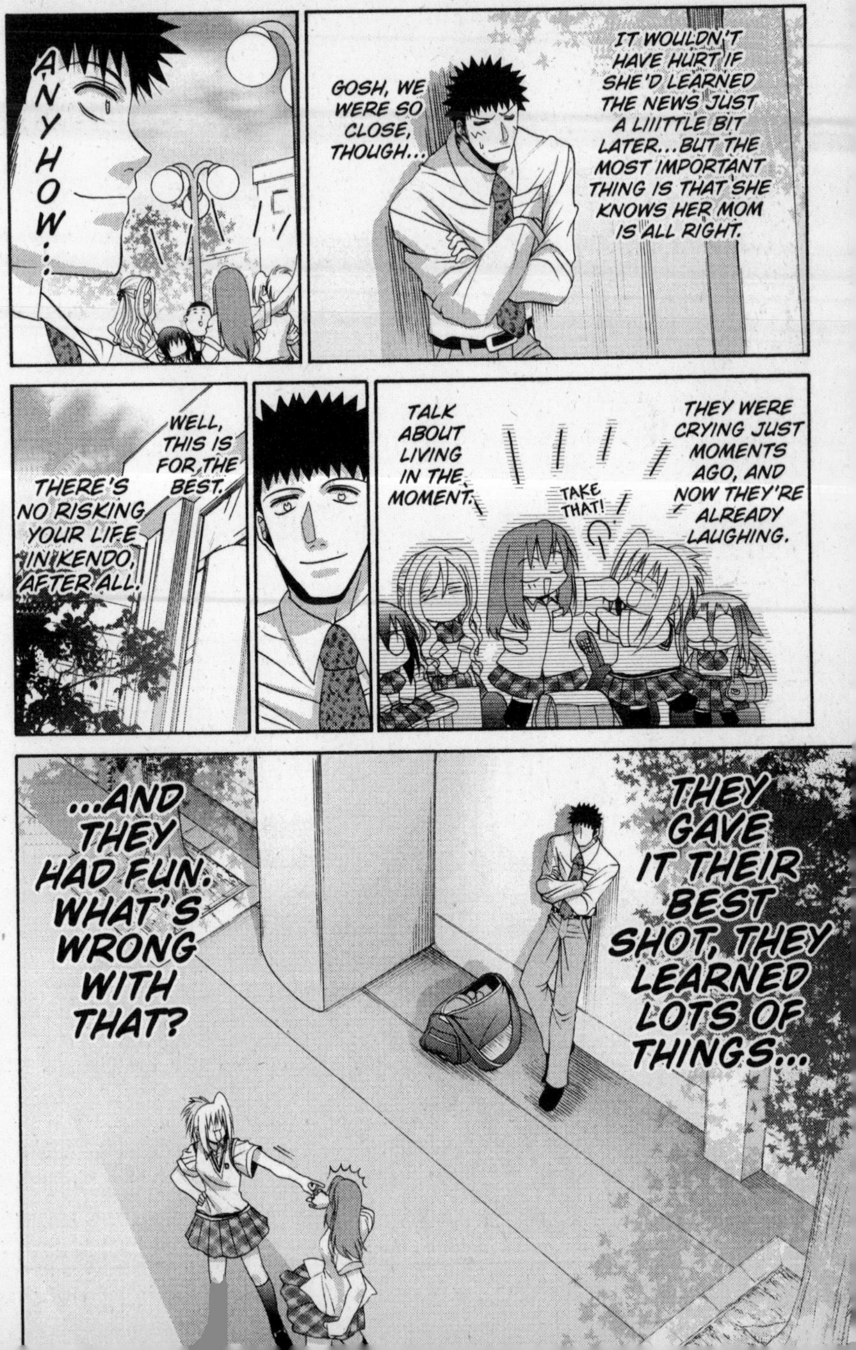
IT WOULDN'T HAVE HURT IF SHE'D LEARNED THE NEWS JUST A LIIITTLE BIT LATER...BUT THE MOST IMPORTANT THING IS THAT SHE KNOWS HER MOM IS ALL RIGHT.
GOSH, WE WERE SO CLOSE, THOUGH...
ANYHOW...
THEY WERE CRYING JUST MOMENTS AGO, AND NOW THEY'RE ALREADY LAUGHING.
TAKE THAT!
TALK ABOUT LIVING IN THE MOMENT.
WELL, THIS IS FOR THE BEST.
THERE'S NO RISKING YOUR LIFE IN KENDO, AFTER ALL.
THEY GAVE IT THEIR BEST SHOT, THEY LEARNED LOTS OF THINGS...
...AND THEY HAD FUN. WHAT'S WRONG WITH THAT?

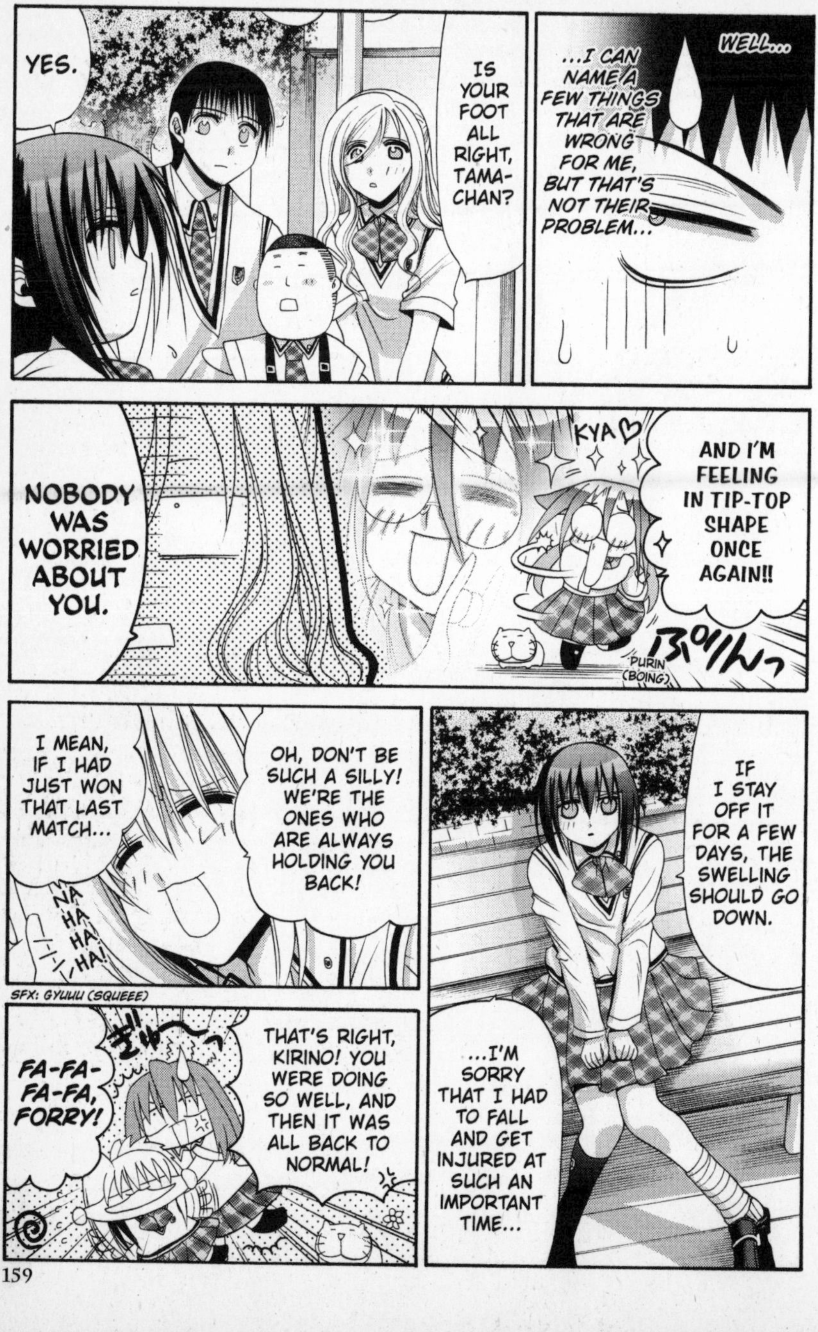
WELL...
...I CAN NAME A FEW THINGS THAT ARE WRONG FOR ME, BUT THAT'S NOT THEIR PROBLEM...
IS YOUR FOOT ALL RIGHT, TAMA-CHAN?
YES.
AND I'M FEELING IN TIP-TOP SHAPE ONCE AGAIN!!
KYA♡
PURIN (BOING)
NOBODY WAS WORRIED ABOUT YOU.
IF I STAY OFF IT FOR A FEW DAYS, THE SWELLING SHOULD GO DOWN.
...I'M SORRY THAT I HAD TO FALL AND GET INJURED AT SUCH AN IMPORTANT TIME...
OH, DON'T BE SUCH A SILLY! WE'RE THE ONES WHO ARE ALWAYS HOLDING YOU BACK!
I MEAN, IF I HAD JUST WON THAT LAST MATCH...
NA HA HA HA!
SFX: GYUUU (SQUEEE)
THAT'S RIGHT, KIRINO! YOU WERE DOING SO WELL, AND THEN IT WAS ALL BACK TO NORMAL!
FA-FA-FA-FA, FORRY!

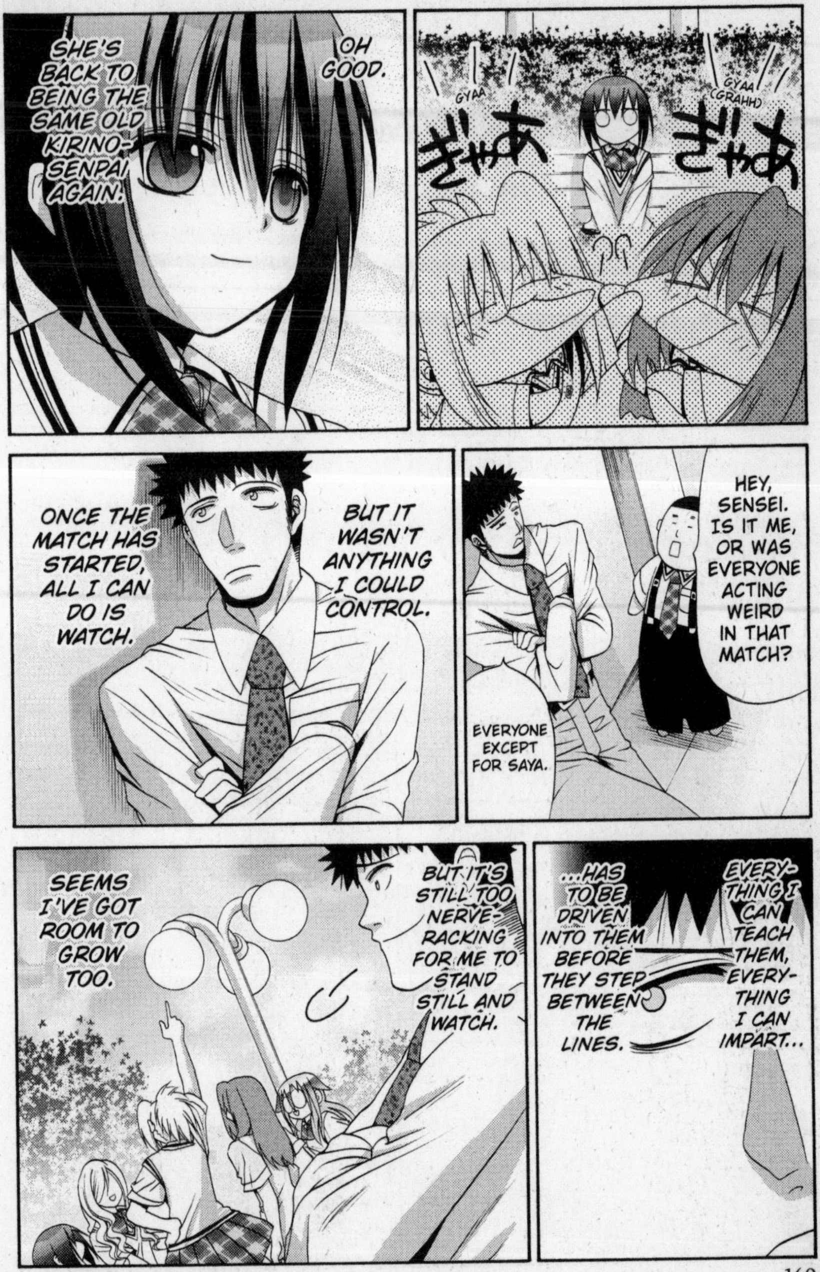
GYAA (GRAHH)
ぎゃあ
GYAA
ぎゃあ
OH GOOD.
SHE'S BACK TO BEING THE SAME OLD KIRINO-SENPAI AGAIN.
HEY, SENSEI. IS IT ME, OR WAS EVERYONE ACTING WEIRD IN THAT MATCH?
EVERYONE EXCEPT FOR SAYA.
BUT IT WASN'T ANYTHING I COULD CONTROL.
ONCE THE MATCH HAS STARTED, ALL I CAN DO IS WATCH.
EVERYTHING I CAN TEACH THEM, EVERYTHING I CAN IMPART...
...HAS TO BE DRIVEN INTO THEM BEFORE THEY STEP BETWEEN THE LINES.
BUT IT'S STILL TOO NERVE-RACKING FOR ME TO STAND STILL AND WATCH.
SEEMS I'VE GOT ROOM TO GROW TOO.

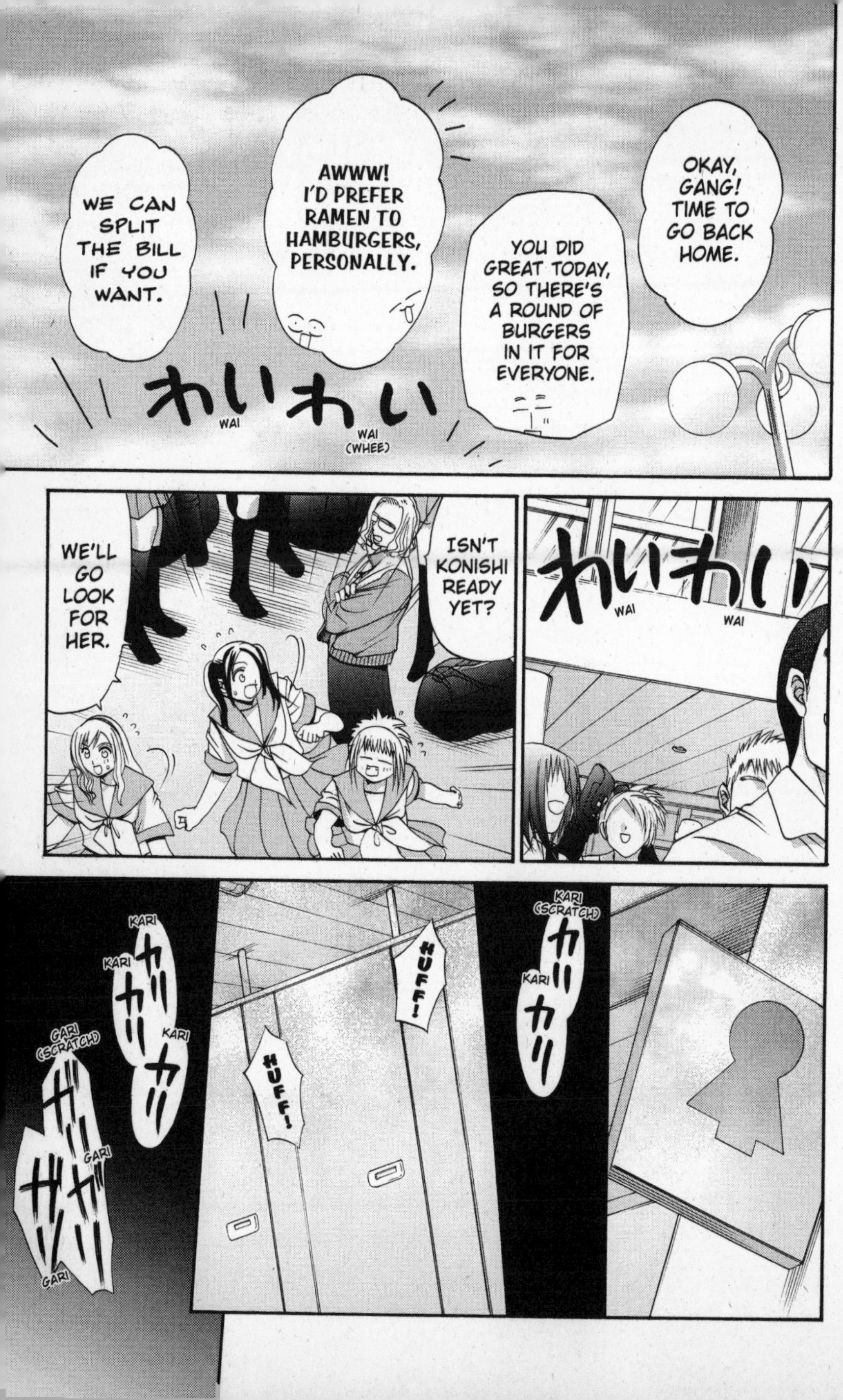
OKAY, GANG! TIME TO GO BACK HOME.
YOU DID GREAT TODAY, SO THERE'S A ROUND OF BURGERS IN IT FOR EVERYONE.
AWWW! I'D PREFER RAMEN TO HAMBURGERS, PERSONALLY.
WE CAN SPLIT THE BILL IF YOU WANT.
わいわい
WAI WAI (WHEE)
わいわい
WAI WAI
ISN'T KONISHI READY YET?
WE'LL GO LOOK FOR HER.
KARI (SCRATCH) カリ
KARI カリ
HUFF!
HUFF!
KARI カリ
KARI カリ
KARI カリ
GARI (SCRATCH) ガリ
GARI ガリ
GARI

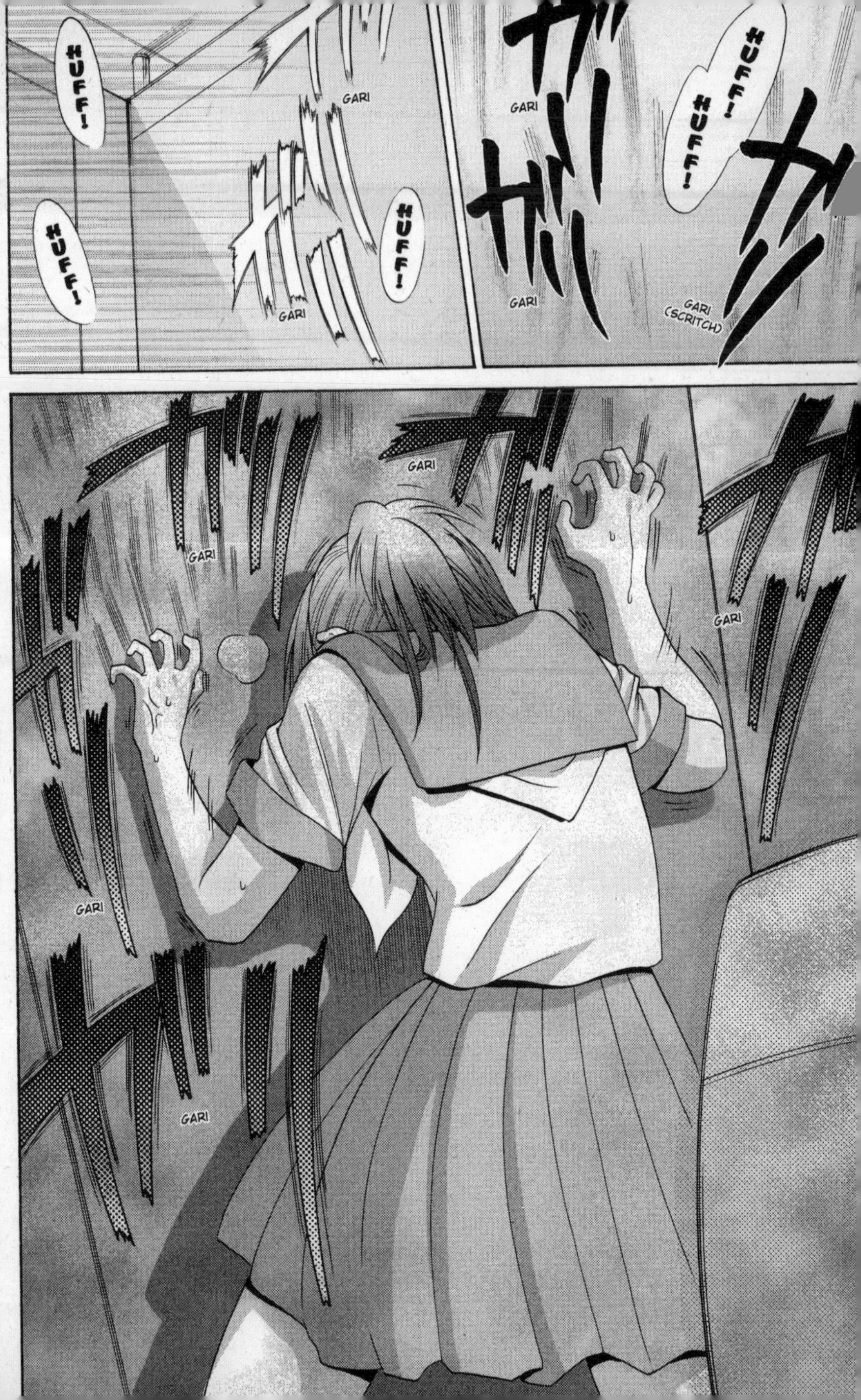
HUFF!
HUFF!
HUFF!
GARI
GARI (SCRITCH)
GARI
GARI
HUFF!
GARI
HUFF!
HUFF!
GARI
GARI
GARI
GARI
GARI

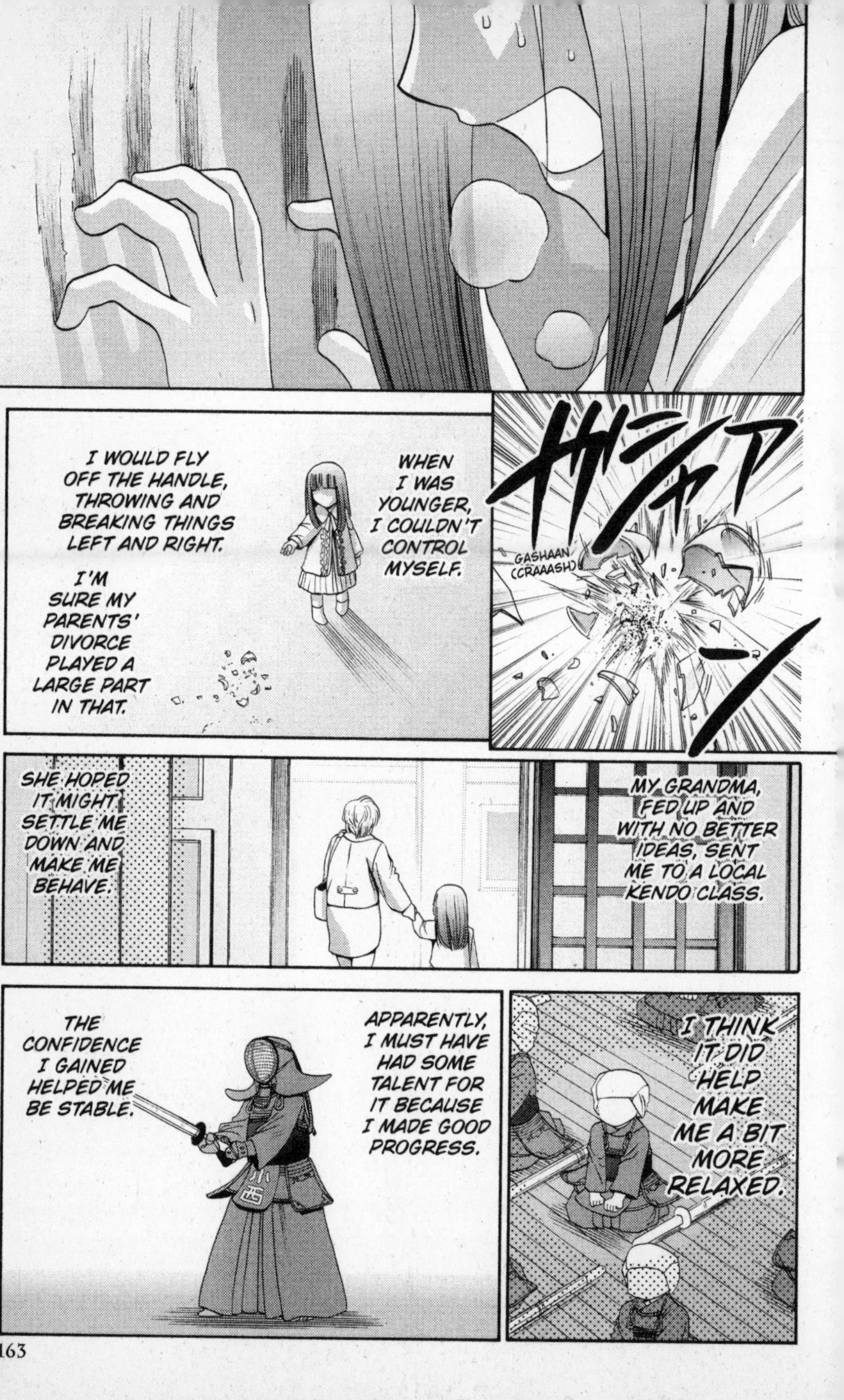
GASHAAN (CRAAASH)
WHEN I WAS YOUNGER, I COULDN'T CONTROL MYSELF.
I WOULD FLY OFF THE HANDLE, THROWING AND BREAKING THINGS LEFT AND RIGHT.
I'M SURE MY PARENTS' DIVORCE PLAYED A LARGE PART IN THAT.
MY GRANDMA, FED UP AND WITH NO BETTER IDEAS, SENT ME TO A LOCAL KENDO CLASS.
SHE HOPED IT MIGHT SETTLE ME DOWN AND MAKE ME BEHAVE.
I THINK IT DID HELP MAKE ME A BIT MORE RELAXED.
APPARENTLY, I MUST HAVE HAD SOME TALENT FOR IT BECAUSE I MADE GOOD PROGRESS.
THE CONFIDENCE I GAINED HELPED ME BE STABLE.

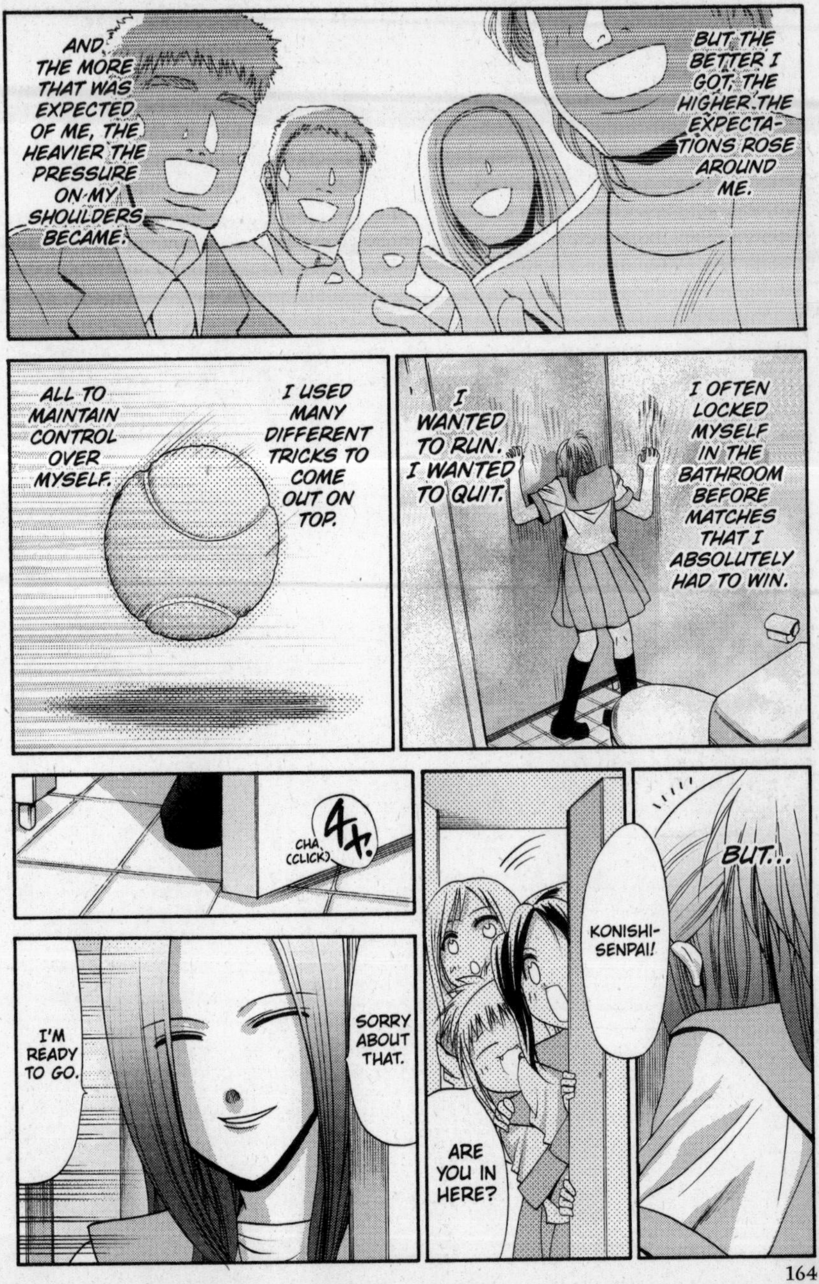
BUT THE BETTER I GOT, THE HIGHER THE EXPECTATIONS ROSE AROUND ME.
AND THE MORE THAT WAS EXPECTED OF ME, THE HEAVIER THE PRESSURE ON MY SHOULDERS BECAME.
I OFTEN LOCKED MYSELF IN THE BATHROOM BEFORE MATCHES THAT I ABSOLUTELY HAD TO WIN.
I WANTED TO RUN. I WANTED TO QUIT.
I USED MANY DIFFERENT TRICKS TO COME OUT ON TOP.
ALL TO MAINTAIN CONTROL OVER MYSELF.
BUT...
KONISHI-SENPAI!
ARE YOU IN HERE?
CHA (CLICK)
SORRY ABOUT THAT.
I'M READY TO GO.

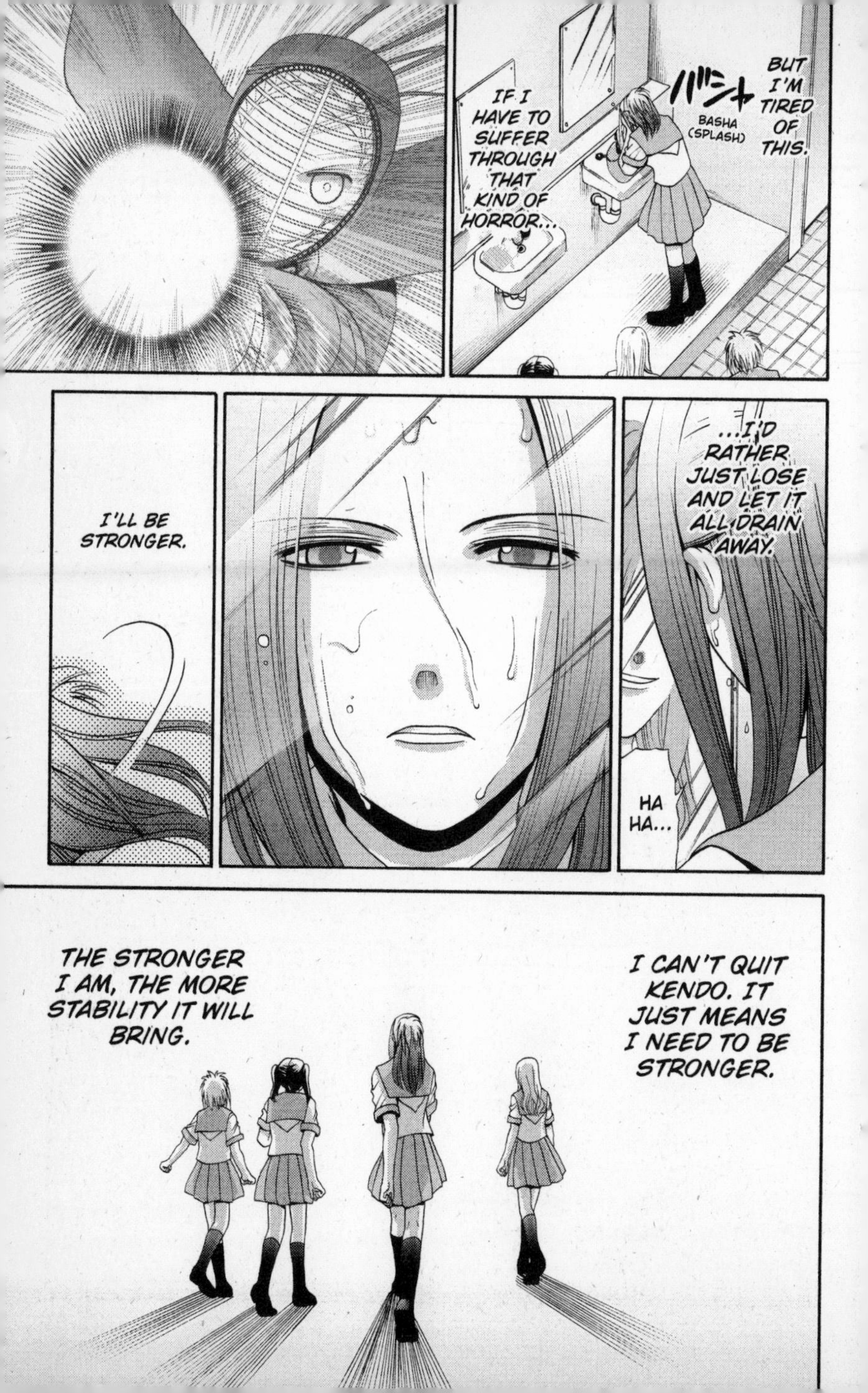
BUT I'M TIRED OF THIS.
バシャ
BASHA (SPLASH)
IF I HAVE TO SUFFER THROUGH THAT KIND OF HORROR...
...I'D RATHER JUST LOSE AND LET IT ALL DRAIN AWAY.
HA HA...
I'LL BE STRONGER.
I CAN'T QUIT KENDO. IT JUST MEANS I NEED TO BE STRONGER.
THE STRONGER I AM, THE MORE STABILITY IT WILL BRING.

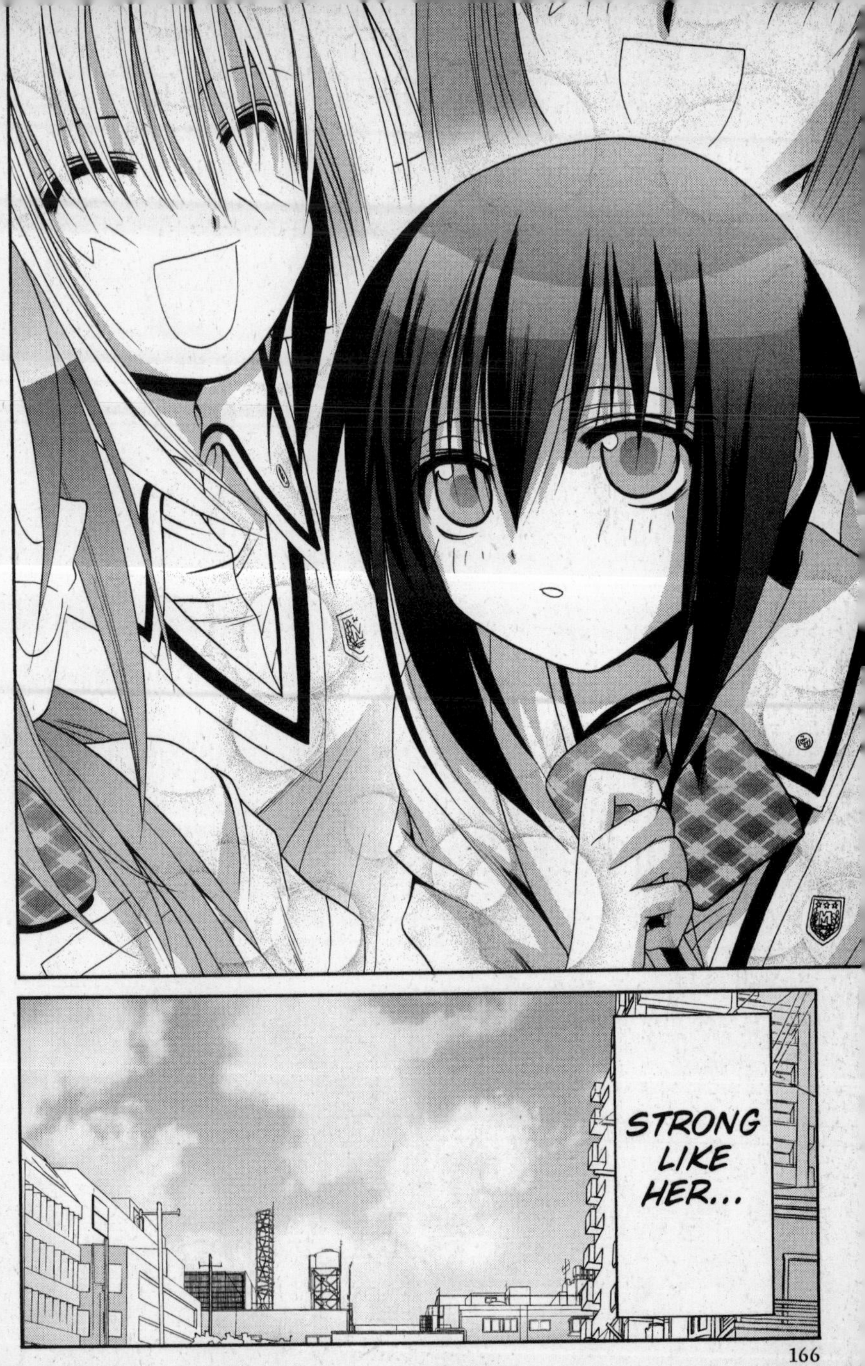
STRONG LIKE HER...

BAMBOO BLADE

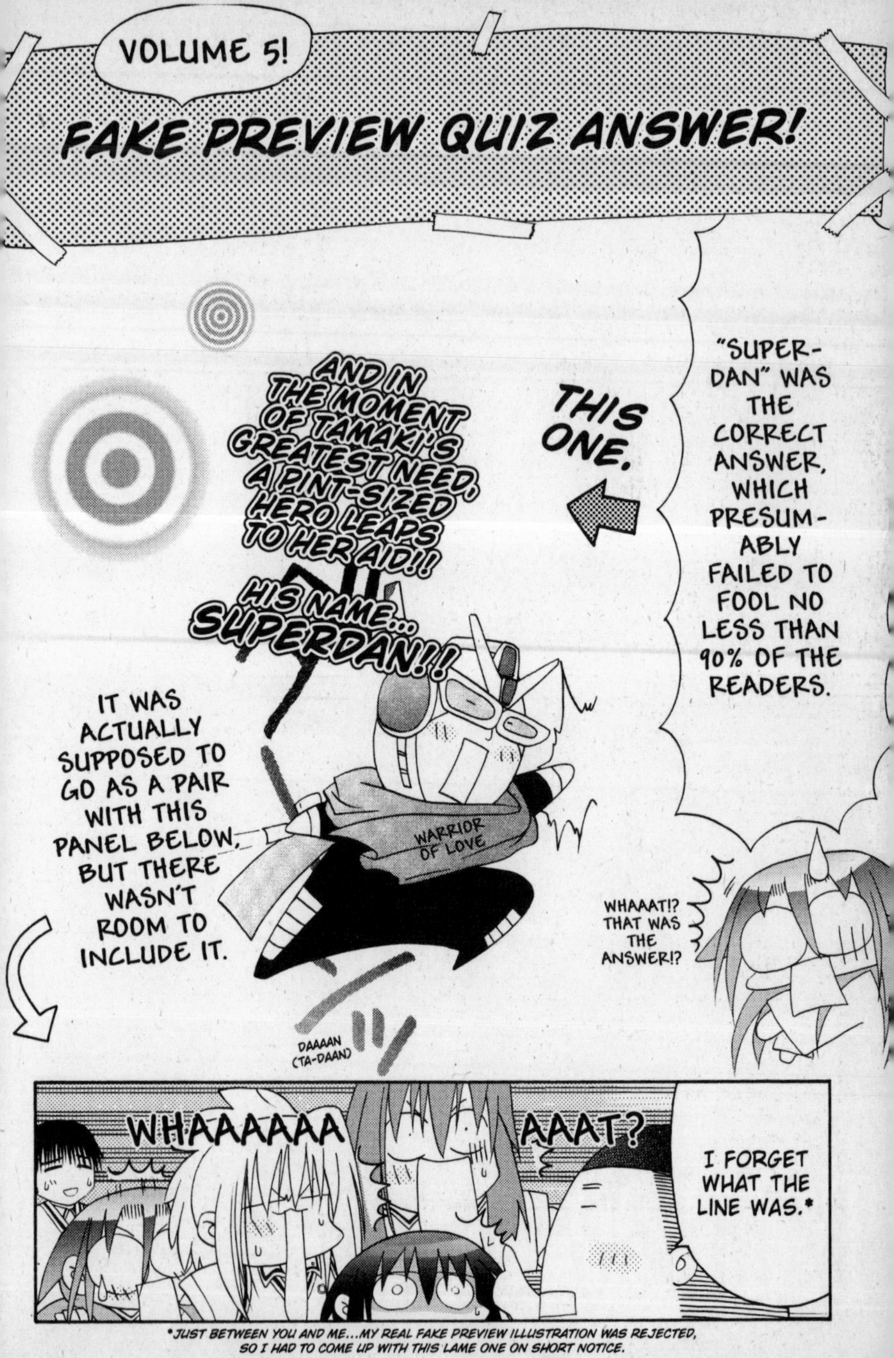
VOLUME 5!
FAKE PREVIEW QUIZ ANSWER!
"SUPER-DAN" WAS THE CORRECT ANSWER, WHICH PRESUMABLY FAILED TO FOOL NO LESS THAN 90% OF THE READERS.
THIS ONE.
AND IN THE MOMENT OF TAMAKI'S GREATEST NEED, A PINT-SIZED HERO LEAPS TO HER AID!!
HIS NAME... SUPERDAN!!
WARRIOR OF LOVE
WHAAAT!? THAT WAS THE ANSWER!?
IT WAS ACTUALLY SUPPOSED TO GO AS A PAIR WITH THIS PANEL BELOW, BUT THERE WASN'T ROOM TO INCLUDE IT.
DAAAAN (TA-DAAN)
I FORGET WHAT THE LINE WAS.*
WHAAAAAAAAAT?

*JUST BETWEEN YOU AND ME...MY REAL FAKE PREVIEW ILLUSTRATION WAS REJECTED, SO I HAD TO COME UP WITH THIS LAME ONE ON SHORT NOTICE.

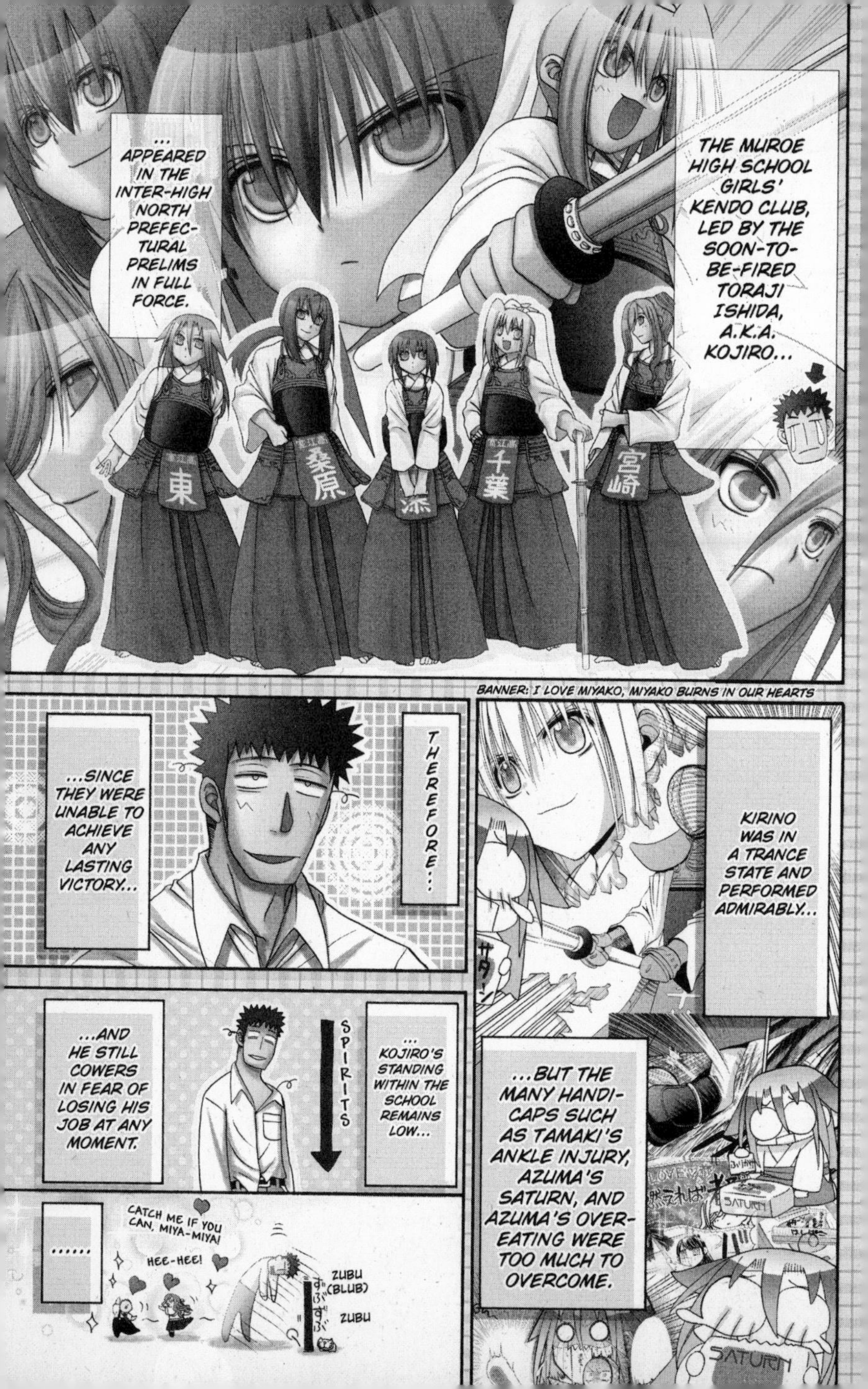
THE MUROE HIGH SCHOOL GIRLS' KENDO CLUB, LED BY THE SOON-TO-BE-FIRED TORAJI ISHIDA, A.K.A. KOJIRO...
...APPEARED IN THE INTER-HIGH NORTH PREFECTURAL PRELIMS IN FULL FORCE.
宮崎
千葉
添
桑原
東
BANNER: I LOVE MIYAKO, MIYAKO BURNS IN OUR HEARTS
KIRINO WAS IN A TRANCE STATE AND PERFORMED ADMIRABLY...
...BUT THE MANY HANDICAPS SUCH AS TAMAKI'S ANKLE INJURY, AZUMA'S SATURN, AND AZUMA'S OVER-EATING WERE TOO MUCH TO OVERCOME.
SATURN
SATURN
THEREFORE...
...SINCE THEY WERE UNABLE TO ACHIEVE ANY LASTING VICTORY...
...KOJIRO'S STANDING WITHIN THE SCHOOL REMAINS LOW...
SPIRITS
...AND HE STILL COWERS IN FEAR OF LOSING HIS JOB AT ANY MOMENT.
ZUBU (BLUB)
ZUBU
CATCH ME IF YOU CAN, MIYA-MIYA!
HEE-HEE!
......

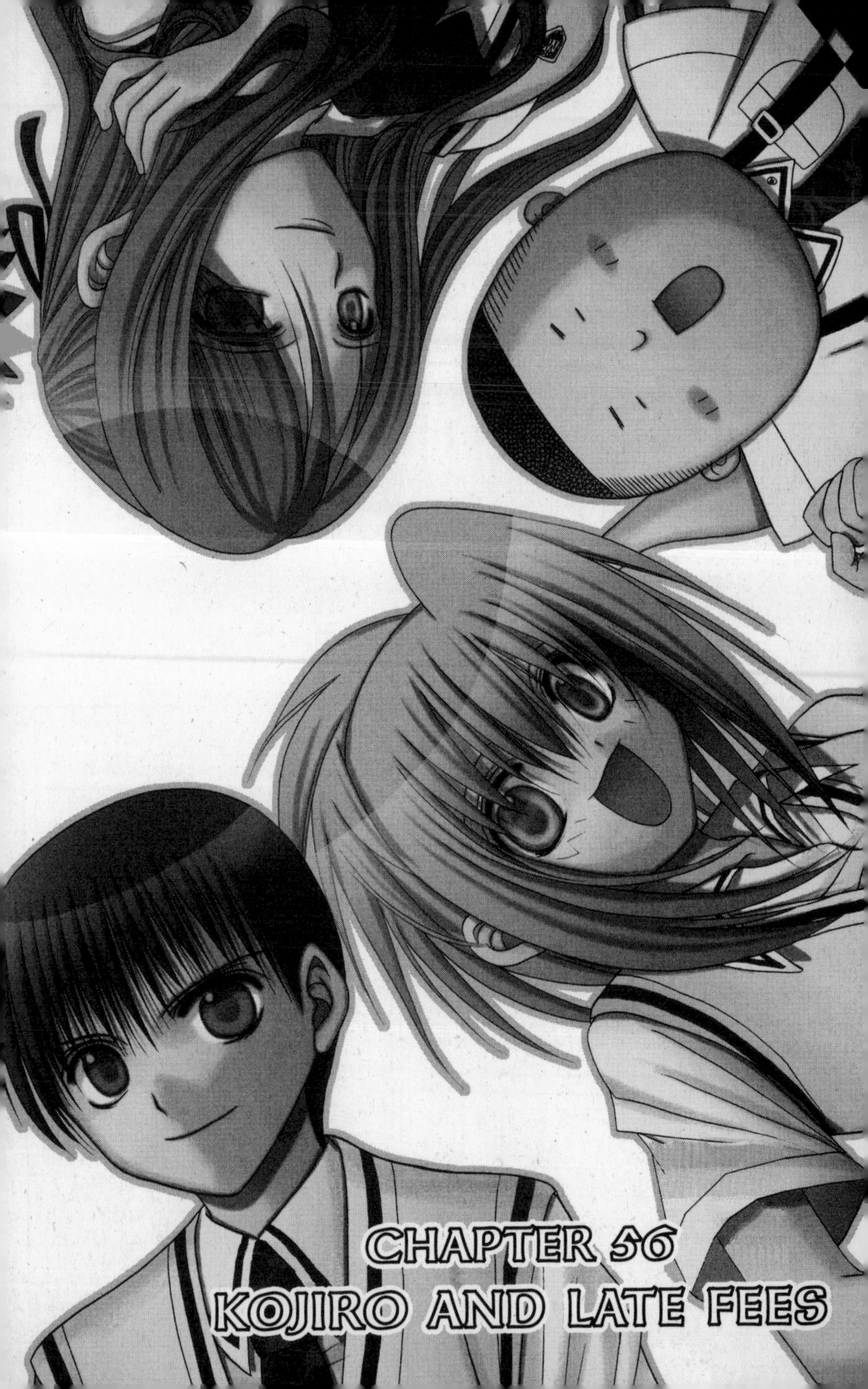
CHAPTER 56
KOJIRO AND LATE FEES

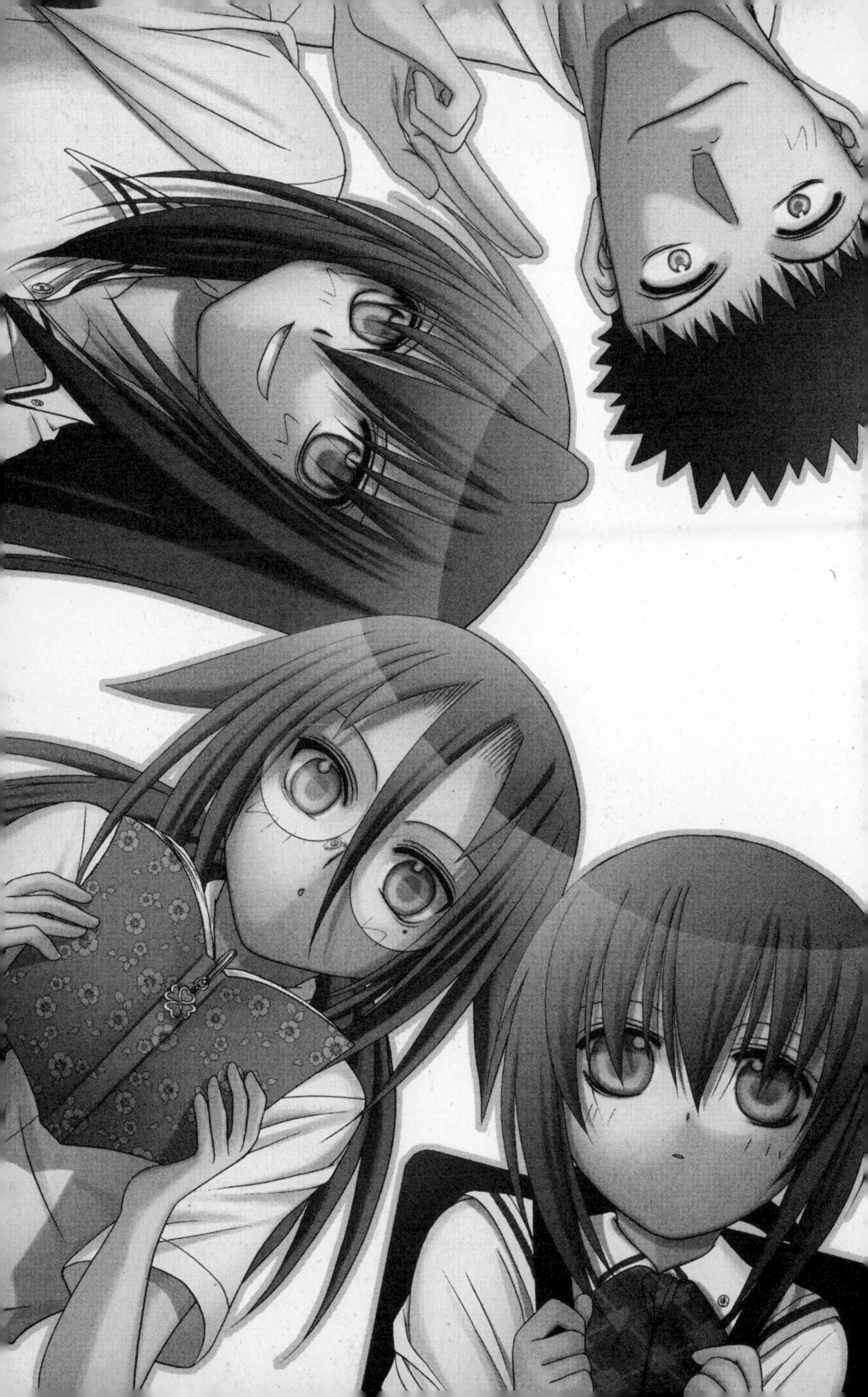

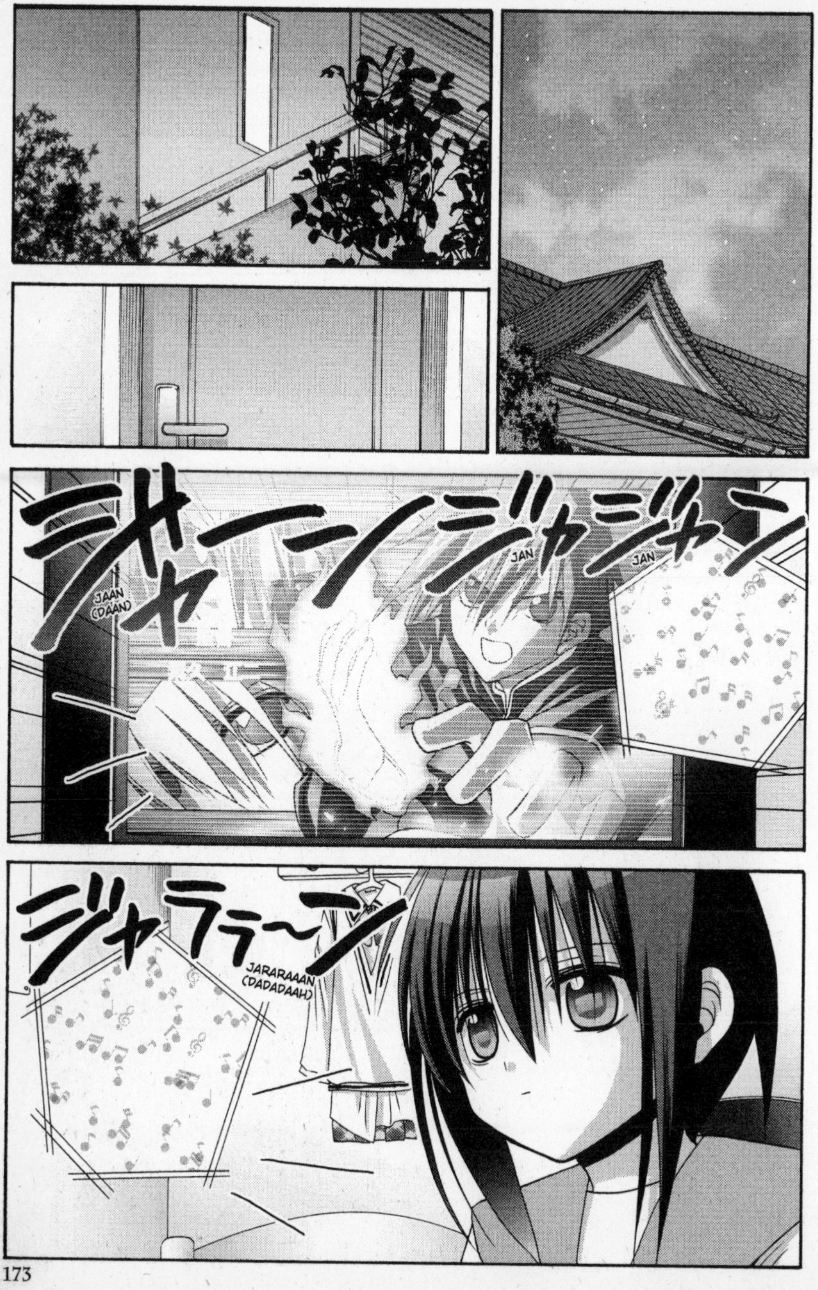
ジャーン
JAAN (DAAN)
ジャン
JAN
ジャン
JAN
ジャララ〜ン
JARARAAAN (DADADAAH)

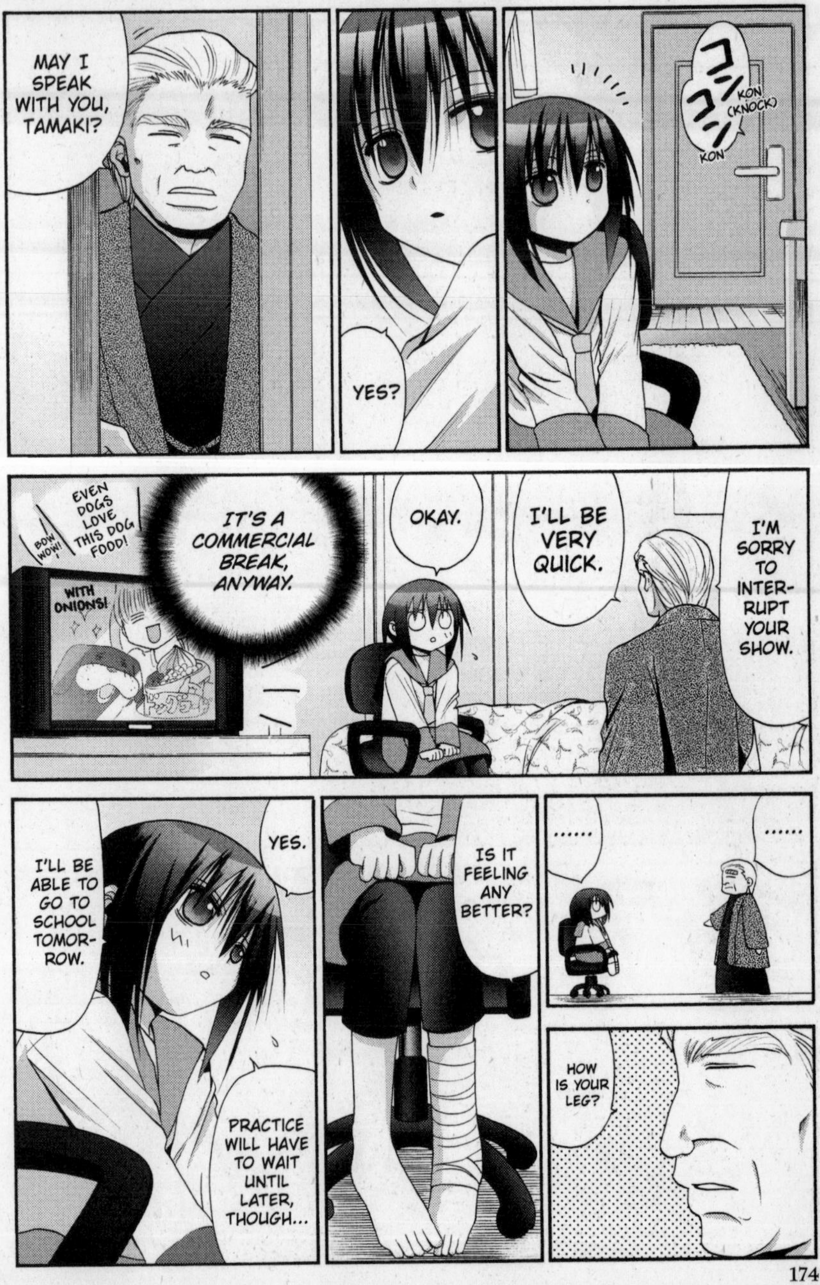
コン
コン
KON
(KNOCK)
KON
YES?
MAY I SPEAK WITH YOU, TAMAKI?
I'M SORRY TO INTER-RUPT YOUR SHOW.
I'LL BE VERY QUICK.
OKAY.
IT'S A COMMERCIAL BREAK, ANYWAY.
EVEN DOGS LOVE THIS DOG FOOD!
BOW WOW!
WITH ONIONS!
......
......
HOW IS YOUR LEG?
IS IT FEELING ANY BETTER?
YES.
I'LL BE ABLE TO GO TO SCHOOL TOMOR-ROW.
PRACTICE WILL HAVE TO WAIT UNTIL LATER, THOUGH...

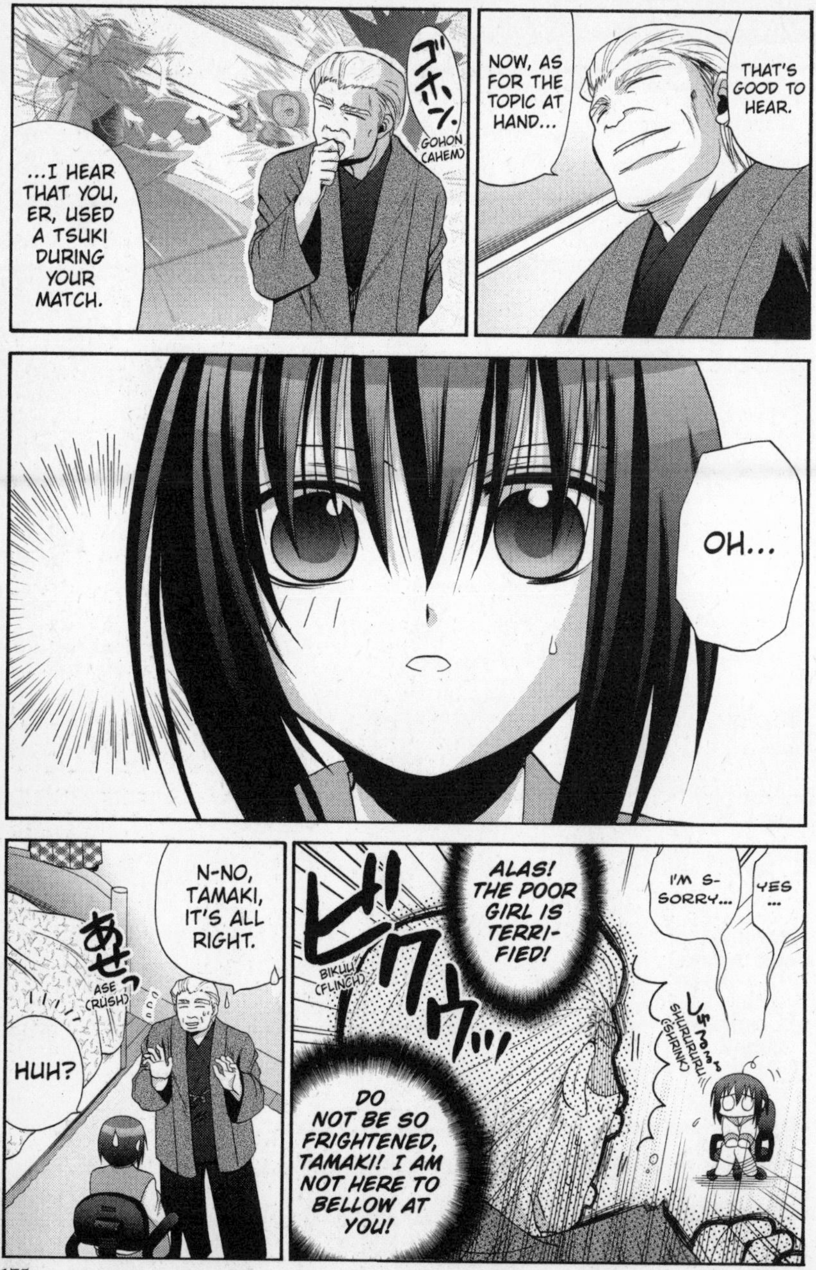
THAT'S GOOD TO HEAR.
NOW, AS FOR THE TOPIC AT HAND...
ゴホン.
GOHON (AHEM)
...I HEAR THAT YOU, ER, USED A TSUKI DURING YOUR MATCH.
OH...
YES ...
I'M S-SORRY...
SHURURURU (SHRINK)
ALAS! THE POOR GIRL IS TERRIFIED!
ビクゥッ
BIKUU (FLINCH)
DO NOT BE SO FRIGHTENED, TAMAKI! I AM NOT HERE TO BELLOW AT YOU!
N-NO, TAMAKI, IT'S ALL RIGHT.
あせっ
ASE (RUSH)
HUH?

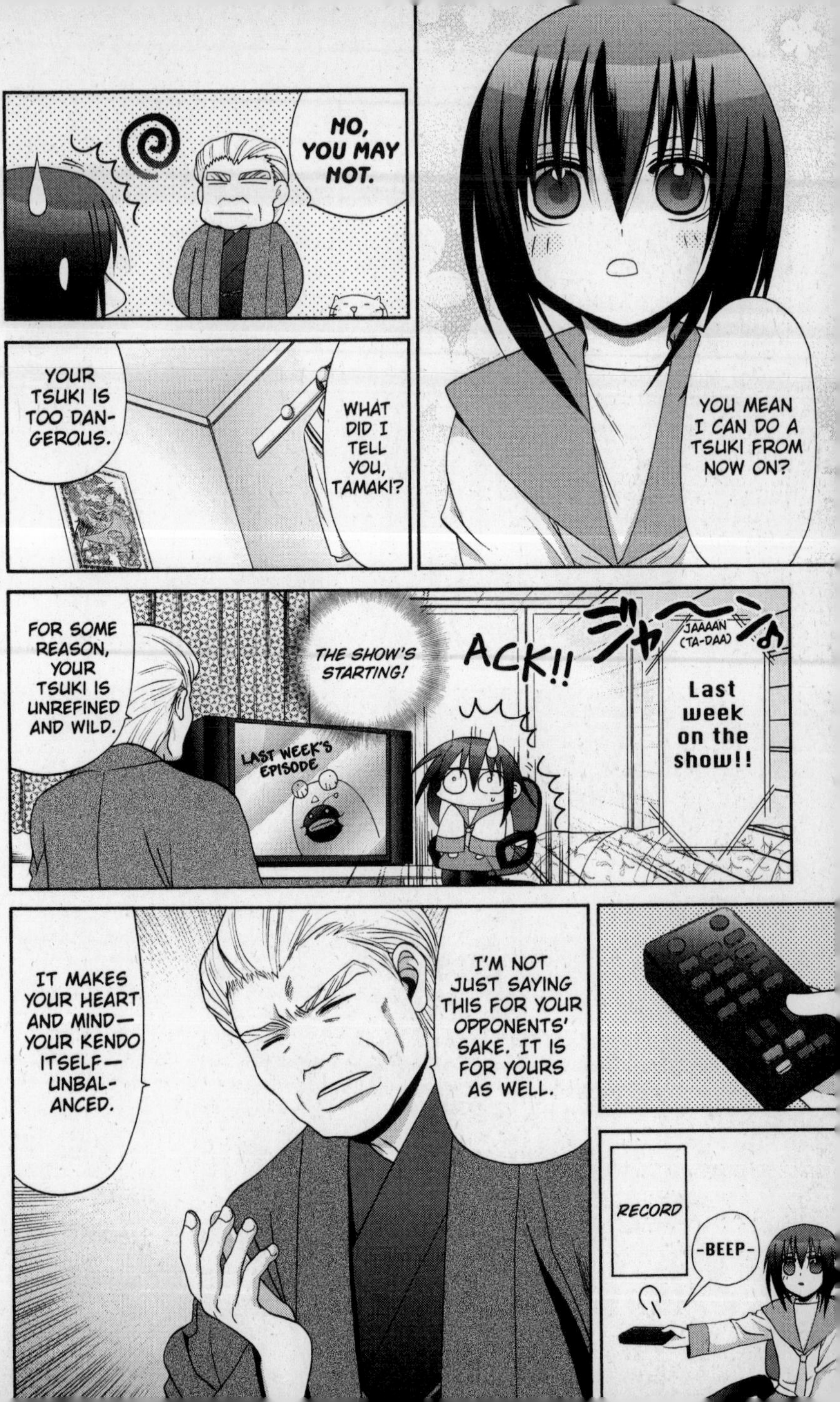
YOU MEAN I CAN DO A TSUKI FROM NOW ON?
NO, YOU MAY NOT.
WHAT DID I TELL YOU, TAMAKI?
YOUR TSUKI IS TOO DAN-GEROUS.
ジャ〜ン
JAAAAN (TA-DAA)
Last week on the show!!
ACK!!
THE SHOW'S STARTING!
FOR SOME REASON, YOUR TSUKI IS UNREFINED AND WILD.
LAST WEEK'S EPISODE
-BEEP-
RECORD
I'M NOT JUST SAYING THIS FOR YOUR OPPONENTS' SAKE. IT IS FOR YOURS AS WELL.
IT MAKES YOUR HEART AND MIND—YOUR KENDO ITSELF—UNBAL-ANCED.

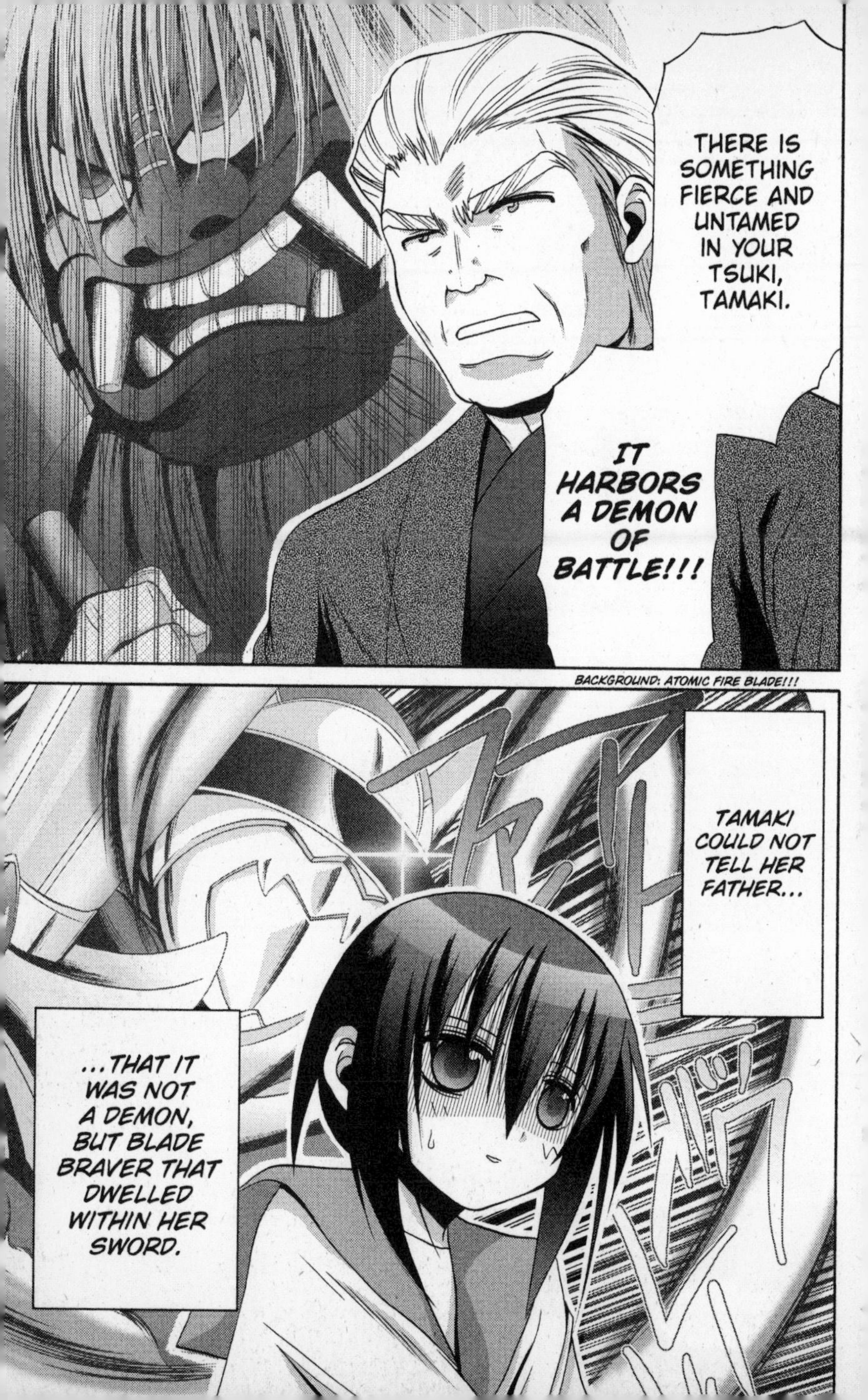
THERE IS SOMETHING FIERCE AND UNTAMED IN YOUR TSUKI, TAMAKI.
IT HARBORS A DEMON OF BATTLE!!!
BACKGROUND: ATOMIC FIRE BLADE!!!
TAMAKI COULD NOT TELL HER FATHER...
...THAT IT WAS NOT A DEMON, BUT BLADE BRAVER THAT DWELLED WITHIN HER SWORD.

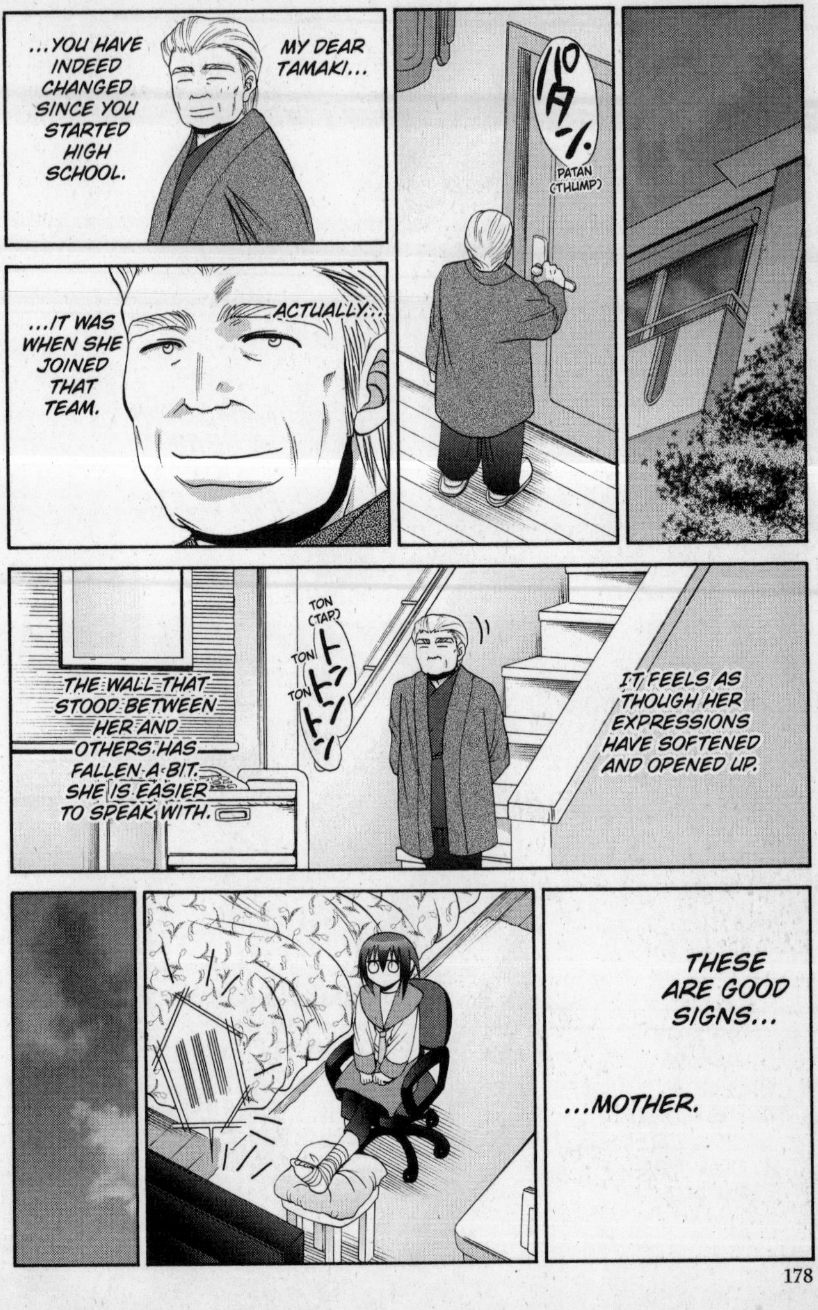
パタン。
PATAN (THUMP)
MY DEAR TAMAKI...
...YOU HAVE INDEED CHANGED SINCE YOU STARTED HIGH SCHOOL.
ACTUALLY...
...IT WAS WHEN SHE JOINED THAT TEAM.
IT FEELS AS THOUGH HER EXPRESSIONS HAVE SOFTENED AND OPENED UP.
トントントン
TON (TAP) TON TON
THE WALL THAT STOOD BETWEEN HER AND OTHERS HAS FALLEN A BIT. SHE IS EASIER TO SPEAK WITH.
THESE ARE GOOD SIGNS...
...MOTHER.

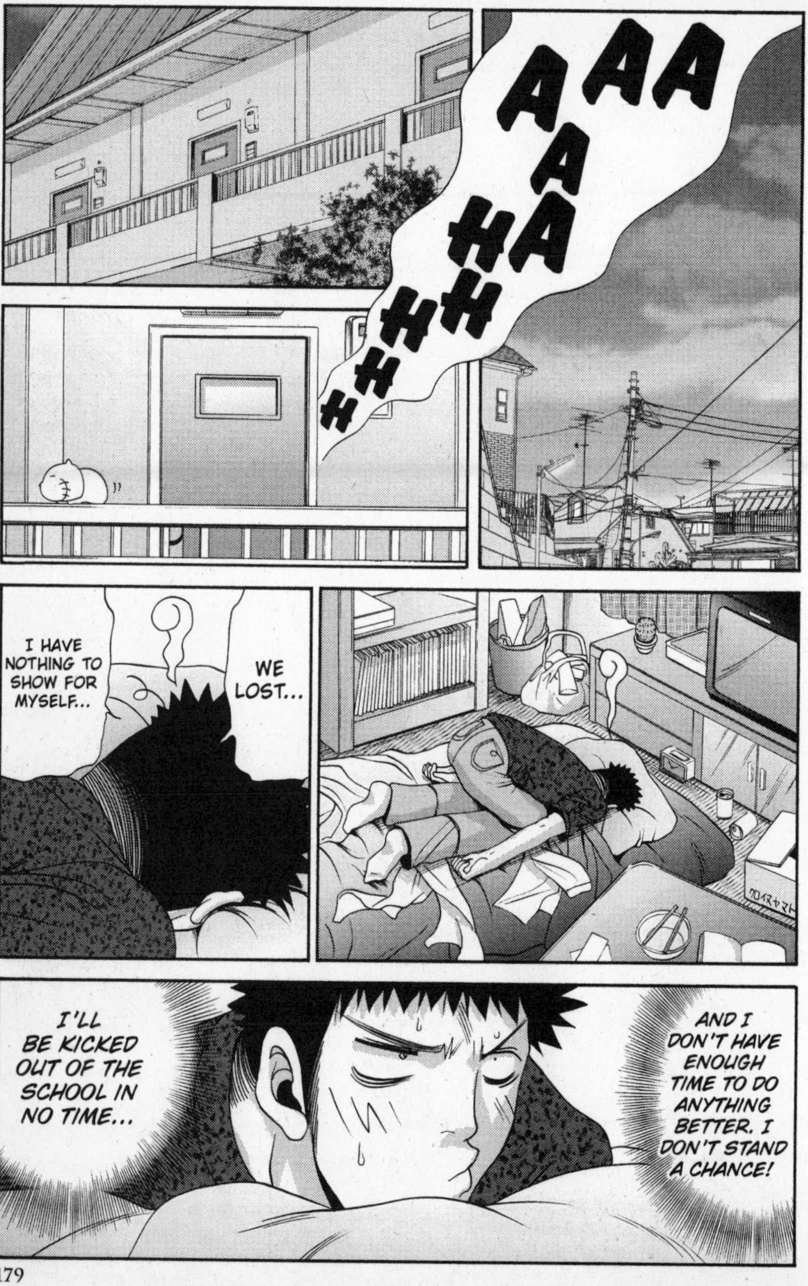

AAAAAAHHHHHH
WE LOST...
I HAVE NOTHING TO SHOW FOR MYSELF...
AND I DON'T HAVE ENOUGH TIME TO DO ANYTHING BETTER. I DON'T STAND A CHANCE!
I'LL BE KICKED OUT OF THE SCHOOL IN NO TIME...

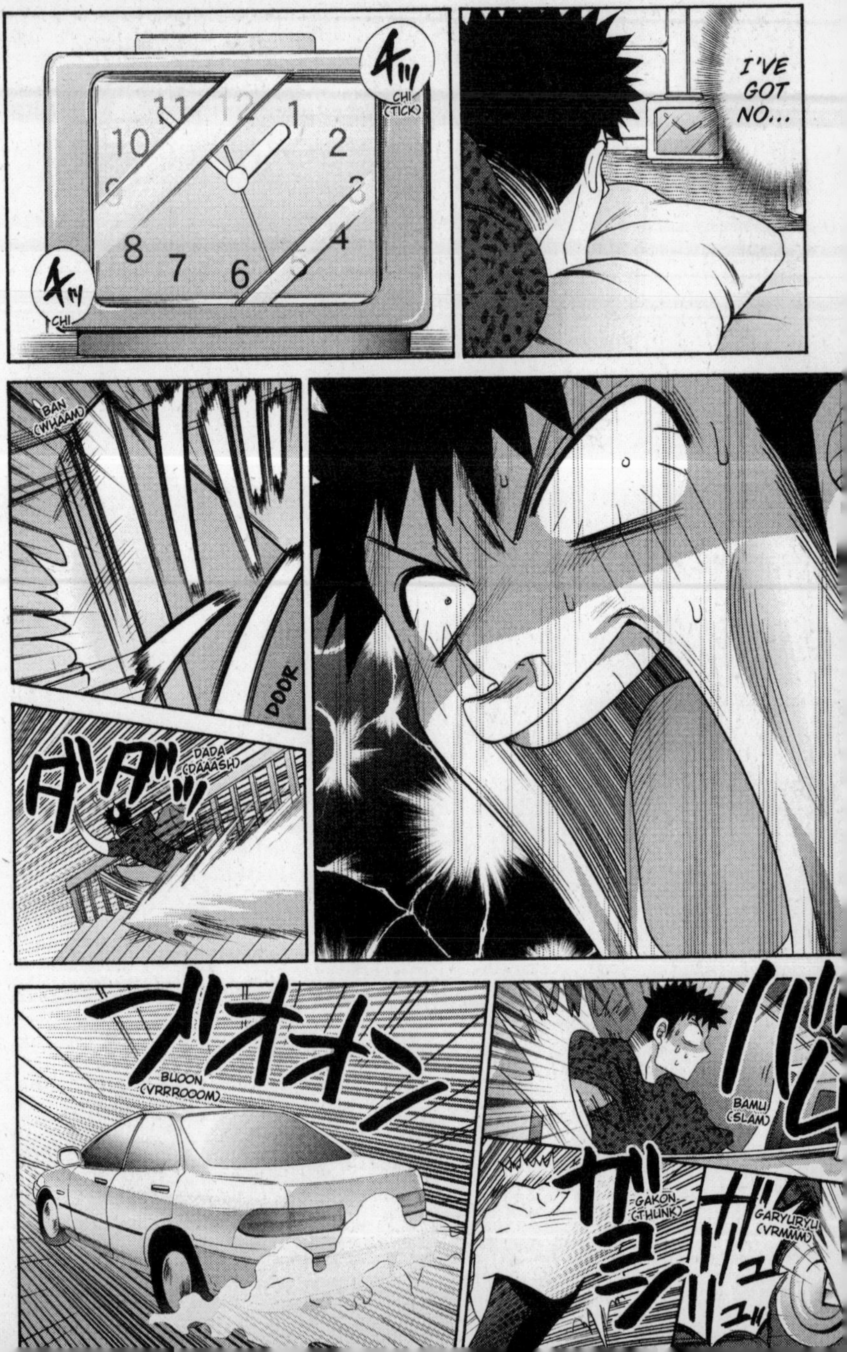
I'VE GOT NO...
チッ
CHI (TICK)
チッ
CHI
BAN (WHAAM)
DOOR
ダダッ
DADA (DAAASH)
バム
BAMU (SLAM)
ガコン
GAKON (THUNK)
GARYURYU (VRMMM)
ブオオン
BUOON (VRRROOOM)

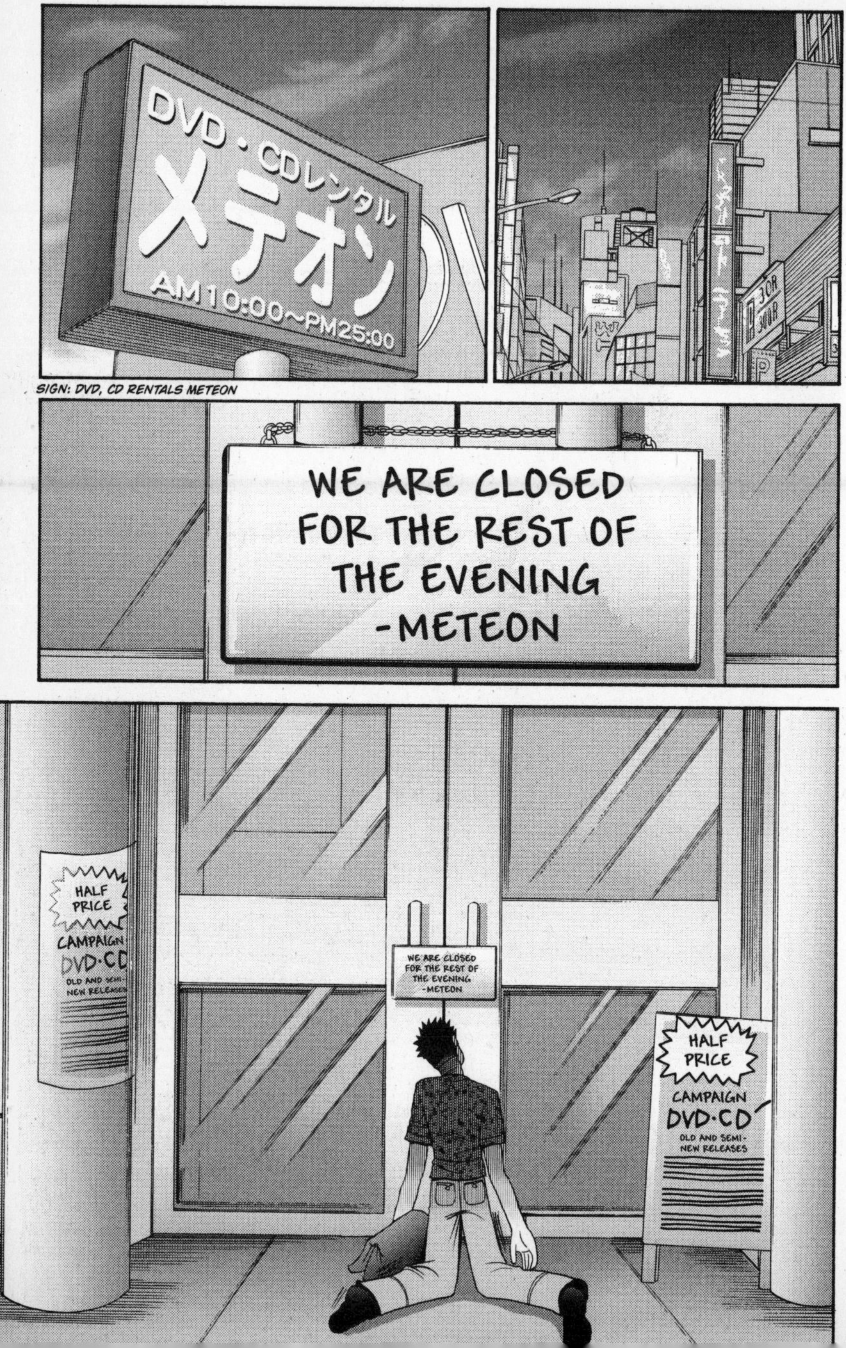
DVD・CDレンタル
メテオン
AM10:00〜PM25:00
SIGN: DVD, CD RENTALS METEON
WE ARE CLOSED FOR THE REST OF THE EVENING -METEON
HALF PRICE
CAMPAIGN
DVD·CD
OLD AND SEMI-NEW RELEASES
WE ARE CLOSED FOR THE REST OF THE EVENING -METEON
HALF PRICE
CAMPAIGN
DVD·CD
OLD AND SEMI-NEW RELEASES

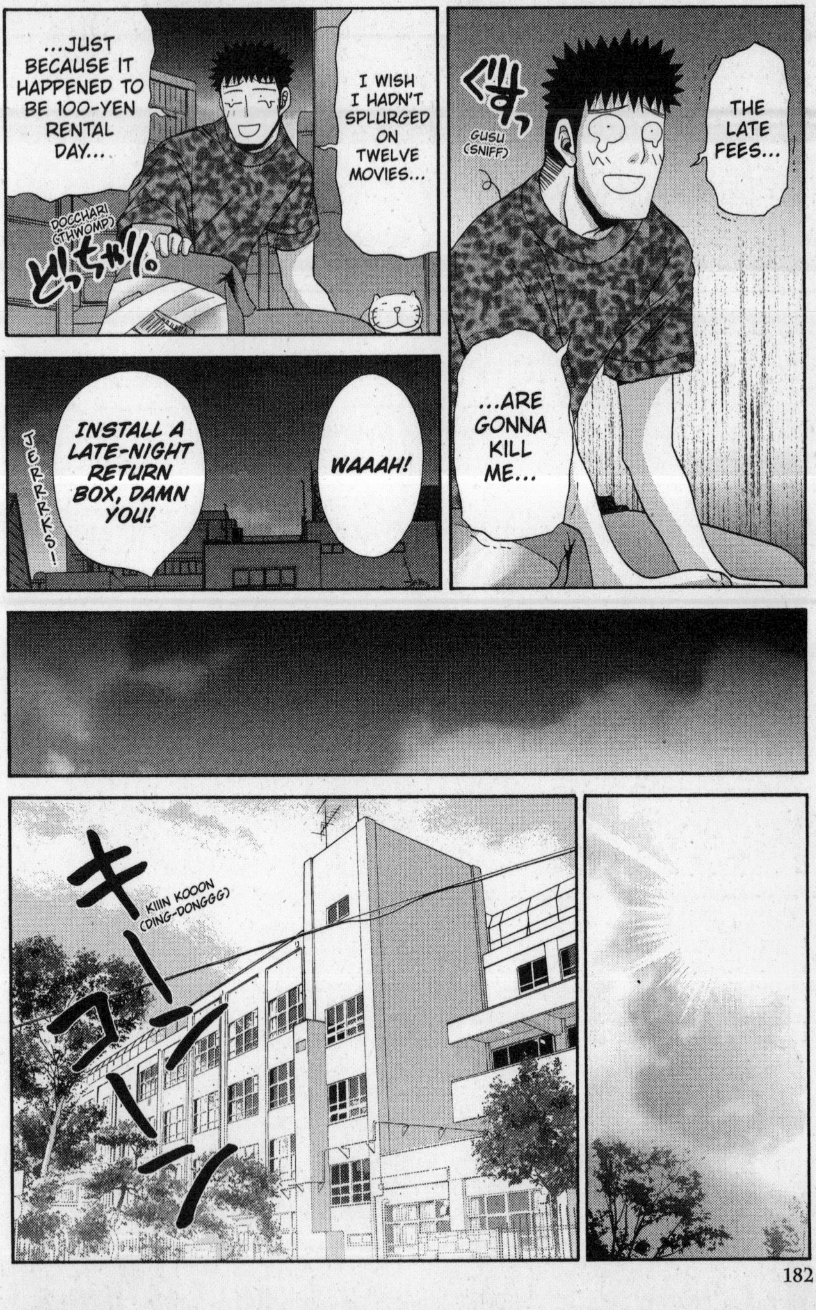
ぐすっ
GUSU (SNIFF)
THE LATE FEES...
...ARE GONNA KILL ME...
I WISH I HADN'T SPLURGED ON TWELVE MOVIES...
...JUST BECAUSE IT HAPPENED TO BE 100-YEN RENTAL DAY...
DOCCHARI (THWOMP)
どっちゃり。
WAAAH!
INSTALL A LATE-NIGHT RETURN BOX, DAMN YOU!
JERRRKS!
キーンコーン
KIIIN KOOON (DING-DONGGG)

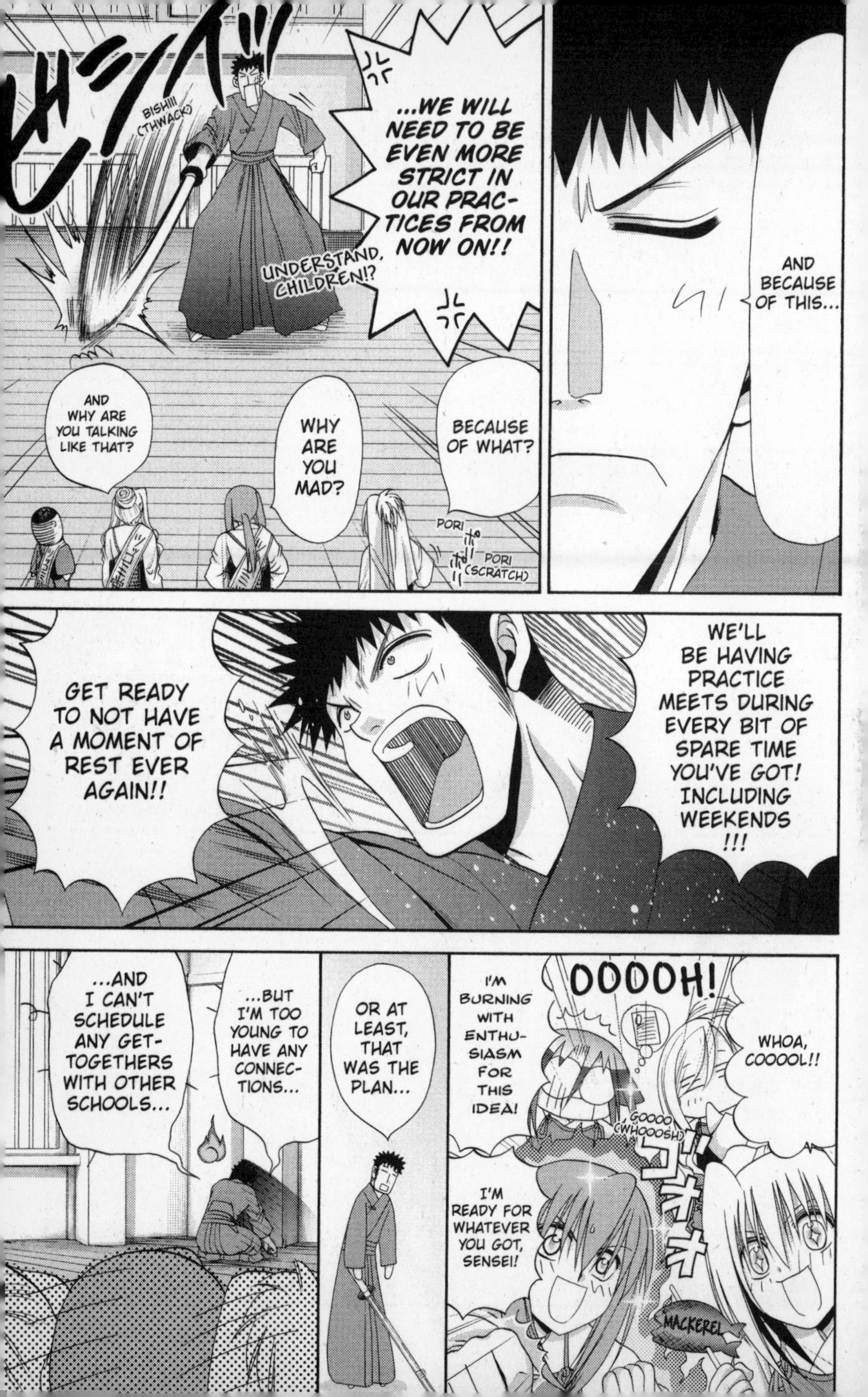
AND BECAUSE OF THIS...
...WE WILL NEED TO BE EVEN MORE STRICT IN OUR PRACTICES FROM NOW ON!!
UNDERSTAND, CHILDREN!?
BISHIII (THWACK)
BECAUSE OF WHAT?
PORI PORI (SCRATCH)
WHY ARE YOU MAD?
AND WHY ARE YOU TALKING LIKE THAT?
WE'LL BE HAVING PRACTICE MEETS DURING EVERY BIT OF SPARE TIME YOU'VE GOT! INCLUDING WEEKENDS!!!
GET READY TO NOT HAVE A MOMENT OF REST EVER AGAIN!!
OOOOH!
WHOA, COOOOL!!
I'M BURNING WITH ENTHUSIASM FOR THIS IDEA!
GOOOO (WHOOOSH)
I'M READY FOR WHATEVER YOU GOT, SENSEI!
MACKEREL
OR AT LEAST, THAT WAS THE PLAN...
...BUT I'M TOO YOUNG TO HAVE ANY CONNECTIONS...
...AND I CAN'T SCHEDULE ANY GET-TOGETHERS WITH OTHER SCHOOLS...

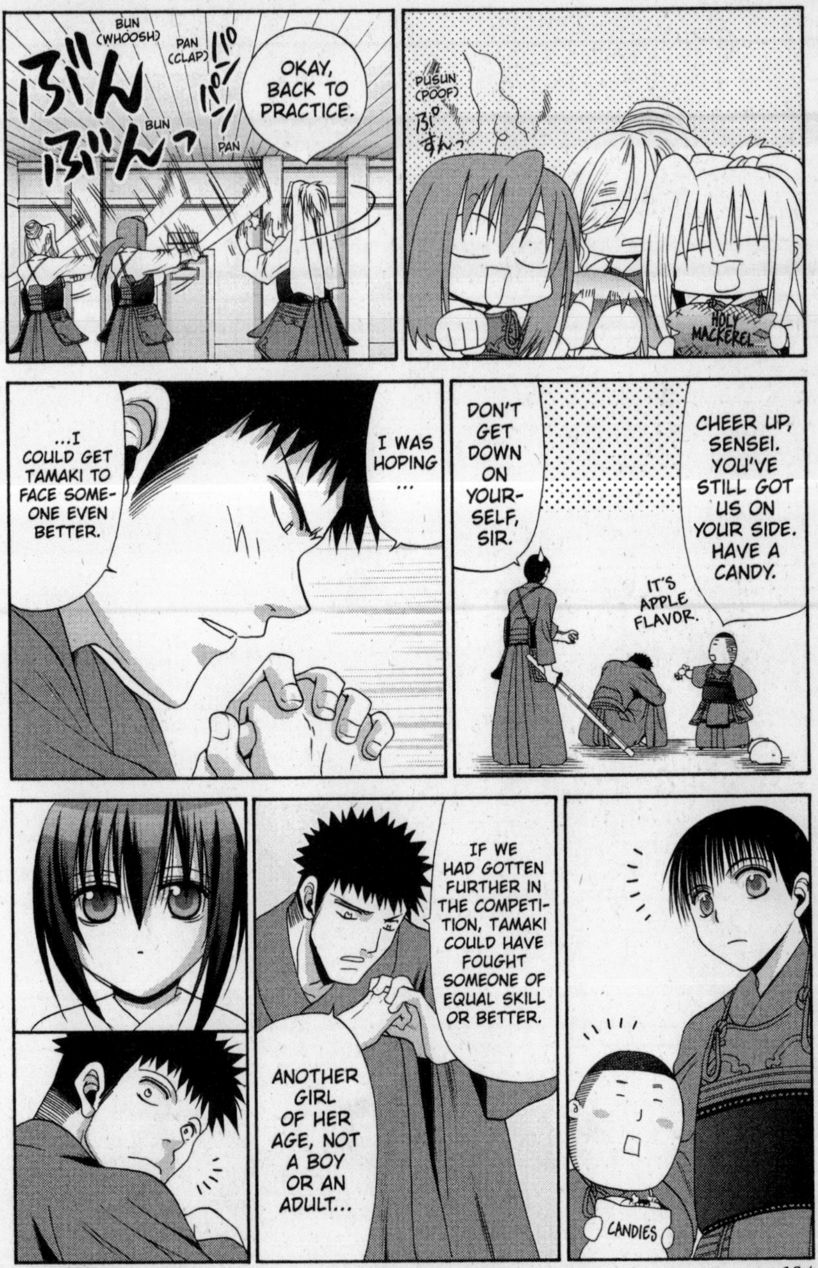
PUSUN (POOF)
ぷすんっ
HOLY MACKEREL
OKAY, BACK TO PRACTICE.
PAN (CLAP)
パンパン
PAN
BUN (WHOOSH)
ぶんぶんっ
BUN
CHEER UP, SENSEI. YOU'VE STILL GOT US ON YOUR SIDE. HAVE A CANDY.
IT'S APPLE FLAVOR.
DON'T GET DOWN ON YOURSELF, SIR.
I WAS HOPING...
...I COULD GET TAMAKI TO FACE SOMEONE EVEN BETTER.
CANDIES
IF WE HAD GOTTEN FURTHER IN THE COMPETITION, TAMAKI COULD HAVE FOUGHT SOMEONE OF EQUAL SKILL OR BETTER.
ANOTHER GIRL OF HER AGE, NOT A BOY OR AN ADULT...

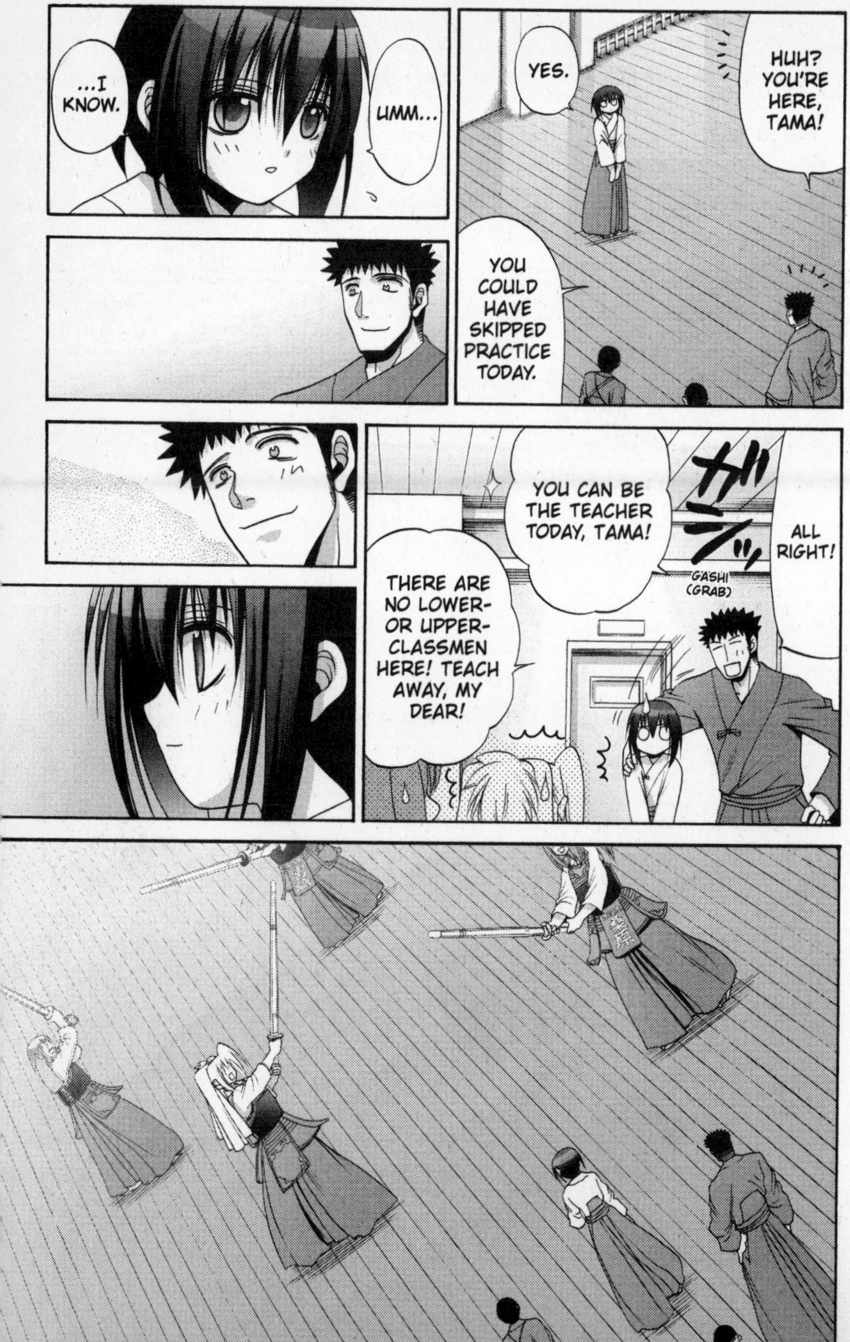
HUH? YOU'RE HERE, TAMA!
YES.
UMM...
...I KNOW.
YOU COULD HAVE SKIPPED PRACTICE TODAY.
ALL RIGHT!
GASHI (GRAB)
YOU CAN BE THE TEACHER TODAY, TAMA!
THERE ARE NO LOWER- OR UPPER-CLASSMEN HERE! TEACH AWAY, MY DEAR!

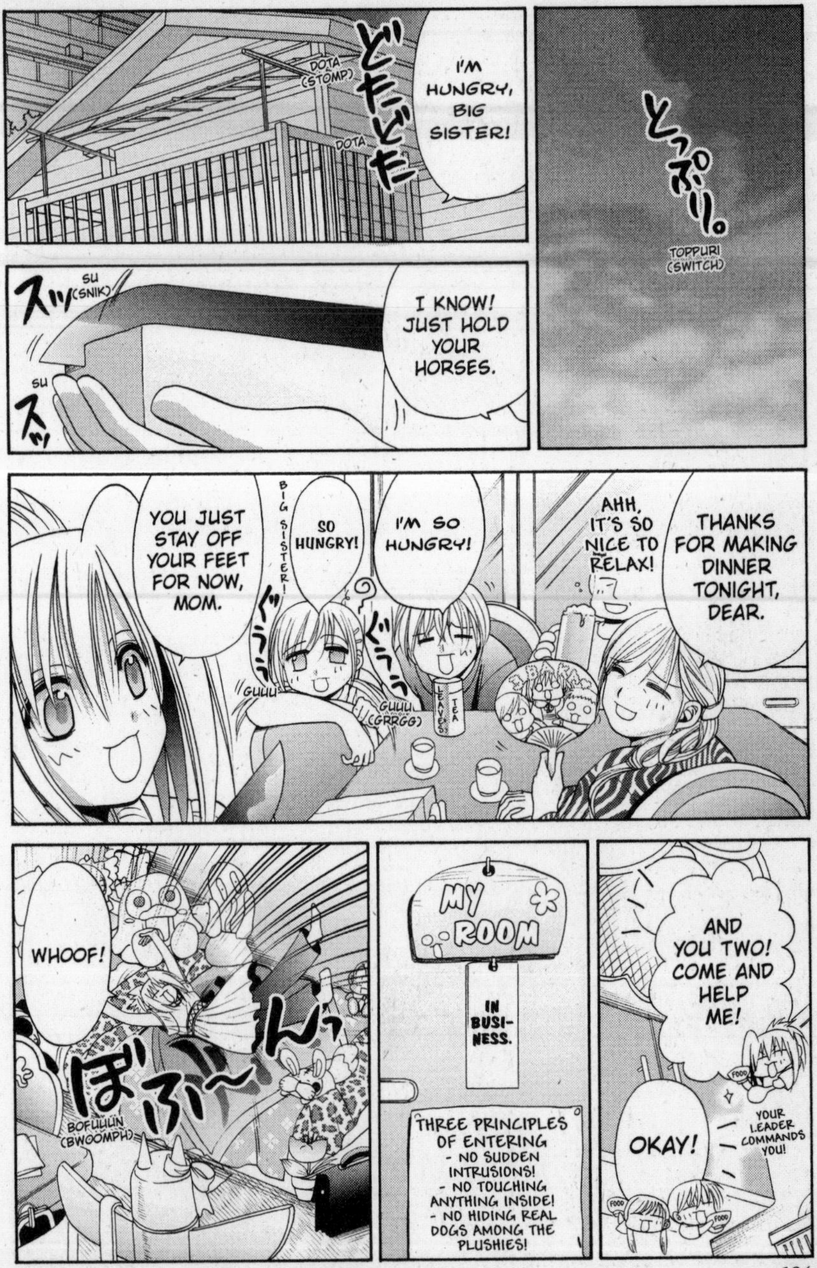
TOPPURI (SWITCH)
I'M HUNGRY, BIG SISTER!
DOTA (STOMP)
DOTA
I KNOW! JUST HOLD YOUR HORSES.
SU (SNIK)
SU
THANKS FOR MAKING DINNER TONIGHT, DEAR.
AHH, IT'S SO NICE TO RELAX!
I'M SO HUNGRY!
SO HUNGRY!
BIG SISTER!
YOU JUST STAY OFF YOUR FEET FOR NOW, MOM.
GUUU (GRRGG)
GUUU
TEA LEAVES
AND YOU TWO! COME AND HELP ME!
YOUR LEADER COMMANDS YOU!
FOOD
OKAY!
FOOD
FOOD
MY ROOM
IN BUSINESS.
THREE PRINCIPLES OF ENTERING
- NO SUDDEN INTRUSIONS!
- NO TOUCHING ANYTHING INSIDE!
- NO HIDING REAL DOGS AMONG THE PLUSHIES!
WHOOF!
BOFUUUN (BWOOMPH)

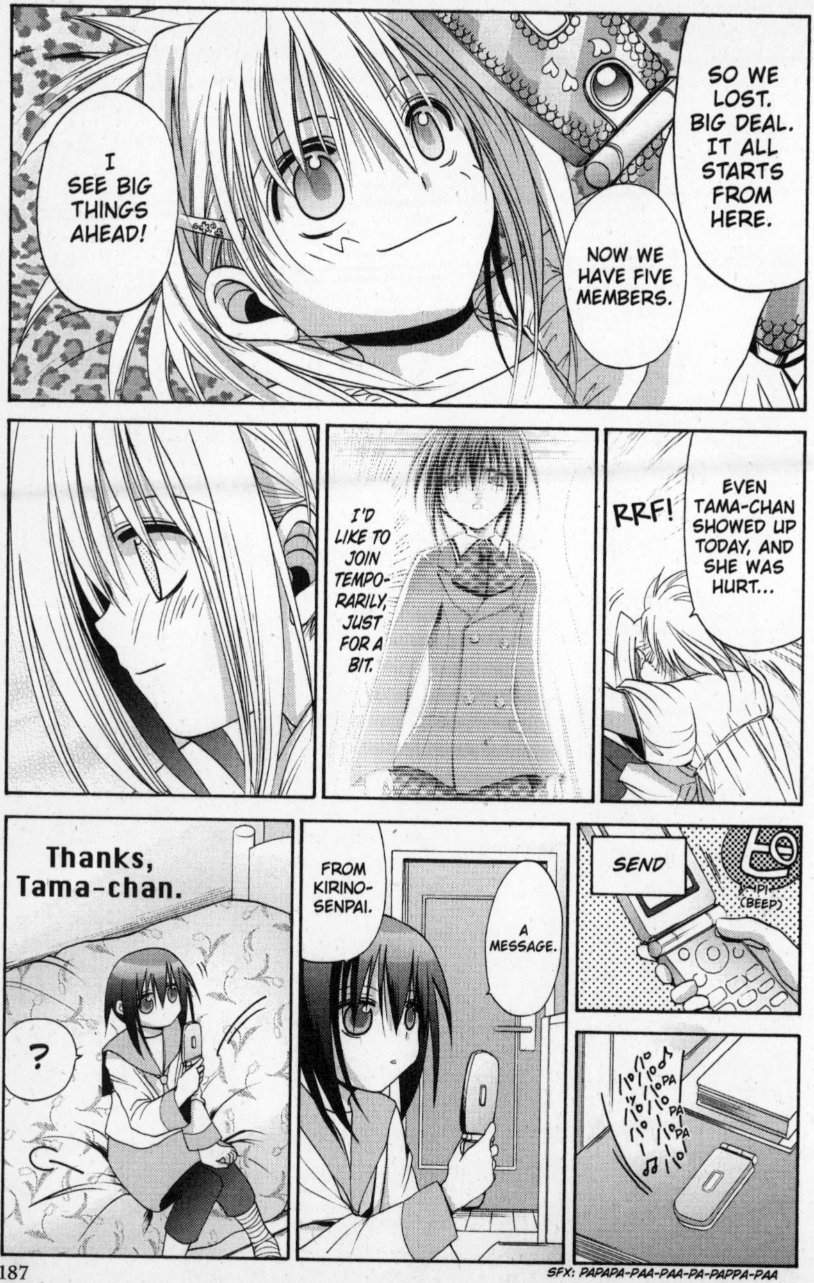
SO WE LOST. BIG DEAL. IT ALL STARTS FROM HERE.
NOW WE HAVE FIVE MEMBERS.
I SEE BIG THINGS AHEAD!
EVEN TAMA-CHAN SHOWED UP TODAY, AND SHE WAS HURT...
RRF!
I'D LIKE TO JOIN TEMPORARILY, JUST FOR A BIT.
SEND
PI (BEEP)
A MESSAGE.
FROM KIRINO-SENPAI.
Thanks, Tama-chan.
?

SFX: PAPAPA-PAA-PAA-PA-PAPPA-PAA

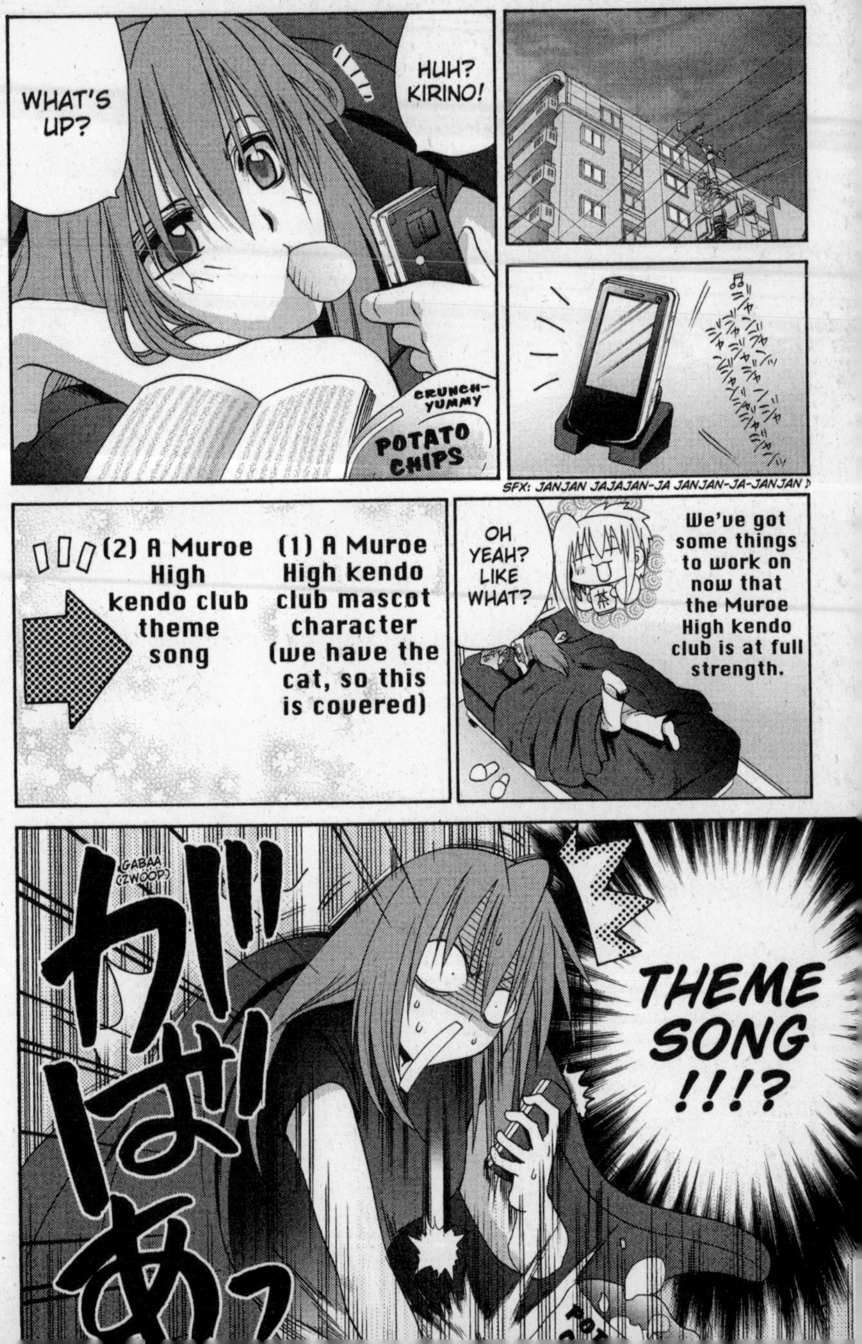
SFX: JANJAN JAJAJAN-JA JANJAN-JA-JANJAN ♪
HUH? KIRINO!
WHAT'S UP?
CRUNCH-YUMMY
POTATO CHIPS
We've got some things to work on now that the Muroe High kendo club is at full strength.
OH YEAH? LIKE WHAT?
(1) A Muroe High kendo club mascot character (we have the cat, so this is covered)
(2) A Muroe High kendo club theme song
THEME SONG!!!?
GABAA (ZWOOP)

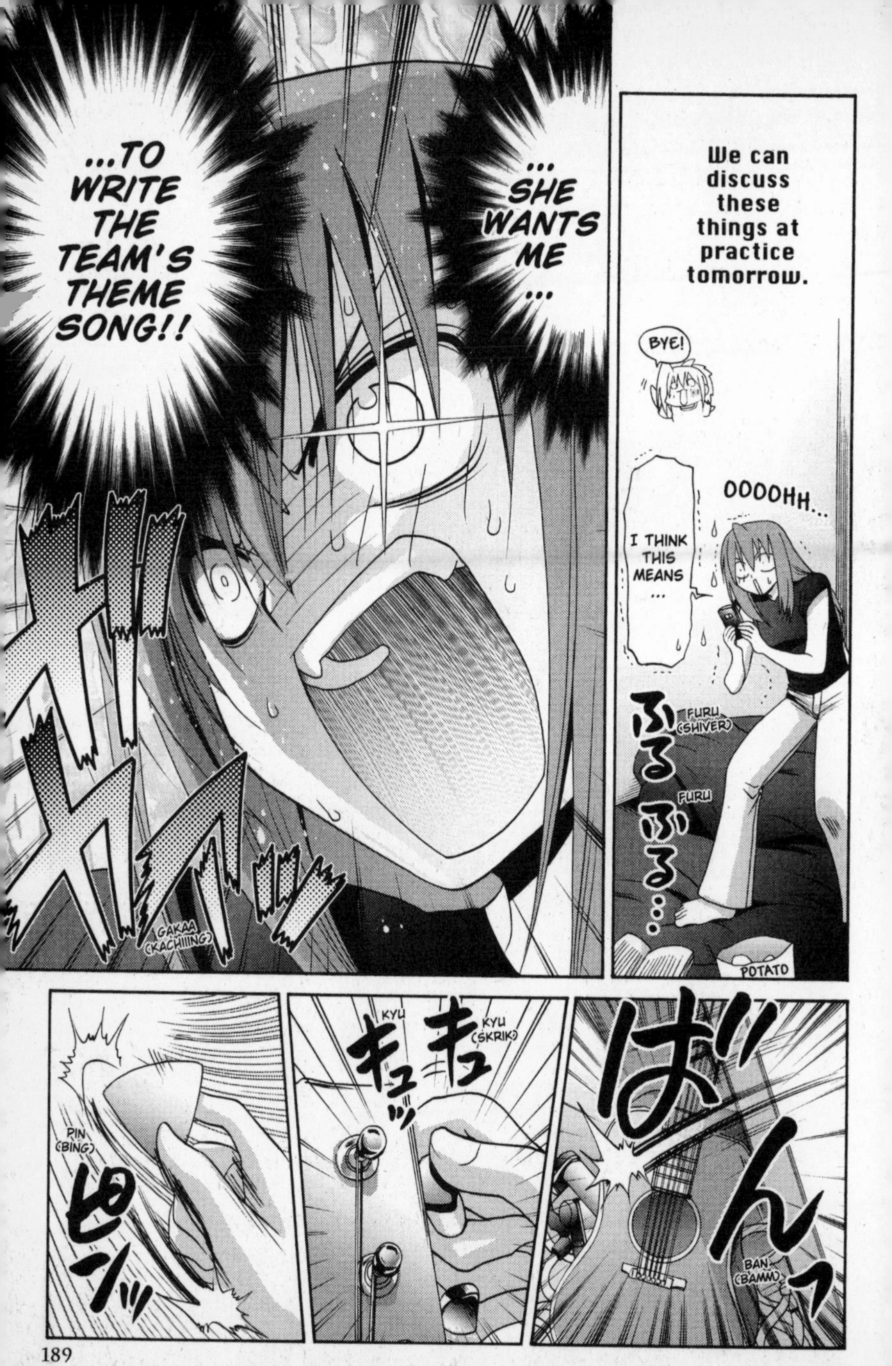
We can discuss these things at practice tomorrow.
BYE!
I THINK THIS MEANS ...
OOOOHH...
ふる
FURU (SHIVER)
ふる
FURU
ふる...
POTATO
... SHE WANTS ME ...
...TO WRITE THE TEAM'S THEME SONG!!
GAKAA (KACHIIING)
ばんっ
BAN (BAMM)
キュ
KYU
キュッ
KYU (SKRIK)
ピンッ
PIN (BING)

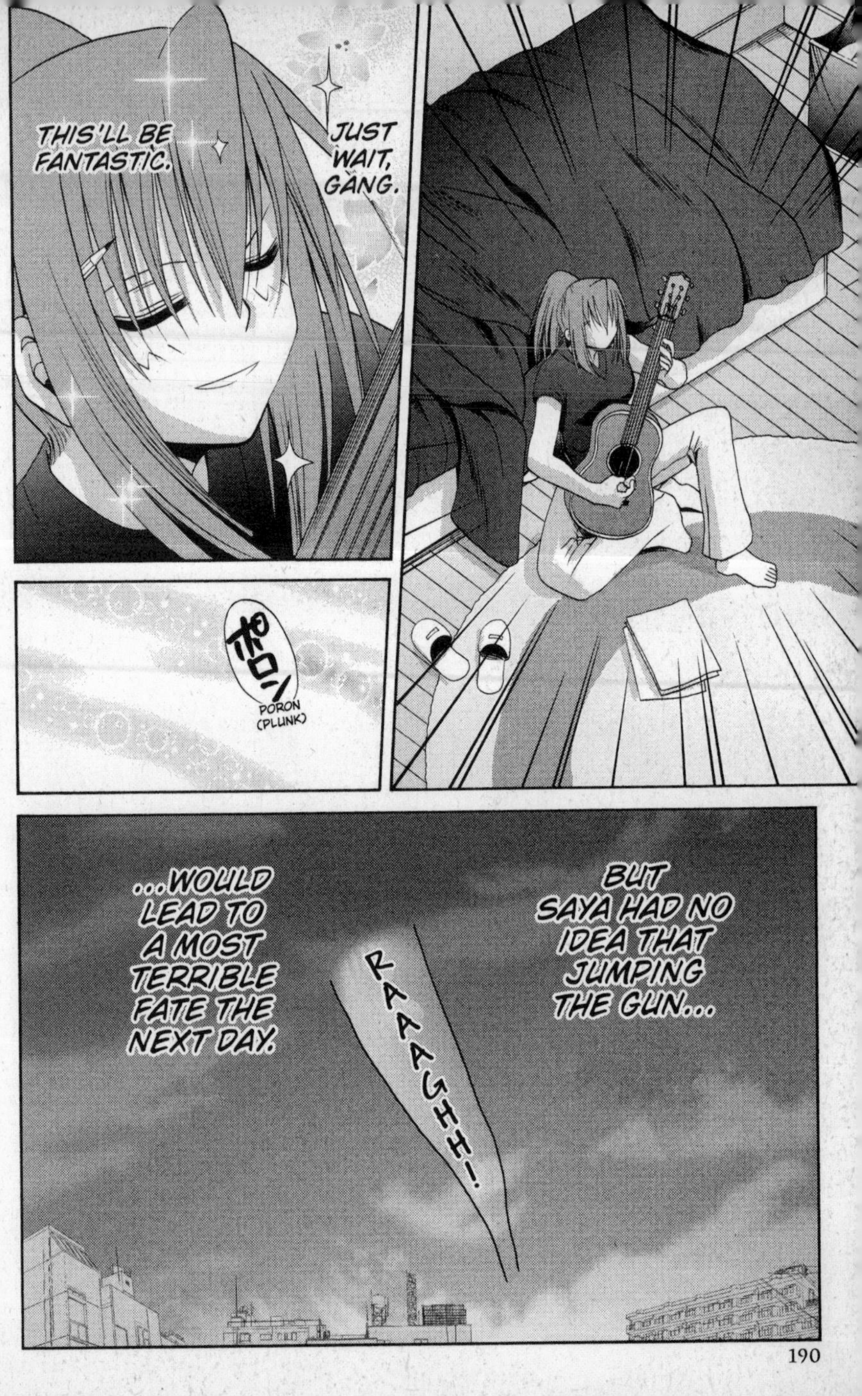
JUST WAIT, GANG.
THIS'LL BE FANTASTIC.
ポロン
PORON (PLUNK)
BUT SAYA HAD NO IDEA THAT JUMPING THE GUN...
...WOULD LEAD TO A MOST TERRIBLE FATE THE NEXT DAY.
RAAAGHH!

BAMBOO BLADE

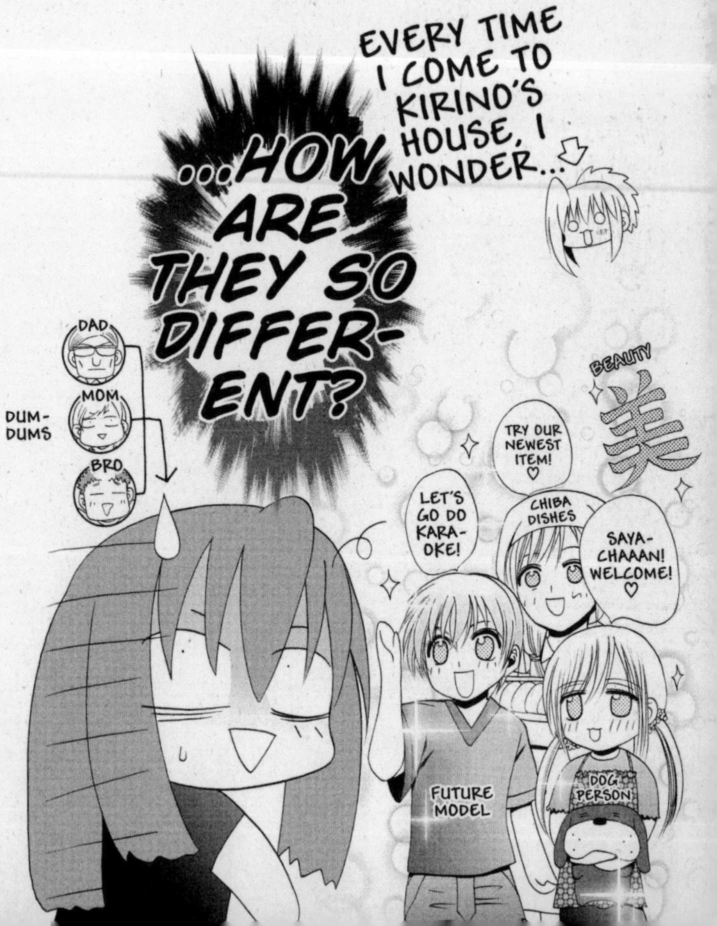
EVERY TIME I COME TO KIRINO'S HOUSE, I WONDER...
...HOW ARE THEY SO DIFFER-ENT?
BEAUTY
美
SAYA-CHAAAN! WELCOME! ♡
TRY OUR NEWEST ITEM! ♡
CHIBA DISHES
LET'S GO DO KARA-OKE!
DAD
MOM
BRO
DUM-DUMS
DOG PERSON
FUTURE MODEL

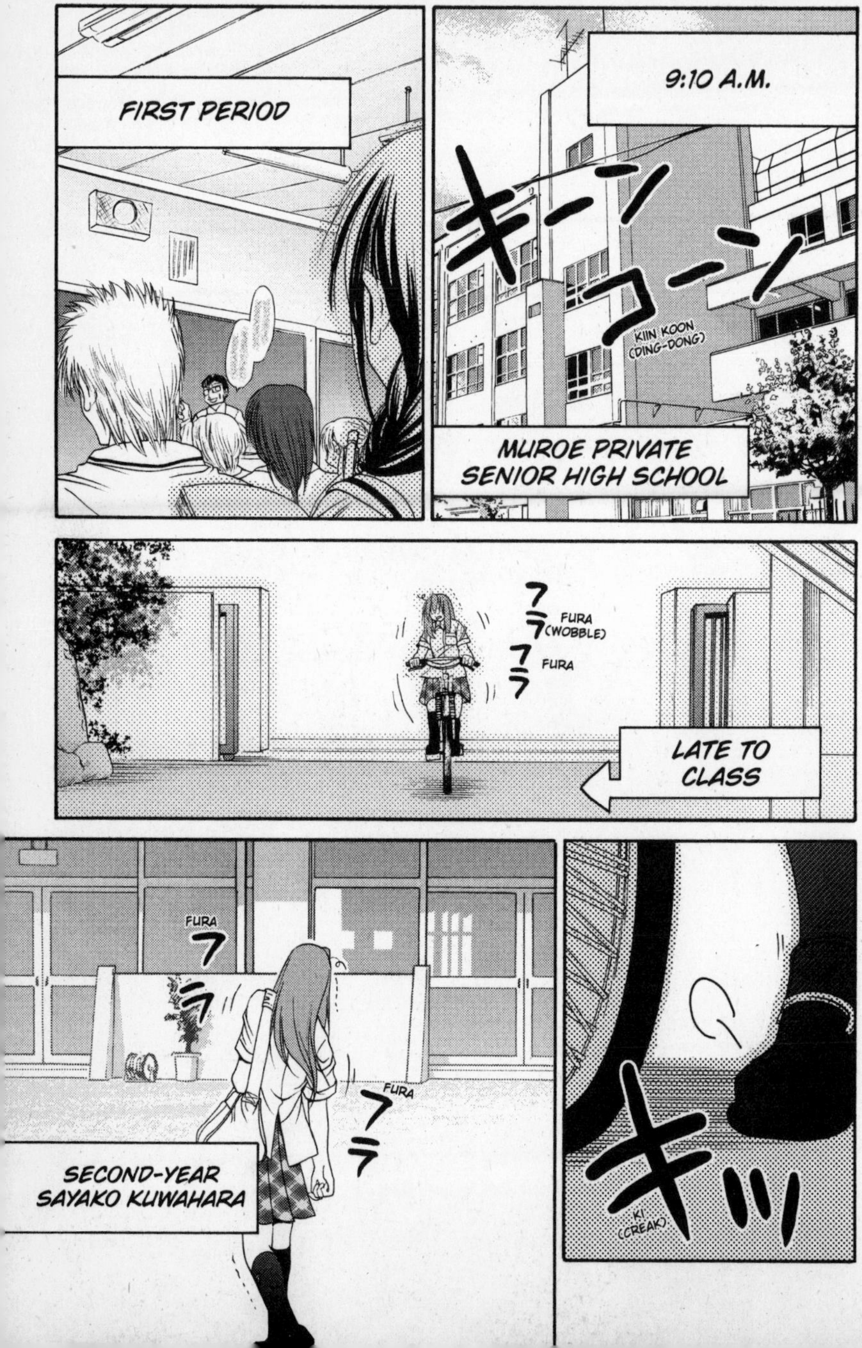
9:10 A.M.
キーンコーン
KIIN KOON (DING-DONG)
MUROE PRIVATE SENIOR HIGH SCHOOL
FIRST PERIOD
フラ
FURA (WOBBLE)
フラ
FURA
LATE TO CLASS
キッ
KI (CREAK)
FURA
フラ
FURA
フラ
SECOND-YEAR SAYAKO KUWAHARA

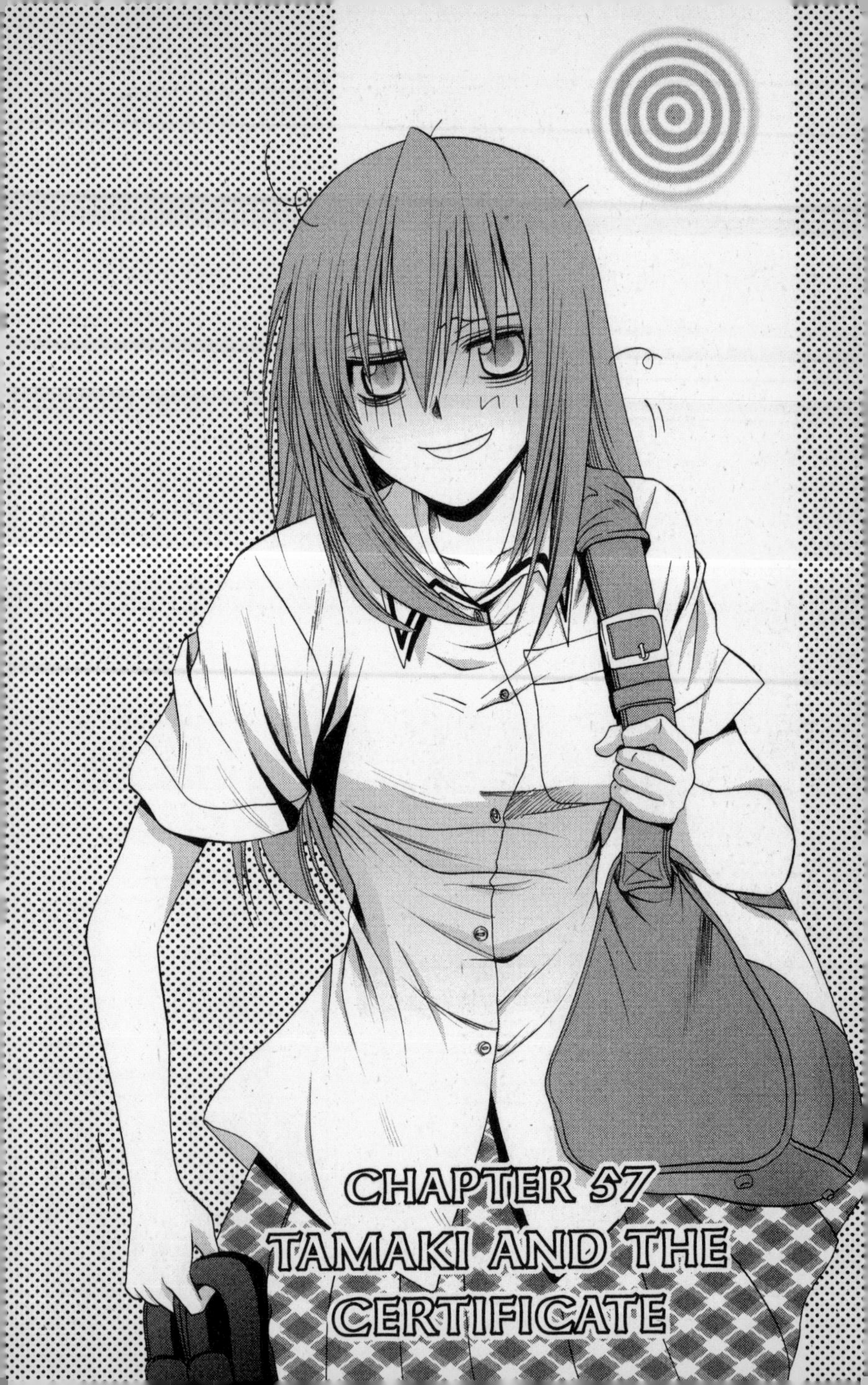
CHAPTER 57
TAMAKI AND THE CERTIFICATE

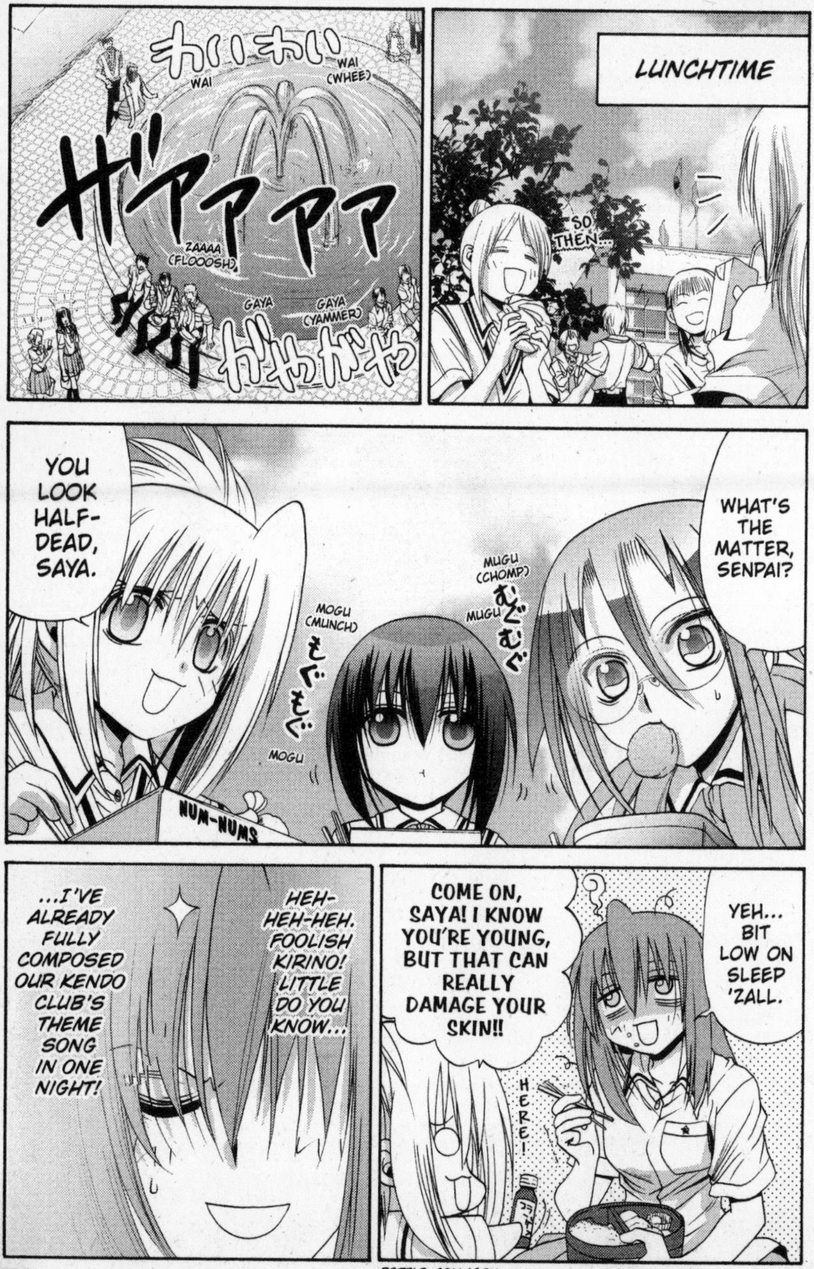
LUNCHTIME
SO THEN...
わいわい
WAI WAI (WHEE)
ザアアアア
ZAAAA (FLOOOSH)
がやがや
GAYA GAYA (YAMMER)
WHAT'S THE MATTER, SENPAI?
むぐむぐ
MUGU (CHOMP) MUGU
もぐもぐ
MOGU (MUNCH) MOGU
YOU LOOK HALF-DEAD, SAYA.
NUM-NUMS
YEH... BIT LOW ON SLEEP 'ZALL.
COME ON, SAYA! I KNOW YOU'RE YOUNG, BUT THAT CAN REALLY DAMAGE YOUR SKIN!!
HERE!
HEH-HEH-HEH. FOOLISH KIRINO! LITTLE DO YOU KNOW...
...I'VE ALREADY FULLY COMPOSED OUR KENDO CLUB'S THEME SONG IN ONE NIGHT!
BOTTLE: COLLAGEN

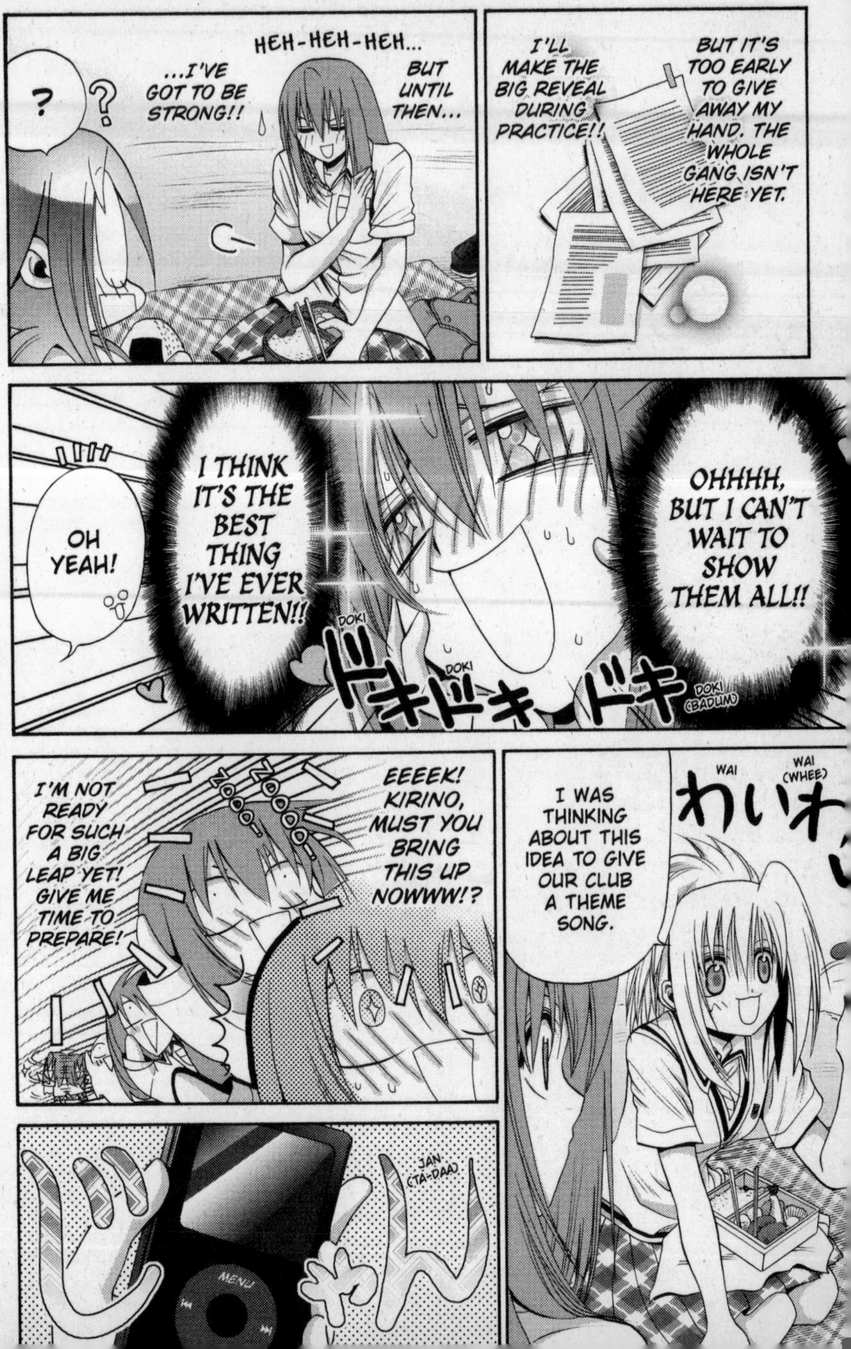
BUT IT'S TOO EARLY TO GIVE AWAY MY HAND. THE WHOLE GANG ISN'T HERE YET.
I'LL MAKE THE BIG REVEAL DURING PRACTICE!!
HEH-HEH-HEH...
BUT UNTIL THEN...
...I'VE GOT TO BE STRONG!!
?
?
OHHHH, BUT I CAN'T WAIT TO SHOW THEM ALL!!
I THINK IT'S THE BEST THING I'VE EVER WRITTEN!!
OH YEAH!
DOKI
DOKI
DOKI (BADUM)
ドキドキドキ
WAI
WAI (WHEE)
わいわ
I WAS THINKING ABOUT THIS IDEA TO GIVE OUR CLUB A THEME SONG.
EEEEK! KIRINO, MUST YOU BRING THIS UP NOWWW!?
I'M NOT READY FOR SUCH A BIG LEAP YET! GIVE ME TIME TO PREPARE!
JAN (TA-DAA)
MENU

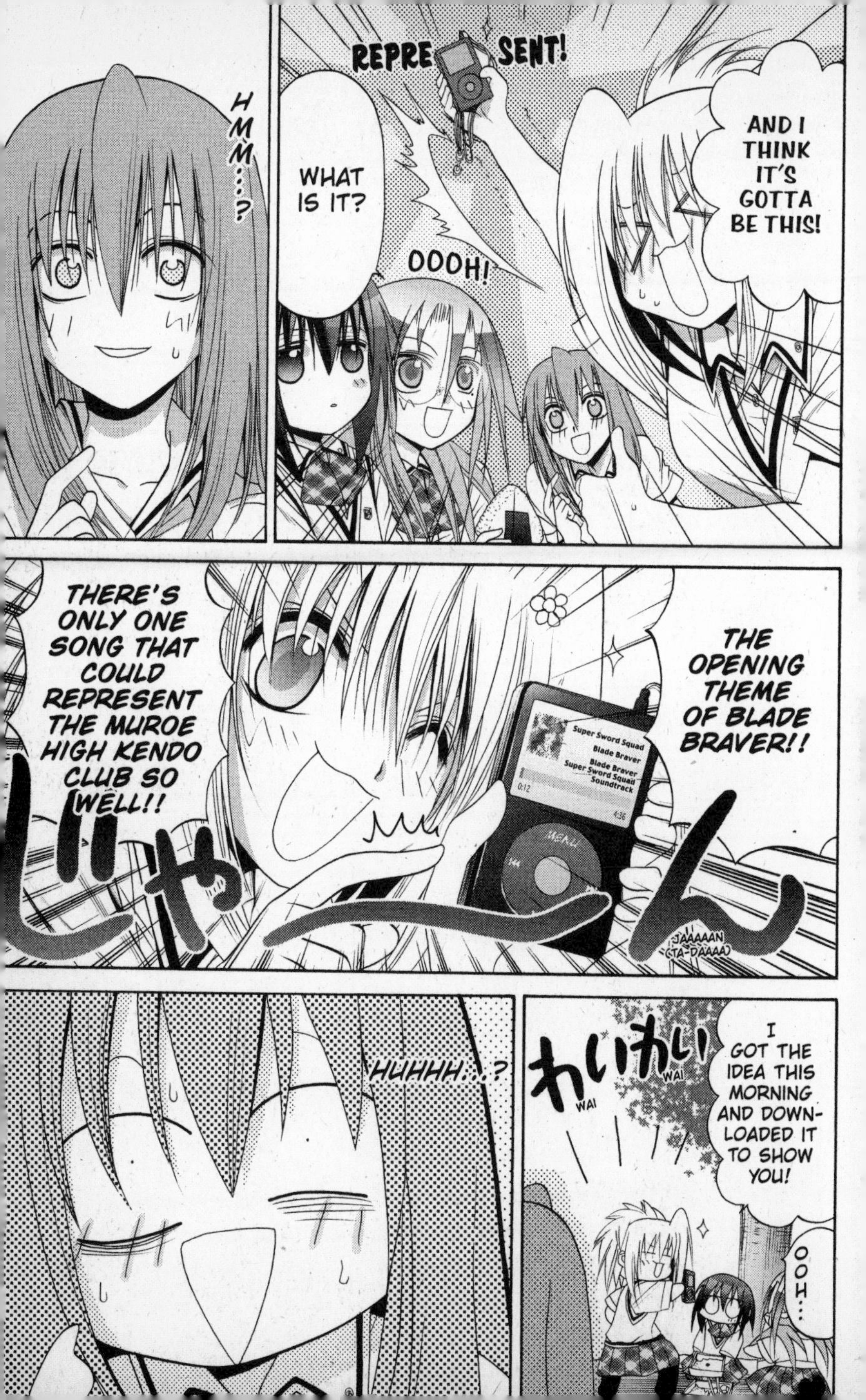
AND I THINK IT'S GOTTA BE THIS!
REPRE SENT!
WHAT IS IT?
OOOH!
HMM...?
THE OPENING THEME OF BLADE BRAVER!!
Super Sword Squad
Blade Braver
Blade Braver Super Sword Squad Soundtrack
0:12
4:56
THERE'S ONLY ONE SONG THAT COULD REPRESENT THE MUROE HIGH KENDO CLUB SO WELL!!
じゃ〜ん
JAAAAAN (TA-DAAAA)
I GOT THE IDEA THIS MORNING AND DOWN-LOADED IT TO SHOW YOU!
わいわい
WAI
WAI
OOOH...
HUHHH...?

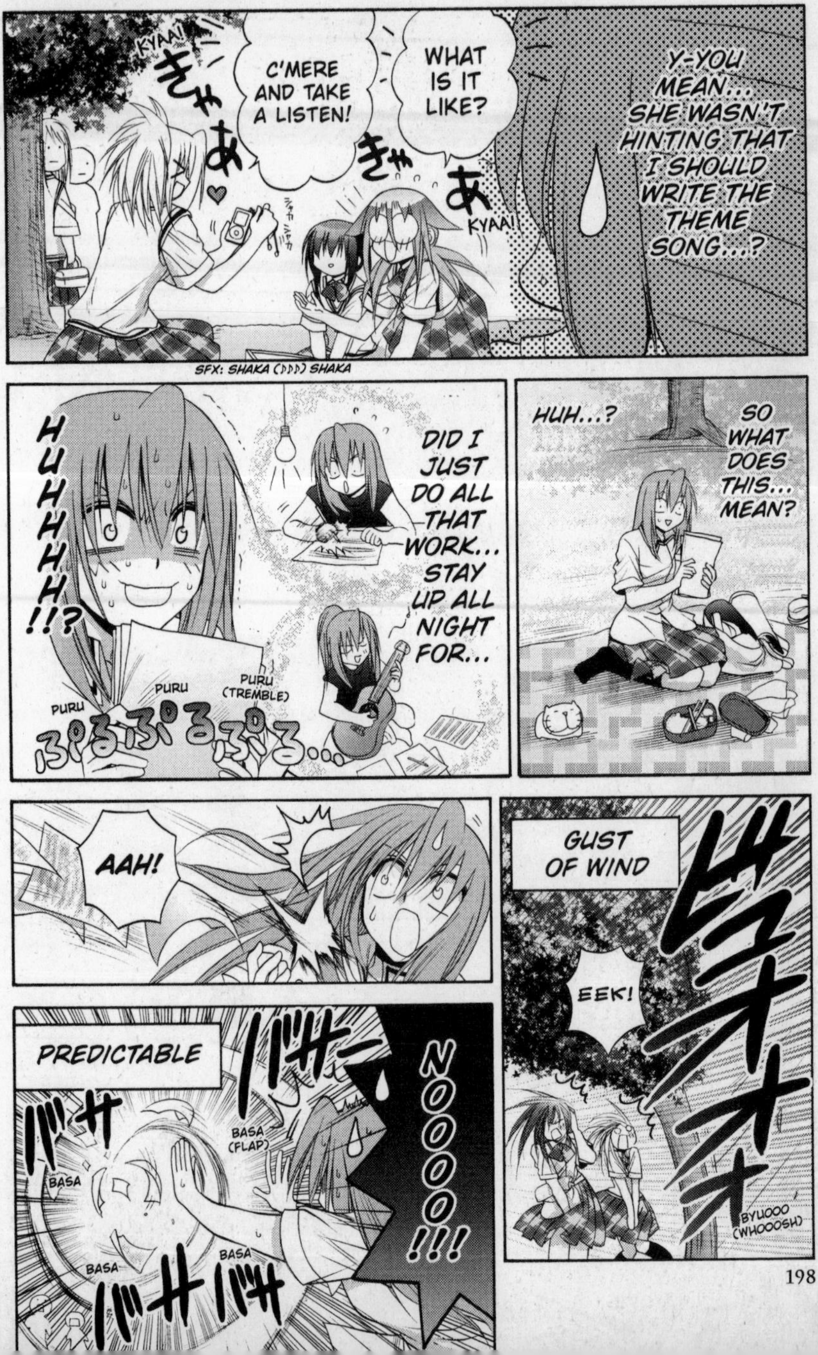
Y-YOU MEAN... SHE WASN'T HINTING THAT I SHOULD WRITE THE THEME SONG...?
WHAT IS IT LIKE?
KYAA!
C'MERE AND TAKE A LISTEN!
KYAA!
SFX: SHAKA (♪♪♪) SHAKA
SO WHAT DOES THIS... MEAN?
HUH...?
DID I JUST DO ALL THAT WORK... STAY UP ALL NIGHT FOR...
HUHHHHHH!!?
PURU (TREMBLE)
PURU
PURU
GUST OF WIND
EEK!
BYUOOO (WHOOOSH)
AAH!
PREDICTABLE
NOOOOOO!!!
BASA (FLAP)
BASA
BASA

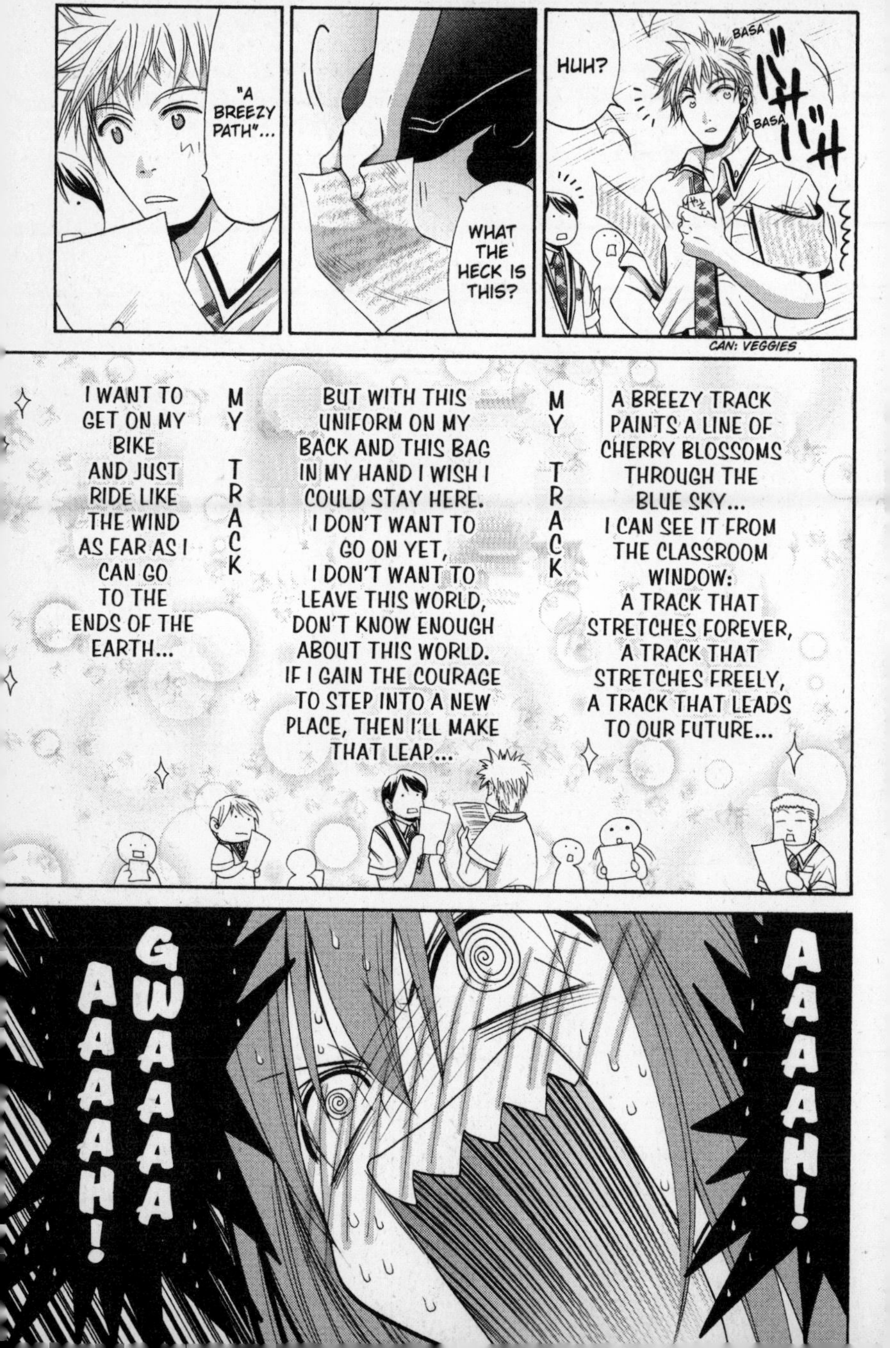
HUH?
BASA
BASA
CAN: VEGGIES
WHAT THE HECK IS THIS?
"A BREEZY PATH"...
A BREEZY TRACK PAINTS A LINE OF CHERRY BLOSSOMS THROUGH THE BLUE SKY... I CAN SEE IT FROM THE CLASSROOM WINDOW: A TRACK THAT STRETCHES FOREVER, A TRACK THAT STRETCHES FREELY, A TRACK THAT LEADS TO OUR FUTURE...
MY TRACK
BUT WITH THIS UNIFORM ON MY BACK AND THIS BAG IN MY HAND I WISH I COULD STAY HERE. I DON'T WANT TO GO ON YET, I DON'T WANT TO LEAVE THIS WORLD, DON'T KNOW ENOUGH ABOUT THIS WORLD. IF I GAIN THE COURAGE TO STEP INTO A NEW PLACE, THEN I'LL MAKE THAT LEAP...
MY TRACK
I WANT TO GET ON MY BIKE AND JUST RIDE LIKE THE WIND AS FAR AS I CAN GO TO THE ENDS OF THE EARTH...
AAAAAH!
GWAAAAA
AAAAAH!

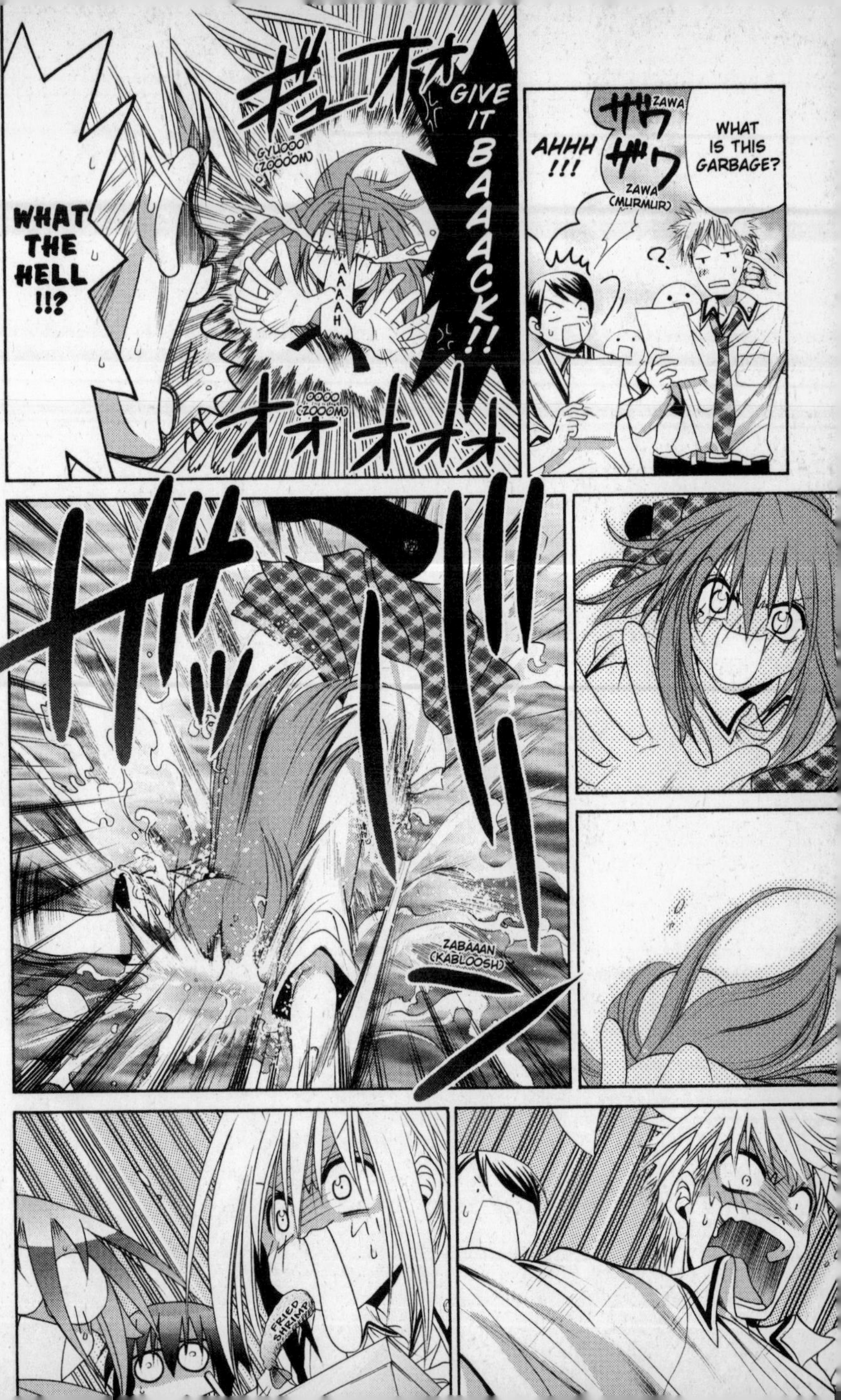
WHAT IS THIS GARBAGE?
ZAWA ZAWA (MURMUR)
AHHH!!!
GIVE IT BAAAACK!!
GYUOOO (ZOOOOM)
AAAAH
WHAT THE HELL!!?
OOOO (ZOOOM)
ZABAAAN (KABLOOSH)
FRIED SHRIMP

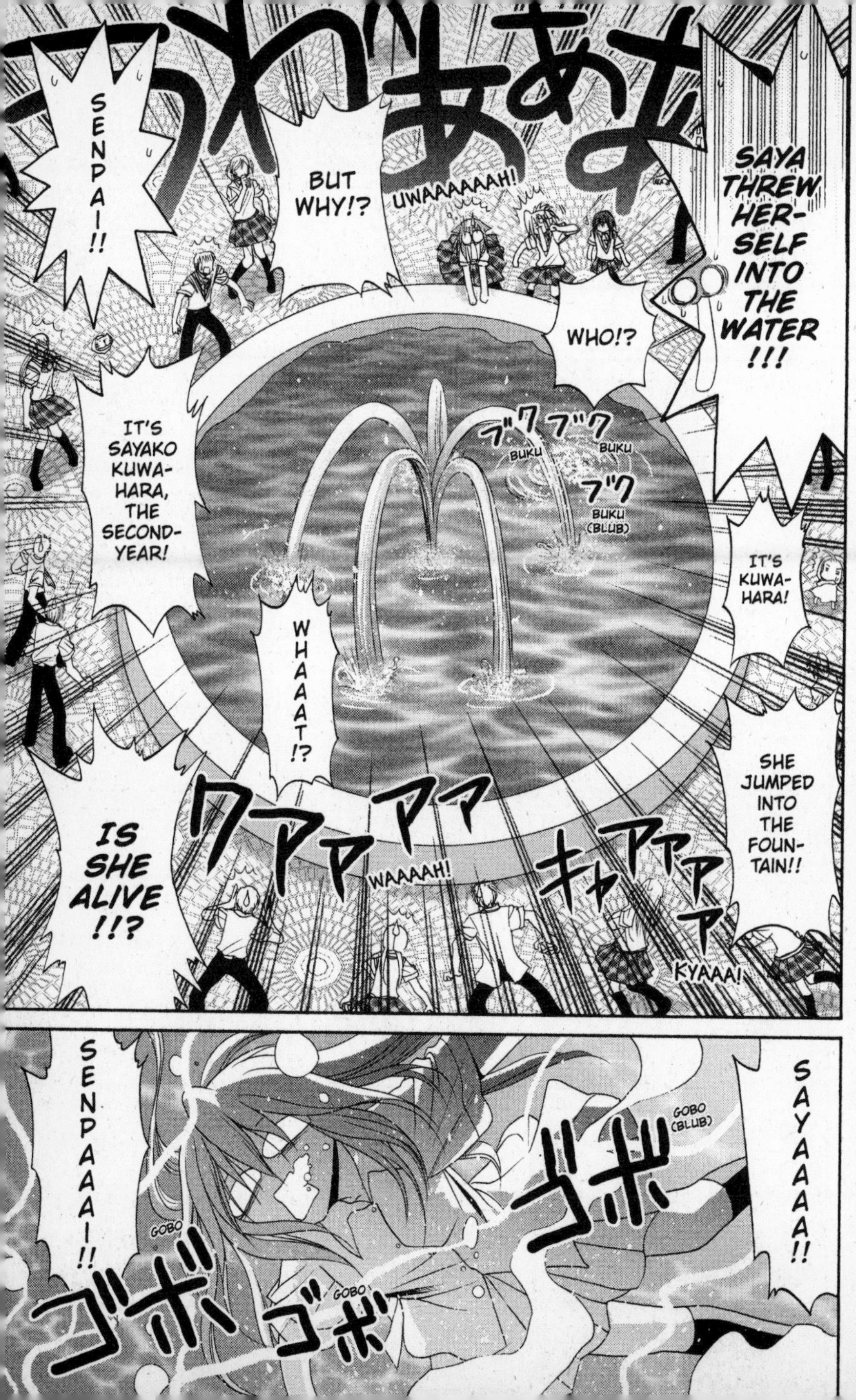
SAYA THREW HERSELF INTO THE WATER!!!
うわああ
UWAAAAAAAH!
BUT WHY!?
SENPAI!!
WHO!?
ブクブク BUKU BUKU
ブク BUKU (BLUB)
IT'S KUWAHARA!
IT'S SAYAKO KUWAHARA, THE SECOND-YEAR!
WHAAAAT!?
SHE JUMPED INTO THE FOUNTAIN!!
キャアアア KYAAA!
ワアアア WAAAAH!
IS SHE ALIVE!!?
SAYAAAAAA!!
ゴボ GOBO (BLUB)
SENPAAAAI!!
ゴボ GOBO
ゴボ GOBO

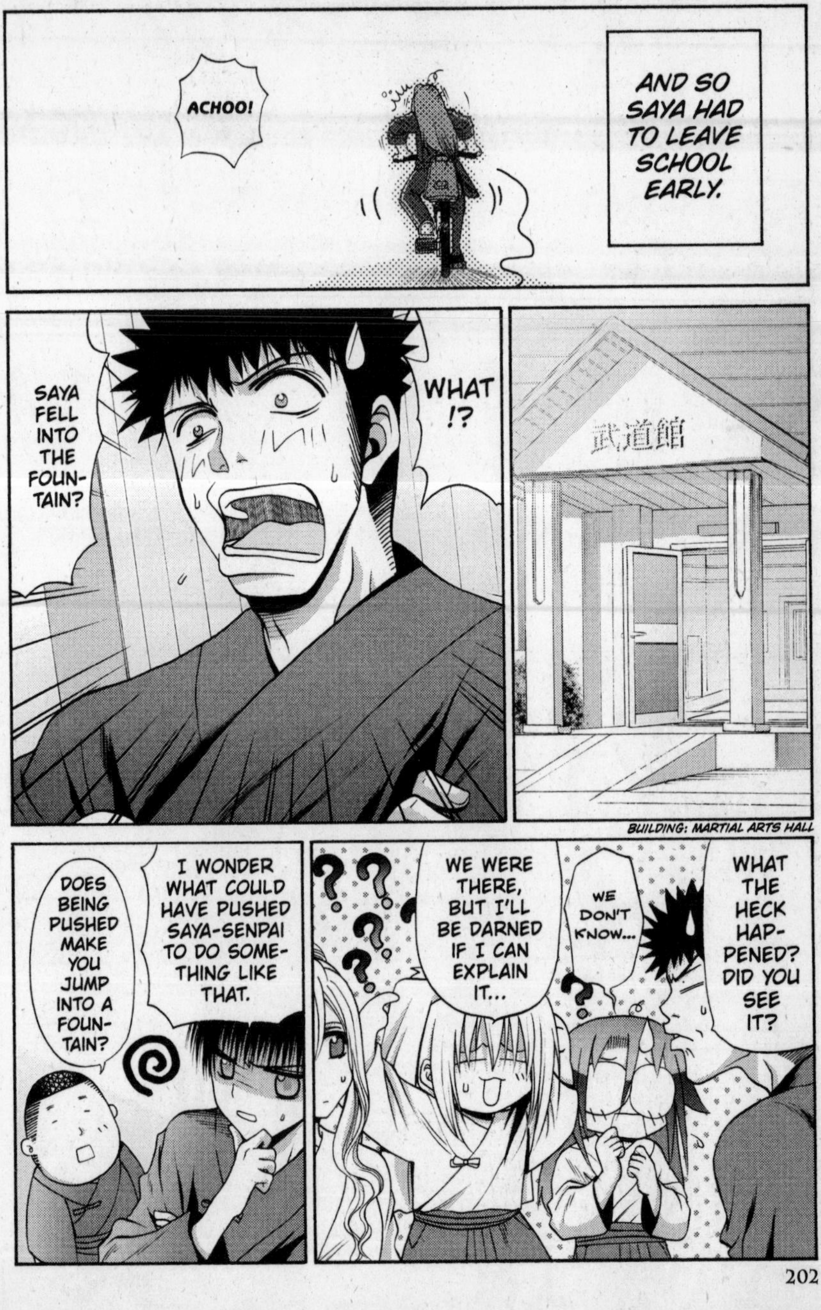
AND SO SAYA HAD TO LEAVE SCHOOL EARLY.
ACHOO!
武道館
BUILDING: MARTIAL ARTS HALL
WHAT!?
SAYA FELL INTO THE FOUN-TAIN?
WHAT THE HECK HAP-PENED? DID YOU SEE IT?
WE DON'T KNOW...
WE WERE THERE, BUT I'LL BE DARNED IF I CAN EXPLAIN IT...
I WONDER WHAT COULD HAVE PUSHED SAYA-SENPAI TO DO SOME-THING LIKE THAT.
DOES BEING PUSHED MAKE YOU JUMP INTO A FOUN-TAIN?

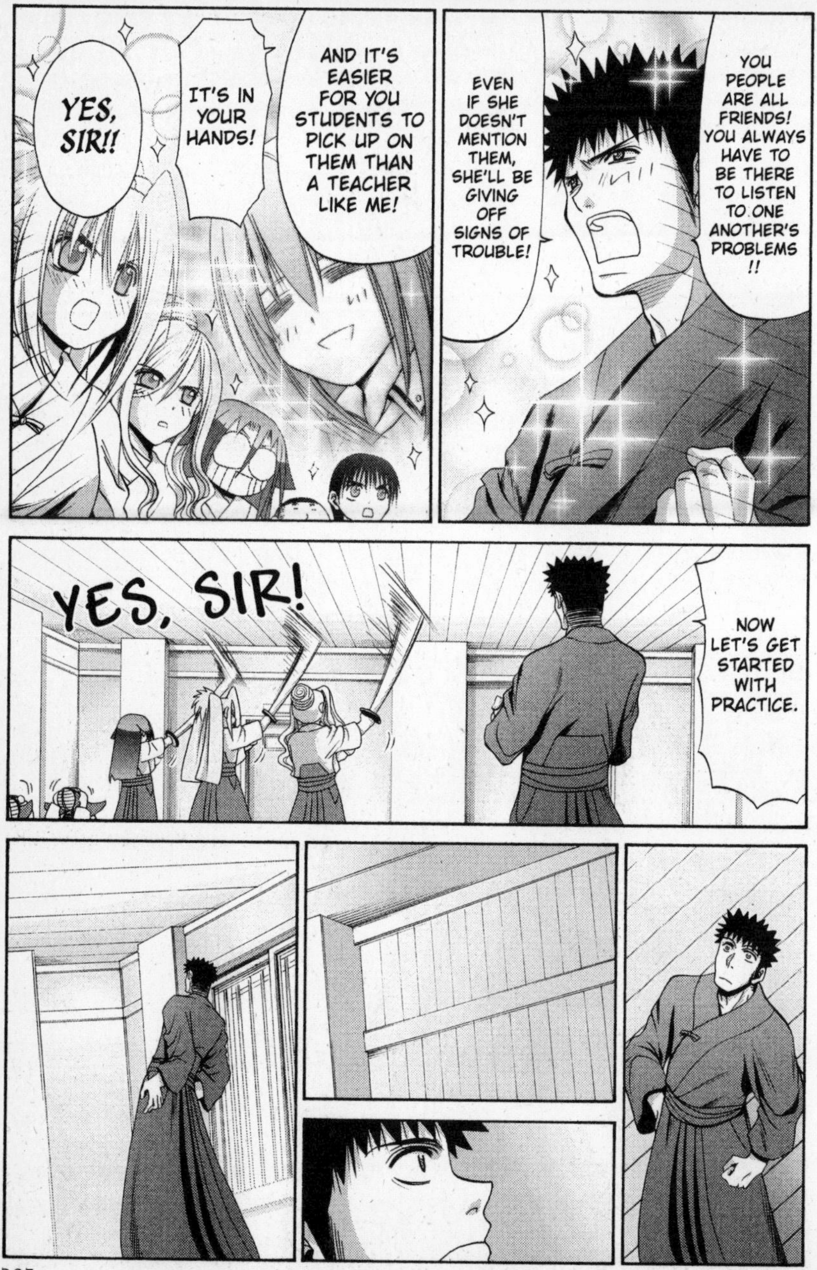
YOU PEOPLE ARE ALL FRIENDS! YOU ALWAYS HAVE TO BE THERE TO LISTEN TO ONE ANOTHER'S PROBLEMS!!
EVEN IF SHE DOESN'T MENTION THEM, SHE'LL BE GIVING OFF SIGNS OF TROUBLE!
AND IT'S EASIER FOR YOU STUDENTS TO PICK UP ON THEM THAN A TEACHER LIKE ME!
IT'S IN YOUR HANDS!
YES, SIR!!
NOW LET'S GET STARTED WITH PRACTICE.
YES, SIR!

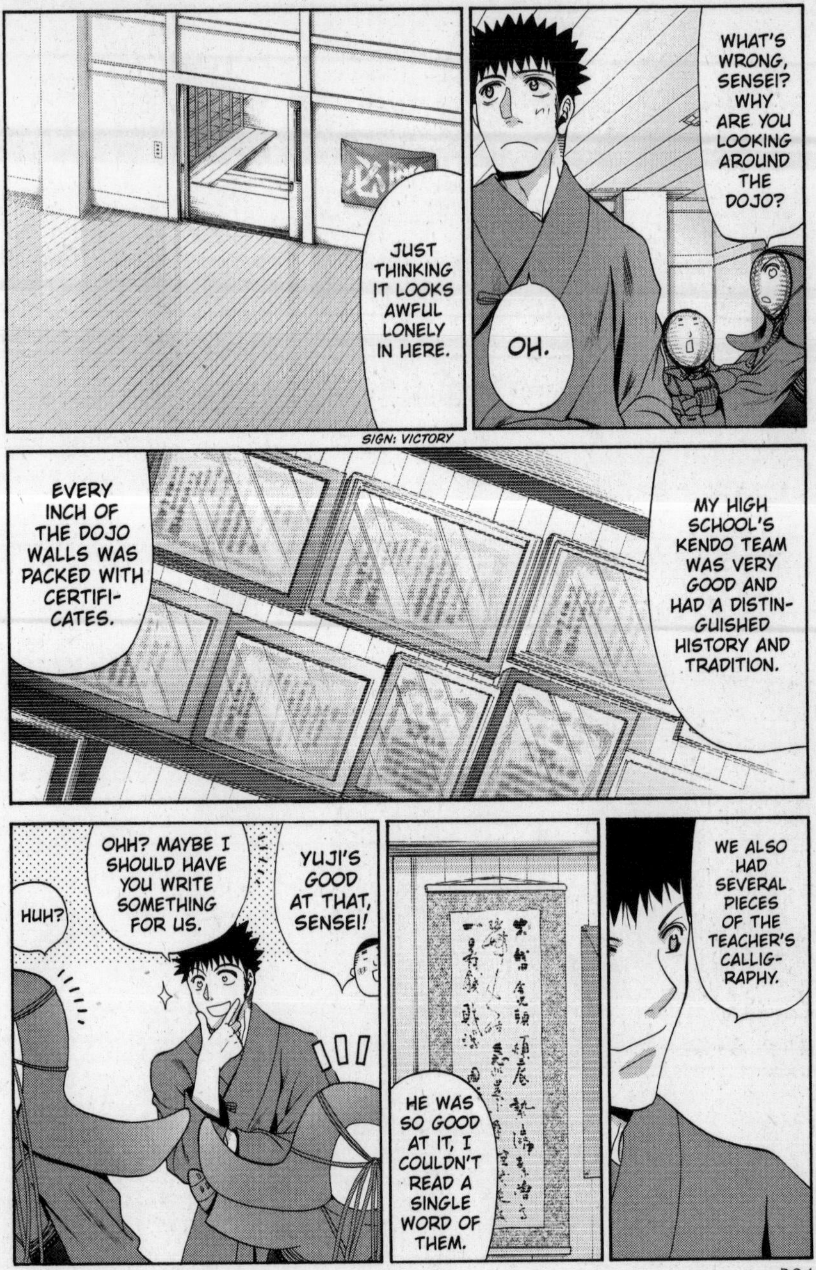
WHAT'S WRONG, SENSEI? WHY ARE YOU LOOKING AROUND THE DOJO?
OH.
JUST THINKING IT LOOKS AWFUL LONELY IN HERE.
MY HIGH SCHOOL'S KENDO TEAM WAS VERY GOOD AND HAD A DISTIN-GUISHED HISTORY AND TRADITION.
EVERY INCH OF THE DOJO WALLS WAS PACKED WITH CERTIFI-CATES.
WE ALSO HAD SEVERAL PIECES OF THE TEACHER'S CALLIG-RAPHY.
HE WAS SO GOOD AT IT, I COULDN'T READ A SINGLE WORD OF THEM.
YUJI'S GOOD AT THAT, SENSEI!
OHH? MAYBE I SHOULD HAVE YOU WRITE SOMETHING FOR US.
HUH?

SIGN: VICTORY

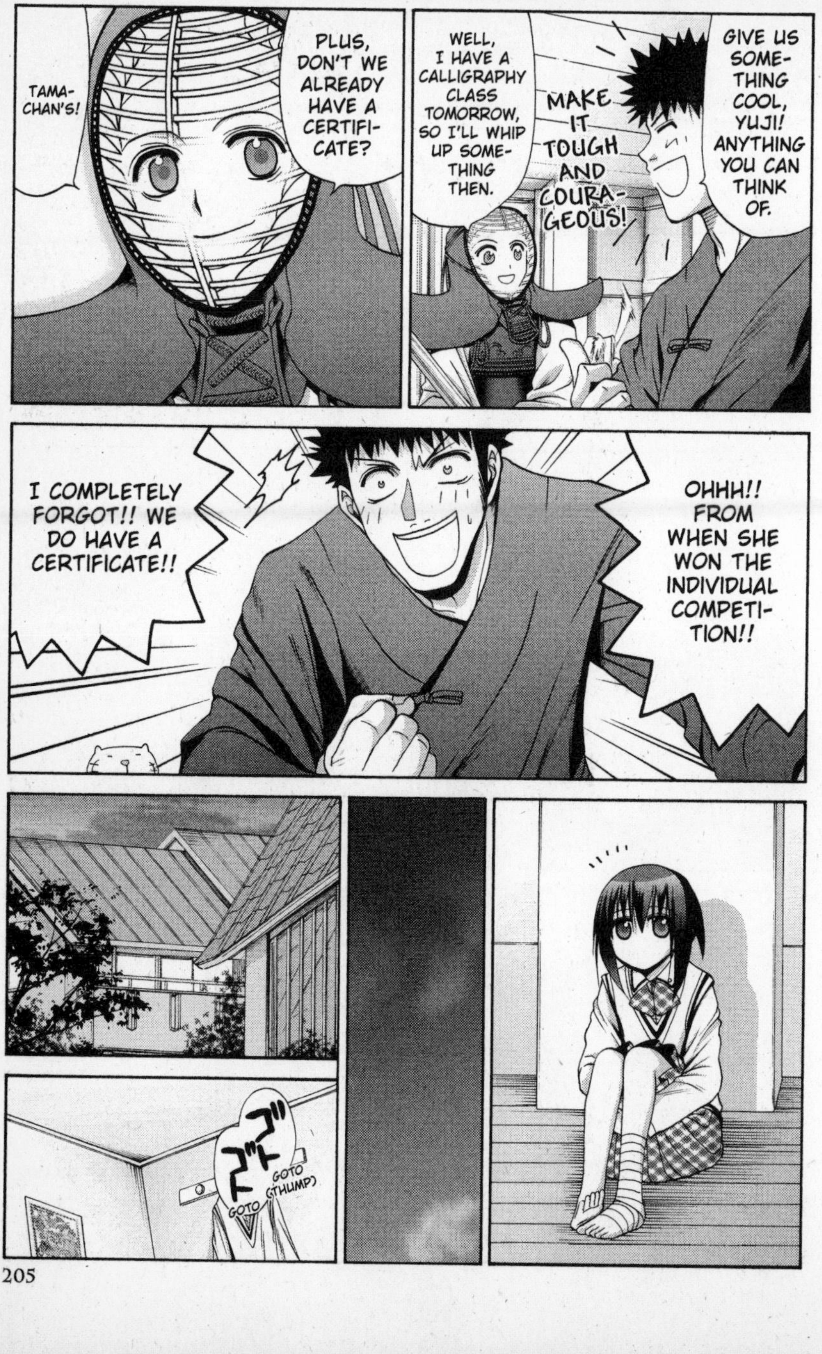

GIVE US SOMETHING COOL, YUJI! ANYTHING YOU CAN THINK OF.
MAKE IT TOUGH AND COURAGEOUS!
WELL, I HAVE A CALLIGRAPHY CLASS TOMORROW, SO I'LL WHIP UP SOMETHING THEN.
PLUS, DON'T WE ALREADY HAVE A CERTIFICATE?
TAMA-CHAN'S!
OHHH!! FROM WHEN SHE WON THE INDIVIDUAL COMPETITION!!
I COMPLETELY FORGOT!! WE DO HAVE A CERTIFICATE!!
GOTO
GOTO (THUMP)

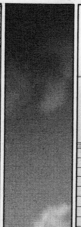

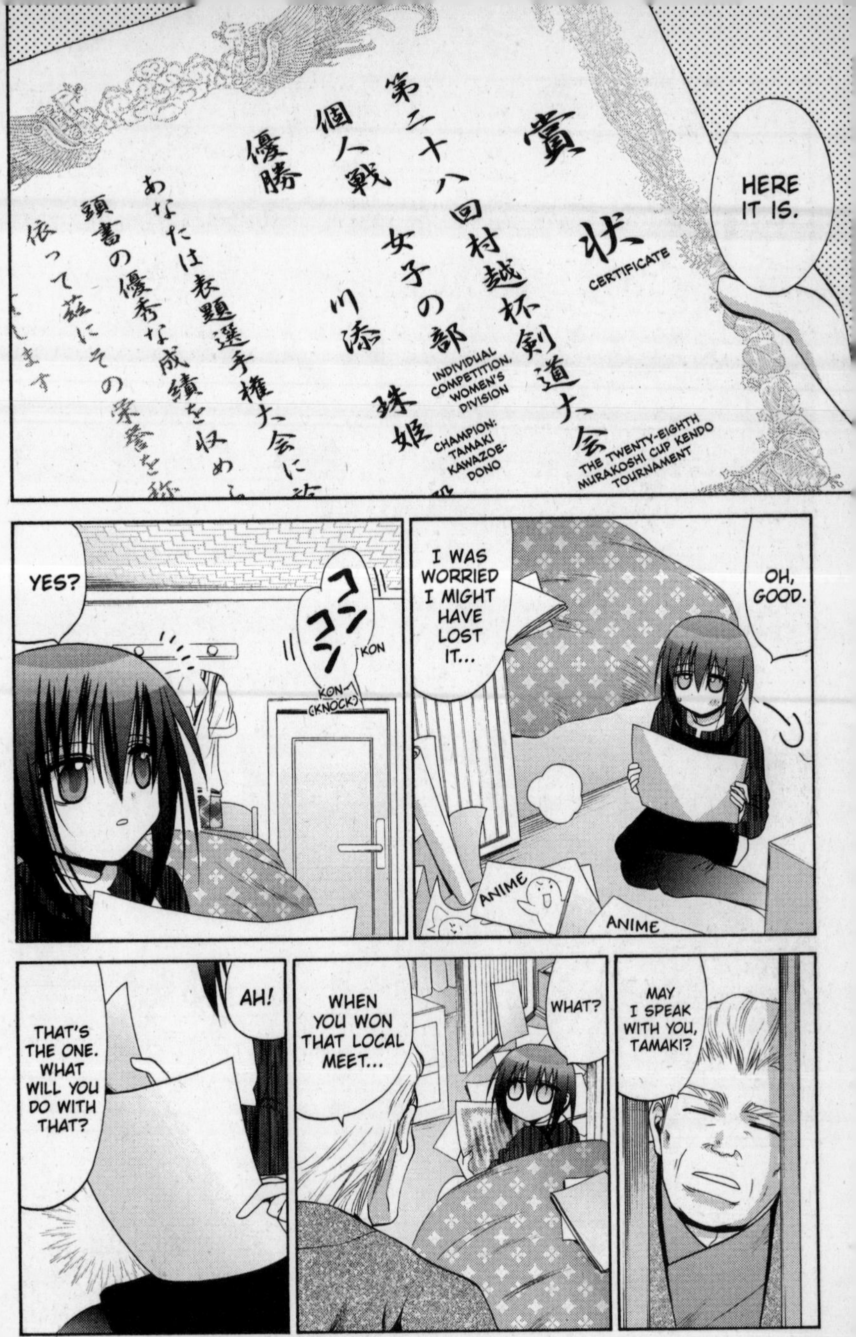
HERE IT IS.
賞状
CERTIFICATE
第二十八回村越杯剣道大会
THE TWENTY-EIGHTH MURAKOSHI CUP KENDO TOURNAMENT
個人戦 女子の部
INDIVIDUAL COMPETITION, WOMEN'S DIVISION
優勝 川添 珠姫
CHAMPION: TAMAKI KAWAZOE-DONO
OH, GOOD.
I WAS WORRIED I MIGHT HAVE LOST IT...
ANIME
ANIME
コンコン
KON KON (KNOCK)
YES?
MAY I SPEAK WITH YOU, TAMAKI?
WHAT?
WHEN YOU WON THAT LOCAL MEET...
AH!
THAT'S THE ONE. WHAT WILL YOU DO WITH THAT?

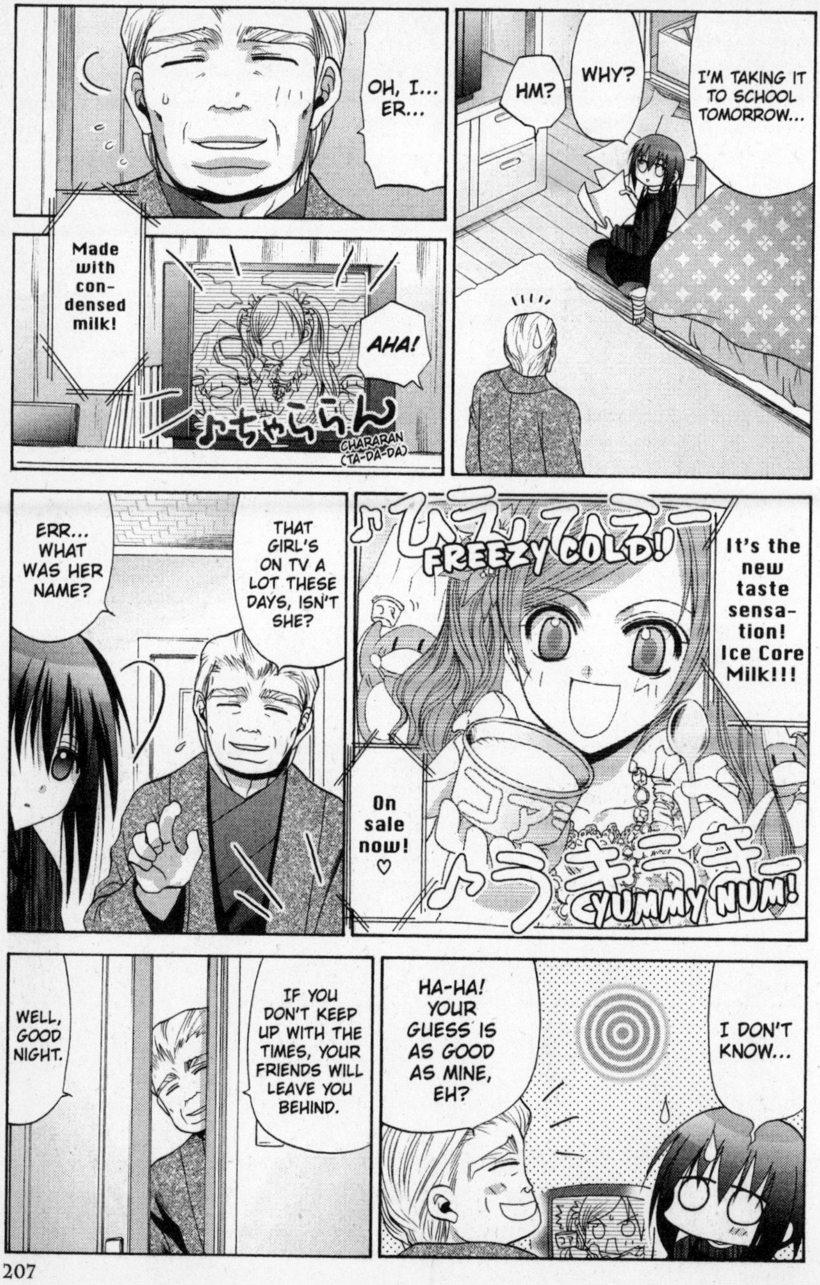
I'M TAKING IT TO SCHOOL TOMORROW...
WHY?
HM?
OH, I... ER...
AHA!
Made with condensed milk!
♪ちゃららん
CHARARAN (TA-DA-DA)
It's the new taste sensation! Ice Core Milk!!!
FREEZY COLD!
On sale now! ♡
YUMMY NUM!
THAT GIRL'S ON TV A LOT THESE DAYS, ISN'T SHE?
ERR... WHAT WAS HER NAME?
I DON'T KNOW...
HA-HA! YOUR GUESS IS AS GOOD AS MINE, EH?
IF YOU DON'T KEEP UP WITH THE TIMES, YOUR FRIENDS WILL LEAVE YOU BEHIND.
WELL, GOOD NIGHT.

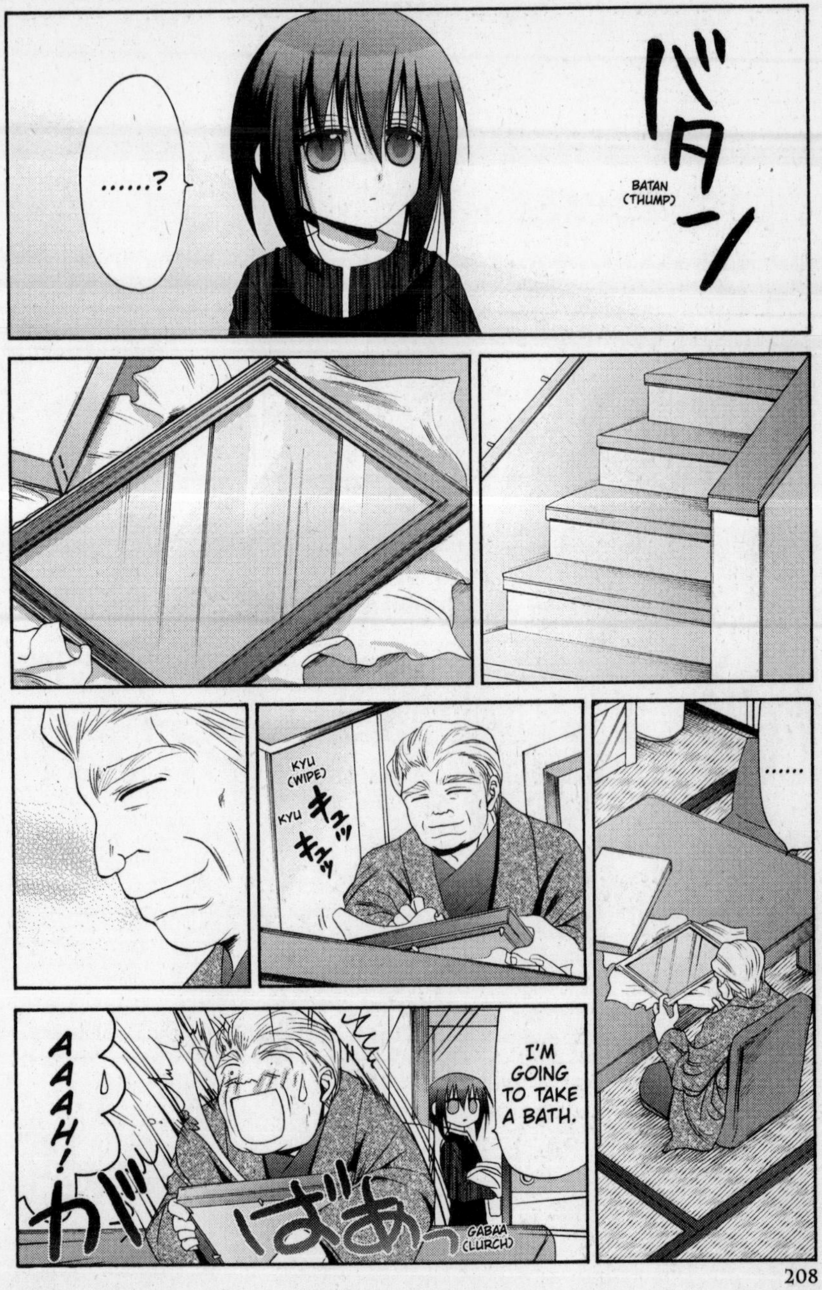
バタン
BATAN (THUMP)
......?
......
KYU (WIPE)
KYU
キュッ
キュッ
I'M GOING TO TAKE A BATH.
GABAA (LURCH)
AAAH!

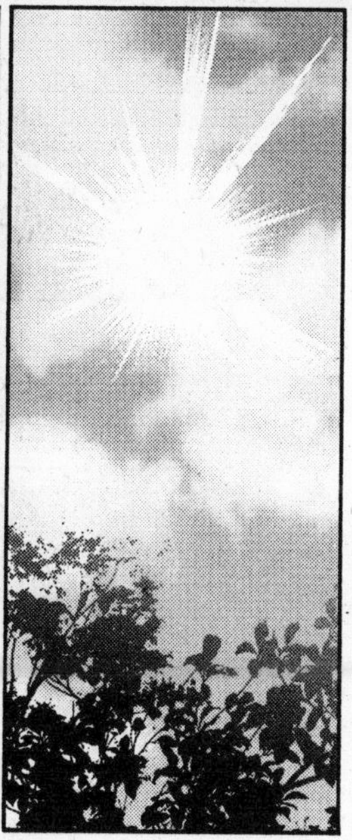

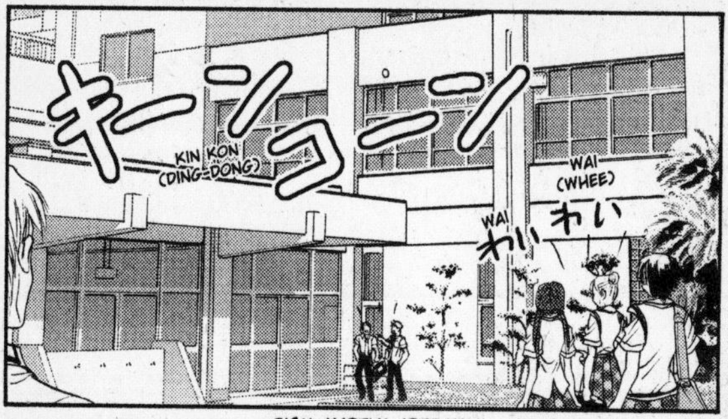
キーンコーン
KIN KON (DING-DONG)
WAI (WHEE)
WAI
わいわい

SIGN: MARTIAL ARTS HALL

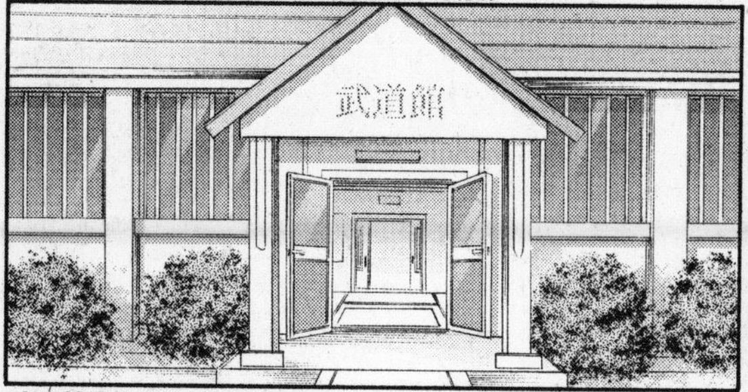
武道館

CALLIGRAPHY: SOUL IN EVERY PITCH

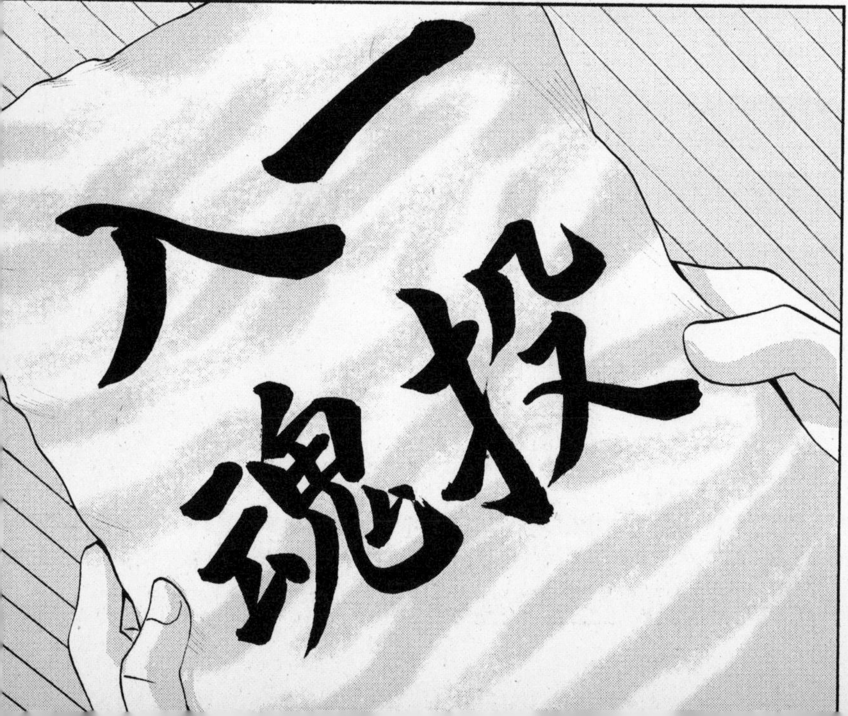
一投入魂

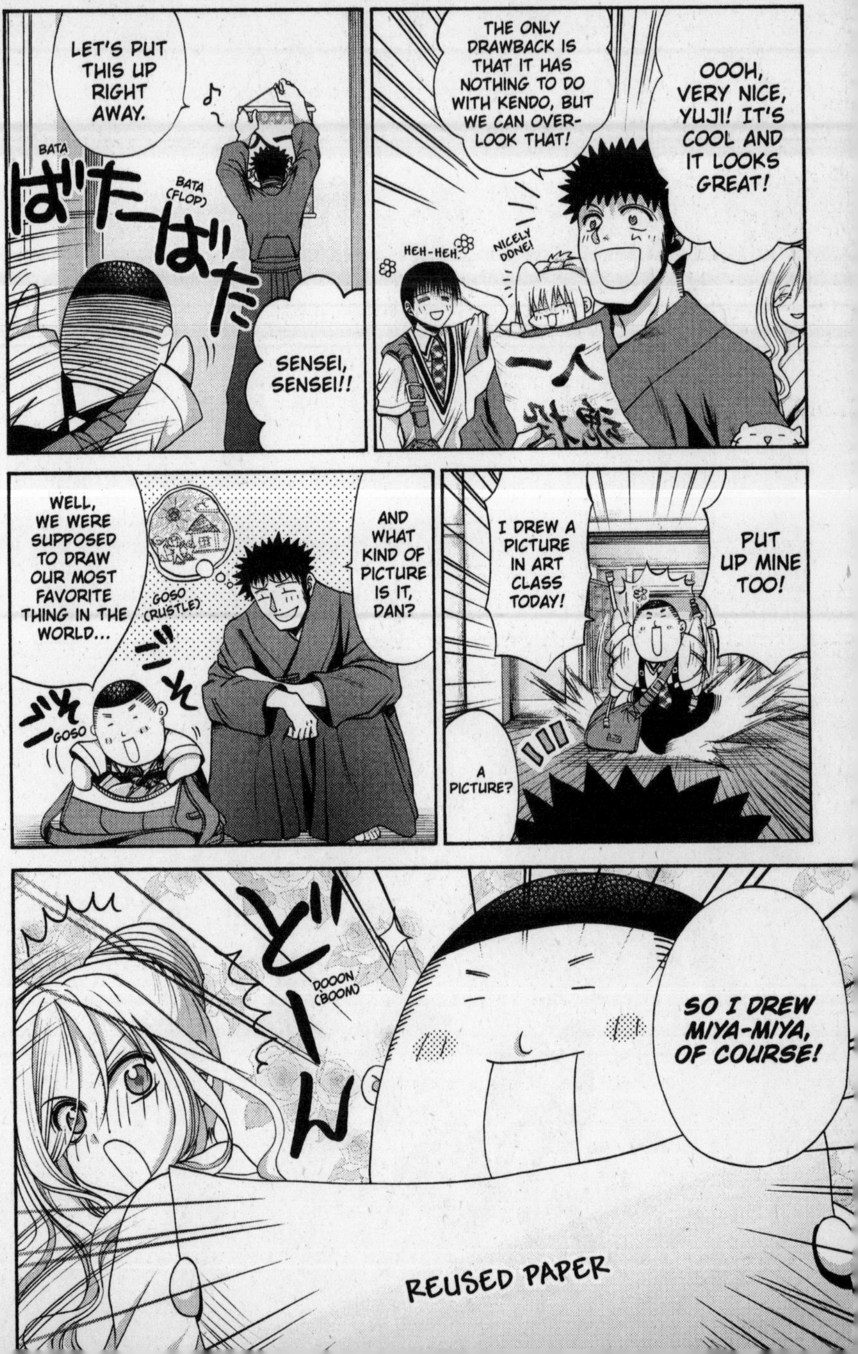
OOOH, VERY NICE, YUJI! IT'S COOL AND IT LOOKS GREAT!
THE ONLY DRAWBACK IS THAT IT HAS NOTHING TO DO WITH KENDO, BUT WE CAN OVER-LOOK THAT!
NICELY DONE!
HEH-HEH.
LET'S PUT THIS UP RIGHT AWAY.
BATA (FLOP)
BATA
SENSEI, SENSEI!!
PUT UP MINE TOO!
I DREW A PICTURE IN ART CLASS TODAY!
A PICTURE?
AND WHAT KIND OF PICTURE IS IT, DAN?
WELL, WE WERE SUPPOSED TO DRAW OUR MOST FAVORITE THING IN THE WORLD...
GOSO (RUSTLE)
GOSO
SO I DREW MIYA-MIYA, OF COURSE!
DOOON (BOOM)
REUSED PAPER

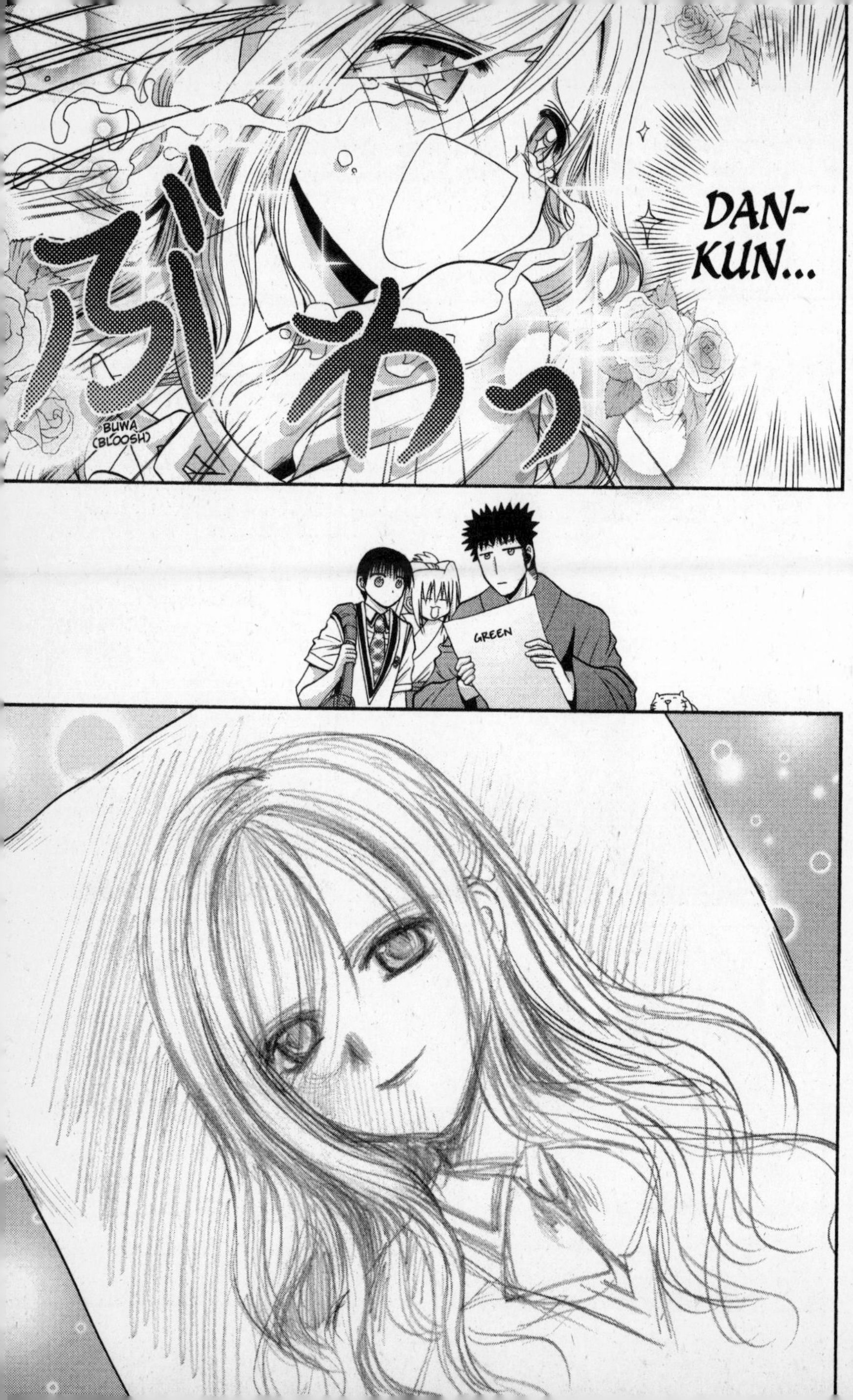
DAN-KUN...
ぶわっ
BUWA (BLOOSH)
GREEN

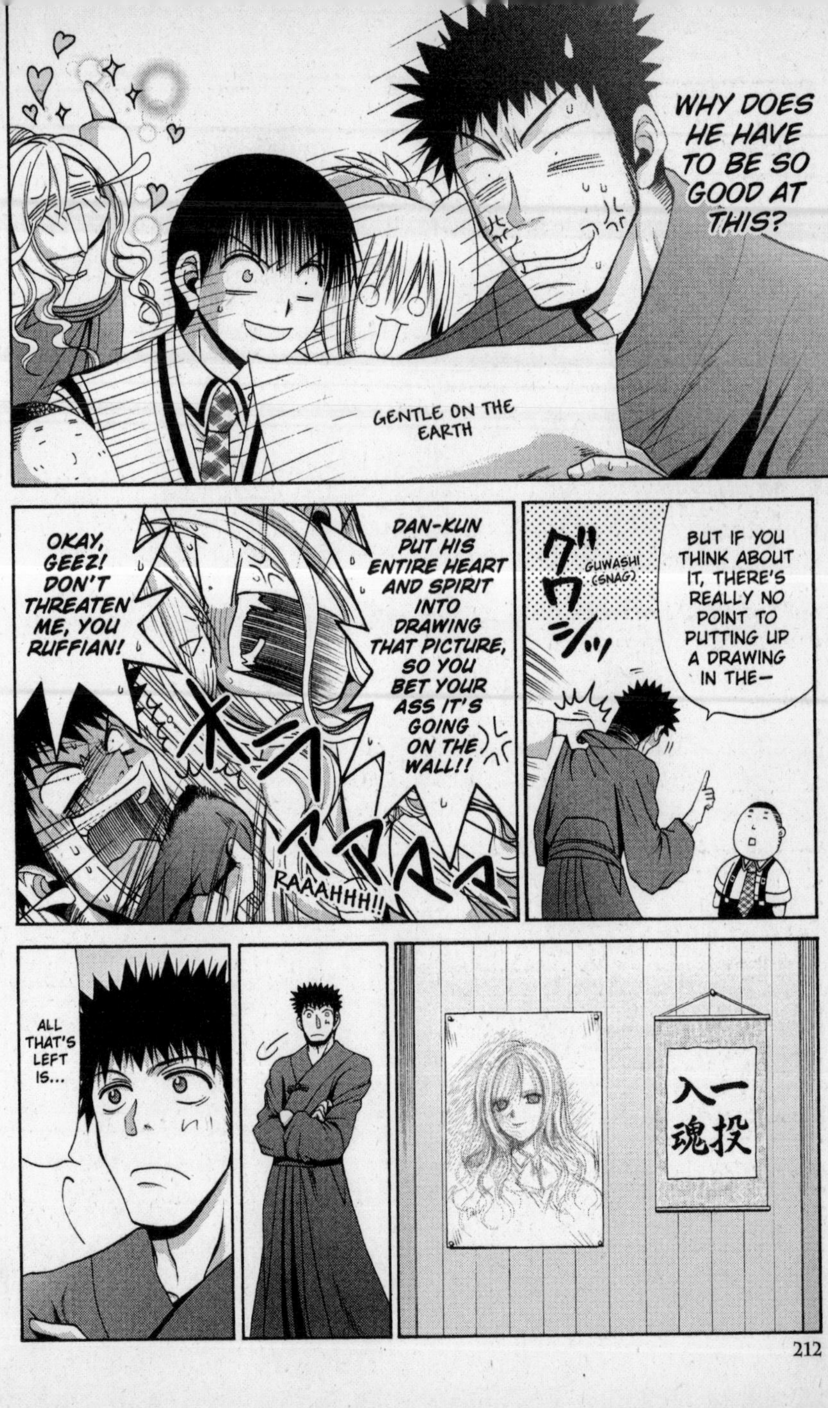
WHY DOES HE HAVE TO BE SO GOOD AT THIS?
GENTLE ON THE EARTH
グワシッ
GUWASHI (SNAG)
BUT IF YOU THINK ABOUT IT, THERE'S REALLY NO POINT TO PUTTING UP A DRAWING IN THE—
DAN-KUN PUT HIS ENTIRE HEART AND SPIRIT INTO DRAWING THAT PICTURE, SO YOU BET YOUR ASS IT'S GOING ON THE WALL!!
OKAY, GEEZ! DON'T THREATEN ME, YOU RUFFIAN!
RAAAHHH!!
一投入魂
ALL THAT'S LEFT IS...

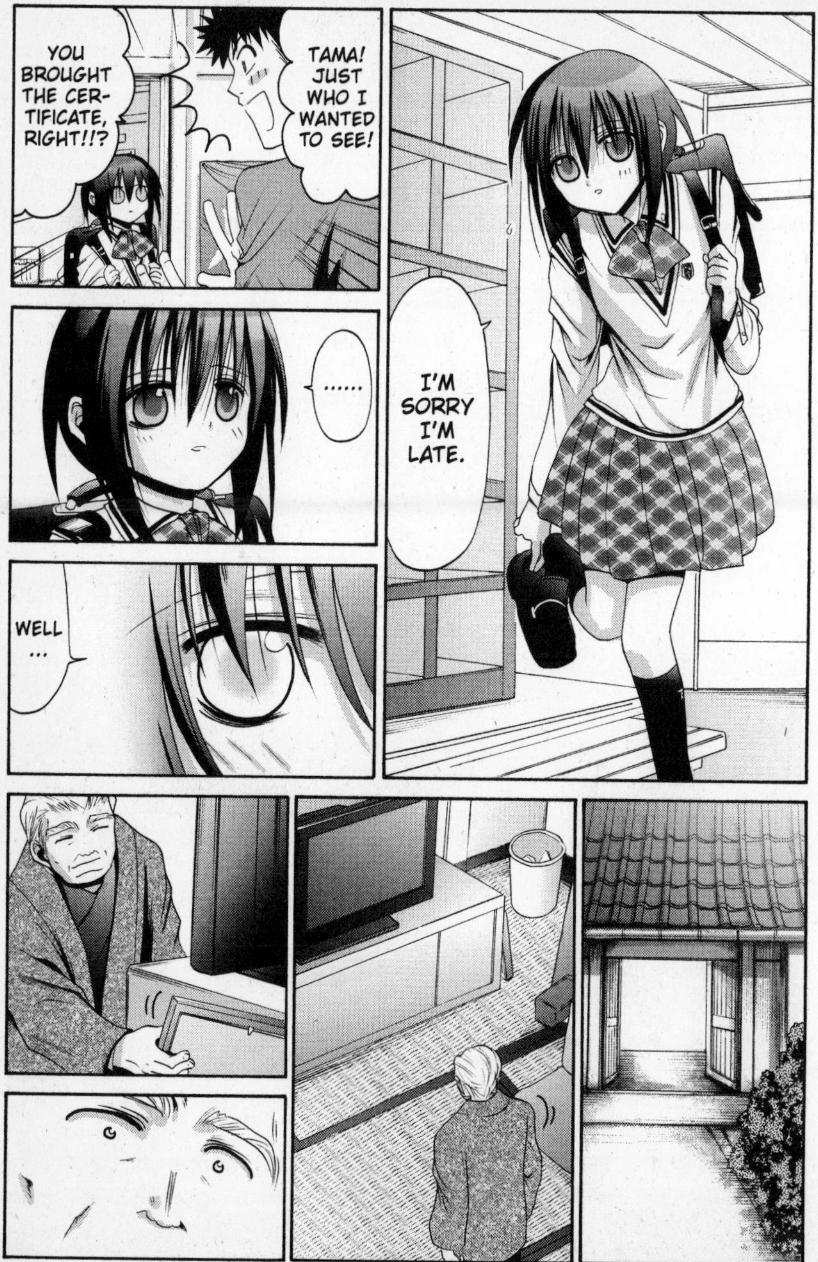
I'M SORRY I'M LATE.
TAMA! JUST WHO I WANTED TO SEE!
YOU BROUGHT THE CER-TIFICATE, RIGHT!!?
......
WELL ...

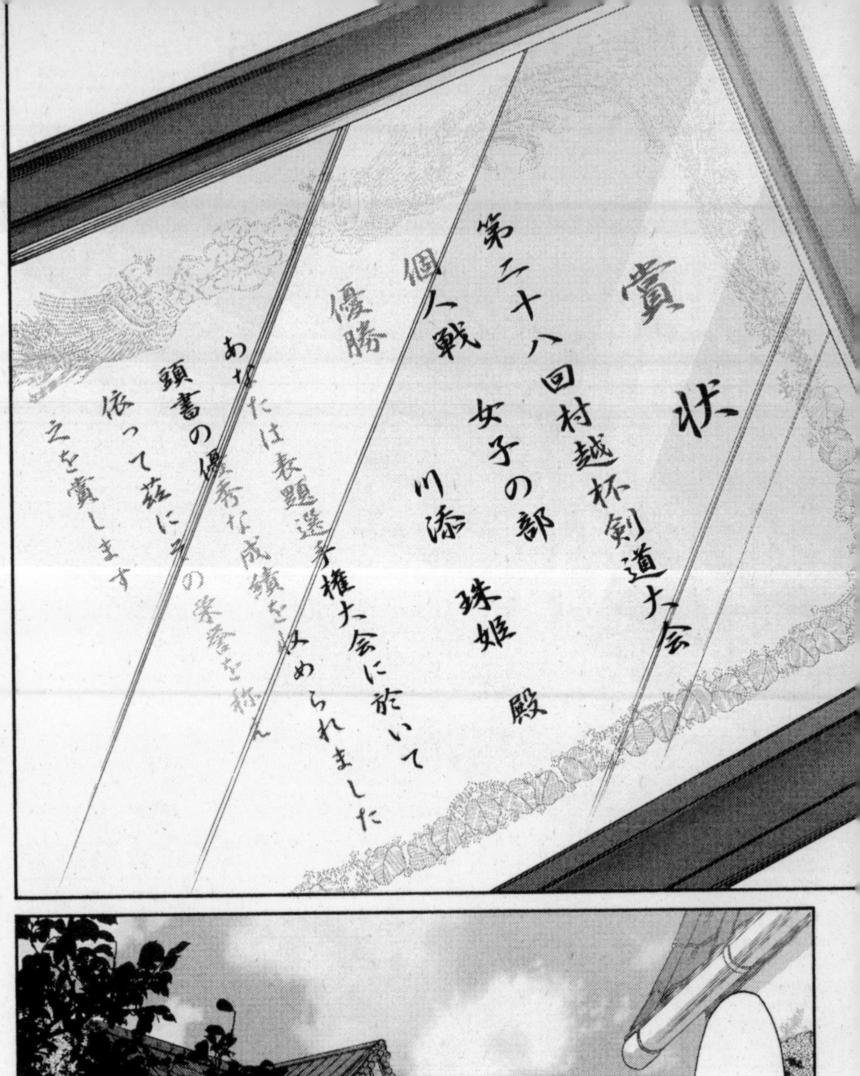
賞状
第二十八回村越杯剣道大会
個人戦　女子の部
川添　珠姫　殿
優勝
あなたは表題選手権大会に於いて
頭書の優秀な成績を収められました
依って茲にその栄誉を称え
之を賞します

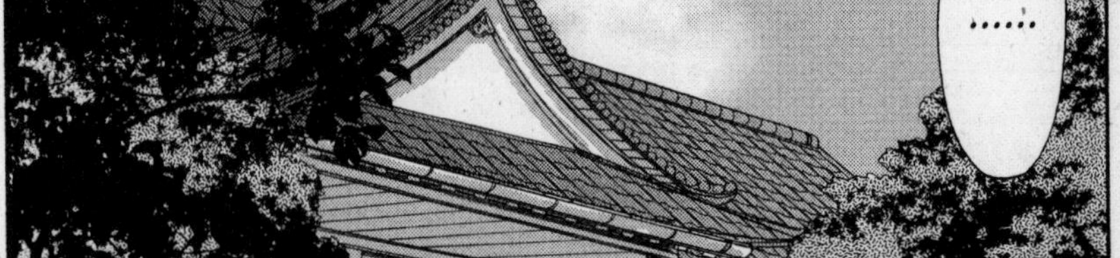
......

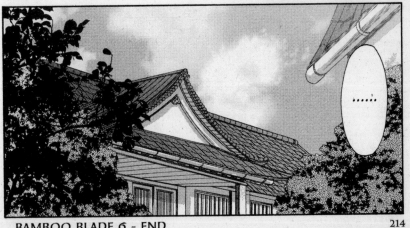

TRANSLATION NOTES

Common Honorifics

No honorific: Indicates familiarity or closeness; if used without permission or reason, addressing someone in this manner would constitute an insult.

-san: The Japanese equivalent of Mr./Mrs./Miss. If a situation calls for politeness, this is the fail-safe honorific.

-sama: Conveys great respect; may also indicate that the social status of the speaker is lower than that of the addressee.

-kun: Used most often when referring to boys, this indicates affection or familiarity. Occasionally used by older men among their peers, but it may also be used by anyone referring to a person of lower standing.

-chan: An affectionate honorific indicating familiarity used mostly in reference to girls; also used in reference to cute persons or animals of either gender.

-senpai: A suffix used in addressing one's upperclassmen.

-sensei: A respectful term for teachers, artists, or high-level professionals.

-dono: A polite, formal honorific used to show respect. Uncommon in modern Japanese.

General Notes

Armor: The guards, or *bogu*, worn in kendo all have their own names: The *men* is the helmet and face mask, the *do* is the breastplate, *tare* refers to the hanging plates worn like a belt, and the *kote* are the gauntlets that protect the hands.

Senpo, Jiho, Chuken, Fukusho, Taisho: These are the five ranks that make up a kendo team and determine the order in which the players appear.

Ari: When a point has been scored, the judge will call out the area struck (*men*, *kote*, *do*, etc.) and then "*ari*," signifying that a point has been scored in the area named.

Shobu ari: The judge calls "*shobu ari*" when the match is over and one combatant has won.

Scoreboard: The letters indicate on which part of the armor the point was scored. The circled letter denotes the first point scored. "F" stands for "foul," and an "X" across the center line means the bout was a draw.

For more information on the formal rules and workings of kendo, see Volume 2 pages 152-154!

Page 3
Hinomaru: The colloquial name for the Japanese flag, meaning "circle of sun." Traditionally, the plainest, cheapest type of bento (boxed) lunch, which consists of a single pickled plum sitting in the middle of a serving of rice, is called "hinomaru" because of its resemblance to the national flag.

Page 65
Footwork: As a reminder, here are the meanings of the four types of footwork:
Okuri-ashi = "Sending steps"
Hiraki-ashi = "Opening steps"
Tsugi-ashi = "Connecting steps"
Ayumi-ashi = "Walking steps"

Page 66
E: In the third panel, Azuma's nameplate says "E." This is because the kanji for "Azuma" can also be read "*higashi*," which means "east."

Page 91
Kendoka: A practitioner of kendo.

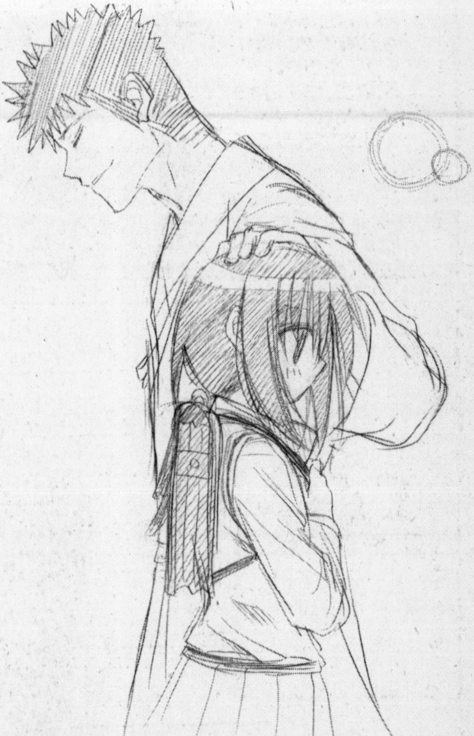

BAMBOO BLADE
バンブーブレード

OMAKE MANGA THEATER 1

TAMAKI AND COOKING (1)

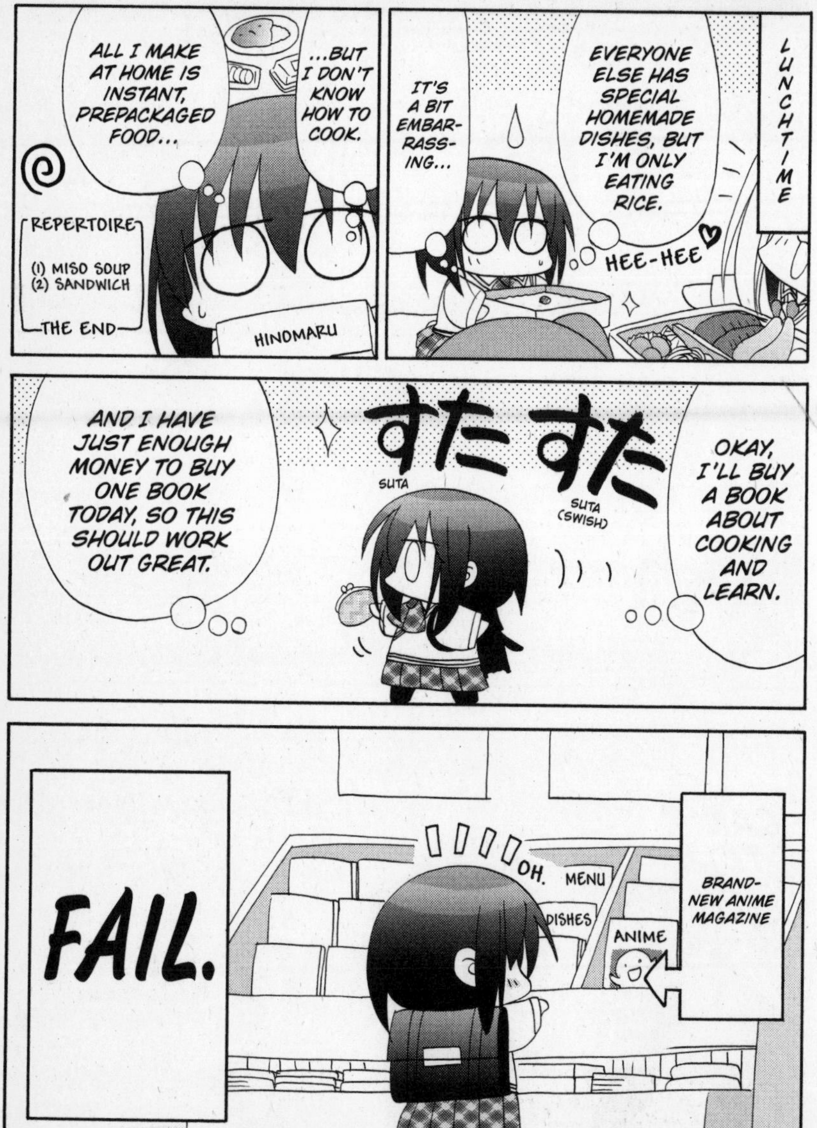

LUNCHTIME
EVERYONE ELSE HAS SPECIAL HOMEMADE DISHES, BUT I'M ONLY EATING RICE.
HEE-HEE
IT'S A BIT EMBARRASSING...
...BUT I DON'T KNOW HOW TO COOK.
ALL I MAKE AT HOME IS INSTANT, PREPACKAGED FOOD...
REPERTOIRE
(1) MISO SOUP
(2) SANDWICH
THE END
HINOMARU
OKAY, I'LL BUY A BOOK ABOUT COOKING AND LEARN.
すたすた
SUTA
SUTA (SWISH)
AND I HAVE JUST ENOUGH MONEY TO BUY ONE BOOK TODAY, SO THIS SHOULD WORK OUT GREAT.
BRAND-NEW ANIME MAGAZINE
ANIME
MENU
DISHES
OH.
FAIL.

OMAKE MANGA THEATER ❷

TAMAKI AND COOKING (2)

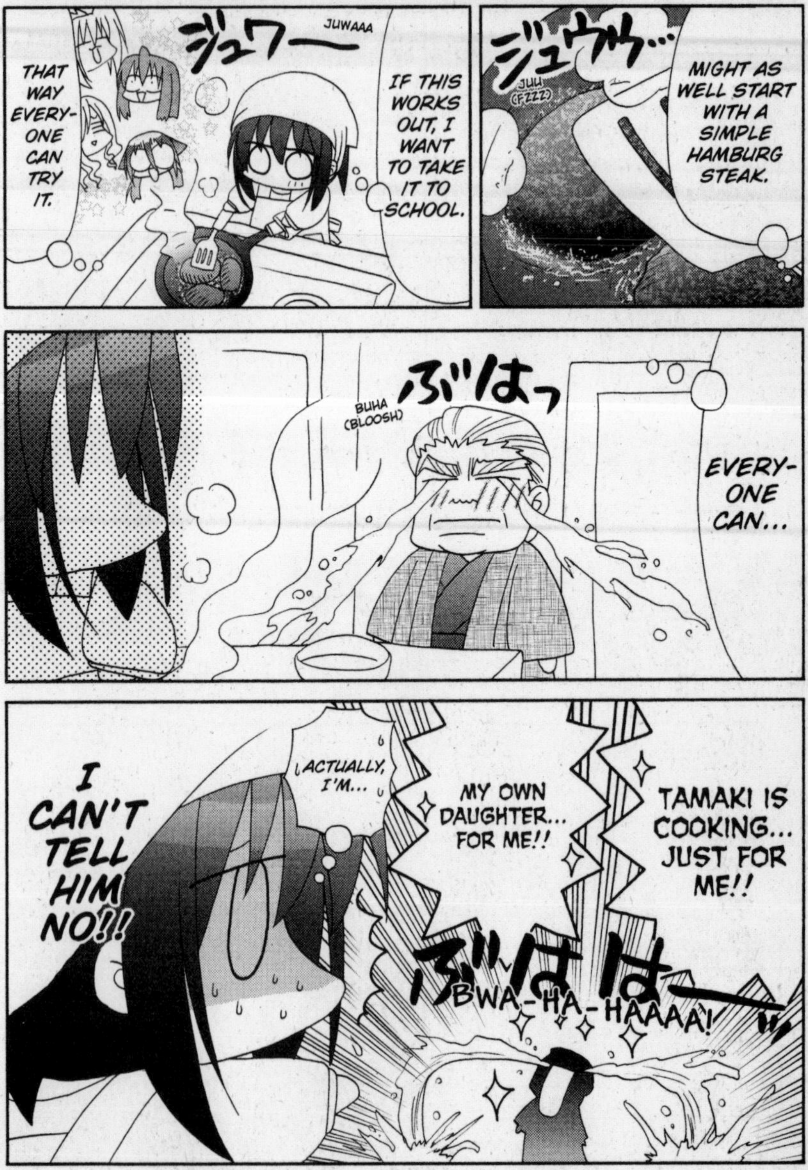
ジュウゥ
JUU (FZZZ)
MIGHT AS WELL START WITH A SIMPLE HAMBURG STEAK.
ジュワー
JUWAAA
IF THIS WORKS OUT, I WANT TO TAKE IT TO SCHOOL.
THAT WAY EVERYONE CAN TRY IT.
EVERYONE CAN...
ぶはっ
BUHA (BLOOSH)
TAMAKI IS COOKING... JUST FOR ME!!
MY OWN DAUGHTER... FOR ME!!
ACTUALLY, I'M...
I CAN'T TELL HIM NO!!!
ぶはは—
BWA-HA-HAAAA!

OMAKE MANGA THEATER ③

MIYA-MIYA AND AZUMA'S CLASSMATES

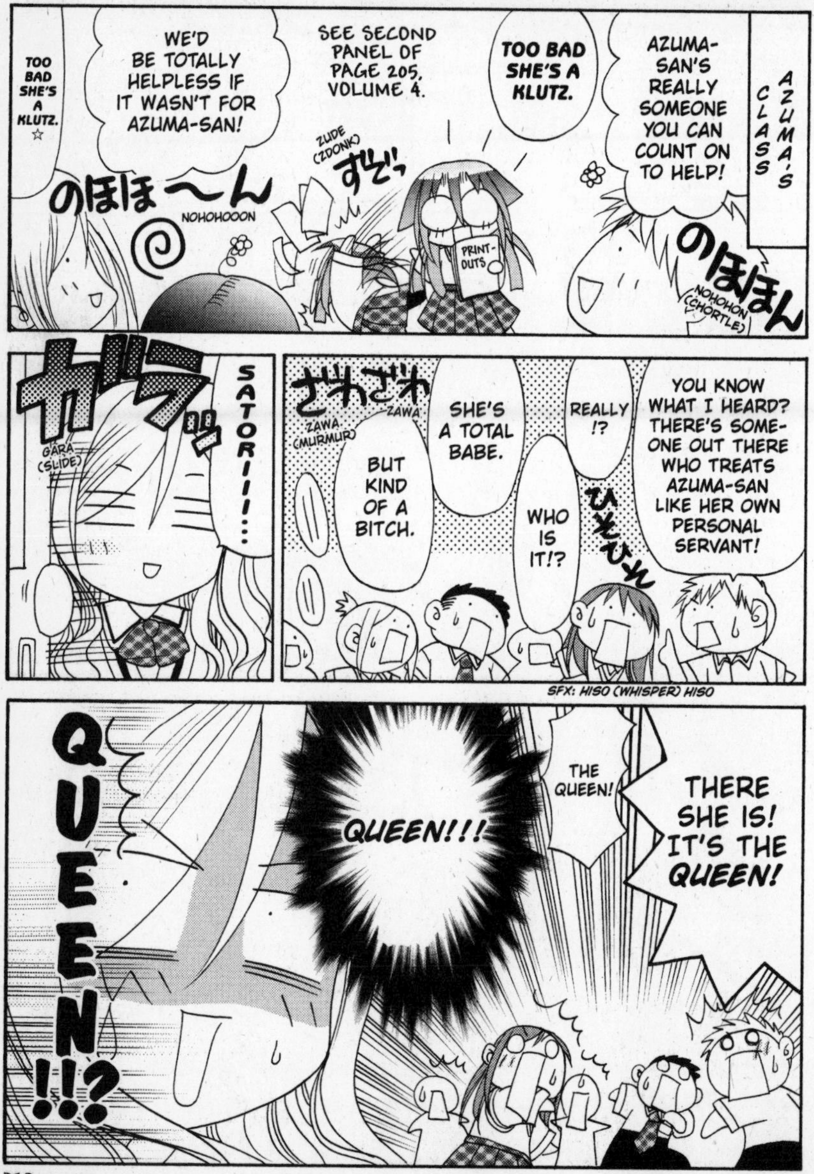
AZUMA'S CLASS
AZUMA-SAN'S REALLY SOMEONE YOU CAN COUNT ON TO HELP!
のほほん
NOHOHON (CHORTLE)
TOO BAD SHE'S A KLUTZ.
ずでっ
ZUDE (ZDONK)
PRINT-OUTS
SEE SECOND PANEL OF PAGE 205, VOLUME 4.
WE'D BE TOTALLY HELPLESS IF IT WASN'T FOR AZUMA-SAN!
のほほ〜ん
NOHOHOOON
TOO BAD SHE'S A KLUTZ. ☆
YOU KNOW WHAT I HEARD? THERE'S SOME-ONE OUT THERE WHO TREATS AZUMA-SAN LIKE HER OWN PERSONAL SERVANT!
ひそひそ
REALLY!?
WHO IS IT!?
SHE'S A TOTAL BABE.
BUT KIND OF A BITCH.
ざわざわ
ZAWA ZAWA (MURMUR)
SATORI!!!...
ガラ
GARA (SLIDE)
THERE SHE IS! IT'S THE QUEEN!
THE QUEEN!
QUEEN!!!
QUEEN!!?

SFX: HISO (WHISPER) HISO

MEANWHILE, AT MACHIDO HIGH 2

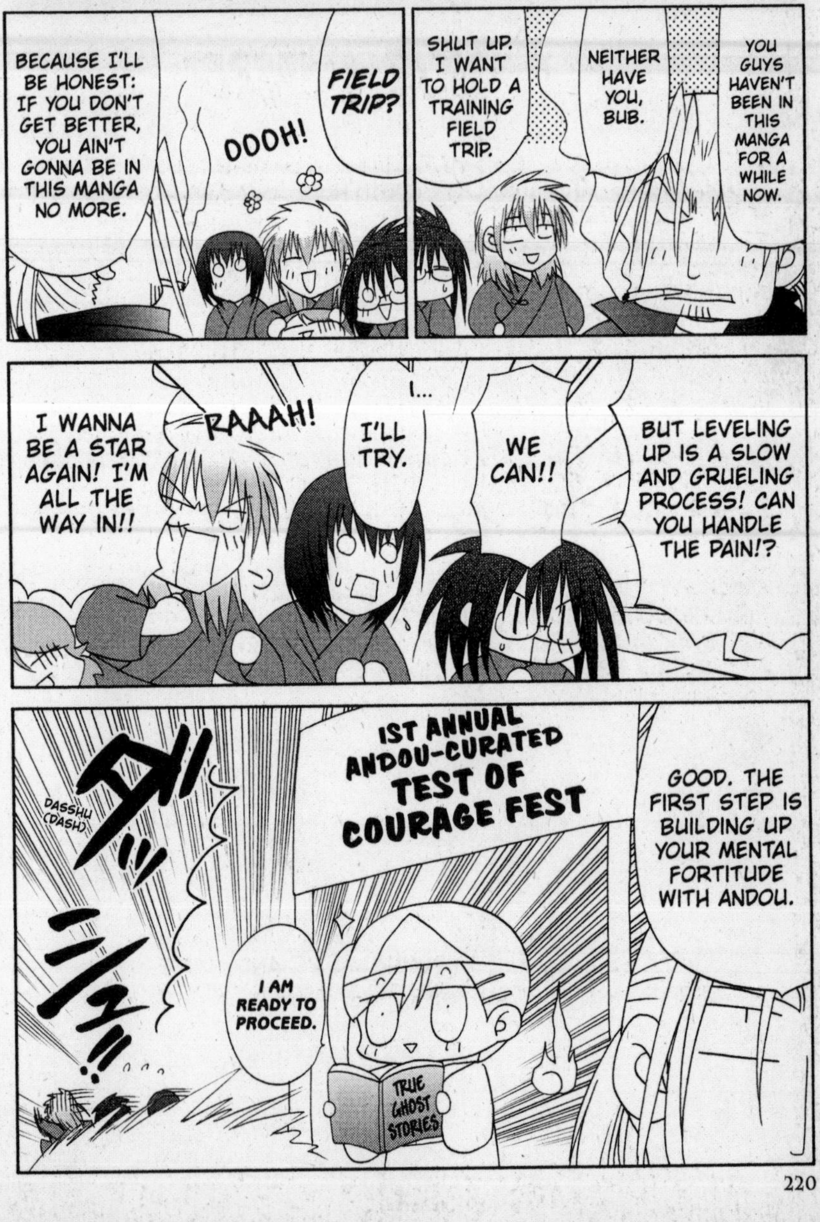
YOU GUYS HAVEN'T BEEN IN THIS MANGA FOR A WHILE NOW.
NEITHER HAVE YOU, BUB.
SHUT UP. I WANT TO HOLD A TRAINING FIELD TRIP.
FIELD TRIP?
OOOH!
BECAUSE I'LL BE HONEST: IF YOU DON'T GET BETTER, YOU AIN'T GONNA BE IN THIS MANGA NO MORE.
BUT LEVELING UP IS A SLOW AND GRUELING PROCESS! CAN YOU HANDLE THE PAIN!?
WE CAN!!
I...
I'LL TRY.
RAAAH!
I WANNA BE A STAR AGAIN! I'M ALL THE WAY IN!!
GOOD. THE FIRST STEP IS BUILDING UP YOUR MENTAL FORTITUDE WITH ANDOU.
1ST ANNUAL ANDOU-CURATED TEST OF COURAGE FEST
I AM READY TO PROCEED.
TRUE GHOST STORIES
DASSHU (DASH)

AFTERWORD

WITH THE TOUJOU HIGH BATTLE IN VOLUME 6, THE FIVE MAIN CHARACTERS ARE FINALLY TOGETHER AND FUNCTIONING AS A SERIOUS UNIT. NEXT VOLUME, ANOTHER CHARACTER WILL BE INTRODUCED. IT'S SOMEONE WHO TOOK A WHILE TO COME AROUND, BUT IT'S FINALLY HAPPENING. HOPE YOU LOOK FORWARD TO IT.

BY THE WAY, IT'S BEEN ANNOUNCED THAT THIS MANGA WILL BE MADE INTO AN ANIME. IT'S STARTING IN JAPAN IN OCTOBER 2007, SO BE ON THE LOOKOUT. (ANIMATION AVAILABLE NOW IN THE U.S. FROM FUNIMATION!) I'M SURE YOU'LL BE ABLE TO FEEL THE STAFF'S ENTHUSIASM FOR THE STORY. EVEN THE CAT MOVES. ALSO, WHILE I DON'T KNOW THE FULL DETAILS, I HEAR THAT "THEY" WILL BE MAKING AN APPEARANCE AS WELL.

ALSO BY THE WAY, MY SERIES CALLED *MATERIAL PUZZLE* IN THE MAGAZINE *SHONEN GANGAN* HAS REACHED THE END OF ACT 2 WITH THE RELEASE OF ITS 20TH VOLUME. IN A LITTLE WHILE I'LL BE STARTING ON THE FINAL ACT, SO IF YOU'RE INTERESTED, TAKE A LOOK.

—MASAHIRO TOTSUKA

BY THE WAY, I'M THINKING MORE AND MORE OF FINALLY GETTING AROUND TO DRAWING "KIYO-SUGI."

BACKSTAGE AFTERWORD

DRAWN BY IGA

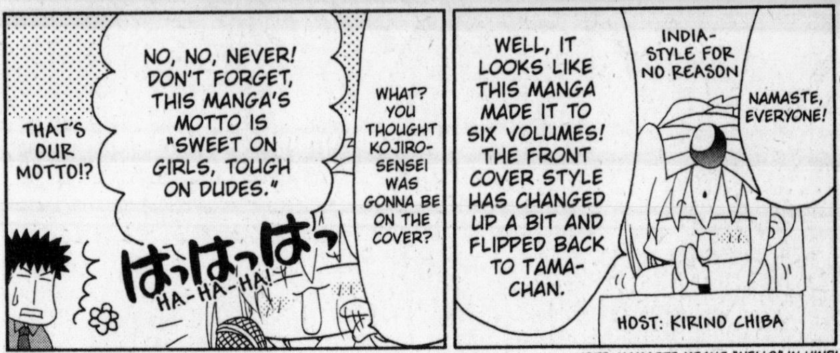
NAMASTE, EVERYONE!
INDIA-STYLE FOR NO REASON
WELL, IT LOOKS LIKE THIS MANGA MADE IT TO SIX VOLUMES! THE FRONT COVER STYLE HAS CHANGED UP A BIT AND FLIPPED BACK TO TAMA-CHAN.
HOST: KIRINO CHIBA
WHAT? YOU THOUGHT KOJIRO-SENSEI WAS GONNA BE ON THE COVER?
NO, NO, NEVER! DON'T FORGET, THIS MANGA'S MOTTO IS "SWEET ON GIRLS, TOUGH ON DUDES."
はっはっはっ
HA-HA-HA!
THAT'S OUR MOTTO!?

NOTE: NAMASTE MEANS "HELLO" IN HINDI

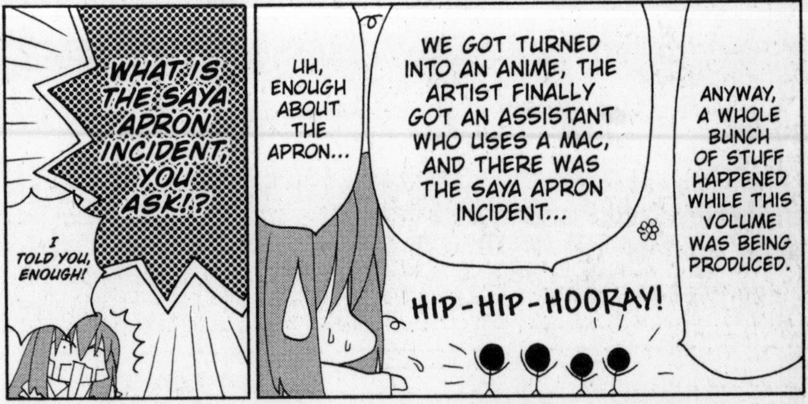
ANYWAY, A WHOLE BUNCH OF STUFF HAPPENED WHILE THIS VOLUME WAS BEING PRODUCED.
WE GOT TURNED INTO AN ANIME, THE ARTIST FINALLY GOT AN ASSISTANT WHO USES A MAC, AND THERE WAS THE SAYA APRON INCIDENT...
HIP-HIP-HOORAY!
UH, ENOUGH ABOUT THE APRON...
WHAT IS THE SAYA APRON INCIDENT, YOU ASK!?
I TOLD YOU, ENOUGH!

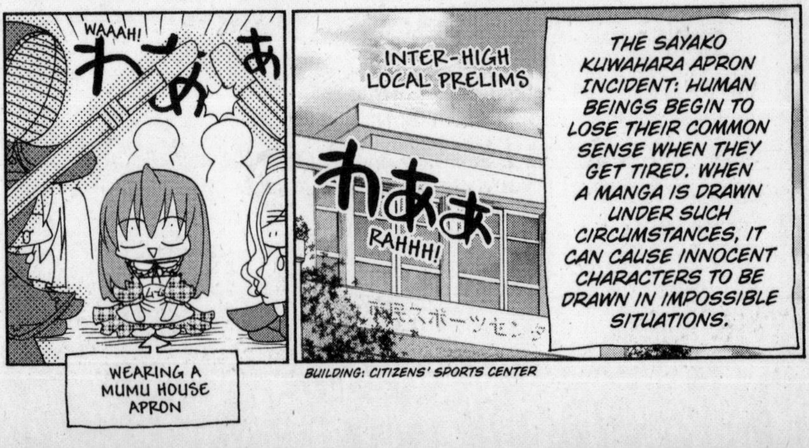
THE SAYAKO KUWAHARA APRON INCIDENT: HUMAN BEINGS BEGIN TO LOSE THEIR COMMON SENSE WHEN THEY GET TIRED. WHEN A MANGA IS DRAWN UNDER SUCH CIRCUMSTANCES, IT CAN CAUSE INNOCENT CHARACTERS TO BE DRAWN IN IMPOSSIBLE SITUATIONS.
INTER-HIGH LOCAL PRELIMS
わあぁ
RAHHH!
WAAAH!
わあぁあ
WEARING A MUMU HOUSE APRON

BUILDING: CITIZENS' SPORTS CENTER

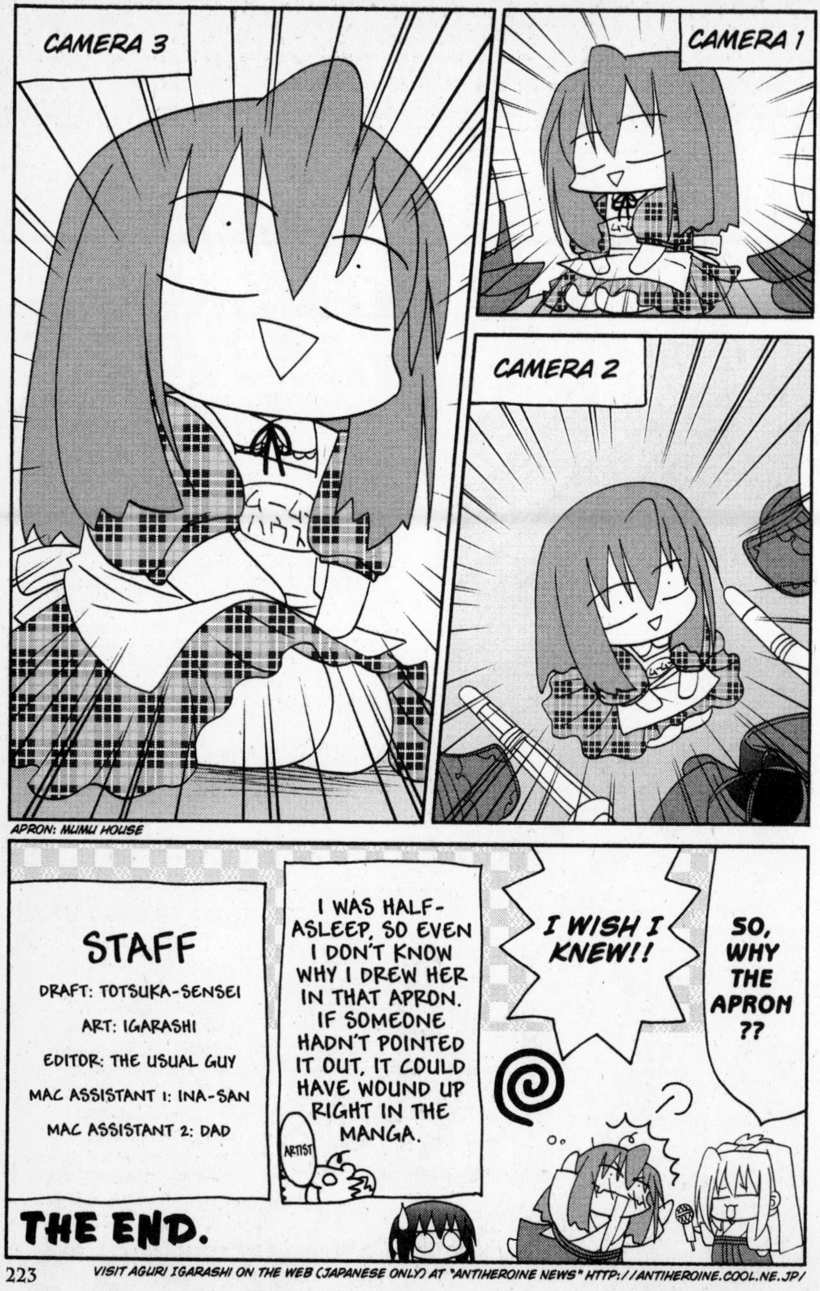
CAMERA 1
CAMERA 2
CAMERA 3
ムームーハウス
APRON: MUMU HOUSE
SO, WHY THE APRON??
I WISH I KNEW!!
I WAS HALF-ASLEEP, SO EVEN I DON'T KNOW WHY I DREW HER IN THAT APRON. IF SOMEONE HADN'T POINTED IT OUT, IT COULD HAVE WOUND UP RIGHT IN THE MANGA.
ARTIST
STAFF
DRAFT: TOTSUKA-SENSEI
ART: IGARASHI
EDITOR: THE USUAL GUY
MAC ASSISTANT 1: INA-SAN
MAC ASSISTANT 2: DAD
THE END.

 VISIT AGURI IGARASHI ON THE WEB (JAPANESE ONLY) AT "ANTIHEROINE NEWS" HTTP://ANTIHEROINE.COOL.NE.JP/

THEIR MEETING... WAS FATE.

NEXT VOLUME PREVIEW

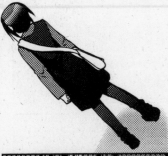